Higginbotham.

D1537097

AURORA FERNÁNDEZ PER
JAVIER MOZAS
JAVIER ARPA

Density **Ho**using **Co**nstruction & Costs

Título **Title**
HoCo

Subtítulo **Subtitle**
Density Housing Construction & Costs

a+t Density series

Autores **Authors**
Aurora Fernández Per
Javier Mozas
Javier Arpa

Maquetación y producción **Layout and production**
Ricardo Unquera
Delia Argote
Dorleta Acosta
Marta Beltrán

Coordinación **Coordination**
Idoia Esteban

Comunicación y Prensa **Communication and Press:**
Edurne Ruiz de Arcaute

Traducciones **Translations**
Wesley Trobaugh
Ken Mortimer
Mireya Sánchez

Publicado por **Edited by**
a+t ediciones

ISBN 978-84-613-3080-5

Impresion **Printing**
Gráficas Santamaría
VI-287/09
Vitoria-Gasteiz, 2009

a+t ediciones. General Álava 15, 2º A. E-01005.
Vitoria-Gasteiz. Spain
www.aplust.net

Agradecimientos **Acknowledgments**
a+t ediciones agradece a todos los autores y
colaboradores de las obras que se incluyen en esta
publicación, su esfuerzo en la comprobación de datos y
en la recopilación de la información.
a+t ediciones thanks the authors of the works
featured in this publication as well as their
collaborators including for their efforts in collecting
information and verifying data.

Elijamos la vivienda como objeto esencial de la ciudad

Echemos un vistazo al lugar donde se implanta (ensanches, centros, extrarradios…).

Verifiquemos los datos de ocupación del territorio en el que se asienta (número de habitantes, densidad…).

Comprobemos la inserción en la trama (ocupación de la parcela, edificabilidad, número de viviendas…).

Sepamos quién la promueve (iniciativa privada, pública, mixta…) .

Quiénes son los usuarios (jóvenes, mayores, cualquiera…).

Con un poco de suerte, puede que haya otros usos en el proyecto (comercios, oficinas, equipamientos…).

Preguntemos amablemente a los autores el coste por metro cuadrado construido.

Adecuemos el coste al poder adquisitivo del país donde se encuentra. Esto es inevitable para comparar en igualdad

Una vez en el interior, veamos cómo se distribuyen los espacios comunes.

Sepamos cuántos tamaños de viviendas hay en cada proyecto (1, 2, 3 o más dormitorios…).

Husmeemos en las secciones constructivas (1:50).

Hurguemos en los detalles (1:20).

Observemos cómo aparecen los materiales en fachada y cubierta.

Analicemos las capas de la envolvente con un sencillo código de colores.

Preguntemos a los autores las estrategias sostenibles que han utilizado (a veces contestan, a veces…).

Añadamos una buena colección de fotos.

Hagamos esto 32 veces y comparemos.

Por último, agreguemos los resultados y unas cuantas reflexiones.

Esto -más o menos- es lo que llamamos HoCo.

Let's choose housing as the essential object of the city

Let's have a look at the place where's it's implemented (urban extensions, downtowns, outskirts...)

Let's check the occupancy data of the territory in which it is located (number of inhabitants, density...)

Let's check the insertion into the urban grid (plot occupancy, planning permission, number of dwellings...)

Let's find out who's doing the development (private initiative, public, mixed...)

Who are the users? (the young, the elderly, anyone...)

With a bit of luck there might be other uses in the project (businesses, offices, facilities...)

Let's ask the authors nicely to let us know the build cost per square metre.

Let's adapt the cost to the purchasing power of the country where it's located. This is inevitable if we want to compare on equal footing

Once inside, let's see how the common spaces are distributed.

Let's find out how many dwelling sizes there are in each project (1, 2, 3 or more bedrooms....)

Let's have a snoop around the building sections (1:50)

Let's rake through the details (1:20)

Let's look at how the materials appear in the facade and on the roof.

Let's analyze the layers of the envelope with a simple colour code.

Let's ask the authors which sustainable strategies they've used (sometimes they reply, sometimes...)

Let's add a good collection of photos.

Let's do this 32 times and compare.

Finally, let's add some thoughts and findings.

This is, more or less, what we call HoCo.

AURORA FERNÁNDEZ PER

ARQUITECTOS ARCHITECTS

La mano que mueve la grúa The hand that moves the crane

JAVIER MOZAS

El lamento es generalizado. La crisis está adelgazando los estudios de arquitectura, devastando las oficinas técnicas y borrando de las páginas amarillas a muchas empresas constructoras. Se está produciendo un cambio de ciclo que va a eliminar, por inanición, toda la grasa superflua que lubrica el negocio inmobiliario.

The lament is generalised. The crisis is downsizing architectural studios, devastating technical offices and removing many construction companies from the yellow pages. A change of cycle is being produced which will starve off all the superfluous fat lubricating the property business.

En los primeros años del siglo XX, Henry Ford hablaba de la racionalidad del proceso productivo y justificaba la extrema proximidad de sus máquinas en la nave de producción –mayor que la de cualquier otra empresa en el mundo–, porque una separación innecesaria de sólo seis pulgadas acababa originando costes extras a los consumidores. El fordismo engordó el consumo de Occidente e inundó el mercado de productos en serie, cebando un cuerpo que fue aumentando de volumen hasta la crisis del petróleo de los años setenta.

In the early years of the 20th Century, Henry Ford spoke of the rationality of the production process and justified the extreme proximity of his machines in the production plant –greater than that of any other company in the world–, for an unnecessary separation of only six inches would end up passing on extra costs to the consumers. Fordism fattened Western consumption and flooded the market with mass-produced products, feeding a body which grew and grew in volume until the petroleum crisis of the seventies.

A mediados del siglo pasado, la empresa de automóviles Toyota[1] ideó la producción ajustada, *lean production* –el término 'lean' en inglés tiene también el significado de menguante, de enjuto, de la carne magra del cuerpo con ausencia de grasa. El modelo fordista sufrió entonces el primer ajuste, basado en el pensamiento a largo plazo. El acuerdo consistía en eliminar todo lo que sobraba –el esfuerzo innecesario y el derroche– y respetar, motivar y engrandecer al personal y a los clientes porque con ello crecía la empresa. El asunto era no quedar nunca conforme con el producto y pensar en mejoras y aprendizajes continuos. La forma oriental de entender la vida se introdujo de este modo, como una dieta de adelgazamiento a base de algas y arroz, en las fábricas y empresas de Occidente.

Esta visión, que lleva más de dos décadas siendo indiscutible en la industria automovilística, no está integrada todavía dentro del sistema de valores de los ejecutores materiales implicados en la construcción de viviendas. Lo que sí está comúnmente aceptado es el concepto general de que la industria es más eficiente que la edificación.

Si después del fordismo se impuso la producción ajustada y menguante, ahora lo que está cambiando es el concepto. Toyota se ha propuesto ser la primera empresa en sacar al mercado el coche enchufable y ha adelantado un año sus previsiones. Esto quiere decir que pretende, de manera generalizada, acelerar el cambio del sistema de obtención de energía motriz en un vehículo, que ha sido de combustión desde el inicio de los

Midway through the last century, the automotive firm Toyota[1] came up with the idea of *lean production* -asociated with the idea of a skinny, lean body meat lacking fat. The Fordist model then suffered the first adjustment, based on long-term thinking. The agreement consisted of removing all that was not necessary, –unnecessary effort and waste– and respecting, motivating and praising staff and clients because with this the company would grow. The theme was never to be completely satisfied with the product and to be always thinking of continuous improvements and learning. The Eastern approach to life was thus introduced, as a slimming diet based on seaweed and rice, into Western companies and factories.

This vision, which has been undisputed for more than two decades in the automotive industry, has still not been integrated into the value system of the material agents in house building. What is commonly accepted is the general concept that the manufacturing industry is more efficient than the construction industry.

If after Fordism tight lean production prevailed, what is changing now is the concept. Toyota has set out to be the first company to market the plug-in car and has brought its forecasts forward by one year. This means that it is attempting, in a generalised way, to accelerate the change of the system of obtaining the driving energy in vehicles, which has been by combustion since the beginning of time, and give way to a rechargeable lith-ion battery. This is not a trivial change, but a substantial one. It is a

1 *The Toyota Way*. Jeffrey Liker. McGraw-Hill. 2004. ISBN 0-07-139231-9

tiempos, y pasar el relevo a una batería recargable de iones de litio. No es un cambio baladí, sino sustancial. Es una transformación que ya está en marcha y que va a obligar a fabricar, tanto automóviles como viviendas, de otra manera.

MMC, OSM, KPI y *Les Compagnons du Devoir*
Hace unos años, se promovieron desde el Ministerio de Vivienda británico nuevos métodos para dinamizar y tecnificar la construcción de viviendas. Los denominaron MMC, *Modern Methods of Construction*[2]. La intención era dar un impulso a la industria edificatoria, sacando el trabajo de la obra e intensificando la OSM, *Off-Site Manufacturing*[3] –nuevo nombre para algo que ya se conocía como prefabricación en taller. El ingrediente nuevo era cumplir con los KPI, Indicadores de Objetivos Fundamentales, como son la satisfacción del cliente, la reducción de defectos, el cumplimiento del plazo y del coste, la rentabilidad, la productividad y la seguridad. El caso cero de este impulso fue el informe de Sir John Egan denominado *Rethinking Construction*[4], dado a conocer en 1998, que explicaba claramente cómo una de las soluciones frente a la escasez de vivienda en el Reino Unido era aumentar la prefabricación de elementos.

Está claro que la construcción de viviendas está presionada para que abandone las malas compañías del arte, la cultura y la tradición y se integre en el grupo de

transformation which is already under way and which will oblige us to build, both cars and housing, in a different way.

MMC, OSM, KPI and *Les Compagnons du Devoir*
Some years ago, new methods to energize and modernize the house building industry were promoted from within the British Ministry of State for Housing. They named them MMC, Modern Methods of Construction[2]. The intention was to give momentum to the construction industry, moving the work off-site and intensifying the OSM, Off-Site Manufacturing[3] –new name for what was previously known as factory pre-fabrication. The new ingredient was to fulfil the KPI, Key Performance Indicators, such as customer satisfaction, reducing defects, meeting deadlines and cost requirements, profitability, productivity and safety. The zero case of this break through was Sir John Egan's report named *Rethinking Construction*[4], released in 1998, which clearly set out that one of the solutions to the housing shortage in the United Kingdom was to increase the prefabrication of elements.

It is clear that the house building industry is under pressure to abandon the bad company of art, culture and tradition and join the group of the serious kids, known as Open Building or Just-in-Time, but how can this transition become a reality in construction work?

MMC, OSM and KPI might find it difficult to fit into the language of *Les Compagnons du Devoir*.

2 'Modern Methods of House Building.' *Postnote*. Parliamentary Office of Science and Technology. December 2003

3 *The Housing Forum. Manufacturing Excellence. UK capacity in offsite manufacturing.* Innovation Studies Centre. Tanaka Business School. Imperial College London. January 2004

4 'The Report of the Construction Task Force.' *Rethinking Construction.* Department of Trade and Industry. Foreword by Sir John Egan

Jean Yves

los chicos serios, conocidos como *Open Building* o *Just-in-Time*, pero ¿cómo se concreta esta transición en la puesta en obra?

MMC, OSM y KPI es difícil que encuentren acomodo en el lenguaje de *Les Compagnons du Devoir*. Son acrónimos anglosajones, que reducen los tiempos de pronunciación y escritura de unas palabras que no existen en el mundo de los oficios gremiales. *Les Compagnons du Devoir*[5] son trabajadores de ese otro tiempo en que la comunicación verbal tenía un valor diferente, porque existía un diálogo permanente entre los miembros de la unión y los aspirantes. Estas cofradías, muy consolidadas en Francia, han estado ligadas a la construcción de catedrales, a la restauración de monumentos con Eugène Viollet le Duc, a la erección de la torre Eiffel y siguen insistentemente presentes como guardianes de los oficios tradicionales.

En su seno están representados la mayoría de los trabajos de la construcción, desde la cantería, hasta la metalistería o la carpintería de armar y siguen conservando el misterio de las asociaciones medievales. Los aspirantes deben hacer suyos los votos de perfeccionamiento, respeto y pasión; emprenden un viaje iniciático de formación con hospedaje y trabajo asegurado, el *Tour de France* le llaman. Así, se hacen con los conocimientos del amplio muestrario de tradiciones locales de las regiones del hexágono. Como examen de admisión, se les exige una maqueta que ponga de manifiesto sus habilidades y que represente su modo particular de resolver, de manera ingeniosa, determinados problemas constructivos.

5 *Les carrières des compagnons du Devoir: entre tradition et modernité.* Annabelle Hulin. CERMAT-IAE de Tours. Université de Tours. 2008

They are acronyms from the English-speaking world, which reduce the pronunciation and writing times of some words which do not exist in the world of professional trades. *Les Compagnons du Devoir*[5] are workers from that other era in which verbal communication had a different value, because there was a permanent dialogue between the guild members and the aspirants. These tradesmen´s guilds, very strong in France, have been linked to cathedral building, to the restoration of monuments with Eugène Viollet le Duc, to the erection of the Eiffel Tower and they remain persistently present as the guardians of traditional trades.

Within this organisation most types of construction work are represented, from masonry, to metalworking or joinery, and it still conserves the mystery of

Pero, ¿qué tienen en común los oficios tradicionales con la construcción industrializada? Las manos y el lugar. Esto es, la imposibilidad de evitar el trabajo manual y la inexcusable necesidad de realizar ciertos trabajos en el propio emplazamiento. La construcción es una manualidad de gran tamaño sujeta al suelo. Las manos desnudas intervienen en la mayoría de los montajes, bien sea en el taller o en la obra. La destreza y las habilidades son necesarias, tanto para levantar una fábrica de ladrillo, como para manejar las grúas de elevación de módulos prefabricados. Actualmente, tanto la artesanía responsable y orgullosa de los gremios tradicionales, como los montadores en obra de elementos prefabricados requieren habilidad manual para obtener resultados de calidad.

El molde de la casa de hormigón

En España, la Empresa Municipal de la Vivienda y Suelo (EMVS) de Madrid –con esa coincidencia de objetivos que muestran los árbitros de las grandes decisiones en temas de vivienda–, lleva años promocionando sistemas constructivos tendentes a la sistematización. Uno de los últimos experimentos se realizó en 2004 con 100 viviendas para jóvenes en Tres Cantos. El arquitecto Rafael de la Hoz planteó una solución de bloque en L con unidades de uno, dos y tres dormitorios en dúplex, ejecutadas con el sistema de molde integral de hormigón armado superfluido y autocompactable. Se empleó un número muy reducido de moldes para todo el conjunto, consiguiendo hormigonar una vivienda completa en cada puesta.

medieval associations. The aspirants must take the vows of self-improvement, respect and passion; setting off on a training voyage of initiation with accommodation and work assured, which they call the *Tour de France*. This way they get to know the many examples of local traditions of the regions of France. As an admission exam they are required to make a model which shows off their skills and which represents their particular way of solving, in an ingenious manner, specific construction problems.

But what do traditional trades have in common with industrialized construction?: Hands and the Site. That is, the impossibility of avoiding manual labour and the unavoidable need to carry out certain tasks on-site. Construction is large-scale craftsmanship attached to the ground. Bare hands intervene in most of the assembly work, be it off-site or on-site. Skill and abilities are necessary, both to build a brick work and to manage the cranes lifting prefabricated modules. Currently, both the responsible and proud craftsmanship of the traditional trades and the on-site assemblers of prefabricated elements require manual skills in order to obtain quality results.

The concrete house mould

In Spain the Municipal Housing and Land Trust (EMVS) of Madrid -with this coincidence of aims that the arbiters of great decisions in housing show-, have spent years promoting construction systems tending towards systematisation. One of the most recent experi-

100 VIVIENDAS PARA JÓVENES.
100 DWELLINGS FOR YOUNG PEOPLE. TRES CANTOS, MADRID
RAFAEL DE LA HOZ 2004

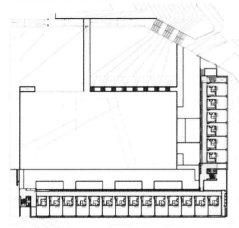

Después de aquel ejemplo, EMVS ha continuado con la serie y en *HoCo* se incluyen dos edificios de viviendas pensados, proyectados y construidos con el sistema de molde integral. Se trata de 102 viviendas en Carabanchel, de dosmasuno arquitectos (pp. 38-55) y del edificio Celosía en Sanchinarro, de MVRDV y Blanca Lleó (pp. 198-217). Ambos edificios, contratados en pleno boom de la construcción en España, estuvieron en espera varios meses por la particular especialización que requiere este proceso constructivo. El ahorro en tiempo, que es pregonado como ventaja por sus comercializadores, se tornó en retrasos por las particularidades del método. Las dos empresas de certificación de la calidad contratadas tampoco lo tenían muy claro, pues manifestaron criterios diferentes y exigieron requisitos dispares a los dos proyectos.

En aquel momento, la escasez de mano de obra en España y el coste de un sistema especializado como éste, obligó a buscar trabajadores fuera del país. La contrata recayó en una empresa colombiana de moldes de aluminio. Los paneles llegaron a España en barco y estuvieron parados en la aduana por los aranceles que se aplican al aluminio. Se tuvo que resolver también la compatibilidad de este material como encofrado, que la norma española no contemplaba, así como la contratación del contingente de trabajadores, quienes como particulares *Compagnons du devoir* del molde americano, investidos así por las circunstancias, realizaron su personal *Tour de España*, ejerciendo sus habilidades allí donde eran requeridas.

ments took place in 2004 with 100 dwellings for young people in Tres Cantos. The architect Rafael de la Hoz proposed the solution of an L-shaped block with units of one, two and three bedrooms on two storeys, carried out with a system of superfluid and self-compacting reinforced concrete integral moulding. A very small number of moulds were used for the whole complex, managing to concrete one whole dwelling in each moulding task.

After that example, EMVS has gone on with the series and in this *HoCo* publication two buildings for housing thought up, planned and built with the integral mould system are included. This is 102 dwellings in Carabanchel, by dosmasuno arquitectos, (pp. 38-55) and the Celosía building in Sanchinarro, by MVRDV and Blanca Lleó (pp. 198-217). Both buildings, commissioned at the height of the construction boom in Spain, were at a standstill for several months due to the particular specialization demanded by this construction process. The time-saving factor, championed as an advantage by its marketers, turned into delays due to the particular nature of the method. The two companies hired to carry out the quality certification were not too clear on the matter, as they showed different criteria and demanded different requirements from the two projects.

At that moment the labour shortage in Spain and the cost of a specialized system such as this meant the obligation of seeking workers from abroad. The contract went out to a Colombian aluminium moulding company. The panels were shipped to Spain and were

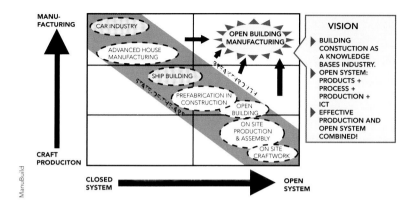

ManuBuild

retained at Customs due to the tariffs applied to aluminium. The problem of the compatibility of this material as formwork had to be solved also, which Spanish regulations did not allow for, as well as the hiring of the contingent of workers, who like private *compagnons du devoir* of American moulding, sworn in as such by circumstance made their own *Tour of Spain*, putting their skills into practise wherever they were required.

Lo mejor de los dos mundos

Artesanado, tradición, oficio, manualidad, deber, capacidad de improvisación, tiempo infinito, compromiso… son conceptos que la crisis va a pasar por un rasero muy fino. Por la malla del tamiz sólo se colarán la pasión y el esfuerzo si pueden justificar la efectividad, el coste y la certeza. El mecanismo injusto de evolución selectiva se aplicará al conjunto de los medios de producción y únicamente sobrevivirán a la prueba los que sean generosos en imaginación y creatividad. El mundo de los oficios y el de la industria están otra vez –no se sabe muy bien si enfrentados o aliados–, en una lucha evolutiva por su propia subsistencia.

Todas las iniciativas que aportan luz en este momento tratan de conjugar lo mejor de los dos mundos para dar respuesta a una demanda masiva y a la vez personalizada. Una casa no es sólo una máquina para vivir, es también el reflejo de un mundo personal, la prolongación espacial del individuo, que se caracteriza precisamente por su condición de no-automatizable.

The best of both worlds

Craftsmanship, tradition, trade, duty, capacity for improvisation, infinite time, commitment... are concepts which the crisis will level out. Passion and effort will only pass through the mesh of the sieve if they can justify effectiveness, cost and certainty. The unfair method of selective evolution will be applied to the set of production means and only those that are rich in imagination and creativity will survive the test. The world of tradesmen and industry are once again –it is not know whether they are opponents or as allies-, in an evolutionary struggle for their very subsistence.

All the initiatives which shed light at this moment try to combine the best of both worlds in order to respond to a demand which is both massive and personalized. A house is not only a machine for living, it is also the reflection of a personal world, the spatial prolongation of the individual, who is characterised precisely for his condition of non-automatizable.

ManuBuild[6] es un proyecto de investigación sobre Construcción Industrializada, financiado por la Unión Europea. Su objetivo es combinar lo imposible: la efectividad de la producción industrializada con la inspiración creadora de una vivienda sin limitaciones. El resultado deberá ofrecer al mercado variadas posibilidades de elección, tanto de materiales y acabados, como de tamaños y configuraciones espaciales.

ManuBuild desea dar un paso adelante respecto al método tradicional, basado en la artesanía, e imponer la construcción del Edificio Abierto, *Open Building Manufacturing*, combinando la fabricación ultra-eficiente en talleres y en la propia obra, con sistemas abiertos de componentes que inunden el mercado con una gran variedad de elementos, aprovechando una especie de red 2.0 de producción global. Esta idea, basada en el *Open Building* –planteada por John Habraken en los años sesenta–[7], separa el soporte, del relleno. El soporte forma parte de la estructura permanente y tiene la característica de inmutable y el relleno aspira a ser alterado, bien porque ha cumplido su vida útil, bien porque así lo desea el usuario.

El Primer Concurso Europeo restringido de Ideas Arquitectónicas[8], convocado en 2006 por la EMVS dentro del proyecto ManuBuild, tiene como misión la construcción de "un edificio experimental que actúe como 'demostrador' de la operatividad y la eficacia de nuevas soluciones constructivas". Fueron invita-

6 ManuBuild. Open Building Manufacturing. Volumen 1. Core Concepts and Industrial Requirements, 2007. Volume 2: Key Technologies, Applications, and Industrial Cases, 2009

7 *Residential Open Building.* Stephen Kendall, Jonathan Teicher. International Council for Building Research, Studies and Documentation. Taylor&Francis. 2000. ISBN 0419238301, 9780419238300

8 *Propuestas del Primer Concurso Europeo Restringido de Ideas Arquitectónicas.* Colección Proyecto ManuBuild. Volumen 1. Empresa Municipal de la Vivienda y Suelo, EMVS. Área de Gobierno de Urbanismo y Vivienda. Ayuntamiento de Madrid. 2009

ManuBuild[6] is a research project on Industrialized Construction, financed by the European Union. Its aim is to combine the impossible: the effectiveness of industrialized production with the creative inspiration of a dwelling without limitations. The result should offer the market several possibilities to choose from, in terms not only of materials and finishing, but also size and spatial configurations.

ManuBuild wants to take a step forward regarding the traditional method, based on craftsmanship, and impose the building of the Open Building Manufacturing, combining the ultra-efficient off-site and on-site fabrication and open systems of components which flood the market with a wide range of elements, taking advantage of a type of web 2.0 of global production. This idea, based on Open Building[7] –set out by John Habraken in the sixties–, separates the support from the infill. The support forms part of the permanent structure and it is of inalterable character, the infill aspires to be altered either because it has come to the end of its useful life or or because it is the desire of the user.

The first restricted European Competition for Architectural Ideas[8], held in 2006 by the EMVS as part of the ManuBuild project, has as its mission the construction of 'an experimental demonstration housing building to showcase the operativity and efficacy of new constructive solutions.' Nine architecture teams were invited with the challenge being to set out new

CTRL [SPACE]
PIERCY CONNER ARCHITECTS 2006

Módulos
Modules

COCINA
KITCHEN

ASEO
WC

EQUIPO MULTIMEDIA
MEDIA UNIT

BAÑO
BATHROOM

ALMACENAMIENTO
STORAGE

Posibles configuraciones
Possible layouts

1 LOSA DE CIMENTACIÓN
DE 70 cm APROX.
COMO SOPORTE DE LA
ESTRUCTURA DE ACERO
SITUADA EN LA RETÍCULA
PRINCIPAL DE 6X6 m
1 APPROX. 700 mm RAFT
FOUNDATION SUPPORTING
RHS FRAME ON 6x6m
PRIMARY GRID

2 PLANCHA DE 1,5 m DE
ANCHO COMO FORJADOS
DE PLANTA Y CUBIERTA
2 1.5 m WIDE HANSON
HOLLOWCOE PC PLANKS
FORM PARTY FLOOR

3 MÓDULOS PRE-INSTALADOS
FABRICADOS EN TALLER
Y LUEGO ENCAJADOS
EN SU SITIO
3 PRE-SERVICED MODULES
FABRICATED OFF-SITE AND
THEN SLID INTO POSITION

4 COLOCACIÓN DE
LOS MÓDULOS DE
ALMACENAMIENTO EN
MUROS MEDIANEROS
Y MONTAJE DEL
REVESTIMIENTO EXTERIOR
4 STORAGE WALL MODULE
PUT INTO LOCATION
AND EXTERNAL
CLADDING ASSEMBLED

5 CALEFACCIÓN
GEOTÉRMICA EMBEBIDA EN
LA CAPA DE COMPRESIÓN
5 GEOTHERMAL HEATING
LAID IN SCREED

6 CINCO AÑOS MÁS
TARDE... SE AÑADE
UNA ENTREPLANTA DE
ACERO CON PERFILES
EN U CADA 40 cm
6 5 YEARS LATER... COLD
FORMED STEEL C
SECTION MEZZANINE
ADDED AT 40 cm

dos nueve equipos de arquitectos con el reto de plantear nuevos métodos constructivos industrializados, flexibles, económicos, seguros, sostenibles y finalmente bellos. ¡Ah, la belleza!

La propuesta ganadora, de Piercy Conner Architects, combina lo mejor de los dos mundos. Su concepto funde lo pragmático y lo sensual con un sentido de integración de opuestos: "Lo que se necesita es un paradigma de viviendas que aproveche las mejores características del modelo industrial y los elementos esenciales de la tradición nacional para crear una vivienda que no sólo sea pragmática y eficaz, sino también sensualmente interesante y receptiva".

Sigue los principios del *Open Building*, con unos elementos fijos, como son la estructura, los servicios y el almacenamiento y otros elementos variables, que corresponden a los tabiques, forjados intermedios y materiales. Esto afecta plenamente a la normativa urbanística, porque la casa deberá ser pensada en metros cúbicos y no en metros cuadrados, con lo que la edificabilidad máxima se ajustará en tres dimensiones, independientemente de la superficie de cada vivienda. El consumidor final podrá elegir entre vivienda en un único piso, o en dos alturas y pensar más en términos de potencial, que en número de dormitorios.

El tercer premio fue para Feilden Clegg Bradley Studios, que construye su propuesta de viviendas con contenedores prefabricados apilables. Propone jardines en todas las plantas y chimeneas de ventilación para que el aire circule verticalmente a través de los apartamentos. El planteamiento se basa en los módulos industrializados en tres di-

industrialized building methods which were to be flexible, economical, safe, sustainable and finally beautiful. Ah, beauty!

The winning proposal, by Piercy Conner Architects, combines the best of both worlds. The concept fuses the pragmatic with the sensual with a sense of integrating opposites: 'What is needed is a housing paradigm that takes the best parts of the industrial model with the essential parts of the domestic tradition to create a dwelling which is not only pragmatic and efficient but also interesting and responsive.'

This follows the principles of Open Building, with some fixed elements, such as the structure, the services and storage and other variable elements, corresponding to the partitions, intermediate framework and materials. This fully affects town-planning laws, because the house should be thought of in terms of cubic metres and not square metres, such that the maximum build space will be adjusted in three dimensions, independent of the surface area of each dwelling. The end-user will be able to choose between a single-storey or double-storey apartment and think more about the potential, than the number of bedrooms.

The third prize went to Feilden Clegg Bradley Studios, which builds its housing proposal with stacked prefabricated shipping containers. They propose gardens on all levels and wind towers for the air to circulate through the apartments. This approach is based on the industrialized 3D modules from the fifties converted now to steel

SKY GARDENS
FEILDEN CLEGG BRADLEY STUDIOS 2006

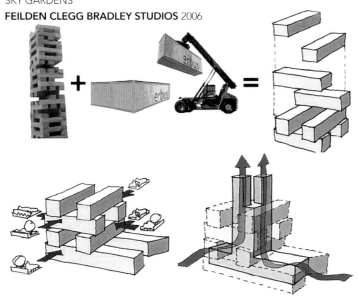

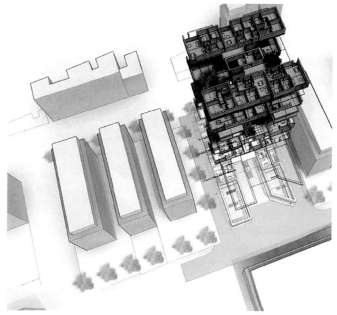

Sistema Verbus
Verbus systems

mensiones de mediados del siglo pasado, convertidos esta vez en contenedores de acero y madera, a los que se añaden tres elementos naturales: aire, tierra y vegetación. Estamos ante otra fusión de opuestos. Por un lado, un producto industrial, el contenedor marítimo fácilmente transportable y por otro, las consideraciones medioambientales, como son su apilado –de manera que se favorezca la ventilación– y sus eco-soluciones verdes y marrones, a base de plantas en altura y de una zona en el subsuelo, rellena de arcilla sin cocer, que actuará como almacén de frescor en verano.

Este sistema presenta a primera vista dos inconvenientes: uno, el coste del transporte del aire en cualquier mercancía hueca, configurada como un contenedor vacío y dos, que la mano de obra local se queda al margen de un proceso de producción que podría desarrollarse a miles de kilómetros de distancia. Junto con las pegas, Feilden Clegg y Bradley aportan sus propias soluciones: aprovechan el vacío del contenedor para transportar las herramientas y los materiales en su interior y sugieren que los trabajos finales de remate y acabado de la vivienda sean ejecutados por mano de obra local, entrenada en el propio emplazamiento.

La ventaja es que se apoya en un fabricante de módulos que ya existe, Verbus Systems[9]. Su método de apilar está probado por la experiencia y se basa en que "la rigidez inherente de las cajas de acero corten permite configurarlas longitudinalmente y en voladizos sin refuerzo de estructural adicional".

and wood containers, to which three natural elements have been added, air, earth and vegetation. We are faced with another fusion of opposites. On the one hand, the easily transported shipping container and on the other hand, the environmental considerations, such as the stacking –so that the ventilation is made easier– and its green and brown eco-solutions, based on plants in the sky and a sub-floor zone, filled with unfired clay bricks, acting as a 'coolth' store in summer.

This system on first sight presents two disadvantages. One, the cost of the transportation of air in any empty cargo, configured as an empty container and two, that local labour is sidelined from a production process which could be carried out thousands of kilometres away. Along with the cons, Feilden Clegg and Bradley contribute their own solutions: they take advantage of the empty space in the container to transport tools and materials and suggest that the final tasks of completion and finishing be performed by local labour, trained on-site.

The advantage is that it is supported by an existing module manufacturer, Verbus Systems[9]. Their stacking system has a proven track record and is based on the fact that 'the corten steel boxes are inherently rigid and are able to span and cantilever with no extra structural stiffening.'

9 Verbus Systems.
   http://www.verbussystems.com

Con la imaginación y la creatividad que aporta un entorno global, seguramente serán las soluciones híbridas las que marquen el camino a seguir. La producción en serie de elementos para la vivienda –fabricados no importa dónde, pero con un elevado nivel de calidad–, va a poner en manos de arquitectos y constructores un enorme abanico de soluciones estandarizadas. Estas unidades, una vez aceptadas y certificadas por los reguladores, serán presentadas al usuario final para que decida entre todas ellas cuál es la que mejor encaja con sus necesidades.

Por eso, cuando aparecen libros como *El Artesano*[10], que ensalza la cultura material y la satisfacción del trabajo bien hecho, cuando se otorga un importante premio de arquitectura al arquitecto-artesano por excelencia y se valora el oficio y la habilidad manual de la disciplina, es el momento de soñar con lo mejor de los dos mundos: la fabricación industrializada de componentes y el saber-hacer de la producción artesanal. Desconectemos el piloto automático y volvamos a agarrar el timón con las manos.

With the imagination and creativity coming from a global setting, it is bound to be hybrid solutions which lead the way. The mass production of housing elements, manufactured no matter where, but of a high standard, will hand architects and builders a huge range of standardized solutions. These units -once accepted and certified by the regulatory bodies-, will be presented to the end-user so that he or she can decide amongst all these units which one best fits their needs.

This is why, when books such as *The Craftsman*[10], which praise material culture and the satisfaction of a job well done, appear, when an important architectural award is given to the architect-craftsman par excellence and the trade and manual skill of the discipline is valued, it is the time to dream of the best of both worlds: the industrialized production of components and the know-how of the craftsman's production. Let's switch off the auto-pilot and get our hands back on the controls.

Translated into English by Ken Mortimer

10 *The Craftsman*. Richard Sennett. Yale University Press. Marzo de 2008. ISBN 0300119097, 978-0300119091
El Artesano. Anagrama. ISBN 978-84-339-6287-4

DENSIDAD DENSITY

Ordenados por densidad de POBLACIÓN, de menor a mayor.
Arranged by RESIDENTIAL density, from lowest to highest.

1:5.000
0 10   50

27,7% OCUPACIÓN COVERED AREA	**11,1%** OCUPACIÓN COVERED AREA	**80%** OCUPACIÓN COVERED AREA	**58,1%** OCUPACIÓN COVERED AREA
1,05 EDIFICABILIDAD FLOOR AREA RATIO	**1,13** EDIFICABILIDAD FLOOR AREA RATIO	**4,77** EDIFICABILIDAD FLOOR AREA RATIO	**1,81** EDIFICABILIDAD FLOOR AREA RATIO

9.278 m²
SUPERFICIE CONSTRUIDA
GROSS FLOOR AREA

13.800 m²
SUPERFICIE CONSTRUIDA
GROSS FLOOR AREA

32.930 m²
SUPERFICIE CONSTRUIDA
GROSS FLOOR AREA

18.240 m²
SUPERFICIE CONSTRUIDA
GROSS FLOOR AREA

6.101 m²
SUPERFICIE DE PARCELA
PLOT AREA

9.200 m²
SUPERFICIE DE PARCELA
PLOT AREA

6.900 m²
SUPERFICIE DE PARCELA
PLOT AREA

8.480 m²
SUPERFICIE DE PARCELA
PLOT AREA

159 ☺/ha

35 ⌂ **57** ⌂/ha

FREI ARCHITEKTEN
ROHR.CH 2007

253 ☺/ha

81 ⌂ **88** ⌂/ha

KASPER DANIELSEN ARCHITECTS / FUTURE SYSTEMS COPENHAGEN.DK 2008

259 ☺/ha

83 ⌂ **120** ⌂/ha

BIG+JDS
COPENHAGEN.DK 2008

267 ☺/ha

95 ⌂ **112** ⌂/ha

POOLEN ARCHITEKTEN
CULEMBORG.NL 2008

74,3%
OCUPACIÓN
COVERED AREA

1,85
EDIFICABILIDAD
FLOOR AREA RATIO

5.104 m²
SUPERFICIE CONSTRUIDA
GROSS FLOOR AREA

2.761 m²
SUPERFICIE DE PARCELA
PLOT AREA

47,7%
OCUPACIÓN
COVERED AREA

3,40
EDIFICABILIDAD
FLOOR AREA RATIO

19.400 m²
SUPERFICIE CONSTRUIDA
GROSS FLOOR AREA

5.378 m²
SUPERFICIE DE PARCELA
PLOT AREA

44,8%
OCUPACIÓN
COVERED AREA

1,58
EDIFICABILIDAD
FLOOR AREA RATIO

13.958 m²
SUPERFICIE CONSTRUIDA
GROSS FLOOR AREA

5.616 m²
SUPERFICIE DE PARCELA
PLOT AREA

21,9%
OCUPACIÓN
COVERED AREA

0,58
EDIFICABILIDAD
FLOOR AREA RATIO

7.731 m²
SUPERFICIE CONSTRUIDA
GROSS FLOOR AREA

9.622 m²
SUPERFICIE DE PARCELA
PLOT AREA

335
☺/ha

23 ⌂   **83** ⌂/ha

ATELIER KEMPE THILL
AMSTERDAM.NL 2007

345
☺/ha

110 ⌂   **204** ⌂/ha

KOKO ARCHITEKTID
TALLINN.EE 2007

400
☺/ha

56 ⌂   **100** ⌂/ha

BEVK PEROVIC ARHITEKTI
LJUBLJANA.SI 2006

410
☺/ha

130 ⌂   **135** ⌂/ha

BEVK PEROVIC ARHITEKTI
MARIBOR.SI 2007

2000
1900
1800
1700
1600
1500
1400
1300
1200
1100
1000
900
800
700
600
500
400
300
200
100
0

2000
1900
1800
1700
1600
1500
1400
1300
1200
1100
1000
900
800
700
600
500
400
300
200
100
0

35,1%
OCUPACIÓN
COVERED AREA

1,30
EDIFICABILIDAD
FLOOR AREA RATIO

5.826 m²
SUPERFICIE CONSTRUIDA
GROSS FLOOR AREA

2.773 m²
SUPERFICIE DE PARCELA
PLOT AREA

59,6%
OCUPACIÓN
COVERED AREA

2,26
EDIFICABILIDAD
FLOOR AREA RATIO

1.577 m²
SUPERFICIE CONSTRUIDA
GROSS FLOOR AREA

698 m²
SUPERFICIE DE PARCELA
PLOT AREA

38,7%
OCUPACIÓN
COVERED AREA

1,69
EDIFICABILIDAD
FLOOR AREA RATIO

5.848 m²
SUPERFICIE CONSTRUIDA
GROSS FLOOR AREA

2.607 m²
SUPERFICIE DE PARCELA
PLOT AREA

29,4%
OCUPACIÓN
COVERED AREA

2,50
EDIFICABILIDAD
FLOOR AREA RATIO

15.400 m²
SUPERFICIE CONSTRUIDA
GROSS FLOOR AREA

6.151 m²
SUPERFICIE DE PARCELA
PLOT AREA

428
⊙/ha

430
⊙/ha

446
⊙/ha

451
⊙/ha

48 ⌂ **173** ⌂/ha

OFIS ARHITEKTI
CERKLJE. SI 2007

8 ⌂ **115** ⌂/ha

ONION FLATS
PHILADELPHIA.US 2009

40 ⌂ **153** ⌂/ha

AVA ARCHITECTS
PORTO.PT 2008

74 ⌂ **120** ⌂/ha

ARONS EN GELAUFF ARCHITECTEN
GRONINGEN.NL 2007

⊙/ha

2000

1900

36,5%
OCUPACIÓN
COVERED AREA

1,66
EDIFICABILIDAD
FLOOR AREA RATIO

18.437 m²
SUPERFICIE CONSTRUIDA
GROSS FLOOR AREA

8.519 m²
SUPERFICIE DE PARCELA
PLOT AREA

100%
OCUPACIÓN
COVERED AREA

1,92
EDIFICABILIDAD
FLOOR AREA RATIO

12.277 m²
SUPERFICIE CONSTRUIDA
GROSS FLOOR AREA

4.446 m²
SUPERFICIE DE PARCELA
PLOT AREA

58%
OCUPACIÓN
COVERED AREA

2,45
EDIFICABILIDAD
FLOOR AREA RATIO

4.590 m²
SUPERFICIE CONSTRUIDA
GROSS FLOOR AREA

1.370 m²
SUPERFICIE DE PARCELA
PLOT AREA

69,8%
OCUPACIÓN
COVERED AREA

2,21
EDIFICABILIDAD
FLOOR AREA RATIO

937 m²
SUPERFICIE CONSTRUIDA
GROSS FLOOR AREA

424 m²
SUPERFICIE DE PARCELA
PLOT AREA

1800

1700

1600

1500

1400

1300

1200

1100

1000

900

800

700

458
⊙/ha

469
⊙/ha

493
⊙/ha

513
⊙/ha

600

500

400

300

200

100

78 ⌂   **92** ⌂/ha

GIGON / GUYER
ZURICH.CH 2007

102 ⌂   **229** ⌂/ha

DOSMASUNO ARQUITECTOS
MADRID.ES 2006

32 ⌂   **234** ⌂/ha

ANA ARCHITECTEN
AMSTERDAM.NL 2007

12 ⌂   **283** ⌂/ha

ADAMO-FAIDEN ARQUITECTOS
BUENOS AIRES.AR 2008

0

2000
1900
1800
1700
1600
1500
1400
1300
1200
1100
1000
900
800
700
600
500
400
300
200
100

40,3%
OCUPACIÓN
COVERED AREA

2,34
EDIFICABILIDAD
FLOOR AREA RATIO

19.800 m²
SUPERFICIE CONSTRUIDA
GROSS FLOOR AREA

6.200 m²
SUPERFICIE DE PARCELA
PLOT AREA

550
☉/ha

112 🏠 **181** 🏠/ha

LEHMANN FIDANZA & ASSOCIÉS
FRIBOURG.CH 2009

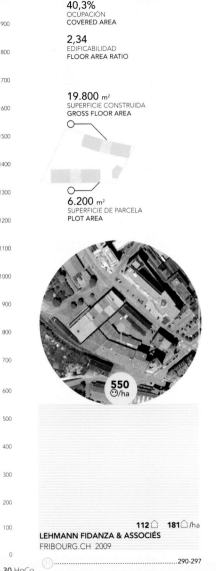

59,6%
OCUPACIÓN
COVERED AREA

7,39
EDIFICABILIDAD
FLOOR AREA RATIO

32.526 m²
SUPERFICIE CONSTRUIDA
GROSS FLOOR AREA

4.162 m²
SUPERFICIE DE PARCELA
PLOT AREA

626
☉/ha

140 🏠 **336** 🏠/ha

OFFICE dA, BURT HILL
BOSTON.US 2007

36,5%
OCUPACIÓN
COVERED AREA

1,84
EDIFICABILIDAD
FLOOR AREA RATIO

11.384 m²
SUPERFICIE CONSTRUIDA
GROSS FLOOR AREA

4.458 m²
SUPERFICIE DE PARCELA
PLOT AREA

665
☉/ha

88 🏠 **197** 🏠/ha

FOREIGN OFFICE ARCHITECTS
MADRID.ES 2007

100%
OCUPACIÓN
COVERED AREA

4,24
EDIFICABILIDAD
FLOOR AREA RATIO

22.070 m²
SUPERFICIE CONSTRUIDA
GROSS FLOOR AREA

5.200 m²
SUPERFICIE DE PARCELA
PLOT AREA

683
☉/ha

108 🏠 **208** 🏠/ha

HVDN ARCHITECTEN
AMSTERDAM.NL 2008

63,8% OCUPACIÓN COVERED AREA	**57,8%** OCUPACIÓN COVERED AREA	**35%** OCUPACIÓN COVERED AREA	**52,5%** OCUPACIÓN COVERED AREA
1,55 EDIFICABILIDAD FLOOR AREA RATIO	**2,97** EDIFICABILIDAD FLOOR AREA RATIO	**2,79** EDIFICABILIDAD FLOOR AREA RATIO	**2,20** EDIFICABILIDAD FLOOR AREA RATIO

9.750 m² SUPERFICIE CONSTRUIDA GROSS FLOOR AREA

5.327 m² SUPERFICIE DE PARCELA PLOT AREA

3.037 m² SUPERFICIE CONSTRUIDA GROSS FLOOR AREA

1.022 m² SUPERFICIE DE PARCELA PLOT AREA

21.550 m² SUPERFICIE CONSTRUIDA GROSS FLOOR AREA

6.021 m² SUPERFICIE DE PARCELA PLOT AREA

4.618 m² SUPERFICIE CONSTRUIDA GROSS FLOOR AREA

1.541 m² SUPERFICIE DE PARCELA PLOT AREA

704 ☺/ha

709 ☺/ha

712 ☺/ha

714 ☺/ha

2000
1900
1700
1600
1500
1400
1300
1200
1100
1000
900
800
700
600
500
400
300
200
100
0

99 ⌂ **186** ⌂/ha

EDOUARD FRANÇOIS
PARIS.FR 2008

31 ⌂ **303** ⌂/ha

dRMM ARCHITECTS
LONDON.UK 2006

146 ⌂ **242** ⌂/ha

MVRDV, BLANCA LLEÓ
MADRID.ES 2009

44 ⌂ **285** ⌂/ha

COLL-LECLERC ARQUITECTOS
LLEIDA.ES 2008

18 252-265   26 340-347   14 198-217   07 104-117

HoCo **31**

2000
1900
1800
1700
1600
1500
1400
1300
1200
1100
1000
900
800
700
600
500
400
300
200
100
0

763
⊙/ha

○ **7.373** m²
SUPERFICIE DE PARCELA
PLOT AREA

○ **13.710** m²
SUPERFICIE CONSTRUIDA
GROSS FLOOR AREA

37,8%
OCUPACIÓN
COVERED AREA

1,60
EDIFICABILIDAD
FLOOR AREA RATIO

287 ⌂ **393** ⌂/ha

URBANUS ARCHITECTURE & DESIGN
GUANGZHOU.CN 2008

781
⊙/ha

2.534 m²
SUPERFICIE CONSTRUIDA
○ GROSS FLOOR AREA

496 m²
○ SUPERFICIE DE PARCELA
PLOT AREA

80%
OCUPACIÓN
COVERED AREA

4,20
EDIFICABILIDAD
FLOOR AREA RATIO

27 ⌂ **544** ⌂/ha

LÓPEZ-RIVERA ARQUITECTOS
BARCELONA.ES 2007

850
⊙/ha

○ **14.963** m²
SUPERFICIE CONSTRUIDA
GROSS FLOOR AREA

○ **4.237** m²
SUPERFICIE DE PARCELA
PLOT AREA

59,6%
OCUPACIÓN
COVERED AREA

3,27
EDIFICABILIDAD
FLOOR AREA RATIO

147 ⌂ **347** ⌂/ha

ALLFORD HALL MONAGHAN MORRIS
LONDON.UK 2007

880
⊙/ha

18.024 m²
SUPERFICIE CONSTRUIDA
GROSS FLOOR AREA
○

○ **5.569** m²
SUPERFICIE DE PARCELA
PLOT AREA

47,6%
OCUPACIÓN
COVERED AREA

2,25
EDIFICABILIDAD
FLOOR AREA RATIO

132 ⌂ **237** ⌂/ha

AGUINAGA Y ASOCIADOS ARQUITECTOS
MADRID.ES 2008

☺/ha

2000

1900

1800

1700

1600

1500

1400

1300

1200

1100

1000

900

800

700

600

500

400

300

200

100

0

1.697 ☺/ha

1.476 ☺/ha

1.119 ☺/ha

886 ☺/ha

1.537 m²
SUPERFICIE CONSTRUIDA
GROSS FLOOR AREA

550 m²
SUPERFICIE DE PARCELA
PLOT AREA

68,2%
OCUPACIÓN
COVERED AREA

2,79
EDIFICABILIDAD
FLOOR AREA RATIO

17 ⌂ 309 ⌂/ha

**EMMANUEL COMBAREL DOMINIQUE
MARREC ARCHITECTES** PARIS.FR 2006

1.740 m²
SUPERFICIE CONSTRUIDA
GROSS FLOOR AREA

726 m²
SUPERFICIE DE PARCELA
PLOT AREA

69,7%
OCUPACIÓN
COVERED AREA

2,40
EDIFICABILIDAD
FLOOR AREA RATIO

65 ⌂ 895 ⌂/ha

HAMONIC + MASSON
PARIS.FR 2008

7.035 m²
SUPERFICIE CONSTRUIDA
GROSS FLOOR AREA

1.050 m²
SUPERFICIE DE PARCELA
PLOT AREA

100%
OCUPACIÓN
COVERED AREA

5,33
EDIFICABILIDAD
FLOOR AREA RATIO

42 ⌂ 400 ⌂/ha

ROLDÁN + BERENGUÉ
BARCELONA.ES 2009

7.470 m²
SUPERFICIE CONSTRUIDA
GROSS FLOOR AREA

1.068 m²
SUPERFICIE DE PARCELA
PLOT AREA

76,4%
OCUPACIÓN
COVERED AREA

5,29
EDIFICABILIDAD
FLOOR AREA RATIO

48 ⌂ 449 ⌂/ha

BECKMANN-N'THÉPÉ ARCHITECTES
PARIS.FR 2007

Coste por m² construido, según paridad de poder adquisitivo per cápita, en dólares internacionales
Cost per built sq metre, according to purchasing power parity per capita, expressed in international dollars

2.000
1900
1800
1700
1600
1500
1400
1300
1200
1100
1000
900
800
700
600
500
400
300
200
100

436   461   507   551   562   619   641   649   760   768   773   802   813   821   838   868

DOSMASUNO ARQUITECTOS MADRID.ES 2006
AVA ARCHITECTS PORTO.PT 2008
FOREIGN OFFICE ARCHITECTS MADRID.ES 2007
FREI ARCHITEKTEN ROHR.CH 2007
AGUINAGA Y ASOCIADOS ARQUITECTOS MADRID.ES 2008
ARONS EN GELAUFF ARCHITECTEN GRONINGEN.NL 2007
COLL-LECLERC ARQUITECTOS LLEIDA.ES 2008
LÓPEZ-RIVERA ARQUITECTOS BARCELONA.ES 2007
URBANUS ARCHITECTURE & DESIGN GUANGZHOU.CN 2008
BEVK PEROVIC ARHITEKTI MARIBOR.SI 2007
BIG+JDS COPENHAGEN.DK 2008
ROLDÁN + BERENGUÉ BARCELONA.ES 2009
POOLEN ARCHITEKTEN CULEMBORG.NL 2008
MVRDV, BLANCA LLEÓ MADRID.ES 2009
OFIS ARHITEKTI CERKLJE.SI 2007
ATELIER KEMPE THILL AMSTERDAM.NL 2007

Subsidised 100%	Subsidised 100%	Subsidised 100%	Subsidised 0%	Subsidised 100%	Subsidised 100%	Subsidised 100%	Subsidised 100%	Subsidised 0%	Subsidised 100%	Subsidised 0%	Subsidised 100%	Subsidised 100%	Subsidised 15%	Subsidised 100%	Subsidised 100%	Subsidised 100%
38-55	56-65	66-75	76-87	88-95	96-103	104-117	118-127	128-143	144-153	154-169	170-183	184-197	198-217	218-229	230-239

$/m²

2.248 not available

1.838

1.688

1.588 1.590

1.562

1.547

1.327

1.303

1.120

1.115

1.089

1.050

1.047

1.030

2.000
1900
1800
1700
1600
1500
1400
1300
1200
1100
1000
900
800
700
600
500
400
300
200
100
0 $/m²

EDOUARD FRANÇOIS PARIS.FR 2008
KOKO ARHITEKTID TALLINN.EE 2007
HVDN ARCHITECTEN AMSTERDAM.NL 2008
LEHMANN FIDANZA & ASSOCIÉS FRIBOURG.CH 2009
ANA ARCHITECTEN AMSTERDAM.NL 2007
EMMANUEL COMBAREL DOMINIQUE MARREC ARCHITECTES PARIS.FR 2006
BEVK PEROVIC ARHITEKTI LJUBLJANA.SI 2006
ADAMO-FAIDEN ARQUITECTOS BUENOS AIRES.AR 2008
dRMM LONDON.UK 2006
ALLFORD HALL MONAGHAN MORRIS LONDON.UK 2007
HAMONIC + MASSON PARIS.FR 2008
KASPER DANIELSEN ARCHITECTS / FUTURE SYSTEMS COPENHAGEN.DK 2008
GIGON / GUYER ZURICH.CH 2007
ONION FLATS PHILADELPHIA.US 2009
OFFICE dA, BURT HILL BOSTON.US 2007

bsidised 64%   240-251
Subsidised 100% (18) 252-265
Subsidised 0% (19) 266-275
Subsidised 0% (20) 276-289
Subsidised 0% (21) 290-297
Subsidised 0% (22) 298-307
Subsidised 100% (23) 308-319
Subsidised 100% (24) 320-329
Subsidised 0% (25) 330-339
Subsidised 61% (26) 340-347
Subsidised 50% (27) 348-357
Subsidised 100% (28) 358-367
Subsidised 0% (29) 368-379
Subsidised 100% (30) 380-391
Subsidised 100% (31) 392-401
Subsidised 0% (32) 402-417 $/m²

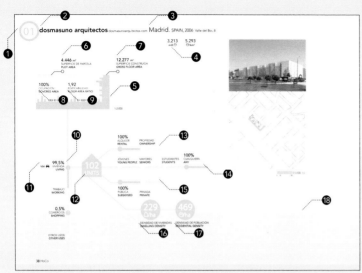

01 dosmasuno arquitectos dosmasunoarquitectos.com **Madrid**. SPAIN, 2006 Valle del Bio, 8

4.446 m²
SUPERFICIE DE PARCELA
PLOT AREA

12.277 m²
SUPERFICIE CONSTRUIDA
GROSS FLOOR AREA

3.213
m/d ⊙

5.293
O/km²

100%
OCUPACIÓN
COVERED AREA

1,92
EDIFICABILIDAD
FLOOR AREA RATIO

1:2.000

100%
ALQUILER
RENTAL

PROPIEDAD
OWNERSHIP

99,5%
VIVIENDA
LIVING

JÓVENES
YOUNG PEOPLE

MAYORES
SENIORS

ESTUDIANTES
STUDENTS

100%
CUALQUIERA
ANY

102 UNITS

TRABAJO
WORKING

100%
PÚBLICA
SUBSIDISED

PRIVADA
PRIVATE

0,5%
COMERCIOS
SHOPPING

22,9
O/ha

469
O/ha

DENSIDAD DE VIVIENDAS
DWELLING DENSITY

DENSIDAD DE POBLACIÓN
RESIDENTIAL DENSITY

OTROS USOS
OTHER USES

38 HoCo

---

❶ NUMERACIÓN Indica el orden de cada obra dentro de la publicación, según el coste por m² construido (según paridad de poder adquisitivo per cápita, en dólares internacionales).

❷ ARQUITECTOS Página web de los arquitectos.

❸ Emplazamiento del proyecto. Fecha final del proyecto.

❹ CIUDAD Número de habitantes de la población en millones. Densidad de la población en número de habitantes por kilómetro cuadrado.

❺ PLANTA DE PARCELA Planta de la parcela con la huella del edificio a escala 1:2.000.

❻ Superficie de parcela.

❼ Superficie construida total en la parcela en todas las plantas.

❽ OCUPACIÓN Porcentaje de superficie ocupada por la edificación en la parcela analizada, respecto a la superficie total de la parcela.

❶ NUMBERING Indicates the order of each work in the publication, according to the cost per built sq metre, according to purchasing power parity per capita, expressed in international dollars.

❷ ARCHITECTS. Architects' web site.

❸ Project location. Completion date.

❹ CITY Number of inhabitants. Population density in the city (inhabitants per km²).

❺ PLAN OF THE PLOT Plan of the plot with the building footprint at a scale of 1:2,000.

❻ Plot area.

❼ Total constructed surface area on the plot and on all floors.

❽ COVERED AREA Percentage of surface area occupied by buildings on the analysed plot, in regard to the total surface area of the plot.

❾ EDIFICABILIDAD Es la relación entre la superficie construida sobre rasante y la total de la parcela en metros cuadrados. El cociente se expresa sin unidades.

❿ USOS Porcentaje de superficie construida de uso residencial, de oficinas, comercial y para otros usos.

⓫ Número de plazas de aparcamiento asignadas a cada uso.

⓬ Número de viviendas.

⓭ RÉGIMEN DE LA VIVIENDA Porcentaje en alquiler o en propiedad.

⓮ USUARIOS DE LA VIVIENDA Porcentaje de jóvenes, mayores, estudiantes o unidades de convivencia multipersonales sin especificar edades.

⓯ PROMOCIÓN DE LA VIVIENDA Porcentaje de promoción pública o privada.

⓰ DENSIDAD DE VIVIENDAS EN LA PARCELA Cociente entre el número de viviendas del proyecto y la superficie neta de la parcela, sin incluir los viales perimetrales. Es una densidad neta y las unidades son viviendas por hectárea.

⓱ DENSIDAD DE POBLACIÓN EN LA PARCELA Se obtiene multiplicando el número de viviendas del proyecto por el número de personas que pueden habitarlas. Para calcular las personas que residen en un edificio se ha aplicado un factor de conversión (Fc) que varía en función del tamaño de la vivienda.
Fc= ** hab/vivienda
Residencias de ancianos o jóvenes, con unidades individuales:
Fc = 1,00 hab/vivienda
Vivienda estudio (un único espacio):
Fc= 1,25 hab/vivienda
Vivienda de 1 dormitorio:
Fc = 1,25 hab/vivienda
Vivienda de 2 dormitorios:
Fc = 2,50 hab/vivienda
Viviendas de 3 dormitorios:
Fc = 3,75 hab/vivienda
Viviendas de 4 o más dormitorios:
Fc = 5,00 hab/vivienda
Densidad residencial neta de parcela en habitantes por hectárea.

⓲ LÍNEA DE FLOTACIÓN Asciende a medida que lo hace el coste de la construcción.

❾ FLOOR AREA RATIO This is the relationship between the constructed surface area above grade and the total surface area of the plot in square metres. The quotient is expressed without units.

❿ USES Percentaje of residential floorspace, office floorspace, commercial floorspace and floorspace for other uses.

⓫ Car park places.

⓬ Number of dwellings.

⓭ TENURE Percentage of rented dwellings or dwellings in ownership.

⓮ USERS Percentaje of young people, seniors, students and multi-personal units of coexistence, without specifying ages.

⓯ PROMOTION Percentaje of subsidised dwellings or private promotion.

⓰ DENSITY OF DWELLINGS ON THE PLOT The quotient of the number of housing units and the net surface area of the plot, not including the perimetral roads. It is a net density and the unit is dwellings per hectare.

⓱ RESIDENTIAL DENSITY ON THE PLOT Obtained by multiplying the number of housing units in the project by the number of people who can inhabit them. To calculate the number of people who live in a building, a factor of conversion (Fc) has been applied. It varies according to the size of the housing unit.
Fc= **inhab/dwelling
Dwellings for the elderly or young people, with individual units:
Fc = 1.00 inhab/dwelling
Studio housing (one single space):
Fc = 1.25 inhab/dwelling
One bedroom dwelling:
Fc = 1,25 inhab/dwelling
Two bedroom dwelling:
Fc = 2.50 inhab/dwelling
Three bedroom dwelling:
Fc = 3.75 inhab/dwelling
Four or more bedroom dwelling:
Fc = 5.00 inhab/dwelling
When referring strictly to the plot, this is a net residential density. The unit is the number of inhabitants per hectare.

⓲ WATERLINE It rises as construction costs go up.

PROYECTOS PROJECTS

3,213
mill.☺

5.293
☺/km²

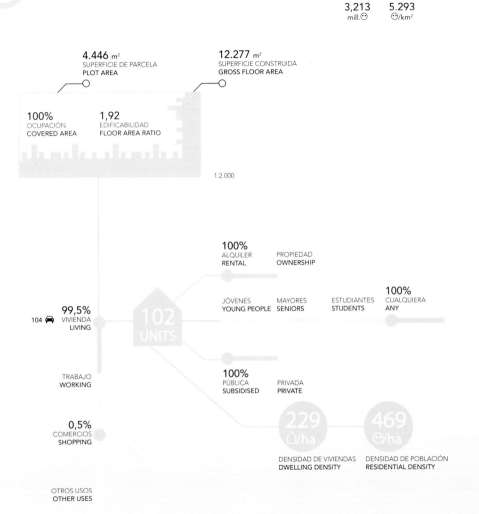

4.446 m²
SUPERFICIE DE PARCELA
PLOT AREA

12.277 m²
SUPERFICIE CONSTRUIDA
GROSS FLOOR AREA

100%
OCUPACIÓN
COVERED AREA

1,92
EDIFICABILIDAD
FLOOR AREA RATIO

1:2.000

100%
ALQUILER
RENTAL

PROPIEDAD
OWNERSHIP

JÓVENES
YOUNG PEOPLE

MAYORES
SENIORS

ESTUDIANTES
STUDENTS

100%
CUALQUIERA
ANY

104 🚗 99,5%
VIVIENDA
LIVING

102
UNITS

TRABAJO
WORKING

100%
PÚBLICA
SUBSIDISED

PRIVADA
PRIVATE

0,5%
COMERCIOS
SHOPPING

229
⌂/ha

469
☺/ha

DENSIDAD DE VIVIENDAS
DWELLING DENSITY

DENSIDAD DE POBLACIÓN
RESIDENTIAL DENSITY

OTROS USOS
OTHER USES

1:5.000
0 10   50

2.000

1900

1800

1700

1600

1500

1400

01

1300

1200

1100

1000

900

800

700

436
$/m²

600

393
€/m²

500

400

300

200

100

0

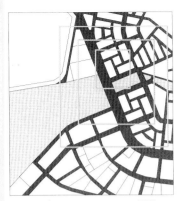

Pausa verde. Nos encontramos en el PAU II-6 Carabanchel, frente a un eje verde que interrumpe la trama edificada del ensanche.

Green interlude. The site is located in the Carabanchel extension plan, opposite a green axis that cuts the built up area.

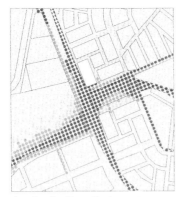

Aproximación al lugar. El solar exento presenta dos alineaciones principales.

Arrival to the site. The building site has two main front facades.

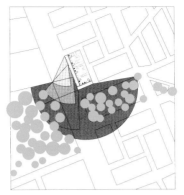

Visuales cercanas. Las viviendas se ajustan a las alineaciones buscando la mejor orientación, y las zonas verdes del entorno.

Close views. Apartments seek for the best orientation and the surrounding green areas.

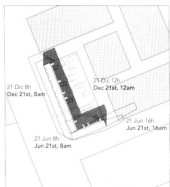

21 Dic 8h
Dec 21st, 8am

21 Dic 12h
Dec 21st, 12am

21 Jun 16h
Jun 21st, 16am

21 Jun 8h
Jun 21st, 8am

Sol y sombra. La sombra arrojada define dos espacios diferentes en el jardín interior, y respeta las edificaciones vecinas.

Sunpath. The shadow of the building determins spaces in the inner courtyard, and respects nearby buildings.

Huella. Orientación y recogimiento

A pesar de las pautas dibujadas sobre los planos, los lugares necesitan expresar su propio ser, surgir naturalmente, construirse a sí mismos. Y concretamente este lugar, alineado frente a la pausa verde, frente a la concatenación de espacios públicos que unen el antiguo Carabanchel con su bosque, a través del ensanche, por delante del solar sobre el que construimos. Como respuesta, las viviendas se comprimen sobre el borde, una única pieza lineal, en una búsqueda de la razón principal del lugar, unas vistas y una orientación óptima donde este y oeste comparten el sur, generando el límite de la actividad, sosegando el interior y definiendo el exterior.

Print. Orientation and meditation

In spite of their drawn guidelines, places need to express their own being, to come about naturally, to build themselves. And specifically in this place, lined up along the green rest, in front of the chain of public spaces that join the old Carabanchel with its forest, through its expansion, past the lot we are building on. In response to this, the housing units are compressed on the edge as one linear piece. They search for the place's reason of being, views and a perfect orientation where east and west share the south, generating limits for activity, calming the interior and defining the exterior.

Atiende también esta situación a las condiciones cercanas.
El entorno inmediato se beneficia de un elemento respetuoso con las edificaciones vecinas, a las que cede el sol, apartándose la construcción sobre un zócalo que mantiene sin embargo la alineación prefigurada en el plan. Este zócalo se convierte en elemento activo y activado. Activado por la propia edificación, que barre con su sombra una zona dura y define en su recorrido la frontera de una superficie con vegetación. Activo, pues además de convertirse en lugar de encuentro y juego, concentra el acceso a los diferentes portales y se relaciona con el estacionamiento que se abre a él, proporcionándole ventilación e iluminación natural.

This situation also attends to nearby conditions. Its immediate surroundings profit from an element that is respectful to neighbouring buildings, who it gives sunlight to, standing back from construction on a base that nonetheless maintains the alignment prefigured on the plan. This base becomes an activated active element. It is activated by the very building, which sweeps a harsh area with its shade and with its path defines the border along a green surface. And it is active because not only does it become a place for social interaction and play, but also concentrates the different building entrances and is connected with the car park, providing natural light and ventilation.

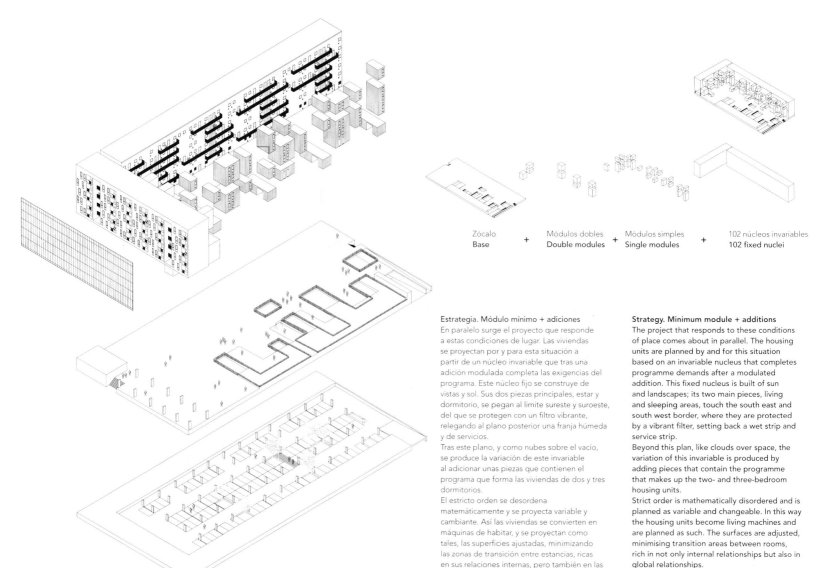

Zócalo
Base +

Módulos dobles
Double modules +

Módulos simples
Single modules +

102 núcleos invariables
102 fixed nuclei

Estrategia. Módulo mínimo + adiciones

En paralelo surge el proyecto que responde a estas condiciones de lugar. Las viviendas se proyectan por y para esta situación a partir de un núcleo invariable que tras una adición modulada completa las exigencias del programa. Este núcleo fijo se construye de vistas y sol. Sus dos piezas principales, estar y dormitorio, se pegan al límite sureste y suroeste, del que se protegen con un filtro vibrante, relegando al plano posterior una franja húmeda y de servicios.

Tras este plano, y como nubes sobre el vacío, se produce la variación de este invariable al adicionar unas piezas que contienen el programa que forma las viviendas de dos y tres dormitorios.

El estricto orden se desordena matemáticamente y se proyecta variable y cambiante. Así las viviendas se convierten en máquinas de habitar, y se proyectan como tales, las superficies ajustadas, minimizando las zonas de transición entre estancias, ricas en sus relaciones internas, pero también en las globales.

Strategy. Minimum module + additions

The project that responds to these conditions of place comes about in parallel. The housing units are planned by and for this situation based on an invariable nucleus that completes programme demands after a modulated addition. This fixed nucleus is built of sun and landscapes; its two main pieces, living and sleeping areas, touch the south east and south west border, where they are protected by a vibrant filter, setting back a wet strip and service strip.

Beyond this plan, like clouds over space, the variation of this invariable is produced by adding pieces that contain the programme that makes up the two- and three-bedroom housing units.

Strict order is mathematically disordered and is planned as variable and changeable. In this way the housing units become living machines and are planned as such. The surfaces are adjusted, minimising transition areas between rooms, rich in not only internal relationships but also in global relationships.

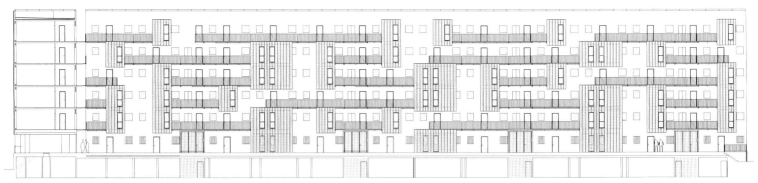

Sección este **East section**

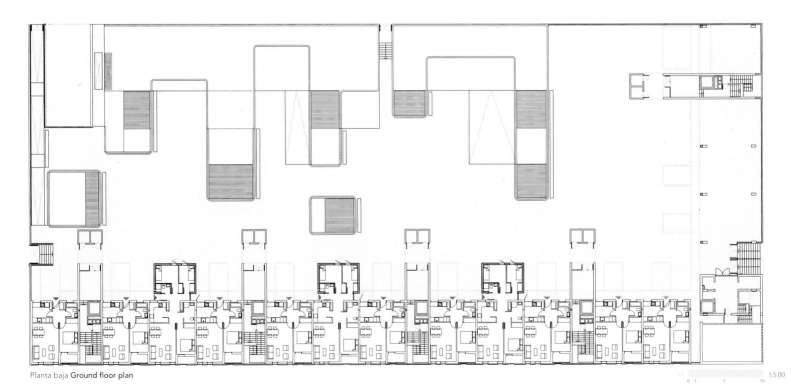

Planta baja **Ground floor plan**

1:5.00

0 1   5   10

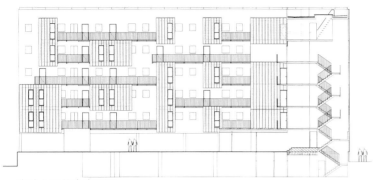

Alzado norte **Noth elevation**

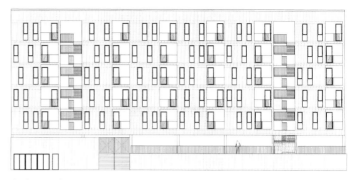

Alzado sur sin la protección de chapa estirada **South elevation without the stretched steel plate**

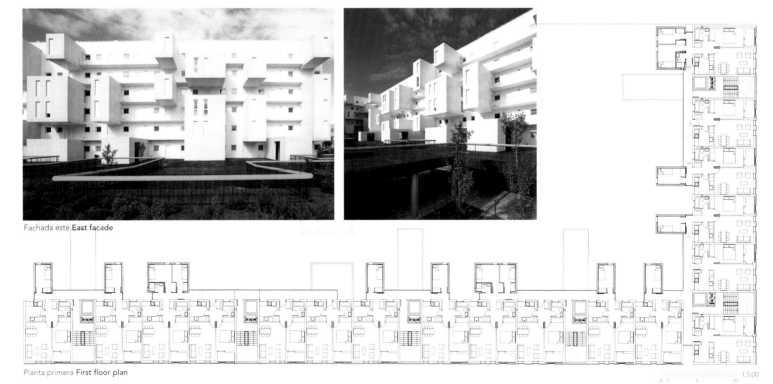

Fachada este **East facade**

Planta primera **First floor plan**

1:5.00

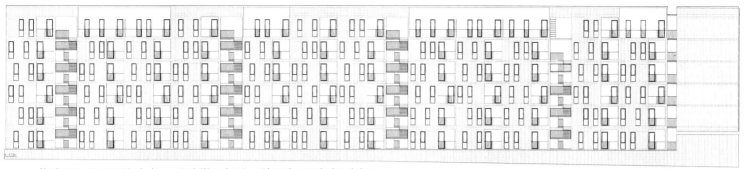

Alzado oeste sin protección de chapa estirada **West elevation without the stretched steel plate**

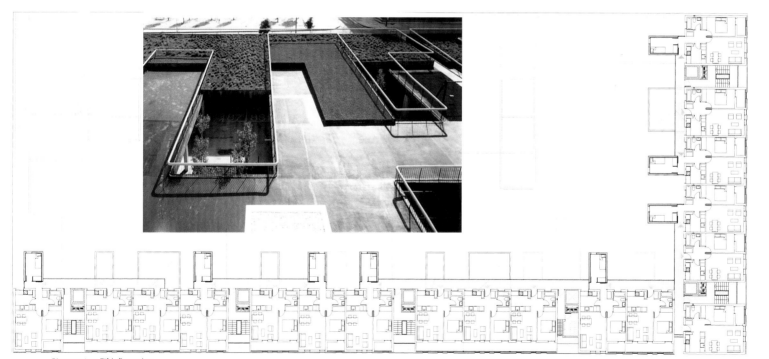

Planta quinta **Fifth floor plan**

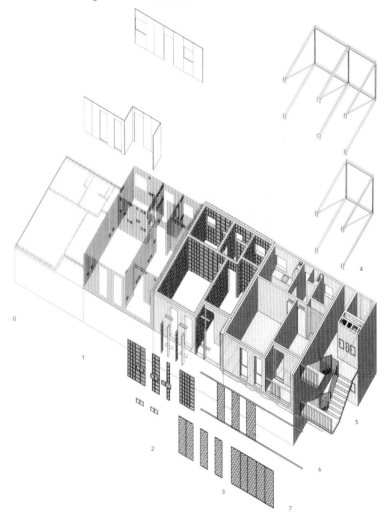

Sistema constructivo.
Encofrado integral a medida

El proyecto propone una sistematización de la vivienda social.

El sistema constructivo empleado es por tanto una consecuencia natural de su organización, que optimiza los valores de la repetición, sin renunciar a la identidad de cada usuario.

Su construcción responde a esta necesidad de optimización industrial. Así, la estabilidad del cuerpo principal se construye en hormigón a partir de un único molde de alta precisión. Mientras, las variaciones suceden gracias a los módulos ligeros en estructura metálica que constituyen los elementos de adición.

Este sistema industrializado facilita la puesta en obra, anula la aparición de escombros en el proceso constructivo, y acelera los plazos de ejecución.

Constructive system.
Customised integrated formwork

The project proposes a systematisation of social housing.

The constructive system used is thus a natural consequence of its organisation, which optimises the value of repetition but does not renounce the identity of the individual user. It construction responds to this need for industrial optimisation. In this way the stability of the main body is built of concrete from a single, highly precise mould.

This industrialised system facilitates construction and eliminates debris in the construction process and reduces execution time.

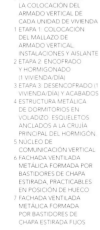

Planta de módulo sencillo
Single module floor plan

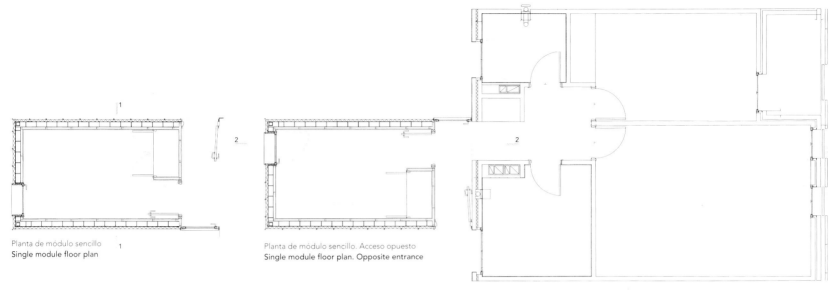

Planta de módulo sencillo. Acceso opuesto
Single module floor plan. Opposite entrance

0 ETAPA 0 ESPERAS PARA LA COLOCACIÓN DEL ARMADO VERTICAL DE CADA UNIDAD DE VIVIENDA
1 ETAPA 1: COLOCACIÓN DEL MALLAZO DE ARMADO VERTICAL, INSTALACIONES Y AISLANTE
2 ETAPA 2: ENCOFRADO Y HORMIGONADO (1 VIVIENDA/DIA)
3 ETAPA 3: DESENCOFRADO (1 VIVIENDA/DIA) Y ACABADOS
4 ESTRUCTURA METÁLICA DE DORMITORIOS EN VOLADIZO. ESQUELETOS ANCLADOS A LA CRUJÍA PRINCIPAL DEL HORMIGÓN.
5 NÚCLEO DE COMUNICACIÓN VERTICAL
6 FACHADA VENTILADA METÁLICA FORMADA POR BASTIDORES DE CHAPA ESTIRADA, PRACTICABLES EN POSICIÓN DE HUECO
7 FACHADA VENTILADA METÁLICA FORMADA POR BASTIDORES DE CHAPA ESTIRADA FIJOS

0 STAGE 0: STEEL RODS DETERMINE THE LOCATION OF THE VERTICAL STEEL REINFORCING BARS
1 STAGE 1: POSITIONING OF THE VERTICAL STEEL REINFORCING BARS, INSTALLATIONS AND THERMAL INSULATION
2 STAGE 2: MOLDS ARE POSITIONED AND CONCRETE IS POURED (1 DWELLING PER DAY)
3 STAGE 3: MOLDS ARE REMOVED (1 DWELLING PER DAY) AND WORK ON INTERIOR FINISHINGS STARTS
4 CANTELIVERED STEEL STRUCTURE FOR THE BEDROOMS. ESKELETONS ARE ANCHORED TO THE MAIN CONCRETE STRUCTURE
5 VERTICAL CIRCULATION CORE
6 VENTILATED FACADE: SLIDING STRETCHED STEEL PANELS IN FRONT OF WINDOWS
7 VENTILATED FACADE: FIXED STRETCHED STEEL PANELS IN FRONT WA

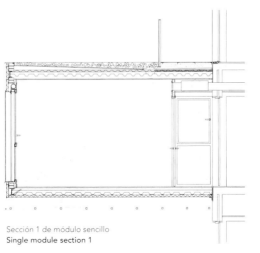

Sección 1 de módulo sencillo
Single module section 1

1:100

0   0.5   1

Sección 2 paralela a fachada de módulo sencillo
Single module paralel to facade section 2

1 ANGULAR DE ACERO
  GALVANIZADO 70 x 40 mm
2 MURO DE FÁBRICA
  DE 1/2 PIE
3 ALBARDILLA DE
  ALUMINIO LACADO
4 ENFOSCADO
5 LANA DE VIDRIO
  HIDROFUGADA CON
  VELO e=5 cm
6 PERFIL UPN 140
7 POLIESTIRENO
  EXTRUIDO e=4 cm
8 DINTEL DE CHAPA PLEGADA
9 PERSIANA
10 DINTEL DE ALUMINIO
   LACADO
11 DOBLE ACRISTALAMIENTO
12 TUBO DE ACERO 20 x 20 mm
13 PERFIL DE ACERO IPE 160
14 CHAPA DE ALUMINIO
   MICRO PERFORADA
15 PERFIL Z DE 55 x 30 mm
16 TUBO DE ACERO 40 x 40 mm
17 TUBO DE ACERO 20 x 20 mm
18 DOBLE LÁMINA ASFÁLTICA
19 GRAVA
20 MORTERO DE PENDIENTES
21 FORJADO DE CHAPA
   COLABORANTE
22 FALSO TECHO DE
   ESCAYOLA
23 CARTÓN YESO
24 CAPIALZADO INTEGRADO
25 CARPINTERÍA DE
   ALUMINIO LACADO
26 RODAPIÉ DM LACADO
27 TARIMA FLOTANTE

1 70 x 40 mm GALVANISED
  STEEL PROFILE
2 BRICKWORK WALL
3 LACQUERED
  ALUMINIUM COPING
4 MORTAR RENDERING
5 5 cm THICK FIREPROOF
  GLASS WOOL
6 UPN 140 STEEL PROFILE
7 4 cm THICK EXTRUDED
  POLYSTYRENE
8 STEEL PLATE LINTEL
9 BLIND
10 LACQUERED
   ALUMINIUM LINTEL
11 DOUBLE GLAZING
12 20 x 20 mm STEEL PROFILE
13 IPE 160 STEEL PROFILE
14 PERFORATED
   ALUMINIUM PLATE
15 55 x 30 mm Z PROFILE
16 40 x 40 mm STEEL PROFILE
17 20 x 20 mm STEEL PROFILE
18 DOUBLE BITUMINOUS
   LAYER
19 GRAVEL
20 SLOPE FORMING MORTAR
21 STEEL PLATE AND
   CONCRETE SLAB
22 PLASTER CEILING
23 PLASTER BOARD
24 INTEGRATED BLIND CASE
25 LACQUERED ALUMINIUM
   FRAMEWORK
26 WOOD FIBRE
   SKIRTING BOARD
27 FLOATING FLOOR

1:20

0   0.5   1

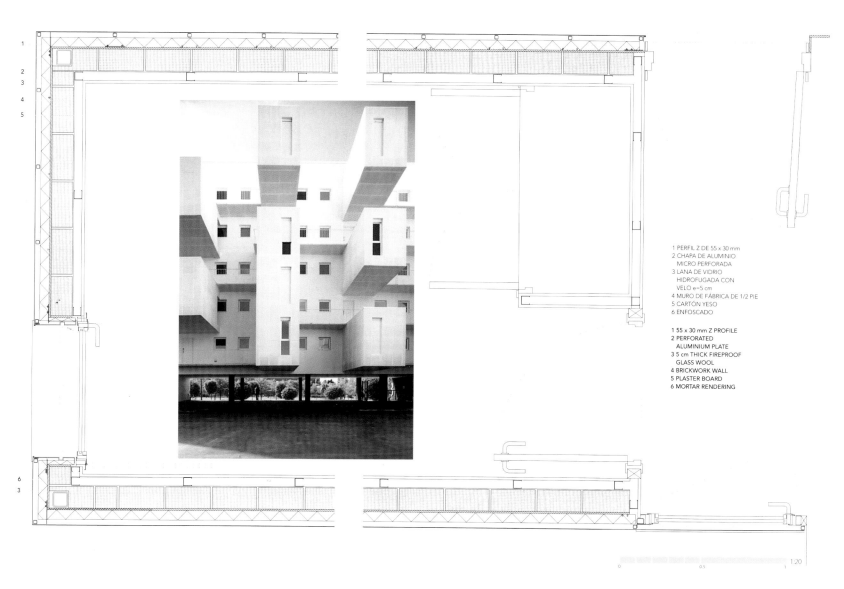

1 PERFIL Z DE 55 x 30 mm
2 CHAPA DE ALUMINIO
  MICRO PERFORADA
3 LANA DE VIDRIO
  HIDROFUGADA CON
  VELO e=5 cm
4 MURO DE FÁBRICA DE 1/2 PIE
5 CARTÓN YESO
6 ENFOSCADO

1 55 x 30 mm Z PROFILE
2 PERFORATED
  ALUMINIUM PLATE
3 5 cm THICK FIREPROOF
  GLASS WOOL
4 BRICKWORK WALL
5 PLASTER BOARD
6 MORTAR RENDERING

1:20

0   0.5   1

A

A

Sección **A** Section   1:500

0.1   5   10

1 CARPINTERÍA DE
  ALUMINIO LACADO
2 ALBARDILLA DE
  ALUMINIO LACADO
3 HERRAJE INFERIOR DE
  CORREDERA EXTERIOR
4 PERFIL DE ACERO IPE 80
5 HERRAJE SUPERIOR DE
  CORREDERA EXTERIOR
6 CHAPA ESTIRADA DE ACERO
  POSGALVANIZADA Y LACADA
7 MURO DE HORMIGÓN
  ARMADO e=10 cm
8 POLIESTIRENO
  EXTRUIDO e=4 cm

1 LACQUERED ALUMINIUM
  FRAMEWORK
2 LACQUERED ALUMINIUM
  COPING
3 LOWER FASTENING FOR
  THE SLIDING PANEL
4 IPE 80 STEEL PROFILE
5 UPPER FASTENING FOR
  THE SLIDING PANEL
6 LACQUERED, GALVANISED
  AND STRETCHED STEEL PLATE
7 10 cm THICK REINFORCED
  CONCRETE WALL
8 4 cm THICK EXTRUDED
  POLYSTYRENE

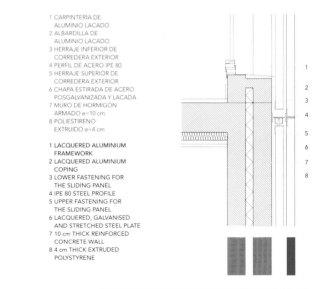

1

2

3

4

5

6

7

8

1   1:20

0   0.1   0.5   1

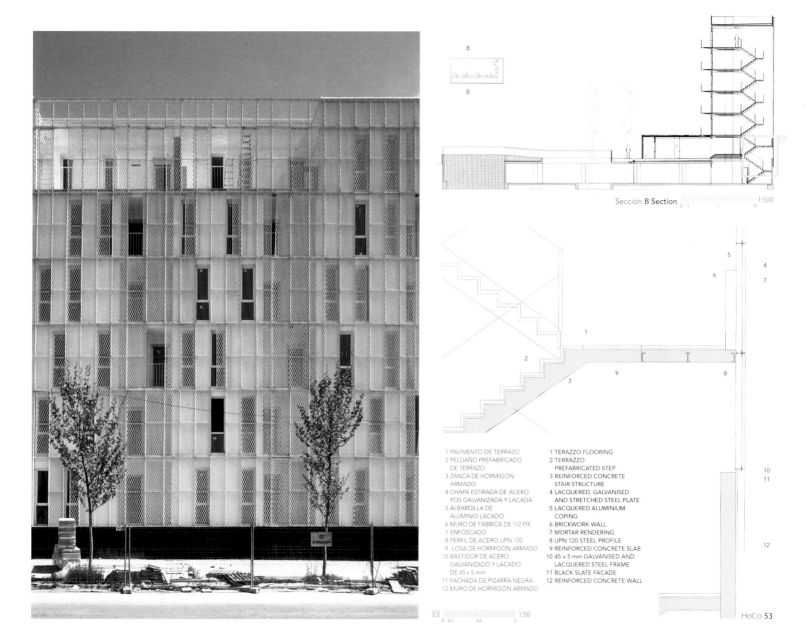

Sección B Section   0 1   10   1:500

1 PAVIMENTO DE TERRAZO
2 PELDAÑO PREFABRICADO
  DE TERRAZO
3 ZANCA DE HORMIGÓN
  ARMADO
4 CHAPA ESTIRADA DE ACERO
  POS GALVANIZADA Y LACADA
5 ALBARDILLA DE
  ALUMINIO LACADO
6 MURO DE FÁBRICA DE 1/2 PIE
7 ENFOSCADO
8 PERFIL DE ACERO UPN 120
9 LOSA DE HORMIGÓN ARMADO
10 BASTIDOR DE ACERO
   GALVANIZADO Y LACADO
   DE 45 x 5 mm
11 FACHADA DE PIZARRA NEGRA
12 MURO DE HORMIGÓN ARMADO

1 TERRAZZO FLOORING
2 TERRAZZO
  PREFABRICATED STEP
3 REINFORCED CONCRETE
  STAIR STRUCTURE
4 LACQUERED, GALVANISED
  AND STRETCHED STEEL PLATE
5 LACQUERED ALUMINIUM
  COPING
6 BRICKWORK WALL
7 MORTAR RENDERING
8 UPN 120 STEEL PROFILE
9 REINFORCED CONCRETE SLAB
10 45 x 5 mm GALVANISED AND
   LACQUERED STEEL FRAME
11 BLACK SLATE FACADE
12 REINFORCED CONCRETE WALL

2   1:50
0 0.1   0.5   1

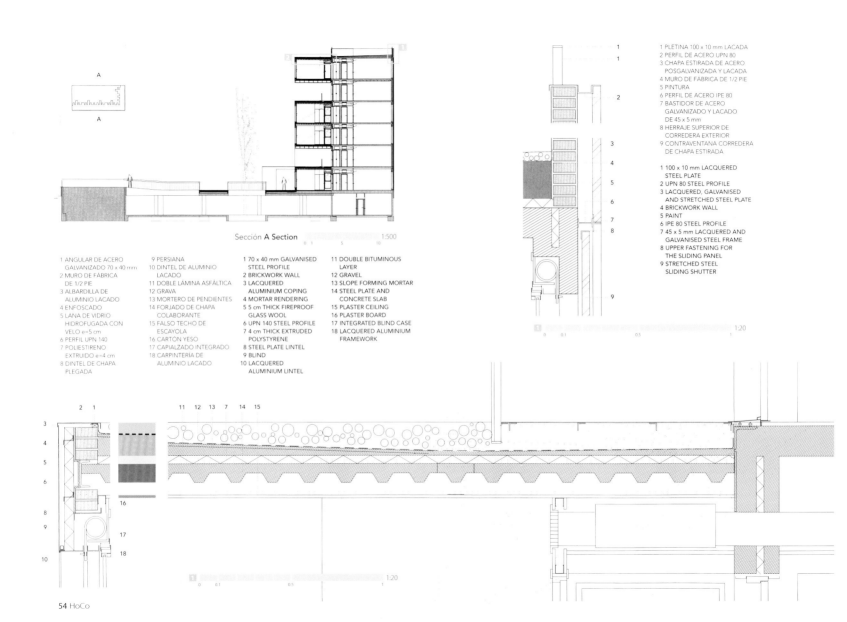

Sección **A** Section   1:500

1 ANGULAR DE ACERO GALVANIZADO 70 x 40 mm
2 MURO DE FÁBRICA DE 1/2 PIE
3 ALBARDILLA DE ALUMINIO LACADO
4 ENFOSCADO
5 LANA DE VIDRIO HIDROFUGADA CON VELO e=5 cm
6 PERFIL UPN 140
7 POLIESTIRENO EXTRUIDO e=4 cm
8 DINTEL DE CHAPA PLEGADA
9 PERSIANA
10 DINTEL DE ALUMINIO LACADO
11 DOBLE LÁMINA ASFÁLTICA
12 GRAVA
13 MORTERO DE PENDIENTES
14 FORJADO DE CHAPA COLABORANTE
15 FALSO TECHO DE ESCAYOLA
16 CARTÓN YESO
17 CAPIALZADO INTEGRADO
18 CARPINTERIA DE ALUMINIO LACADO

1 70 x 40 mm GALVANISED STEEL PROFILE
2 BRICKWORK WALL
3 LACQUERED ALUMINIUM COPING
4 MORTAR RENDERING
5 5 cm THICK FIREPROOF GLASS WOOL
6 UPN 140 STEEL PROFILE
7 4 cm THICK EXTRUDED POLYSTYRENE
8 STEEL PLATE LINTEL
9 BLIND
10 LACQUERED ALUMINIUM LINTEL
11 DOUBLE BITUMINOUS LAYER
12 GRAVEL
13 SLOPE FORMING MORTAR
14 STEEL PLATE AND CONCRETE SLAB
15 PLASTER CEILING
16 PLASTER BOARD
17 INTEGRATED BLIND CASE
18 LACQUERED ALUMINIUM FRAMEWORK

1 PLETINA 100 x 10 mm LACADA
2 PERFIL DE ACERO UPN 80
3 CHAPA ESTIRADA DE ACERO POSGALVANIZADA Y LACADA
4 MURO DE FÁBRICA DE 1/2 PIE
5 PINTURA
6 PERFIL DE ACERO IPE 80
7 BASTIDOR DE ACERO GALVANIZADO Y LACADO DE 45 x 5 mm
8 HERRAJE SUPERIOR DE CORREDERA EXTERIOR
9 CONTRAVENTANA CORREDERA DE CHAPA ESTIRADA

1 100 x 10 mm LACQUERED STEEL PLATE
2 UPN 80 STEEL PROFILE
3 LACQUERED, GALVANISED AND STRETCHED STEEL PLATE
4 BRICKWORK WALL
5 PAINT
6 IPE 80 STEEL PROFILE
7 45 x 5 mm LACQUERED AND GALVANISED STEEL FRAME
8 UPPER FASTENING FOR THE SLIDING PANEL
9 STRETCHED STEEL SLIDING SHUTTER

1:20

1:20

1 PLETINA CALIBRADA
   80 x 10 mm
2 BARROTE ACERO LACADO
   DE 20 mm DE DIÁMETRO
3 CHAPA LAGRIMADA
   GALVANIZADA Y LACADA
4 PERFIL DE ACERO 80 x 80 mm
5 PERIL DE ACERO HEB 100
6 ELECTRICIDAD
7 TELECOMUNICACIONES
8 AGUA
9 CHAPA DE ALUMINIO
   MICRO PERFORADA
10 ANGULAR DE ACERO
   30 x 30 mm
11 PERFIL DE ACERO 120 x 120 mm
12 ALBARDILLA DE
   ALUMINIO LACADO
13 PUERTA METÁLICA LACADA
   CON GOTERÓN INFERIOR
14 PAVIMENTO DE TERRAZO
15 LOSA DE HORMIGÓN
   ARMADO e=16 cm
16 MURO DE HORMIGÓN
   ARMADO e=10 cm
17 POLIESTIRENO
   EXTRUIDO e=4 cm

1 80 x 10 mm STEEL PLATE
2 Ø 20 mm LACQUERED
   STEEL ROD
3 LACQUERED GALVANISED
   STEEL PLATE
4 80 x 80 mm STEEL ANGLE
5 HEB 100 STEEL PROFLE
6 ELECTRICITY
7 VOICE AND DATA
8 WATER
9 PERFORATED
   ALUMINIUM PLATE
10 30 x 30 mm STEEL PROFILE
11 120 x 120 mm STEEL ANGLE
12 LACQUERED ALUMINIUM
   COPING
13 LACQUERED METAL DOOR
   WITH LOWER GUTTER
14 TERAZZO FLOORING
15 16 cm REINFORCED
   CONCRETE FLOOR SLAB
16 10 cm THICK REINFORCED
   CONCRETE WALL
17 4 cm THICK EXTRUDED
   POLYSTYRENE

B

B

Sección B Section   1:500

0 1   5   10

LAYERS

GRAVA
GRAVEL

CERÁMICA
TERRACOTTA

MADERA
WOOD

CEMENTO
CEMENT

VEGETACIÓN
PLANTING

METAL
METAL

AISLAMIENTO
INSULATION

MEMBRANA
MEMBRANE

HORMIGÓN
CONCRETE

MADERA
WOOD

CERÁMICA
TERRACOTTA

CARTÓN-YESO
PLASTER-BOARD

ENLUCIDO
PLASTER

METAL
METAL

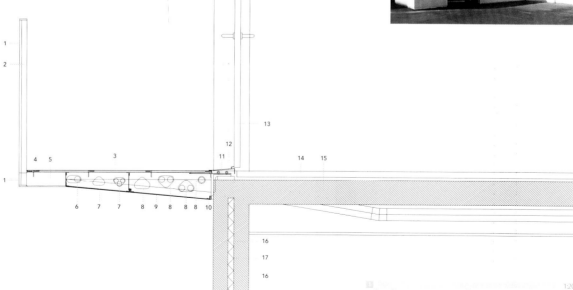

1

2

1

4   5   3   11

6   7   7   8 9 8   8 8   10

13

12

14   15

16

17

16

0   0.1   0.5   1:20

0,240
mill.☺

5.785
☺/km²

2.607 m²
SUPERFICIE DE PARCELA
PLOT AREA

5.848 m²
SUPERFICIE CONSTRUIDA
GROSS FLOOR AREA

1:2.000

38,7%
OCUPACIÓN
COVERED AREA

1,69
EDIFICABILIDAD
FLOOR AREA RATIO

100%
ALQUILER   PROPIEDAD
RENTAL   OWNERSHIP

JÓVENES   MAYORES   ESTUDIANTES   100%
YOUNG PEOPLE SENIORS   STUDENTS   CUALQUIERA
                                          ANY

40 🚗   83%
VIVIENDA
LIVING

40
UNITS

TRABAJO
WORKING

100%
PÚBLICA   PRIVADA
SUBSIDISED   PRIVATE

17%
COMERCIOS
SHOPPING

153
⌂/ha

446
☺/ha

DENSIDAD DE VIVIENDAS
DWELLING DENSITY

DENSIDAD DE POBLACIÓN
RESIDENTIAL DENSITY

OTROS USOS
OTHER USES

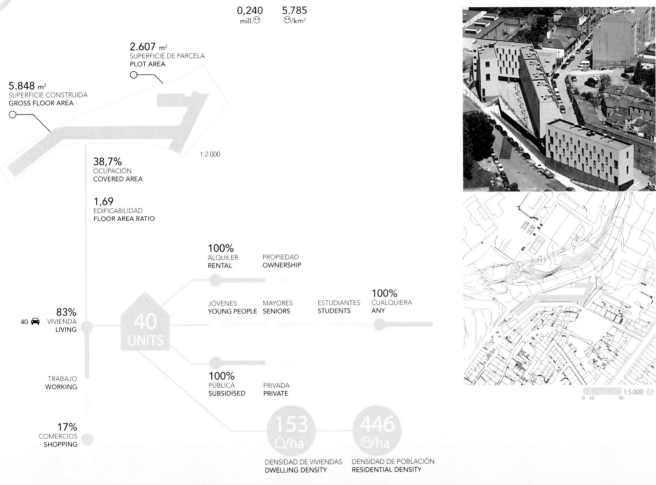

1:5.000

0 10   50

2.000

1.900

1.800

1.700

1.600

1.500

1.400

1.300

1.200

1.100

1.000

900

800

700

02

461
$/m²

600

376
€/m²

500

400

300

200

100

0

El (re)diseño de esta parte de ciudad tuvo como punto de partida el reconocimiento de las permanencias significativas de la estructura urbana circundante.

El edificio propuesto se adapta llenando el vacío urbano, buscando una unidad urbana de fragmentos nuevos y antiguos que son producto de diferentes momentos, y que nunca podrán ser "reducidos" a una unidad inmediata, pero que han de coexistir como realidades paralelas. Hemos procurado que las fachadas exteriores no reproduzcan de forma mimética la unidad buscada, sino que representen una imagen plástica resultante de la articulación e integración de la envolvente edificada más próxima (Lapa) y alejada (Leja).

La propuesta se asienta en la colmatación de los límites de la parcela, adaptando el edificio a la calle y afirmando el reconocimiento de los puntos significativos de la realidad urbana.

Las diversas alturas de la volumetría sirven para responder al contexto y la variación de la escala, produciendo un edificio/espacio significativo que media entre dos modos de hacer ciudad.

Por cuestiones económicas nos parece consecuente una tipología basada en el esquema "izquierdo-derecho". Además, las características morfológicas del solar, su poca profundidad permitida y la poca

The (re)designing of this part of the city had its starting point at the recognition of the significant permanence of the surrounding urban structure.

The proposed building adapts by filling urban empty space, searching for an urban unit of new and old fragments, products of different moments. These fragments can never be 'reduced' to an immediate unit, but must coexist as parallel realities.

We sought to make sure that exterior facades would not simply mimic the desired unit, but would reproduce an artistic image resulting from the articulation and integration of the nearest enclosure (Lapa) and the furthest (Leja).

The proposal is established on the overflow of the limits of the lot, adapting the building to the street and affirming the recognition of the significant points of urban reality.

The different heights of the volumetry respond to the context and variation of scale, producing a significant building/space that mediates between two ways of creating a city.

For economic reasons, we find it consistent to use a typology based on the 'left-right' outline. Furthermore, the morphological characteristics of the lot, the little depth it allows and the little depth desired for the building impede any other sort of typology. Therefore

profundidad deseada del edificio, impiden otra tipología.

Por consiguiente, hemos implantado una racionalidad tipológica en la distribución de las viviendas que sólo se rompe en los puntos de giro de la planta.

Los accesos están directamente relacionados con la tipología de vivienda propuesta, y al mismo tiempo, de acuerdo con la organización programática y funcional.

Los accesos se sitúan en torno del espacio central, fundamental en la articulación de las diferentes escalas urbanas. El acceso al aparcamiento se realiza desde el patio y las calles adyacentes (en las esquinas y en medio del edificio).

La distribución de las viviendas sigue un esquema con espacios a ambos lados de un pasillo, se identifica con el tejido que le es contiguo y es fruto de una aproximación a la tipología a partir de los elementos de composición de la fachada.

Dada la diferencia de cota entre las calles, es casi obligatorio orientar los dormitorios hacia el patio y las zonas húmedas hacia la calle Salgueiros. De esta forma se reduce el tamaño de la ventana, lo que redunda en una mayor privacidad.

El aparcamiento, que aloja una plaza por vivienda, tiene acceso desde las dos calles colindantes y se distribuye en dos niveles.

we have introduced typological rationality in the distribution of the housing units that is only broken at turning points on the floor plan. The entrances are directly related to the proposed housing typology and, at the same time, in accordance with the programmatic and functional organisation. The entrances are located around the central space, fundamental in the articulation of the different urban scales. Access to the car park is from the patio and adjacent streets (on corners and in the middle of the building).

The distribution of the housing units follows an outline on both sides of a hall. It identifies with the adjoining fabric and is the result of an approximation to the typology based on the composition elements of the facade. Given the differences in elevation of the streets, facing the bedrooms towards the patio and the wet areas towards calle Salgueiros is almost compulsory. In this way, window size is reduced, providing more privacy.

The car park, with one parking place per housing unit, has entrances on both adjacent streets and is distributed on two levels.

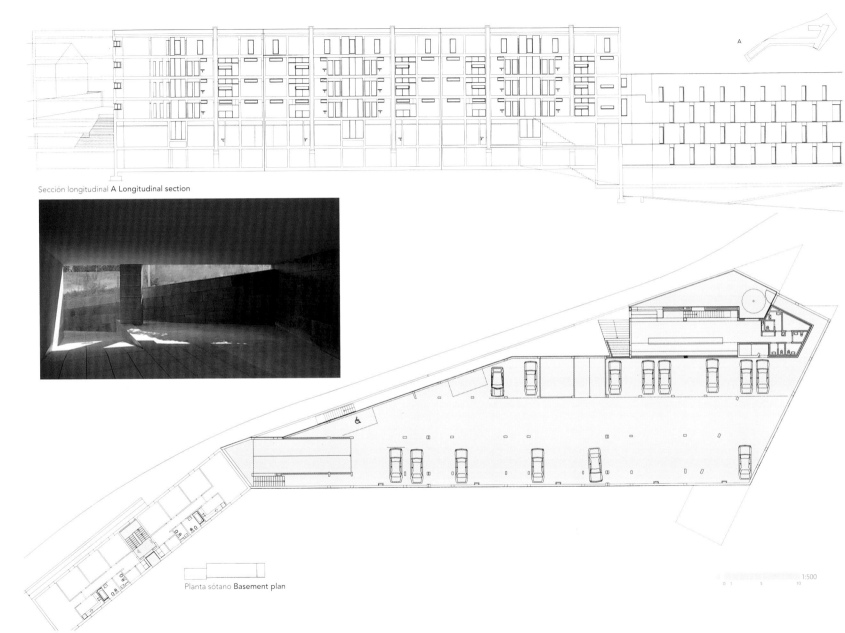

Sección longitudinal A Longitudinal section

Planta sótano Basement plan

1:500
0 1   5   10

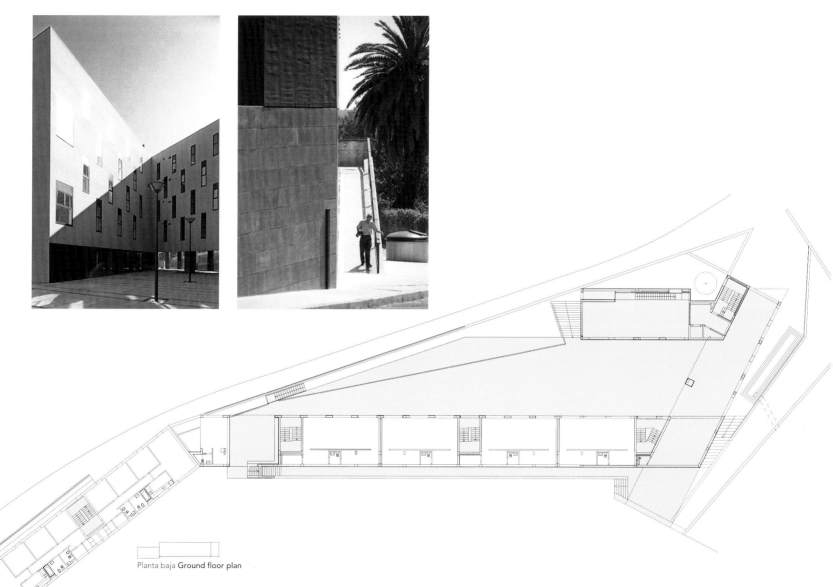

Planta baja **Ground floor plan**

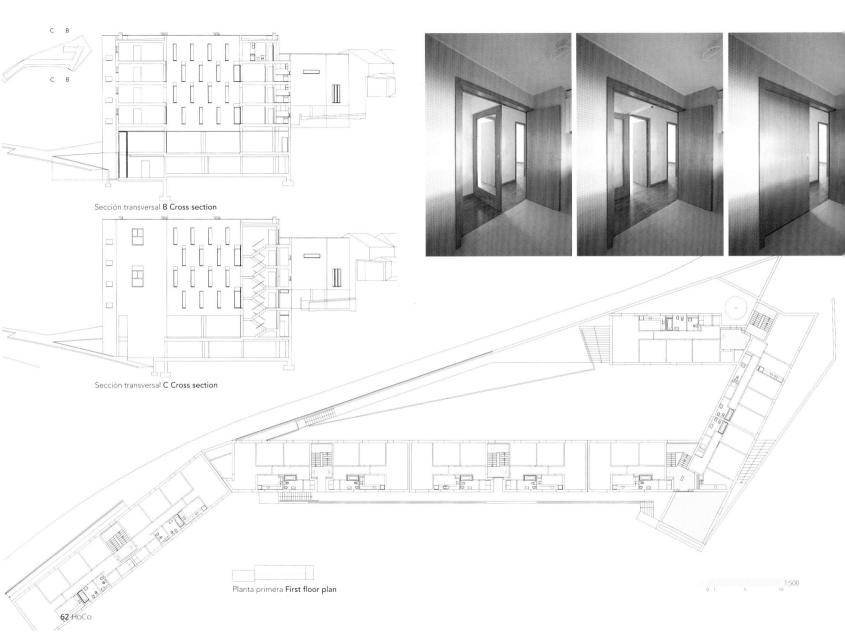

Sección transversal B **Cross section**

Sección transversal C **Cross section**

Planta primera **First floor plan**

1:500

0 1   5   10

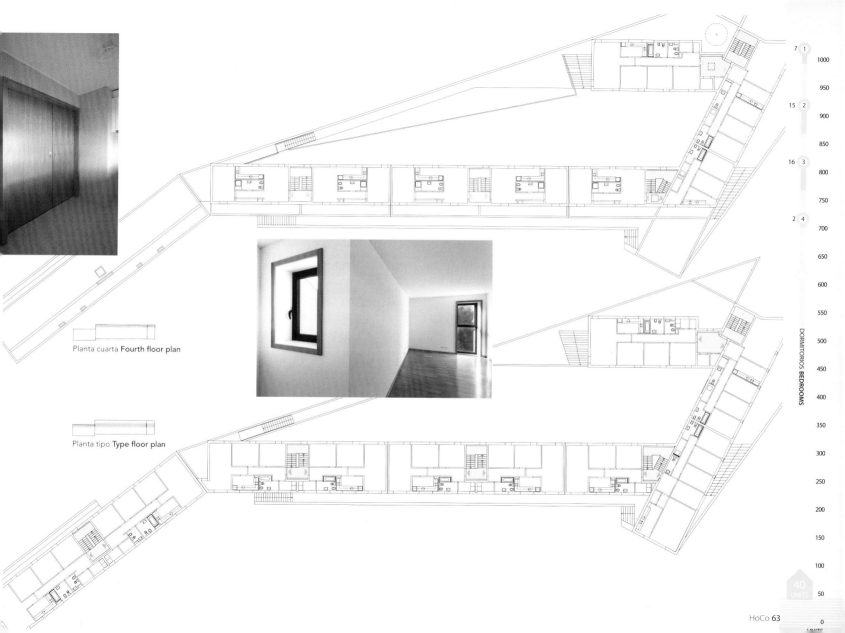

Planta cuarta **Fourth floor plan**

Planta tipo **Type floor plan**

DORMITORIOS BEDROOMS

7 1   1000
       950
15 2   900
       850
16 3   800
       750
2 4   700
       650
       600
       550
       500
       450
       400
       350
       300
       250
       200
       150
       100
       50
       0

40 UNITS

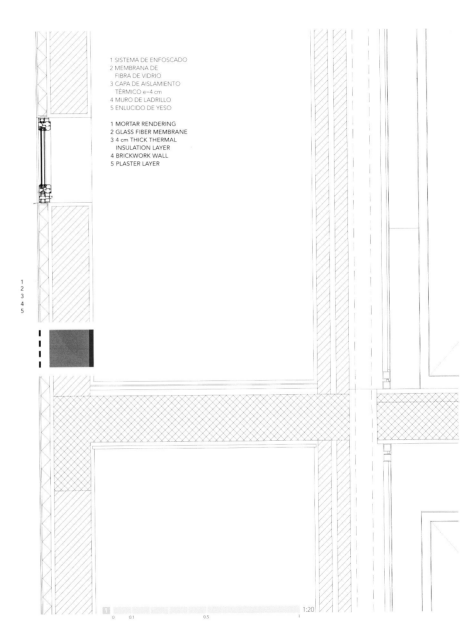

LAYERS

EXTERNAL

CERÁMICA
BRICKWORK

HORMIGÓN
CONCRETE

MADERA
WOOD

CEMENTO
CEMENT

METAL
METAL

COMPUESTO
COMPOSITE

VIDRIO
GALSS

ENFOSCADO/
ESTUCO
MORTAR/
STUCCO

AISLAMIENTO
INSULATION

MEMBRANA
MEMBRANE

PRINCIPAL

CERÁMICA
BRICKWORK

VIDRIO
GALSS

HORMIGÓN
CONCRETE

MADERA
WOOD

COMPUESTO
COMPOSITE

INTERNAL

CARTÓN-YESO
PLASTER-BOARD

CERÁMICA
BRICKWORK

ENLUCIDO
PLASTER

Sección de fachada 1
1 Facade section

1:200

0   1   5   10

1 SISTEMA DE ENFOSCADO
2 MEMBRANA DE
   FIBRA DE VIDRIO
3 CAPA DE AISLAMIENTO
   TÉRMICO e=4 cm
4 MURO DE LADRILLO
5 ENLUCIDO DE YESO

1 MORTAR RENDERING
2 GLASS FIBER MEMBRANE
3 4 cm THICK THERMAL
   INSULATION LAYER
4 BRICKWORK WALL
5 PLASTER LAYER

1
2
3
4
5

1:20

0   0.1   0.5   1

LAYERS

EXTERNAL

GRAVA
GRAVEL

CERÁMICA
TERRACOTTA

MADERA
WOOD

CEMENTO
CEMENT

VEGETACIÓN
PLANTING

METAL
METAL

AISLAMIENTO
INSULATION

MEMBRANA
MEMBRANE

PRINCIPAL

HORMIGÓN
CONCRETE

MADERA
WOOD

CERÁMICA
TERRACOTTA

INTERNAL

CARTÓN-YESO
PLASTER-BOARD

ENLUCIDO
PLASTER

METAL
METAL

1 MURO DE HORMIGÓN
2 CAPA DE AISLAMIENTO TÉRMICO e=4 cm
3 ENFOSCADO
4 LOSA DE CEMENTO
5 CAPA DE AISLAMIENTO TÉRMICO DE POLIESTIRENO EXTRUIDO e=3 cm
6 IMPERMEABILIZACIÓN CON DOBLE TELA ASFÁLTICA
7 CAPA DE FORMACIÓN DE PENDIENTE
8 FIELTRO GEOTEXTIL
9 LOSA DE HORMIGÓN
10 CARTÓN-YESO
11 GRAVA

1 CONCRETE WALL
2 4 cm THICK THERMAL INSULATION LAYER
3 MORTAR RENDERING
4 CEMENT PAVER
5 3 cm THICK EXTRUDED POLYSTYRENE THERMAL INSULATION LAYER
6 2-SHEETS ASPHALT WATERPROOF LAYER
7 SCREED TO FORM ROOF SLOPE
8 GEOTEXTILE FELT
9 CONCRETE SLAB
10 GYPSUM BOARD
11 GRAVEL

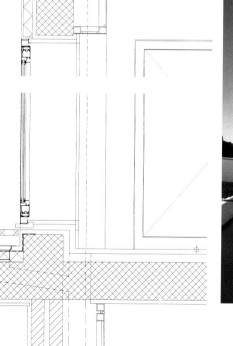

1:20

0   0.1   0.5   1

3,213
mill.☺

5.293
☺/km²

4.458 m²
SUPERFICIE DE PARCELA
PLOT AREA

11.384 m²
SUPERFICIE CONSTRUIDA
GROSS FLOOR AREA

1:2.000

36,5%
OCUPACIÓN
COVERED AREA

1,84
EDIFICABILIDAD
FLOOR AREA RATIO

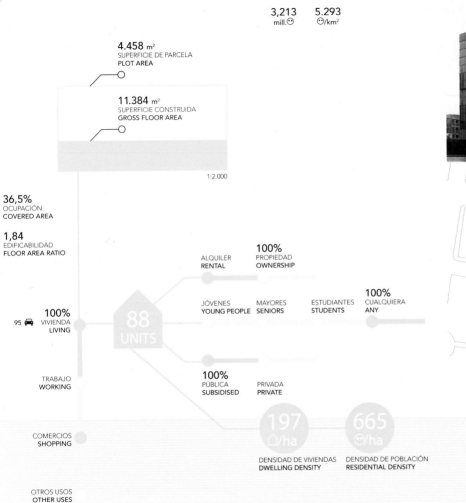

100%
VIVIENDA
LIVING

95 🚗

TRABAJO
WORKING

COMERCIOS
SHOPPING

OTROS USOS
OTHER USES

88
UNITS

ALQUILER
RENTAL

100%
PROPIEDAD
OWNERSHIP

JÓVENES
YOUNG PEOPLE

MAYORES
SENIORS

ESTUDIANTES
STUDENTS

100%
CUALQUIERA
ANY

100%
PÚBLICA
SUBSIDISED

PRIVADA
PRIVATE

197
⌂/ha

665
☺/ha

DENSIDAD DE VIVIENDAS
DWELLING DENSITY

DENSIDAD DE POBLACIÓN
RESIDENTIAL DENSITY

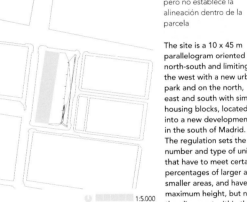

1:5.000
0 10   50

El lugar es un paralelogramo de 100 x 45 m orientado norte-sur, limitando al oeste con un nuevo parque urbano y al norte, este y sur con otras manzanas similares, situadas en un nuevo ensanche del sur de Madrid. La normativa establece la cantidad y el tipo de unidades, ciertos porcentajes de tamaños máximos y mínimos, así como una altura máxima, pero no establece la alineación dentro de la parcela

The site is a 10 x 45 m parallelogram oriented north-south and limiting on the west with a new urban park and on the north, east and south with similar housing blocks, located into a new development in the south of Madrid. The regulation sets the number and type of units that have to meet certain percentages of larger and smaller areas, and have a maximum height, but not the alignment within the rectangular plot.

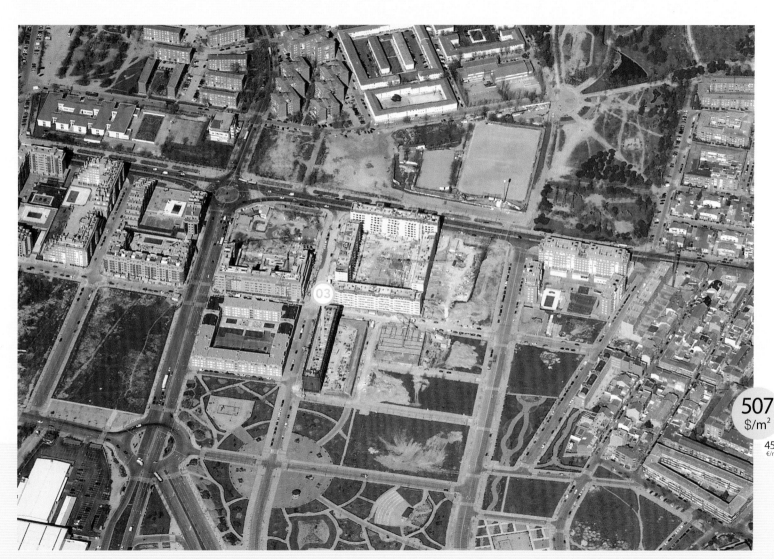

03

507
$/m²

457
€/m²

2.000

1.900

1.800

1.700

1.600

1.500

1.400

1.300

1.200

1.100

1.000

900

800

700

600

500

400

300

200

100

0

Como respuesta a la presencia del futuro parque en los terrenos colindantes y la orientación norte-sur de la parcela, decidimos proponer un volumen compacto que respetase la máxima altura permitida. De esta manera, cada vivienda goza de una doble orientación este-oeste. Para ello, las unidades se desarrollan sobre una planta de 13,40 m de longitud que conecta ambas fachadas, libre de elementos estructurales en las divisiones entre apartamentos. Esta concentración de la edificación en el lado oeste del solar permite construir un jardín común en el lado este, encima del aparcamiento para residentes.

Todas las viviendas miran a un jardín por cada lado y su cerramiento es enteramente de vidrio. Además, están dotadas de una galería perimetral de 1,5 m de ancho que puede ser usada como estancia semi-exterior durante parte del año. El cerramiento de esta galería es una celosía de bambú montada sobre un bastidor metálico practicable, que protege del intenso sol, proporciona seguridad y puede ser abierta a los jardines cuando se desee.

Given the adjacency to the future urban park and the North-South orientation of the site, our proposal was to compact the volume within the given height so that every unit will have double orientation east-west. In order to achieve this, the units become a sort of 13.40 m long 'tubes' that connect both facades and avoid any type of structure in the partitions between apartments.

This concentration on the western side of the plot allows us the possibility of providing a private garden for the units on the eastern side, to be located above the parking belonging to the units.

The residential units are therefore opened to two different gardens on each orientation, and are fully glazed in the facades. Each side of the building is provided with a 1.5 m wide terrace along the full facade that will make possible a semi-exterior type of use during certain seasons. These terraces are enclosed with bamboo louvers mounted on folding frames that will provide with the necessary protection from the strong East-West sun exposure, provide security to the units and open entirely to the side gardens when desired.

There has been much talk in the past few years about exploring the potentials of customised residential typologies, and the possibility of

En los últimos años, se ha debatido mucho sobre la posibilidad de explorar el potencial de las tipologías residenciales individualizadas, permitiendo a cada residente la posibilidad de identificarse con su vivienda. Si bien se trata de un enfoque legítimo e interesante, las experiencias llevadas a cabo hasta la fecha son poco más que una serie cosmética de ajustes arbitrarios de color para lograr la diferenciación. Esta tendencia corre el peligro de caer en una especie de ideología provinciana por la que los habitantes de la ciudad contemporánea esperan residir en viviendas diferenciadas y específicas cuando, de hecho, una de las ventajas de la vida metropolitana consiste en poder ser anónimo y perder esa identificación rural o burguesa entre vivienda y habitante. Este tipo de contorsiones cosméticas absorbe importantes recursos, muchas veces a costa de la calidad del detalle y la calidad del espacio. Nuestra investigación en estas de viviendas de bajo coste se centró en procurar la máxima cantidad de espacio, flexibilidad y calidad a las viviendas, borrando las diferencias entre ellas dentro de un único volumen con una piel homogénea. Las diferenciaciones dependerán de los deseos de los habitantes, no de la visión del arquitecto.

a differentiated appearance of the units so that inhabitants would have the opportunity to acquire some form of personal identification with their residences. Even if the approach is a legitimate and interesting one, the experiments developed so far have evolved into rather arbitrary arrangements of difference where some of these identities become purely colourful and cosmetic. The risk of this approach is to fall into some sort of provincial ideology in which contemporary urban inhabitants are looking to their homes to be different and specific, while in fact one of the advantages of metropolitan living lies in the possibility of being anonymous, of losing the sort of rural or bourgeois identification between the home and its inhabitant.

These sort of developments absorb substantial resources in this sort of cosmetic contortions sometimes at the expense of quality of detail and quality of space. Our experiment with this project of low-cost residences was to provide the maximum amount of space, flexibility and quality to the residences, and to erase the visibility of the units and their differences into a single volume with a homogeneous skin able to incorporate some gradation of differences not dependent on the architect's vision, but on each inhabitants desires.

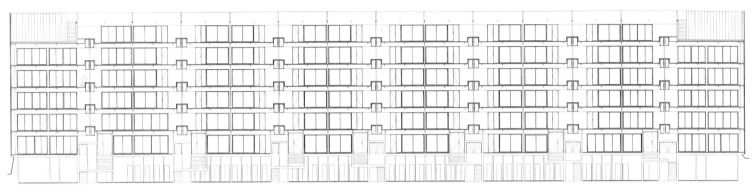

Sección longitudinal **A** Longitudinal section

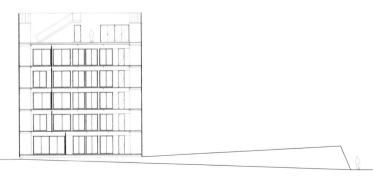

Sección transversal **B** Cross section

1:500

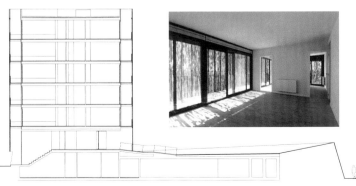

Sección transversal **C** Cross section

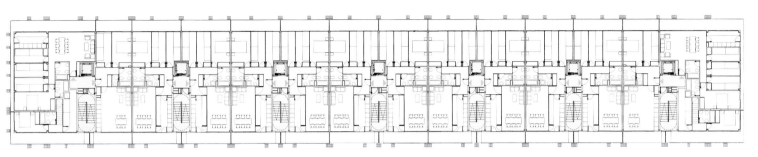

Planta tipo **Type plan**

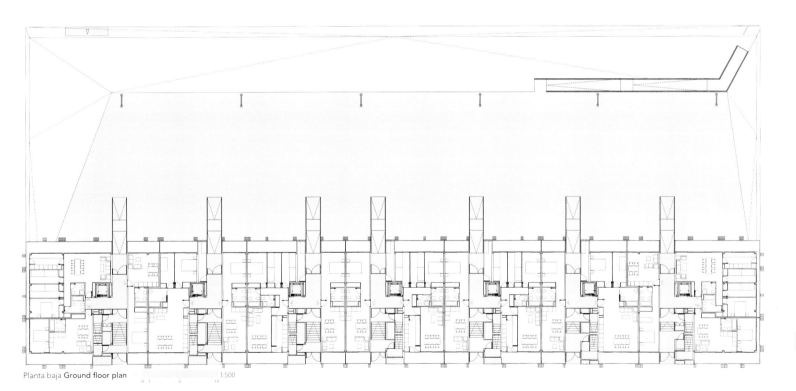

Planta baja **Ground floor plan**   0 1   5   10   1:500

DORMITORIOS **BEDROOMS**

9	1	1000
		950
17	2	900
		850
54	3	800
		750
8	4	700
		650
		600
		550
		500
		450
		400
		350
		300
		250
		200
		150
		100
		50
		0

UNITS

CERÁMICA
BRICKWORK

HORMIGÓN
CONCRETE

MADERA
WOOD

CEMENTO
CEMENT

METAL
METAL

COMPUESTO
COMPOSITE

VIDRIO
GALSS

ENFOSCADO/
ESTUCO
**MORTAR/
STUCCO**

AISLAMIENTO
INSULATION

MEMBRANA
MEMBRANE

PRINCIPAL

CERÁMICA
BRICKWORK

VIDRIO
GALSS

HORMIGÓN
CONCRETE

MADERA
WOOD

COMPUESTO
COMPOSITE

INTERNAL

CARTÓN-YESO
PLASTER-BOARD

CERÁMICA
BRICKWORK

ENLUCIDO
PLASTER

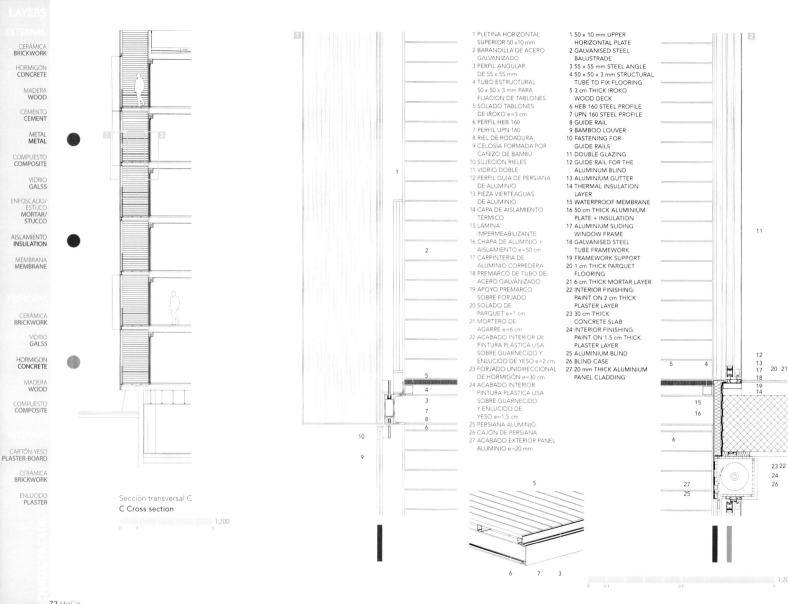

Sección transversal C
C Cross section

1:200

0   1   5

1 PLETINA HORIZONTAL
  SUPERIOR 50 x10 mm
2 BARANDILLA DE ACERO
  GALVANIZADO
3 PERFIL ANGULAR
  DE 55 x 55 mm
4 TUBO ESTRUCTURAL
  50 x 50 x 3 mm PARA
  FIJACIÓN DE TABLONES
5 SOLADO TABLONES
  DE IROKO e=3 cm
6 PERFIL HEB 160
7 PERFIL UPN 160
8 RIEL DE RODADURA
9 CELOSÍA FORMADA POR
  CAÑIZO DE BAMBÚ
10 SUJECIÓN RIELES
11 VIDRIO DOBLE
12 PERFIL GUÍA DE PERSIANA
  DE ALUMINIO
13 PIEZA VIERTEAGUAS
  DE ALUMINIO
14 CAPA DE AISLAMIENTO
  TÉRMICO
15 LÁMINA
  IMPERMEABILIZANTE
16 CHAPA DE ALUMINIO +
  AISLAMIENTO e=50 cm
17 CARPINTERÍA DE
  ALUMINIO CORREDERA
18 PREMARCO DE TUBO DE
  ACERO GALVANIZADO
19 APOYO PREMARCO
  SOBRE FORJADO
20 SOLADO DE
  PARQUET e=1 cm
21 MORTERO DE
  AGARRE e=6 cm
22 ACABADO INTERIOR DE
  PINTURA PLÁSTICA LISA
  SOBRE GUARNECIDO Y
  ENLUCIDO DE YESO e=2 cm
23 FORJADO UNIDIRECCIONAL
  DE HORMIGÓN e=30 cm
24 ACABADO INTERIOR
  PINTURA PLÁSTICA LISA
  SOBRE GUARNECIDO
  Y ENLUCIDO DE
  YESO e=1,5 cm
25 PERSIANA ALUMINIO
26 CAJÓN DE PERSIANA
27 ACABADO EXTERIOR PANEL
  ALUMINIO e=20 mm

1 50 x 10 mm UPPER
  HORIZONTAL PLATE
2 GALVANISED STEEL
  BALUSTRADE
3 55 x 55 mm STEEL ANGLE
4 50 x 50 x 3 mm STRUCTURAL
  TUBE TO FIX FLOORING
5 3 cm THICK IROKO
  WOOD DECK
6 HEB 160 STEEL PROFILE
7 UPN 160 STEEL PROFILE
8 GUIDE RAIL
9 BAMBOO LOUVER
10 FASTENING FOR
  GUIDE RAILS
11 DOUBLE GLAZING
12 GUIDE RAIL FOR THE
  ALUMINUM BLIND
13 ALUMINIUM GUTTER
14 THERMAL INSULATION
  LAYER
15 WATERPROOF MEMBRANE
16 50 cm THICK ALUMINIUM
  PLATE + INSULATION
17 ALUMINIUM SLIDING
  WINDOW FRAME
18 GALVANISED STEEL
  TUBE FRAMEWORK
19 FRAMEWORK SUPPORT
20 1 cm THICK PARQUET
  FLOORING
21 6 cm THICK MORTAR LAYER
22 INTERIOR FINISHING:
  PAINT ON 2 cm THICK
  PLASTER LAYER
23 30 cm THICK
  CONCRETE SLAB
24 INTERIOR FINISHING:
  PAINT ON 1.5 cm THICK
  PLASTER LAYER
25 ALUMINIUM BLIND
26 BLIND CASE
27 20 mm THICK ALUMINIUM
  PANEL CLADDING

1:20

0   0.1   0.5   1

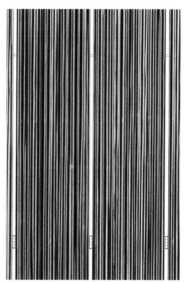

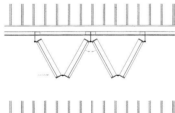

1 RASTRELES PERFORADOS
2 CARPINTERIA DE ALUMINIO
 CORREDERA DE DOS HOJAS
3 PREMARCO DE TUBO DE
 ACERO GALVANIZADO
4 APOYO PREMARCO
 SOBRE FORJADO
5 SOLADO DE PARQUET e=1 cm
 SOBRE LÁMINA ANTI-IMPACTO
6 MORTERO DE AGARRE e=8 cm
7 MURO HORMIGÓN
 ARMADO e=30 cm
8 RELLENO DE MURO
 ZONA INTERNA
9 RELLENO DE MURO: TIERRA
 VEGETAL ZONA EXTERNA
10 MALLA TRIDIMENSIONAL
11 MALLA DE POLIESTER Y PVC
12 LOSA DE HORMIGÓN
 ARMADA e=22 cm
13 REMATE CON CHAPA DE
 ALUMINIO e=2 cm
14 RELLENO AISLAMIENTO
 TÉRMICO
15 PERFIL METÁLICO UPN 80
16 SUJECIÓN RIELES
17 CELOSÍA FORMADA POR
 CAÑIZO DE BAMBÚ CON
 MALLA GALVANIZADA
18 CHAPA DE ALUMINIO e=2 mm
19 BASTIDOR DE ALUMINIO
20 PERFIL ANGULAR DE 55 x 55 mm
21 BARANDILLA DE ACERO
 GALVANIZADO

1 PERFORATED WOODEN PLANKS
2 SLIDING ALUMINIUM
 WINDOW FRAME
3 GALVANISED STEEL
 TUBE FRAMEWORK
4 FRAMEWORK SUPPORT
5 1 cm THICK PARQUET
 FLOORING ON ANTISHOCK MAT
6 8 cm THICK MORTAR LAYER
7 30 cm THICK REINFORCED
 CONCRETE WALL
8 INTERIOR WALL FILLER
9 EXTERIOR WALL FILLER:
 NATURAL SOIL
10 THREE-DIMENSIONAL MESH
11 POLYESTER MESH AND PVC
12 22 cm THICK REINFORCED
 CONCRETE SLAB
13 2 cm THICK ALUMINIUM CAP
14 THERMAL INSULATION INFILL
15 UPN 80 STEEL PROFILE
16 GUIDE RIALS FASTENING
17 BAMBOO LOUVER WITH
 GALVANISED WIRE MESH
18 2 mm THICK ALUMINIUM PLATE
19 ALUMINIUM FRAME
20 55 x 55 mm STEEL ANGLE
21 GALVANISED STEEL
 BALUSTRADE

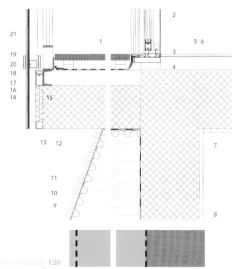

1:20

0.1   0.5   1

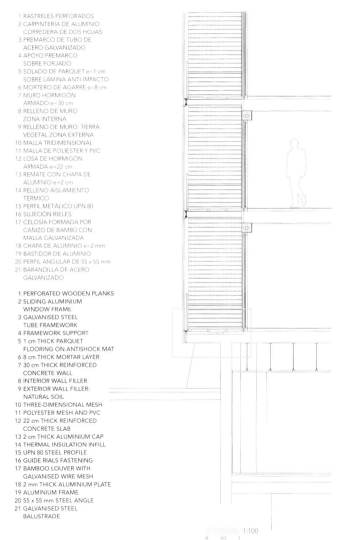

1:100

0   0.5   1

LAYERS

EXTERNAL

GRAVA
GRAVEL

CERÁMICA
TERRACOTTA

MADERA
WOOD

CEMENTO
CEMENT

VEGETACIÓN
PLANTING

METAL
METAL

AISLAMIENTO
INSULATION

MEMBRANA
MEMBRANE

STRUCTURAL

HORMIGÓN
CONCRETE

MADERA
WOOD

CERÁMICA
TERRACOTTA

INTERNAL

CARTÓN-YESO
PLASTER-BOARD

ENLUCIDO
PLASTER

METAL
METAL

0,003
mill.☺

897
☺/km²

9.278 m²
SUPERFICIE CONSTRUIDA
GROSS FLOOR AREA

6.101 m²
SUPERFICIE DE PARCELA
PLOT AREA

27,7%
OCUPACIÓN
COVERED AREA

1,05
EDIFICABILIDAD
FLOOR AREA RATIO

1:2.000

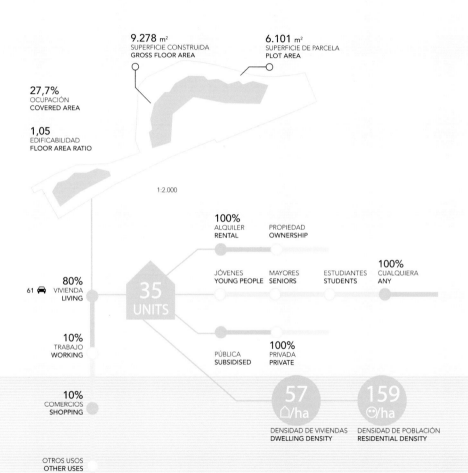

100%
ALQUILER
RENTAL

PROPIEDAD
OWNERSHIP

JÓVENES
YOUNG PEOPLE

MAYORES
SENIORS

ESTUDIANTES
STUDENTS

100%
CUALQUIERA
ANY

61 🚗 80%
VIVIENDA
LIVING

35
UNITS

10%
TRABAJO
WORKING

PÚBLICA
SUBSIDISED

100%
PRIVADA
PRIVATE

10%
COMERCIOS
SHOPPING

57
⌂/ha

159
☺/ha

DENSIDAD DE VIVIENDAS
DWELLING DENSITY

DENSIDAD DE POBLACIÓN
RESIDENTIAL DENSITY

OTROS USOS
OTHER USES

1:5.000
0 10   50

04

2.000
1900
1800
1700
1600
1500
1400
1300
1200
1100
970 1000
CHF/m²
900
800
700
600
500
400
300
200
100

551
$/m²

0

Concepto urbanístico. Organización

El conjunto de viviendas Quellenpark se encuentra en el centro del municipio de Rohr, en un área caracterizada por un lado por su espectacular enclave, un paisaje boscoso, escarpado e idílico, un terreno en pendiente apenas construido que recorre la región en dirección oeste-este, y por otra parte por la forma de joroba de camello de la parcela: dos grandes curvas hacia el norte y una estrecha franja intermedia no edificable. El límite sur del área en cuestión es la calle principal del municipio.

Dos edificios distintos en forma y volumen ocupan la parcela. Ambos se adaptan al recorrido del montículo, así como al tamaño específico de la curva del solar en que se ubican. Mientras que el edificio que ocupa el lado este, más pequeño y compacto, se alinea y adapta también al trazado de la calle principal, el bloque que ocupa el flanco oeste, más grande y con múltiples pliegues, retrocede liberando el espacio y conformando una plaza que recoge el arbolado preexistente. Estas zonas verdes, que discurren a lo largo de la calle principal de Rohr, son un rasgo distintivo de la misma, que queda reforzado por la disposición que adopta el edificio.

La concepción de las fachadas hace de ambos edificios un conjunto coherente al tiempo que tiene en cuenta la marcada dualidad de la parcela ocupada.

Urban planning concept. Organisation

The Quellenpark set of housing units is located in the centre of the city of Rohr. This area is characterised by its spectacular surroundings, a rugged and idyllic forest landscape and hills with little construction that run from West to East. It is also greatly characterised by the camel-hump shape of the lot, two large curves toward the North and a narrow intermediate strip where nothing can be built. The southern limit of the area is the city's main street.

Two buildings, different in shape and volume, occupy the lot. Both adapt to the route of the hill as well as the specific size of the curve of the lot where they are located. While the building that takes up the East side, smaller and more compact, is lined up and adapts to the route of the main street, the block that occupies the West side, larger and with several folds, stands back, freeing space and creating a wooded plaza that uses existing trees. These green areas, which run along the main street of Rohr, are a distinguishing characteristic of the city and are reinforced by the disposition that the building takes on.

The concept of the facades makes the two buildings a coherent set as it considers the marked duality of the lot used.

In face of the consolidated urban surroundings to the South, East and West, the facades stand out as

Frente al entorno urbano consolidado al sur, este y oeste, las fachadas se manifiestan como superficies compactas y precisas. La disposición de los huecos da vida a las fachadas y hace que los edificios parezcan más pequeños de lo que son en realidad. Por el contrario, en la cara norte, boscosa, aparecen balcones, obteniéndose así profundidad y una vista directa hacia la naturaleza circundante. El empleo de materiales constructivos como la madera resta frialdad a la construcción y contribuye a su integración en el entorno.

Distribución interior

La distribución interior de ambos edificios es flexible, aloja oficinas en planta baja y viviendas de distintos tipos en las plantas superiores. Todas las viviendas tienen dos frentes, disfrutando así, tanto de las vistas de la naturaleza en la cara norte, como del pueblo en la cara sur. Las unidades del lado oeste, más grandes, son viviendas de alquiler de entre 3,5 y 4,5 habitaciones y un salón pasante, mientras que el bloque más pequeño, en la parte este de la parcela, alberga viviendas-estudio articuladas a través de un núcleo compacto de baño y cocina que organiza un espacio único. El aparcamiento está resuelto mayoritariamente bajo rasante.

compact and precise surfaces. The layout of the wall openings gives life to the facades and makes the buildings look smaller than they really are. On the contrary, on the North side facing the forest, there are balconies, providing depth and a direct view of the natural surroundings. The use of building materials like wood adds warmth to the construction and contributes to its integration with its surroundings.

Interior Layout

The interior layout of both buildings is flexible. It houses offices on the ground floor and different types of flats on the upper floors. All housing units have two sides, thus enjoying views of nature to the North and the city to the South. The flats on the west side are larger, 3.5- and 4.5-bedroom rental units with a passing living room. Meanwhile, the smaller block, on the east side, holds studio apartments articulated by means of a compact nucleus with bathroom and kitchen that organises a single space. Car park is mostly taken care of underground.

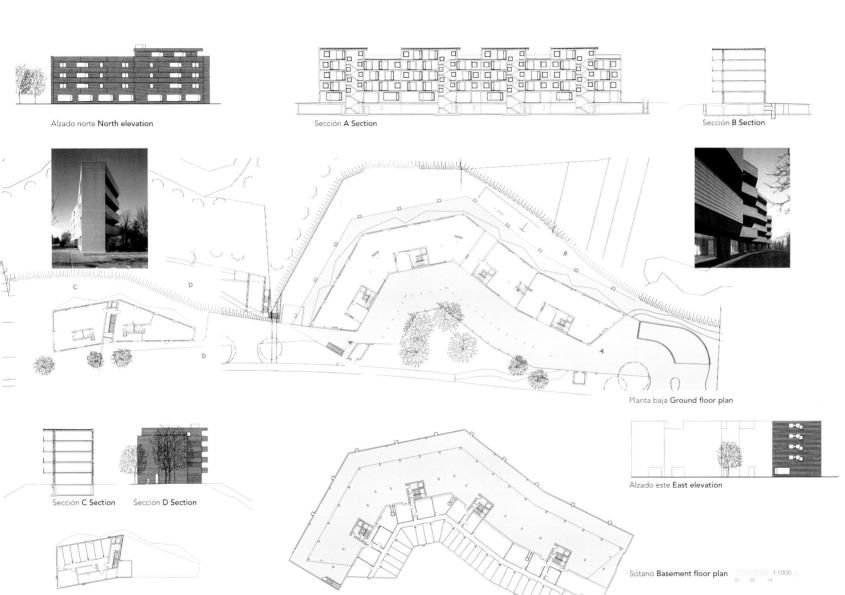

Alzado norte **North elevation**

Sección **A Section**

Sección **B Section**

Planta baja **Ground floor plan**

Sección **C Section**   Sección **D Section**

Alzado este **East elevation**

Sótano **Basement floor plan**   1:1000

01 05 10

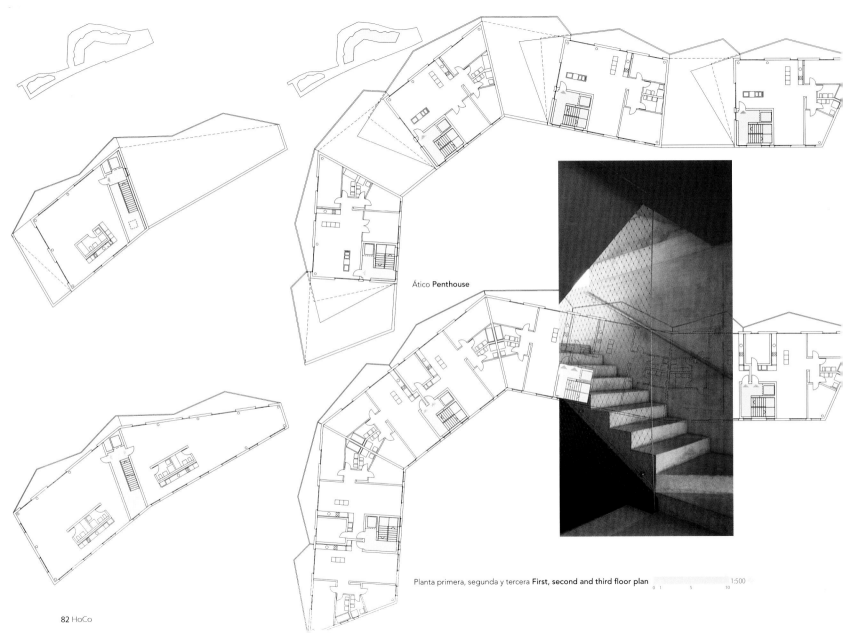

Ático **Penthouse**

Planta primera, segunda y tercera **First, second and third floor plan**

1:500

0 1   5   10

1000

950

12 2 900

850

16 3 800

750

700

650

7 600

550

DORMITORIOS **BEDROOMS**

500

450

400

350

300

250

200

150

100

50

0

UNITS

LAYERS

EXTERNAL

CERÁMICA
BRICKWORK

HORMIGON
CONCRETE

MADERA
WOOD

CEMENTO
CEMENT

METAL
METAL

COMPUESTO
COMPOSITE

VIDRIO
GALSS

ENFOSCADO/
ESTUCO
**MORTAR/
STUCCO**

AISLAMIENTO
INSULATION

MEMBRANA
MEMBRANE

CERÁMICA
BRICKWORK

VIDRIO
GALSS

HORMIGON
CONCRETE

MADERA
WOOD

COMPUESTO
COMPOSITE

INTERNAL

CARTÓN-YESO
PLASTER-BOARD

CERÁMICA
BRICKWORK

ENLUCIDO
PLASTER

Sección **B** Section

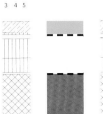

Fachada sur **South facade**   1:1000
01 05 10

20 9

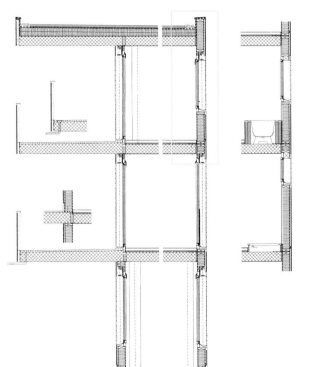

1 ALBARDILLA DE CHAPA
  DE ACERO e=2 mm
2 TABLERO AGLOMERADO
  e=1,5 cm
3 AJARDINAMIENTO. CAPA DE
  SUSTRATO MINERAL e=6 cm
4 LÁMINA PROTECTORA e=1 cm
5 DOBLE MEMBRANA DE
  IMPERMEABILIZACIÓN e=2 cm
6 CAPA DE AISLAMIENTO
  TÉRMICO e=10 cm
7 CAPA DE POLIESTIRENO
  e= 2-18 cm
8 BARRERA DE VAPOR e=1 cm
9 LOSA DE HORMIGÓN e=24 cm
10 TABLERO DE ABETO
   IMPERMEABILIZADO e=1,8 cm
11 CÁMARA VENTILADA
12 PANEL DE MADERA e=1,5 cm
13 CAPA DE AISLAMIENTO
   TÉRMICO DE LANA
   MINERAL e=18 cm
14 PANEL DE CARTÓN-YESO
   e=1,5 cm PARA RECIBIDO
   DEL REVOCO LISO
15 PAVIMENTO e=1,5 cm
16 CAPA DE MORTERO
   AUTONIVELANTE e=5,5 cm
17 CAPA DE AISLAMIENTO
   ACÚSTICO e=2 cm
18 CAPA DE AISLAMIENTO
   TÉRMICO e=2 cm
19 LOSA DE HORMIGÓN e=24 cm
20 ENLUCIDO DE YESO

1 2 mm THICK STEEL
  PLATE WALL CAP
2 1.5 cm THICK PLYWOOD
3 6 cm MINERAL
  PLANTING BED
4 1 cm THICK
  PROTECTION MAT
5 2 cm THICK DOUBLE
  WATERPROOF MEMBRANE
6 10 cm THICK THERMAL
  INSULATION LAYER
7 2 TO 18 THICK
  POLYESTYRENE LAYER
8 1 cm THICK VAPOUR BARRIER
9 24 cm THICK CONCRETE SLAB
10 1.8 cm FIR WOOD PANEL
   WITH WATERPROOF
   FINISHING
11 AIR CAVITY
12 1.5 cm THICK
   WOODEN PANEL
13 18 cm THICK MINERAL
   WOOL INSULATION LAYER
14 1.5 cm THICK GYPSUM FIBRE
   PANEL TO BE COATED WITH
   A LAYER OF LIME RENDERING
15 1.5 cm THICK FLOORING
16 5.5 cm THICK
   MORTAR SCREED
17 2 cm THICK NOISE
   INSULATION LAYER
18 2 cm THICK THERMAL
   INSULATION LAYER
19 24 cm THICK CONCRETE SLAB
20 PLASTER RENDERING

1:100
0 0.5 1

15
16
17
18
19

20

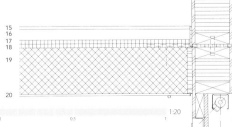

10
11
12
13
14

1:20
0 0.1 0.5

LAYERS

GRAVA
GRAVEL

CERÁMICA
TERRACOTTA

MADERA
WOOD

CEMENTO
CEMENT

VEGETACIÓN
PLANTING

METAL
METAL

AISLAMIENTO
INSULATION

MEMBRANA
MEMBRANE

HORMIGÓN
CONCRETE

MADERA
WOOD

CERÁMICA
TERRACOTTA

CARTÓN-YESO
PLASTER-BOARD

ENLUCIDO
PLASTER

METAL
METAL

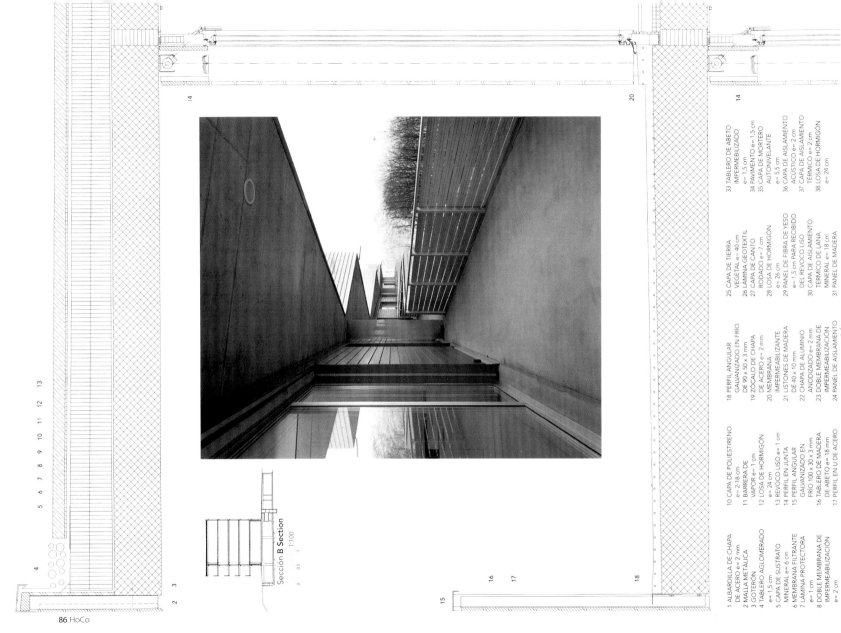

Sección B Section 1:100

0   0,5   1

1 ALBARDILLA DE CHAPA
DE ACERO e= 2 mm
2 MALLA METÁLICA
3 GOTERÓN
4 TABLERO AGLOMERADO
e= 1,5 cm
5 CAPA DE SUSTRATO
MINERAL e= 6 cm
6 MEMBRANA FILTRANTE
7 LÁMINA PROTECTORA
e= 1 cm
8 DOBLE MEMBRANA DE
IMPERMEABILIZACIÓN
e= 2 cm

10 CAPA DE POLIESTIRENO
e= 2-18 cm
11 BARRERA DE
VAPOR e= 1 cm
12 LOSA DE HORMIGÓN
e= 24 cm
13 REVOCO LISO e= 1 cm
14 PERFIL EN JUNTA
15 PERFIL ANGULAR
GALVANIZADO EN
FRÍO 100 x 30 x 3 mm
16 TABLERO DE MADERA
DE ABETO e= 18 mm
17 PERFIL EN U DE ACERO

18 PERFIL ANGULAR
GALVANIZADO EN FRÍO
DE 90 x 50 x 3 mm
19 ZÓCALO DE CHAPA
DE ACERO e= 2 mm
20 MEMBRANA
IMPERMEABILIZANTE
21 LISTONES DE MADERA
DE 40 x 10 mm
22 CHAPA DE ALUMINIO
ANODIZADO e= 2 mm
23 DOBLE MEMBRANA DE
IMPERMEABILIZACIÓN
24 PANEL DE AISLAMIENTO

25 CAPA DE TIERRA
VEGETAL e= 40 cm
26 LÁMINA GEOTEXTIL
27 CAPA DE CANTO
RODADO e= 7 cm
28 LOSA DE HORMIGÓN
e= 26 cm
29 PANEL DE FIBRA DE YESO
e= 1,5 cm PARA RECIBIDO
DEL REVOCO LISO
30 CAPA DE AISLAMIENTO
TÉRMICO DE LANA
MINERAL e= 18 cm
31 PANEL DE MADERA

33 TABLERO DE ABETO
IMPERMEABILIZADO
e= 1,5 cm
34 PAVIMENTO e= 1,5 cm
35 CAPA DE MORTERO
AUTONIVELANTE
e= 5,5 cm
36 CAPA DE AISLAMIENTO
ACÚSTICO e= 2 cm
37 CAPA DE AISLAMIENTO
TÉRMICO e= 2 cm
38 LOSA DE HORMIGÓN
e= 24 cm

Sección vertical por el muro
Wall vertical section

1 2 mm THICK STEEL WALL CAP
2 METAL MESH
3 GUTTER
4 1.5 cm THICK PLYWOOD
5 6 cm MINERAL PLANTING BED
6 FILTERING MAT
7 1 cm THICK PROTECTION MAT
8 2 cm THICK DOUBLE WATERPROOF MEMBRANE
9 10 cm THICK THERMAL INSULATION LAYER

10 2 TO 18 cm THICK POLYESTYRENE LAYER
11 1 cm THICK VAPOUR BARRIER
12 24 cm THICK CONCRETE SLAB
13 1 cm THICK LIME RENDERING
14 JOINT PROFILE
15 100 x 30 x 3 mm COLD GALVANISED STEEL ANGLE
16 18 mm THICK FIR WOOD BOARD
17 60 x 60 x 4 mm COLD GALVANISED STEEL U-PROFILE

18 90 x 50 x 3 mm COLD GALVANISED STEEL PROFILE
19 2 mm THICK STEEL PLATE
20 WATERPROOF LAYER
21 40 x 10 mm TIMBER BATTENS
22 2 mm THICK ANODIZED ALUMINIUM WINDOWSILL
23 DOUBLE WATERPROOF MEMBRANE
24 5 cm THICK THERMAL INSULATION AND WATERPROOF PANEL

25 40 cm THICK PLANTING BED
26 GEOTEXTILE MAT
27 7 cm THICK PEBBLE LAYER
28 26 cm THICK CONCRETE SLAB
29 1.5 cm THICK GYPSUM FIBRE PANEL TO BE COATED WITH A LAYER OF LIME RENDERING
30 18 cm THICK MINERAL WOOL INSULATION LAYER
31 1.5 cm THICK WOODEN PANEL

32 AIR CAVITY
33 1.8 cm FIR WOOD PANEL WITH WATERPROOF FINISHING
34 1.5 cm THICK FLOORING
35 5.5 cm THICK MORTAR SCREED
36 2 cm THICK NOISE INSULATION LAYER
37 2 cm THICK THERMAL INSULATION LAYER
38 24 cm THICK CONCRETE SLAB

1:20

0   0.1   0.5   1

Aguinaga y Asociados Arquitectos e-aguinaga.com Madrid. SPAIN, 2008 Bulevar de la Naturaleza, Ensanche de Vallecas

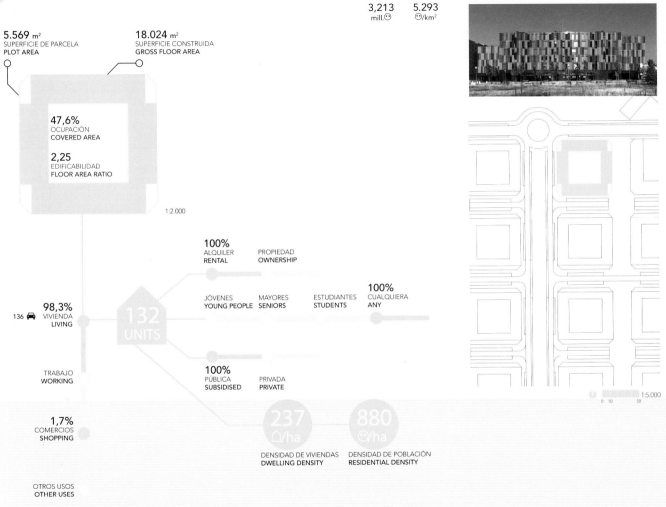

3,213 mill.☉

5.293 ☺/km²

5.569 m²
SUPERFICIE DE PARCELA
PLOT AREA

18.024 m²
SUPERFICIE CONSTRUIDA
GROSS FLOOR AREA

47,6%
OCUPACIÓN
COVERED AREA

2,25
EDIFICABILIDAD
FLOOR AREA RATIO

1:2.000

100%
ALQUILER
RENTAL

PROPIEDAD
OWNERSHIP

136 🚗 **98,3%**
VIVIENDA
LIVING

JÓVENES
YOUNG PEOPLE

MAYORES
SENIORS

ESTUDIANTES
STUDENTS

100%
CUALQUIERA
ANY

132
UNITS

TRABAJO
WORKING

100%
PÚBLICA
SUBSIDISED

PRIVADA
PRIVATE

1,7%
COMERCIOS
SHOPPING

237
🏠/ha

880
☺/ha

DENSIDAD DE VIVIENDAS
DWELLING DENSITY

DENSIDAD DE POBLACIÓN
RESIDENTIAL DENSITY

OTROS USOS
OTHER USES

1:5.000
0   10   50

05

562
$/m²

507
€/m²

2.000

1.900

1.800

1.700

1.600

1.500

1.400

1.300

1.200

1.100

1.000

900

800

700

600

500

400

300

200

100

0

Se trata de un conjunto de viviendas, destinadas al alquiler, que combina una tipología repetitiva de viviendas pasantes con doble orientación, con variedad en el tratamiento de las fachadas combinando una matizada paleta de colores inspirada en alguna de las obras de Paul Klee.

Se han evitado cuidadosamente los chaflanes previstos por el planeamiento urbanístico tan inapropiados y fuera de escala para esta tipología de viviendas, sustituyéndolos por un diseño "en canto de pilastra" que evita distorsiones en la geometría de los pilares en las esquinas de la manzana. El conjunto de la edificación forma una manzana cerrada cuyo gran patio central tapizado de césped recuerda vagamente los grandes "courts" de las Universidades inglesas.

El basamento de soportales en pizarra gris permite enterrar desde las calles perimetrales este jardín interior. Estas vistas sólo quedan interrumpidas en las fachadas norte y sur por unos pequeños locales destinados al comercio al por menor en servicio de la zona. El arquitecto, partidario de la mezcla de usos en la ciudad, hubiera querido una mayor presencia del comercio en los bajos de la manzana, al estilo de los antiguos Ensanches, pero lamentablemente el planeamiento no lo ha hecho posible.

Se han utilizado unas luces entorno a los 5,50 m, se ha resuelto la fachada con módulos de mortero monocapa

The project involves a set of rental units, which combine a repetitive typology of horizontal flats facing two directions and with a rich variety in the treatment of the facades combining a blended colour palette inspired by works of Paul Klee.

The chamfers foreseen by urban planning were carefully avoided, as they are inappropriate and out of scale for this typology of housing. They have been replaced by design in recessed-angle block corners which avoids distortion in the geometry of the pillars.

The whole of the building forms a closed block whose large central grassy patio is reminiscent of the great courts of English universities. The base of arcades in grey slate allows the inner garden to be buried by the surrounding streets. These views are only interrupted on the north and south facades by small wholesale commercial premises on ground floor. The architect, in favour of mixing uses in the city, would have liked more commercial space on street level, as in 19th century urban expansion projects. Unfortunately official urban planning did not allow for it.

Spans of approximately 5.5 metres were used, and the facade was resolved with modules of single layer mortar of different colours which not only reduce costs but also lack the need for repainting over time. Periodic cleaning of the facade, every five to ten years,

de diferentes colores que, además de aportar economía en su ejecución, no necesitan labores de repintado con el paso del tiempo: será suficiente la limpieza periódica de la fachada cada 5 ó 10 años dependiendo de la polución ambiental que se produzca en su momento. Las carpinterías de las ventanas tampoco necesitan de un mantenimiento especial.

depending on the pollution at each given moment; window frames also do not need special maintenance.

Planta baja **Ground floor plan**

1:1000

01 05 10

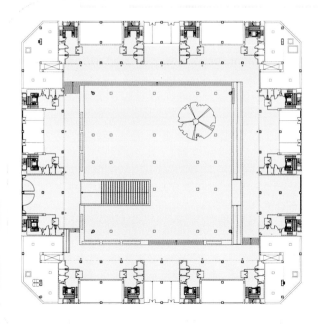

Alzado este East elevation

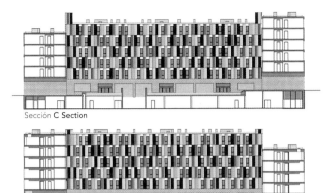

Sección C Section

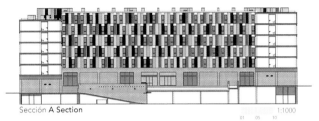

Sección A Section

1:1000
01 05 10

Sección F Section

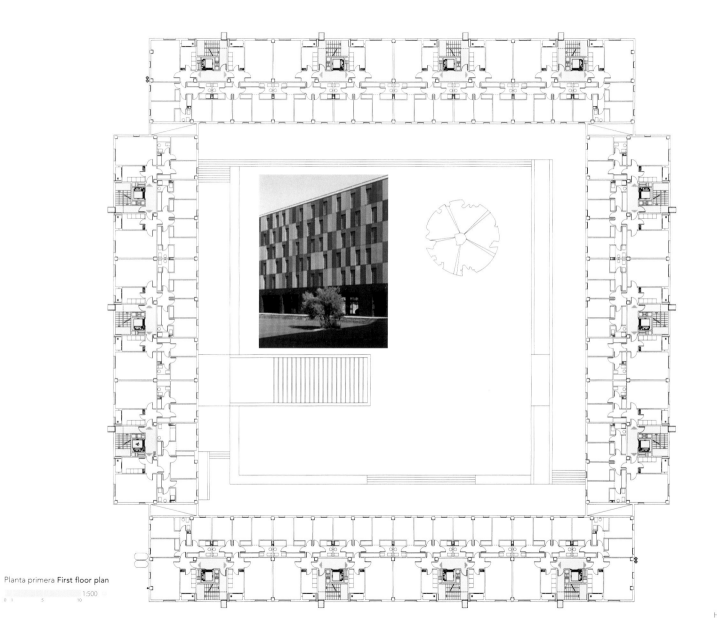

Planta primera **First floor plan**

0 1   5   10   1:500

DORMITORIOS **BEDROOMS**

1000
950
30 ② 900
850
76 ③ 800
750
26 ④ 700
650
600
550
500
450
400
350
300
250
200
150
100
50

132
UNITS

0
UNITS

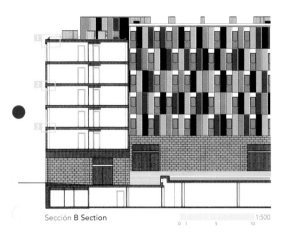

Sección **B** Section

1:500

0 1   5   10

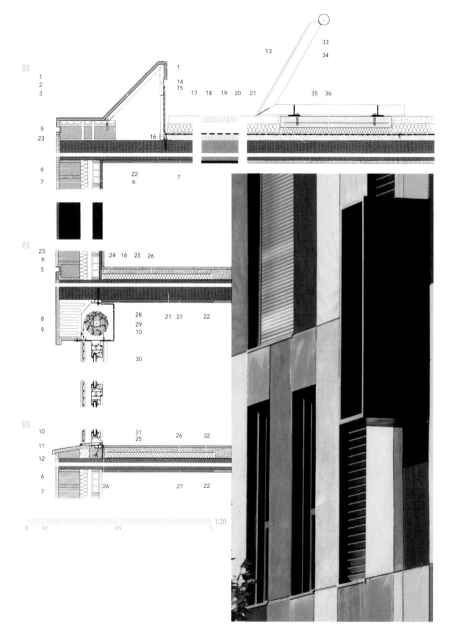

1:20

0   0.1   0.5   1

FACHADA FAÇADE

1 REMATE DE CUBIERTA DE CHAPA PLEGADA DE ALUMINIO e=2 mm
2 TABLERO COMPUESTO DE CEMENTO Y MADERA e=19 mm
3 PERFIL DE CHAPA DE ACERO GALVANIZADO EN FORMA DE L
4 CAPA DE MORTERO e=1,5 cm
5 PERFIL "L" DE 20 x 20 mm DE ACERO GALVANIZADO
6 MURO DE LADRILLO
7 CAPA DE AISLAMIENTO TÉRMICO e=40 mm
8 CHAPA DE ALUMINIO e=2 mm REFORZADA CON POLIESTIRENO EXPANDIDO e=20 mm COMO CIERRE DEL CAJÓN DE PERSIANA
9 SELLADO DE ESPUMA DE POLIURETANO INYECTADO
10 PERSIANA DE ALUMINIO LACADO EN COLOR GRIS OSCURO
11 CHAPA DE ALUMINIO e=2 mm PARA FORMACIÓN DE VIERTEAGUAS
12 CAPA DE MORTERO e=1,5 cm
13 SELLADO
14 ORIFICIO DE VENTILACIÓN
15 REMATE DE CUBIERTA
16 JUNTA DE DILATACIÓN
17 LOSA COMPUESTA DE CEMENTO Y CAPA DE AISLAMIENTO TÉRMICO
18 FIELTRO SEPARADOR
19 LÁMINA IMPERMEBILIZANTE
20 MORTERO DE REGULARIZACIÓN
21 FORJADO DE HORMIGÓN
22 GUARNECIDO Y ENLUCIDO DE YESO
23 ENFOSCADO DE CEMENTO COLOREADO SEGÚN CÓDIGO DE COLORES DEL ALZADO
24 RODAPIÉ EN MADERA
25 SOLADO DE PARQUET DE MADERA DE ROBLE
26 BANDA DE AISLAMIENTO TÉRMICO DE 60 cm DE ANCHO A LO LARGO DE LAS FACHADAS
27 AISLAMIENTO TÉRMICO PROYECTADO
28 PREMARCO
29 CAJÓN DE PERSIANA
30 VIDRIO DOBLE
31 CARPINTERÍA DE ALUMINIO
32 LAMINA DE ESPUMA DE POLIETILENO e=3 mm
33 PERFIL TUBULAR HUECO
34 PERFIL T
35 SOLERA e=6 cm DE HORMIGÓN ARMADO
36 AISLAMIENTO DE FORJADO

1 2 mm THICK ALUMINIUM CAP
2 19 mm THICK WOOD-CEMENT PANEL
3 L-SHAPED GALVANISED ALUMINIUM PROFILE
4 1.5 cm THICK MORTAR LAYER
5 20 x 20 mm L- SHAPED GALVANISED ALUMINIUM PROFILE
6 BRICK WORK WALL
7 40 mm THICK THERMAL INSULATION LAYER
8 BLIND CASE: 2 mm THICK ALUMINIUM PLATE REINFORCED WITH A 20 mm THICK EXPANDED POLYSTYRENE LAYER
9 INJECTED POLYURETHANE SEALING
10 GRAY LACQUERED ALUMINIUM BLIND
11 2 mm THICK ALUMINIUM PLATE GUTTER
12 1.5 cm THICK MORTAR LAYER
13 SEALING
14 VENTILATION GAP
15 ROOF CAP
16 DILATATION JOINT
17 FLOOR SLAB CONSISTING OF A CEMENT LAYER OVER A THERMAL INSULATION LAYER
18 FELT
19 WATERPROOF MEMBRANE
20 SCREED MORTAR
21 CONCRETE SLAB
22 PLASTER FINISHING
23 CEMENT RENDERING, TAINTED ACCORDING TO THE COLOUR CODE ESTABLISHED FOR THE FACADES
24 WOODEN SKIRTING BOARD
25 OAK WOOD FLOORING
26 60 cm WIDE INSULATION LAYER ALONG FACADES
27 PROJECTED THERMAL INSULATION FOAM
28 WINDOWFRAME
29 BLIND CASE
30 DOUBLE GLAZING
31 ALUMINIUN FRAMEWORK
32 3 mm THICK POLYETHYLENE FOAM
33 HOLLOW STEEL TUBE
34 T PROFILE
35 REINFORCED CONCRETE SCREED
36 SLAB INSULATION

LAYERS
EXTERNAL

GRAVA
GRAVEL

CERÁMICA
TERRACOTTA

MADERA
WOOD

CEMENTO
CEMENT

VEGETACIÓN
PLANTING

METAL
METAL

AISLAMIENTO
INSULATION

MEMBRANA
MEMBRANE

HORMIGÓN
CONCRETE

MADERA
WOOD

CERÁMICA
TERRACOTTA

INTERNAL

CARTÓN-YESO
PLASTER-BOARD

ENLUCIDO
PLASTER

METAL
METAL

CUBIERTA ROOF

0,182 mill.☺   2.171 ☺/km²

6.151 m²
SUPERFICIE DE PARCELA
PLOT AREA

15.400 m²
SUPERFICIE CONSTRUIDA
GROSS FLOOR AREA

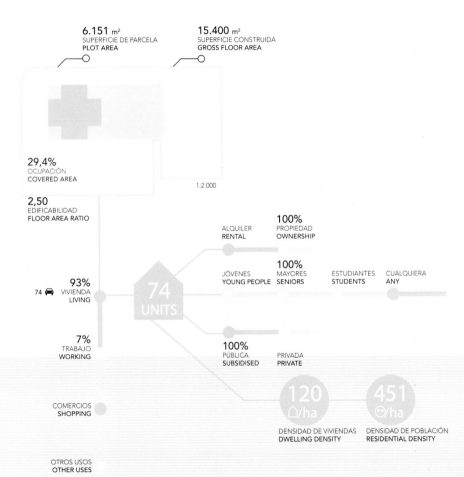

29,4%
OCUPACIÓN
COVERED AREA

1:2.000

2,50
EDIFICABILIDAD
FLOOR AREA RATIO

ALQUILER
RENTAL

100%
PROPIEDAD
OWNERSHIP

74 🚗 93%
VIVIENDA
LIVING

74
UNITS

JÓVENES
YOUNG PEOPLE

100%
MAYORES
SENIORS

ESTUDIANTES
STUDENTS

CUALQUIERA
ANY

7%
TRABAJO
WORKING

100%
PÚBLICA
SUBSIDISED

PRIVADA
PRIVATE

COMERCIOS
SHOPPING

120
⌂/ha

451
☺/ha

DENSIDAD DE VIVIENDAS
DWELLING DENSITY

DENSIDAD DE POBLACIÓN
RESIDENTIAL DENSITY

OTROS USOS
OTHER USES

En el año 2003, el Ayuntamiento de Groningen lanzó "Ciudad Intensa" para mantener la compacidad mediante el aumento de la densidad edificatoria de los distritos cercanos al centro. El edificio de viviendas Rokade se encuentra en una de las primeras zonas que cuya densidad ha sido incrementada, en la esquina de las calles Corpus den Hoor y Sportlaan, la vía de acceso al distrito de Hoornse Meer.

In 2003, Groningen municipal council launched a project 'The Intense City' to keep the city compact by increasing the building density of districts around the Centre. The Rokade Residential Tower Block is situated on one of the first increased density locations, and marks the corner of the Corpus den Hoorn Laan and the Sportlaan, the avenue providing access to the Hoornse Meer district.

1:5.000
0 10   50

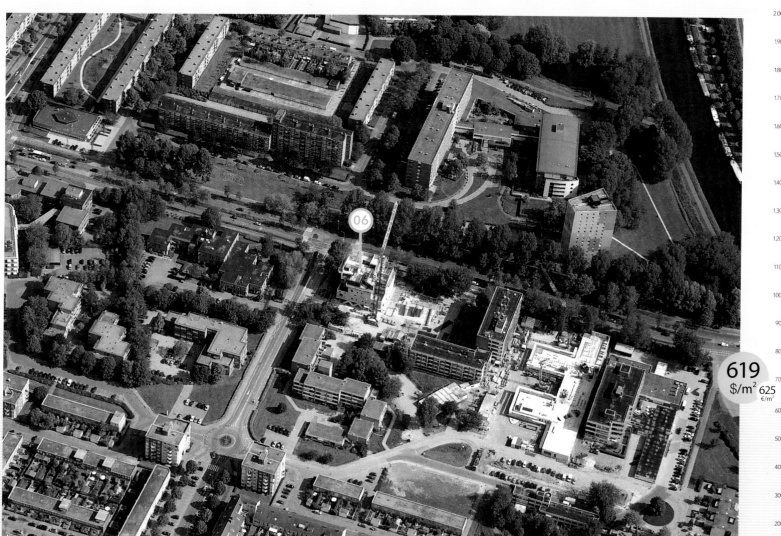

06

619
$/m² 625
€/m²

2.000
1.900
1.800
1.700
1.600
1.500
1.400
1.300
1.200
1.100
1.000
900
800
700
600
500
400
300
200
100

Torre Rokade
Rokade Tower

El edificio colinda con una guardería y un centro de día que ha sido renovado completamente: el centro Maartenshof. Las viviendas son en propiedad para personas de edad avanzada que aún son independientes y mantienen una estrecha pero sutil vinculación con el centro de día apenas perceptible desde el exterior.

Las torres de viviendas en los Países Bajos disponen normalmente, por motivos de presupuesto, de cuatro viviendas por planta. El edificio Rokade no es una excepción: cuatro apartamentos ocupan cada uno de los 21 niveles dispuestos sobre una planta en forma de cruz. Cada uno, con forma de L, se dispone en los ángulos interiores de la cruz y goza de estupendas vistas y una relativa privacidad.

De Rokade is immediately adjacent to the nursing and care home, Maartenshof, which has been extensively renovated. The apartments for purchase are intended for the 'younger seniors'. The building is linked to Maartenshof in a subtle way. In this way, Maartenshof can supply diverse forms of care to the buyers, without this delicate relationship being visible to the outside world. Towers in the Netherlands often have a minimum of four dwellings per layer for budgetary reasons. This is also true of De Rokade. The building is 21 floors high and seems very slim due to the cross-shaped ground plan. The four apartments are situated in L-form around the inside angles of the tower. In this way, the dwellings combine the beautiful view with an introverted quality.

Los sistemas de fachada, estructurales y de instalaciones permiten tres distribuciones distintas a elegir por los compradores.

El edificio, según las directivas de calidad residencial de Groningen, es muy sostenible. En vez de un oscuro y costoso aparcamiento subterráneo, el proyecto plantea dos niveles de aparcamiento situados sobre las consultas de fisioterapia a los que se accede mediante un ascensor para coches. El garaje se ventila naturalmente y dispone de iluminación natural. Con un coste de 15.000 euros por plaza, se trata de una opción mucho más barata que la tradicional caja subterránea de aparcamiento.

The apartments' facades, load bearing construction and installations have been made ready for three different layout possibilities. The present and future inhabitants will be able to determine their own ground plan in this way. The building is extra sustainable according to Groninger Residential Quality directives. Instead of an expensive and dark underground car park, we have elevated car park to the two floors above the physiotherapists' practice accommodation. The inhabitants reach their parking place on the first or second floor with a car lift. The garage is naturally ventilated, has daylight and a view and, with construction costs of €15,000 per parking place, is cheaper than the traditional underground car park box.

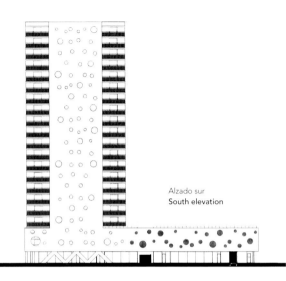

Alzado sur
South elevation

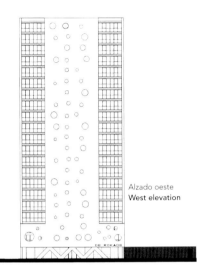

Alzado oeste
West elevation

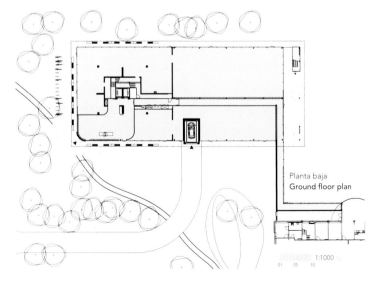

Planta baja
Ground floor plan

1:1000
01   05   10

Planta tercera **Third floor plan**

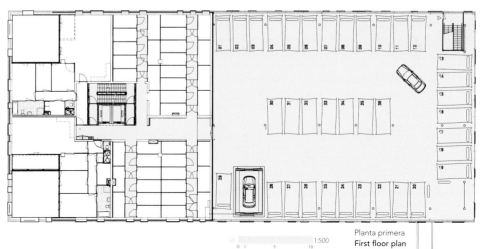

Planta primera
First floor plan

1:500

0 1   5   10

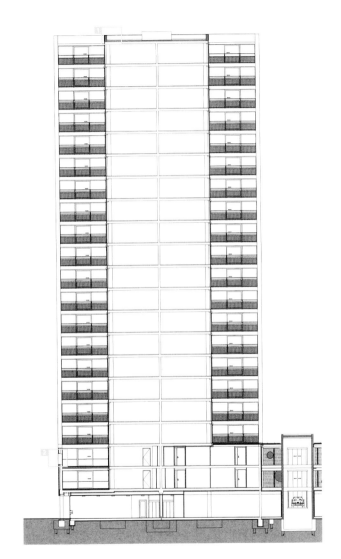

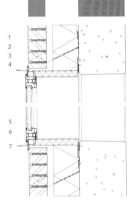

1 REVESTIMIENTO
  EXTERIOR DE LADRILLO
  VITRIFICADO BLANCO
2 CAPA DE AISLAMIENTO
  TÉRMICO DE LANA DE ROCA
3 MEMBRANA
  IMPERMEABILIZANTE
4 MURO DE HORMIGÓN IN SITU
5 ALFÉIZAR CIRCULAR DE
  ALUMINIO RECUBIERTO,
  COLOR RAL 9006
6 CARINTERÍA CIRCULAR
7 MARCO PREFABRICADO CON
  AISLAMIENTO INTEGRADO

1 MASONRY, WHITE
  GLAZED BRICK
2 MINERAL WOOL THERMAL
  INSULATION LAYER
3 WATERPROOF FOIL
4 IN-SITU CONCRETE WALL
5 CIRCULAR WINDOWSILL, RAL
  9006 COATED ALUMINIUM
6 CIRCULAR WINDOW FRAME
7 PREFABRICATED INSULATED
  WINDOW MOUNTING

2   1:20
  0   0.1   0.5   1

A ———————— A

Sección longitudinal A
A long section   1:500
  0 1   5   10

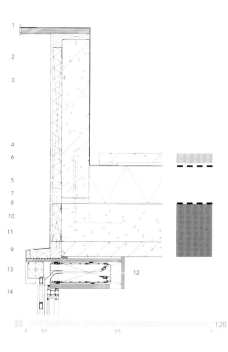

1:20

0   0.1   0.5   1

1 REMATE DE CUBIERTA EN ALUMINIO	1 ALUMINIUM ROOF TRIM
2 CHAPA DE ALUMINIO, COLOR RAL 7026	2 ALUMINIUM PLATE, RAL 7026
3 PIEZA DE HORMIGÓN PREFABRICADO	3 PREFAB ELEMENT, CONCRETE
4 MEMBRANA ASFÁLTICA	4 BITUMINOUS ROOF COVERING
5 AISLAMIENTO TÉRMICO RESISTENTE A LA PRESIÓN	5 PRESSURE RESISTENT INSULATION
6 ÁREA TRANSITABLE DE LOSAS DE CEMENTO	6 TILES INSPECTION PATH, CONCRETE
7 ANCLAJE	7 FIXTURE
8 BARRERA DE VAPOR	8 WATERPROOF FOIL
9 TAPA DESMONTABLE DE ALUMINIO PARA LA CAJA DE PERSIANA	9 ALUMINIUM REMOVABLE SUNSCREEN COVER
10 FORJADO DE HORMIGÓN IN SITU	10 IN-SITU CONCRETE FLOOR
11 LOSA PREFABRICADA DE HORMIGÓN PARA EL FORJADO	11 PREFABRICATED FLOOR ELEMENT, CONCRETE
12 CONDUCTO DE VENTILACIÓN NATURAL PROTEGIDO CONTRA EL RUIDO	12 NOISE INSULATING, NATURAL VENTILATION
13 PERSIANA DISPONIBLE EN ROJO, AMARILLO O NARANJA	13 SUNSCREEN, AVAILABLE IN RED, YELLOW AND ORANGE
14 CARPINTERÍA DE ALUMINIO	14 ALUMINIUM WINDOW FRAME

GRAVA
GRAVEL

CERÁMICA
TERRACOTTA

MADERA
WOOD

CEMENTO
CEMENT

VEGETACIÓN
PLANTING

METAL
METAL

AISLAMIENTO
INSULATION

MEMBRANA
MEMBRANE

HORMIGÓN
CONCRETE

MADERA
WOOD

CERÁMICA
TERRACOTTA

CARTÓN-YESO
PLASTER-BOARD

ENLUCIDO
PLASTER

METAL
METAL

0,127
mill.☺

600
☺/km²

1.541 m²
SUPERFICIE DE PARCELA
PLOT AREA

4.618 m²
SUPERFICIE CONSTRUIDA
GROSS FLOOR AREA

1:2.000

52,5%
OCUPACIÓN
COVERED AREA

2,20
EDIFICABILIDAD
FLOOR AREA RATIO

100%
ALQUILER   PROPIEDAD
RENTAL   OWNERSHIP

44 🚗 **73%**
VIVIENDA
LIVING

JÓVENES   MAYORES   ESTUDIANTES   **100%**
YOUNG PEOPLE   SENIORS   STUDENTS   CUALQUIERA
                                              ANY

44
UNITS

TRABAJO
WORKING

100%
PÚBLICA   PRIVADA
SUBSIDISED   PRIVATE

COMERCIOS
SHOPPING

285
⌂/ha

714
☺/ha

DENSIDAD DE VIVIENDAS   DENSIDAD DE POBLACIÓN
DWELLING DENSITY   RESIDENTIAL DENSITY

27%
VIVIENDA-TRABAJO
LIVEWORK UNITS

1:5.000
0 10   50

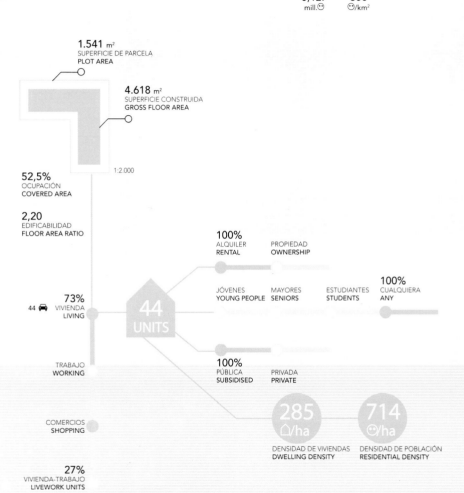

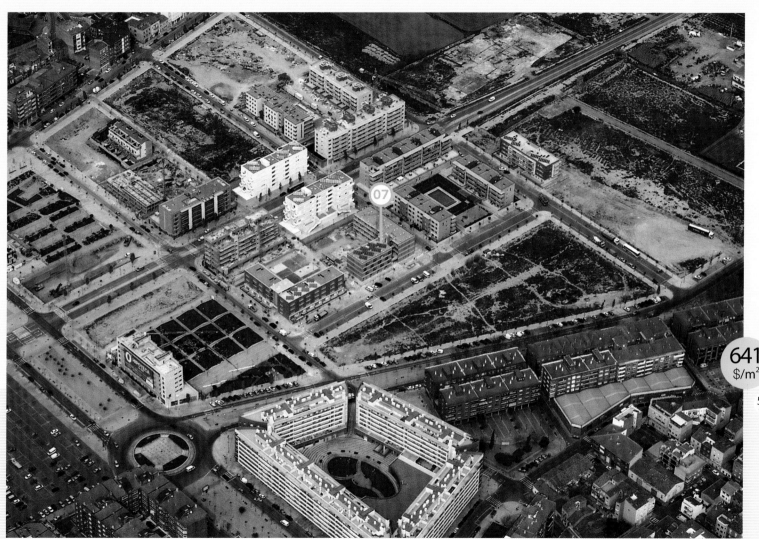

07

641
$/m²

578
€/m²

2.000
1.900
1.800
1.700
1.600
1.500
1.400
1.300
1.200
1.100
1.000
900
800
700
600
500
400
300
200
100
0

Asoleo **Sunlight**

4 VIVIENDAS (9%)
Orientación noreste/suroeste reciben 45
minutos solares entre las 10:00 y las 11:00 h.
40 VIVIENDAS (91%) orientación sureste/
suroeste y noreste/suroeste reciben, al menos,
1 hora solar entre las 11:00 y las 14:00 h en el
solsticio de invierno.

4 DWELLINGS (9%)
North East/South West orientation.
They receive sunlight for 45 minutes beetwen
10 a.m. and 11 a.m.
40 DWELLINGS (91%) South East/South
West orientation and North East/South West
orientation. They receive at least sunlight for
1 hour beetwen 11 a.m. and 2 p.m. on the
winter solstice.

1:2000

14:00
13:00
12:00
11:00

21 Diciembre 10:00 h
December 21st 10:00 a.m.

10:00

21st June
N
21st December
10
11
12
13
14
S

14:00 h

Latitud media: 41°36' N Lleida
Latitude: 41°36' N Lleida

Como respuesta a las condiciones
del solar y a los criterios de
sostenibilidad especificados en el
programa (1 hora de sol entre las
10:00 y las 14:00 horas en el solsticio
de invierno para el 91 % de las
viviendas), la propuesta plantea
un solo edificio formado por dos
bloques separados (A y B), con
vestíbulo y escalera común, acceso
por pasarela y 44 viviendas (11 por
planta) de un solo tipo, pero que
cambia según el bloque (gira 180
grados según la orientación, sea
bloque A o B) y según la altura (de
una planta a otra se le aplica una
simetría especular).
Esta vivienda tipo, de 60 m² útiles
(5,65 x 11,80 metros) tiene una
distribución interior que se puede
adaptar según el usuario (edad

To answer to the conditions of the
lot and the sustainability criteria
specified in the programme (one
hour of sunlight between 10:00 am
and 2:00 pm at the winter solstice
for 91% of housing units), the
proposal presents a single building
made up of two separate blocks
(A and B), with a common hall and
stairway, a walkway entrance and 44
housing units (11 per floor).
There is only one housing type which
changes in each block, turning 180
degrees depending its orientation,
A or B, or depending on its level,
applying a specular symmetry to one
floor or another.
This housing unit type, with 60
usable metres (5.65 x 11.8 m²)
has an interior layout that can be
adapted to different users (age and

y número de personas), según
la orientación deseada (permite
intercambiar la sala por el comedor
según se desee patio o calle, en
invierno o verano). También se
pueden permutar los dormitorios o
transformarlos en estudios.
La vivienda se abre al exterior (a
calle y a pasarela de acceso) por
dos porches o patios abiertos a
fachada. Son espacios de transición
(no queríamos terrazas) que acercan
las condiciones de relación con el
exterior a aquellas de una vivienda
unifamiliar, accediendo por puertas
correderas de aluminio. Por tanto
toda la vivienda se cierra o abre al
exterior por dos huecos en fachada,
ganando en control climático, control
de visuales y ganando en seguridad.

number of people), to the desired
orientation (changing the location of
the living room and the dining room
as patio or street views are desired,
in winter or summer). Bedrooms can
also be changed around or turned
into studios.
The housing unit opens up to
the exterior (street and entrance
walkway) by means of two porches
or patios facing the facade. They are
transition spaces (we did not want
terraces), which make relationships
with the exterior more similar to
those of a single family house,
through aluminium sliding doors.
The entire house is thus opened or
closed to the outside by means of
two openings on the facade, gaining
climatic control, visual control and
security.

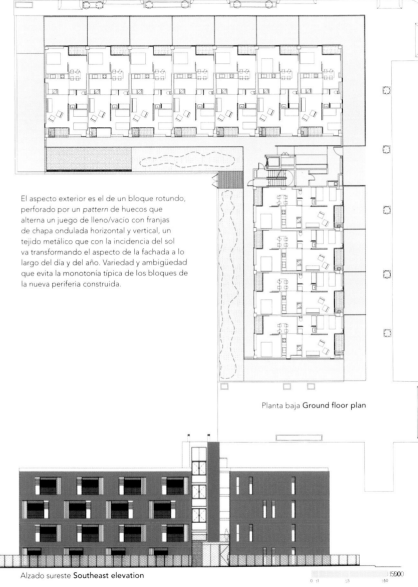

El aspecto exterior es el de un bloque rotundo, perforado por un *pattern* de huecos que alterna un juego de lleno/vacío con franjas de chapa ondulada horizontal y vertical, un tejido metálico que con la incidencia del sol va transformando el aspecto de la fachada a lo largo del día y del año. Variedad y ambigüedad que evita la monotonía típica de los bloques de la nueva periferia construida.

Planta baja **Ground floor plan**

Alzado sureste **Southeast elevation**

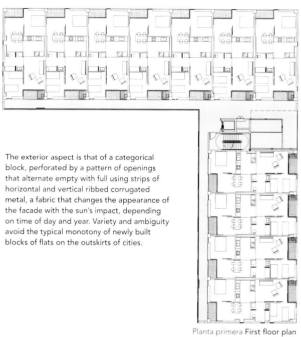

The exterior aspect is that of a categorical block, perforated by a pattern of openings that alternate empty with full using strips of horizontal and vertical ribbed corrugated metal, a fabric that changes the appearance of the facade with the sun's impact, depending on time of day and year. Variety and ambiguity avoid the typical monotony of newly built blocks of flats on the outskirts of cities.

Planta primera **First floor plan**

1:500

0 1   5   10

A ⌐ A

Sección **A Section**

1000
950
900
850
800
750
700
650
600
550
500
450
400
350
300
250
200
150

44
UNITS

100
50
0
UNITS

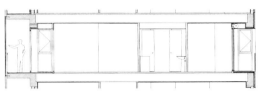

Sección longitudinal A Long section

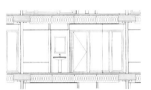

Sección transversal B Cross section

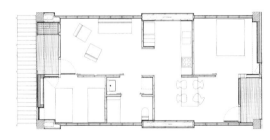

B

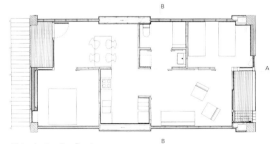

B

Viviendas tipo Dwelling types

1:200

0　1　　　　5　　　　　10

EDAD AGE

Tipo 1 **Tipo 1**

LOFT/ESPACIO
CONTINUO
45,9 m² ESPACIO
ABIERTO
SOLTERO/PAREJA
JOVEN

LOFT/CONTINUOUS
SPACE
45.9 m² OPEN SPACE
SINGLE/YOUNG COUPLE

Tipo 2 **Type**

VIVIENDA+ESTUDIO
15,5 m² ESPACIO
ABIERTO
PAREJA PROFESIONAL
(SIN HIJOS)

APARTEMENT+STUDY
15.5 m² OPEN SPACE
PROFESSIONAL COUPLE
(NO CHILDREN)

Tipo 3 (verano) **3 Type (summer)**

CORREDERA CERRADA
GALERÍA ESPACIO
INTERIOR
VENTILACIÓN CRUZADA
34.6 m² ESPACIO ABIERTO
PAREJA+2 HIJOS

SLINDING PANELS CLOSED
GALLERY, INTERIOR SPACE
CROSS VENTILATION
34.6 m² OPEN SPACE
COUPLE+2 CHILDREN

Tipo 3 (invierno) **3 Type (winter)**

CORREDERA CERRADA
GALERÍA ESPACIO
INTERIOR
VENTILACIÓN CRUZADA
27,4 m² ESPACIO ABIERTO
PAREJA+2 HIJOS

SLINDING PANELS CLOSED
GALLERY, INTERIOR SPACE
CROSS VENTILATION
27.4 m² OPEN SPACE
COUPLE+2 CHILDREN

1:500
0 1   5   10

EXTERNAL

CERÁMICA
BRICKWORK

HORMIGON
CONCRETE

MADERA
WOOD

CEMENTO
CEMENT

METAL
METAL

COMPUESTO
COMPOSITE

VIDRIO
GALSS

ENFOSCADO/
ESTUCO
MORTAR/
STUCCO

AISLAMIENTO
INSULATION

MEMBRANA
MEMBRANE

CERÁMICA
BRICKWORK

VIDRIO
GALSS

HORMIGON
CONCRETE

MADERA
WOOD

COMPUESTO
COMPOSITE

CARTÓN-YESO
PLASTER-BOARD

CERÁMICA
BRICKWORK

ENLUCIDO
PLASTER

1 PAVIMENTO INTERIOR
  DE LOSAS DE TERRAZO
  DE 40 cm DE LADO
2 FORJADO DE LOSAS
  ALVEOLARES
3 CHAPA PLEGADA DE ACERO
  GALVANIZADO e=1,5 mm
4 CARTÓN-YESO e=13 mm
5 CAPA DE AISLAMIENTO
  TÉRMICO DE POLIESTIRENO
  EXTRUIDO DE ALTA
  DENSIDAD
6 CAJA DE PERSIANA
7 FALSO TECHO EXTERIOR
8 CARPINTERÍA DE ALUMINIO
9 MARCO DE ACERO
  GALVANIZADO
10 IMPERMEABILIZACIÓN CON
   DOS LÁMINAS BITUMINOSAS
11 HORMIGÓN CELULAR
   PARA LA FORMACIÓN
   DE PENDIENTES
12 PAVIMENTO EXTERIOR
   DE HORMIGÓN
13 VIDRIO CON BUTIRAL
   DE COLOR
14 CHAPA DE ACERO
   PLEGADA e=5 mm
15 LÁMINA GEOTEXTIL
16 GUÍA
17 PANEL DE CHAPA DE
   ACERO ONDULADA
18 CANALÓN

19 ESTRUCTURA DE
   HORMIGÓN IN SITU
20 IMPRIMACIÓN BITUMINOSA
21 PUERTA CORREDERA
   DE BASTIDOR DE TUBO
   DE ACERO DE 50 x 50
   mm Y RELLENO DE
   MALLA METÁLICA
22 TABLERO CONTRACHAPADO
   DE ABEDUL CON UN
   ACABADO DE PROPILENO
   IMPRESO DE COLOR GRIS
23 ACABADO CON
   RECUBRIMIENTO DE
   RESINA EPOXI

1 INTERIOR FLOORING
  OF 40 x 40 cm LONG
  TERRAZZO TILES
2 HOLLOW CORE SLAB
3 1.5 mm THICK GALVANISED
  STEEL BENT PLATE
4 13 mm THICK
  GYPSUM BOARD
5 HIGH DENSITY EXTRUDED
  POLYSTYRENE THERMAL
  INSULATION
6 BLIND CASE
7 EXTERIOR CEILING
8 ALUMINIUM FRAMEWORK
9 GALVANISED STEEL FRAME
10 2 SHEETS OF BITUMINOUS
   WATERPROOFING
11 LIGHT CONCRETE SCREED
   AS ROOF SLOPE
12 CONCRETE EXTERIOR
   PAVING
13 DOUBLE GLAZING WITH A
   COLORED BUTIRAL SHEET
14 5 mm THICK BENT
   STEEL PLATE

15 GEOTEXTILE MAT
16 RAIL GUIDE
17 CORRUGATED STEEL
   SHEETING
18 GUTTER
19 CAST IN PLACE
   CONCRETE STRUCTURE
20 BITUMINOUS LAYER
21 SLIDING DOOR: STEEL
   MESH WITHIN A 50 x 50
   mm STEEL TUBE FRAME
22 BIRCH PLYWOOD
   COATED WITH GRAY
   PROPYLENE COATING
23 EPOXI RESIN FINISHING

1:50

0 0.1   0.5   1

FACHADA/FACADE

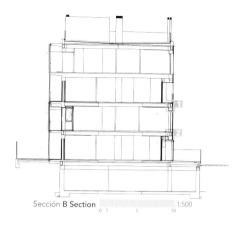

Sección B Section   1:500

0 1   5   10

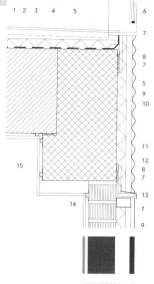

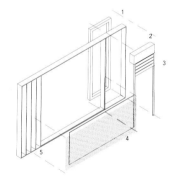

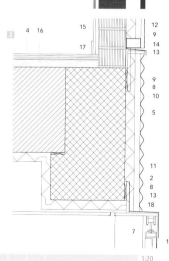

0 0,1   0,5   1   1:20

1 MARCO DE ACERO GALVANIZADO
2 CAJA DE PERSIANA
3 PERSIANA ENROLLABLE
4 VIDRIO CON LÁMINA DE BUTIRAL DE COLOR
5 LAMAS DE ACERO GALVANIZADO

1 GALVANISED STEEL FRAME
2 BLIND CASE
3 ROLL-UP BLIND
4 GLASS WITH BUTIRAL INTERMEDIATE SHEET
5 GALVANISED STEEL LOUVERS

1 TABLERO CONTRACHAPADO DE ABEDUL CON UN ACABADO DE PROPILENO IMPRESO DE COLOR GRIS
2 CAPA DE AISLAMIENTO TÉRMICO DE POLIESTIRENO EXTRUIDO DE ALTA DENSIDAD
3 IMPRIMACIÓN BITUMINOSA
4 FORJADO DE LOSAS ALVEOLARES
5 ESTRUCTURA DE HORMIGÓN IN SITU
6 VIDRIO CON BUTIRAL DE COLOR
7 PLETINA DE ACERO e=8 mm
8 SELLADO DE ESPUMA DE POLIURETANO IMPREGNADA CON BITUMEN ASFÁLTICO
9 CAPA DE AISLAMIENTO

TÉRMICO DE POLIURETANO PROYECTADO e=40 mm
10 CHAPA ONDULADA
11 CINTA DE NEOPRENO e=10 mm
12 LADRILLO DE 15 cm
13 CHAPA PLEGADA DE ACERO GALVANIZADO e=1,5 mm
14 RASTRELES DE SUJECCIÓN DE LA CHAPA ONDULADA
15 PANELES DE CARTÓN YESO e=13 mm APOYADOS SOBRE PERFILES OMEGA DE 16 mm CADA 400 mm
16 PAVIMENTO INTERIOR DE LOSAS DE TERRAZO DE 40 cm DE LADO
17 RODAPIÉ DE RESINA DE 70 mm DE ALTO
18 GUÍA
19 PERFIL L DE 40 x 40 mm

1 BIRCH PLYWOOD COATED WITH GRAY PROPYLENE COATING
2 HIGH DENSITY EXTRUDED POLYSTYRENE THERMAL INSULATION
3 BITUMINOUS LAYER
4 HOLLOW CORE SLAB
5 CAST IN PLACE CONCRETE STRUCTURE
6 DOUBLE GLAZING WITH A COLORED BUTIRAL SHEET
7 8 mm THICK STEEL PLATE
8 POLYURETHANE FOAM SEALING, IMPREGNATED WITH ASPHALTIC BITUMEN
9 40 mm SPRAYED POLYURETHANE THERMAL INSULATION LAYER
10 CORRUGATED STEEL SHEET

11 10 mm THICK NEOPRENE TAPE
12 15 cm BRICK WALL
13 1.5 mm THICK GALVANISED STEEL BENT PLATE
14 FIXATION SUBSTRUCTURE OF THE CORRUGATED PLATE
15 13 mm THICK GYPSUM BOARD PANELS ON 16 mm OMEGA PROFILES POSITIONED EVERY 400 mm
16 INTERIOR FLOORING OF 40 x 40 cm LONG TERRAZZO TILES
17 70 mm HIGH RESIN SKIRTING
18 RAIL GUIDE
19 40 x 40 mm L-PROFILE

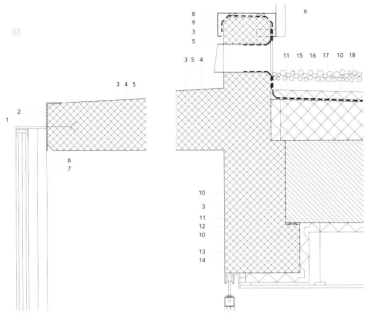

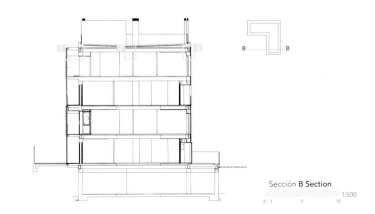

Sección **B Section**

1:500

0 1   5   10

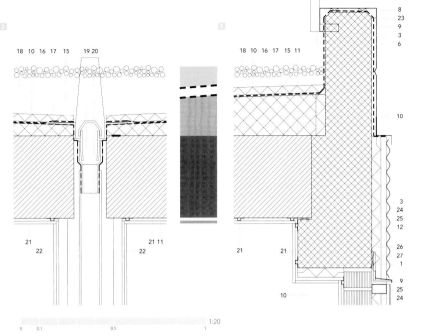

1 PLETINA DE ACERO e=8 mm
2 CHAPA DE ACERO PLEGADA e=5 mm
3 ESTRUCTURA DE HORMIGÓN IN SITU
4 CAPA SUPERIOR PULIDA CON CUARZO
5 CAPA DE CAUCHO
6 BARANDILLA DE BASTIDOR DE TUBO DE ACERO DE 50 mm DE DIÁMETRO Y RELLENO DE MALLA DE SIMPLE TORSIÓN
7 PANEL DE POLICARBONATO CELULAR DE 400 mm DE ANCHO Y e=40 mm
8 LISTÓN DE MADERA
9 CHAPA PLEGADA DE ACERO GALVANIZADO e=1,5 mm
10 CAPA DE AISLAMIENTO TÉRMICO DE POLIESTIRENO EXTRUIDO DE ALTA DENSIDAD
11 FORJADO DE LOSAS ALVEOLARES
12 CINTA DE NEOPRENO e=10 mm
13 PERFIL L DE ACERO DE 70 x 70 mm
14 GUÍA
15 HORMIGÓN CELULAR PARA LA FORMACIÓN DE PENDIENTES
16 LÁMINA SEPARADORA DE FIELTRO DE POLIPROPILENO
17 IMPERMEABILIZACIÓN CON DOS LÁMINAS BITUMINOSAS
18 GRAVA
19 BOTE SIFÓNICO DE PVC RÍGIDO 110 mm DE DIÁMETRO
20 BAJANTE DE PVC RÍGIDO DE 110 mm DE DIÁMETRO
21 PANELES DE CARTÓN YESO e=13 mm APOYADOS SOBRE PERFILES OMEGA DE 16 mm CADA 400 mm
22 TABIQUE DE CARTÓN YESO
23 LÁMINA IMPERMEABILIZANTE
24 CAPA DE AISLAMIENTO TÉRMICO DE POLIURETANO PROYECTADO e=40 mm
25 CHAPA ONDULADA
26 LADRILLO DE 15 cm
27 SELLADO DE ESPUMA DE POLIURETANO IMPREGNADA CON BITUMEN ASFÁLTICO

1 8 mm THICK STEEL PLATE
2 5 mm THICK BENT STEEL PLATE
3 CAST IN PLACE CONCRETE STRUCTURE
4 UPPER SIDE QUARTZ POLISHED
5 RUBBER LAYER
6 BALUSTRADE: STEEL MESH WITHIN A Ø 50 mm STEEL TUBE FRAME
7 400 mm WIDE, 40 mm THICK CELLULAR POLYCARBONATE PANEL
8 TIMBER BATTEN
9 1,5 mm THICK GALVANISED STEEL BENT PLATE
10 HIGH DENSITY EXTRUDED POLYSTYRENE THERMAL INSULATION
11 HOLLOW CORE SLAB
12 10 mm THICK NEOPRENE TAPE
13 70 x 70 mm L-PROFILE
14 RAIL GUIDE
15 LIGHT CONCRETE SCREED AS ROOF SLOPE
16 POLYPROPYLENE FELT SEPARATING SHEET
17 2 SHEETS OF BITUMINOUS WATERPROOFING
18 GRAVEL
19 Ø 110 mm RIGID PVC SIPHON TRAP
20 Ø 110 mm RIGID PVC PIPE
21 13 mm THICK GYPSUM BOARD PANELS ON 16 mm OMEGA PROFILES POSITIONED EVERY 400 mm
22 GYPSUM BOARD LIGHT WALL
23 WATERPROOF MEMBRANE
24 40 mm THICK SPRAYED POLYURETHANE THERMAL INSULATION LAYER
25 CORRUGATED STEEL SHEET
26 15 cm WALL BRICK
27 POLYURETHANE FOAM SEALING, IMPREGNATED WITH ASPHALTIC BITUMEN

GRAVA **GRAVEL**
CERÁMICA **TERRACOTTA**
MADERA **WOOD**
CEMENTO **CEMENT**
VEGETACIÓN **PLANTING**
METAL **METAL**
AISLAMIENTO **INSULATION**
MEMBRANA **MEMBRANE**
HORMIGÓN **CONCRETE**
MADERA **WOOD**
CERÁMICA **TERRACOTTA**
CARTÓN-YESO **PLASTER-BOARD**
ENLUCIDO **PLASTER**
METAL **METAL**

1:20

Construcción

Estructura de pilares y jácenas de hormigón paralelas a fachada sobre las que se apoyan las placas alveolares de 45 cm que cubren una luz de 11,00 metros, quedando el interior de las viviendas sin soportes.

Fachada exterior a sur y este, ventilada de chapa galvanizada PL 18/76 minionda colocada verticalmente entre huecos y horizontalmente entre dintel y pavimento, lacada en taller plata RAL 9006, sobre proyectado de poliuretano y ladrillo perforado de 14 cm.

La fachada interior al norte (a las pasarelas) está acabada con revoco pintado de gris antracita, con los accesos a las viviendas protegidos del viento de norte por unos paneles de policarbonato de color verde.

Construction

A structure of pillars and concrete beams parallel to the facade on which 45 cm alveolar plates are supported and which cover a span of 11.00 metres on the interior of the housing units without pillars.

Exterior ventilated facade faces South and East, and is in galvanised sheet metal PL 18/76 'narrow ribbed', placed vertically between openings and horizontally between the lintel and pavement, lacquered in silver RAL 9006, on sprayed polyurethane and 14 cm perforated brick.

The interior facade faces North (towards the walkways) and is finished in rendering painted anthracite grey, with the entrances to housing units protected from northern wind by green polycarbonate panels.

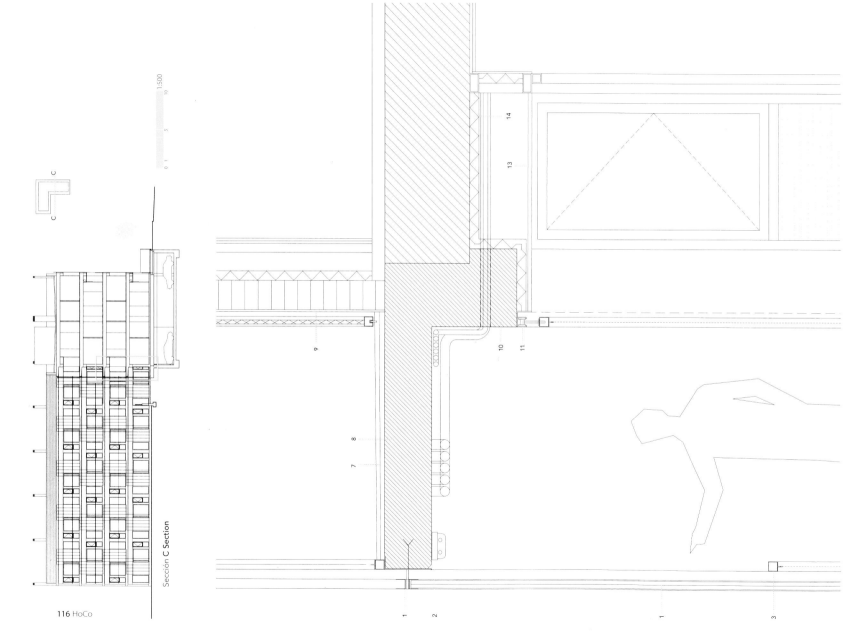

1:500

C C

C C

Sección C Section

7 8

9

10 11

13 14

1 2

1 3

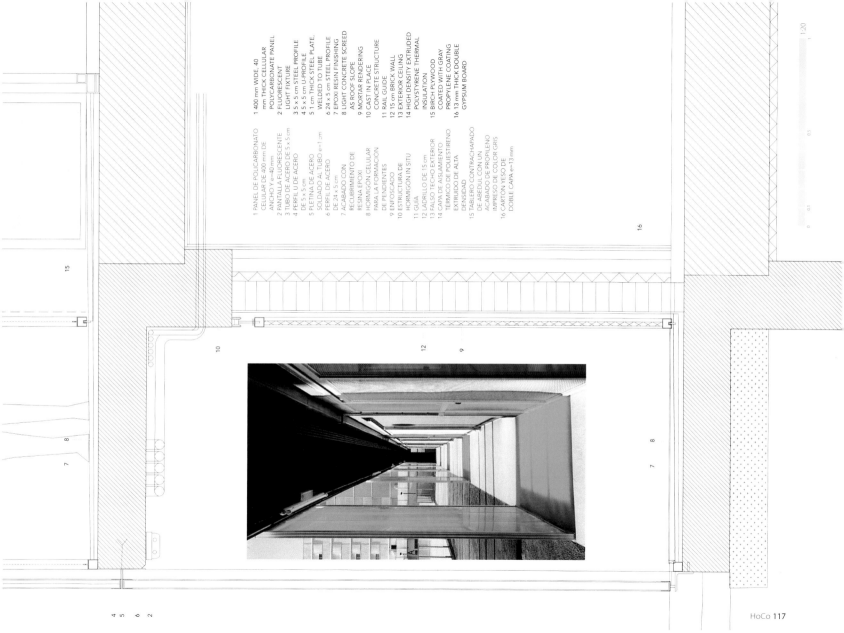

1 400 mm WIDE, 40 mm THICK CELLULAR POLYCARBONATE PANEL
2 FLUORESCENT LIGHT FIXTURE
3 5 x 5 cm STEEL PROFILE
4 5 x 5 cm U-PROFILE
5 1 cm THICK STEEL PLATE, WELDED TO TUBE
6 24 x 5 cm STEEL PROFILE
7 EPOXI RESIN FINISHING
8 LIGHT CONCRETE SCREED AS ROOF SLOPE
9 MORTAR RENDERING
10 CAST IN PLACE CONCRETE STRUCTURE
11 RAIL GUIDE
12 15 cm BRICK WALL
13 EXTERIOR CEILING
14 HIGH DENSITY EXTRUDED POLYSTYRENE THERMAL INSULATION
15 BIRCH PLYWOOD COATED WITH GRAY PROPYLENE COATING
16 13 mm THICK DOUBLE GYPSUM BOARD

1 PANEL DE POLICARBONATO CELULAR DE 400 mm DE ANCHO Y e=40 mm
2 PANTALLA FLUORESCENTE
3 TUBO DE ACERO DE 5 x 5 cm
4 PERFIL U DE ACERO DE 5 x 5 cm
5 PLETINA DE ACERO SOLDADO AL TUBO e=1 cm
6 PERFIL DE ACERO DE 24 x 5 cm
7 ACABADO CON RECUBRIMIENTO DE RESINA EPOXI
8 HORMIGÓN CELULAR PARA LA FORMACION DE PENDIENTES
9 ENFOSCADO
10 ESTRUCTURA DE HORMIGÓN IN SITU
11 GUÍA
12 LADRILLO DE 15 cm
13 FALSO TECHO EXTERIOR
14 CAPA DE AISLAMIENTO TÉRMICO DE POLIESTIRENO EXTRUIDO DE ALTA DENSIDAD
15 TABLERO CONTRACHAPADO DE ABEDUL CON UN ACABADO DE PROPILENO IMPRESO DE COLOR GRIS
16 CARTÓN YESO DE DOBLE CAPA e=13 mm

1:20

López-Rivera Arquitectos lopez-rivera.com Barcelona. SPAIN, 2007 Sant Adriá 33, Sant Andreu

1,603 mill.☺

15.810 ☺/km²

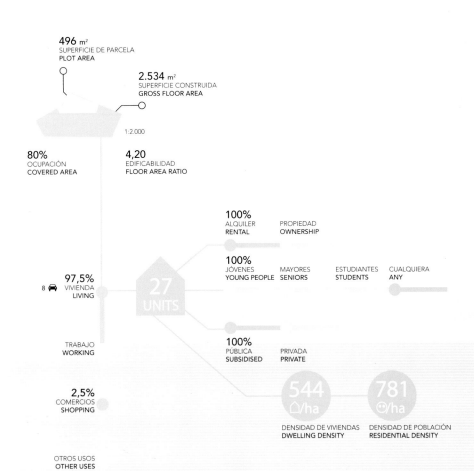

496 m²
SUPERFICIE DE PARCELA
PLOT AREA

2.534 m²
SUPERFICIE CONSTRUIDA
GROSS FLOOR AREA

1:2.000

80%
OCUPACIÓN
COVERED AREA

4,20
EDIFICABILIDAD
FLOOR AREA RATIO

100%
ALQUILER
RENTAL

PROPIEDAD
OWNERSHIP

100%
JÓVENES
YOUNG PEOPLE

MAYORES
SENIORS

ESTUDIANTES
STUDENTS

CUALQUIERA
ANY

97,5%
8 🚗 VIVIENDA
LIVING

27
UNITS

TRABAJO
WORKING

100%
PÚBLICA
SUBSIDISED

PRIVADA
PRIVATE

2,5%
COMERCIOS
SHOPPING

544
⌂/ha

781
☺/ha

DENSIDAD DE VIVIENDAS
DWELLING DENSITY

DENSIDAD DE POBLACIÓN
RESIDENTIAL DENSITY

OTROS USOS
OTHER USES

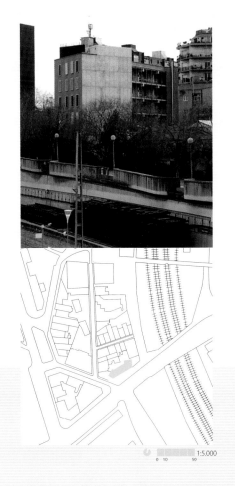

1:5.000
0 10 50

08

649
$/m²

585
€/m²

AUTHOR'S DESCRIPTION

Se trata de un proyecto de veintisiete viviendas para jóvenes resultado de un concurso organizado en 2003 por la Generalitat de Catalunya y el COAC para arquitectos menores de 40 años. El programa pedía 6 viviendas por rellano: 5 para 1 o 2 personas de 40 m² útiles y una para 2-3 personas de 50 m² útiles. Las viviendas resultantes son 5 de 44 m² útiles y una de 51 m² útiles. El edificio se ubica en un solar trapezoidal en el barrio barcelonés de Sant Andreu.

Nuestra aproximación al proyecto fue comenzar desde adentro hacia afuera, prestando especial atención a las cualidades espaciales del interior, un aspecto, al que creemos que no se le presta la atención suficiente en vivienda social hoy en día. Entendemos los lugares de transición entre interior y exterior como limites gruesos. Estos límites están compuestos por intersticios amortiguadores de pequeña escala, que le dan a la vivienda una mayor variedad de espacios.

Tanto la ventilación natural, como la abundante luz natural en todos los espacios, están garantizadas por la distribución interior y por disponer todas las unidades de dos fachadas opuestas abiertas.

Aprovechando el clima mediterráneo, la entrada a los apartamentos se realiza mediante una pasarela abierta en la parte posterior del edificio, que mira hacia un típico patio interior de manzana barcelonés.

This project for twenty-seven low-rent dwelling units for young people was a result of a competition for architects under 40 years of age, organised in 2003 by the Catalonian Architect's Association (COAC) and the Catalonian Government. The brief called for six units (5 of 40 m² of net usable area for 1 or 2 people and one of 50 m² for 2-3 people) per storey, to be accommodated in an odd shaped site located in Sant Andreu, Barcelona. The resulting units are 44 m² (for 1-2 persons) and 51m² (for 2-3 persons).

Our approach to the project was to work from inside out, carefully considering the spatial qualities and adjacencies of the interior spaces, an aspect we feel is not given enough attention currently in social housing. We intended for the places of transition between interior and exterior to become thick boundaries composed of small scale buffer zones or 'almost-rooms' providing the dwelling with a richer variety of spaces.

Natural cross ventilation and abundant daylight in all spaces is guaranteed by the interior distribution and by having two opposite facades. Taking advantage of the mild weather in Barcelona, entry from the street to the apartments is made from an open walkway located on the back facade of the building overlooking a typical Barcelona interior court.

La cocina y el lavabo se colocan adyacentes a esta fachada, mientras que la zona principal de estar se encuentra en la fachada sureste opuesta, con el fin de cumplir con el decreto local de eco-eficiencia. Este decreto pide que el 80% de las viviendas dispongan de al menos una hora de sol directo en la sala de estar de 10:00 a 14:00 en el solsticio de invierno.

Funcionando como amortiguador climático y acústico entre la calle y el estar y recuperando una tradición barcelonesa, colocamos una pequeña galería en el extremo sur del estar. Ésta galería se genera entre dos superficies vidriadas y funciona como captador solar pasivo en el invierno. En verano, debido a la verticalidad de la incidencia solar, abriendo las lamas vidriadas exteriores y cerrando las puertas plegables interiores, la galería se transforma en un balcón. Adyacente a la sala de estar y separada por dos grandes puertas corredizas, se encuentra la habitación. Hacia la fachada de la calle se encuentra un espacio alcoba generado por la profundidad de la galería. En este espacio una ventana de dimensiones más reducidas, con lamas orientables filtra la luz de sur según las necesidades del usuario. La ventana se coloca en el centro del espacio para liberar las dos esquinas, con el fin de poder colocar armarios o escritorios a ambos lados. Este espacio puede usarse también como rincón para dormir, y así disponer del resto de la habitación para otros usos.

The kitchen and bathroom are located adjacent to this facade while the main living spaces are on the opposite south-eastern facade facing the street, in order to comply with the local eco-efficiency decree that demands that 80% of the dwellings have at least 1 hour of direct sunlight in the living room from 10:00 am to 2 pm in winter solstice.

Acting as a climactic and acoustic buffer zone between the street and the living room space, and recuperating a Barcelonan tradition, there is a small gallery space between two glazed enclosures that acts as a sunroom providing passive solar heat gain in the winter. In the summer, by means of the overhang that protects it from the high sun, it becomes a balcony when opening the exterior glass louvers and closing the interior folding glass doors. Adjacent to the living area and separated by large sliding doors, is an elongated bedroom. On the bedroom's street facade side, an alcove-like space is generated by the depth of the sunroom. In this space within the sleeping area, a smaller window with movable opaque louvers protects and filters the southern light according to user's desires and needs. Its central position provides two corners which allow it to be furnished with closets or a desk on either side. It could be used as a sleeping nook as well, freeing up the rest of the bedroom for other uses.

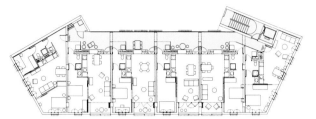

Planta tipo Typical floor plan

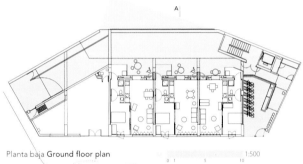

Planta baja Ground floor plan

1:500

0 1 5 10

A

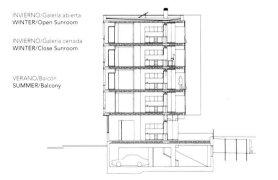

INVIERNO/Galería abierta
WINTER/Open Sunroom

INVIERNO/Galería cerrada
WINTER/Close Sunroom

VERANO/Balcón
SUMMER/Balcony

Sección transversal A Cross section

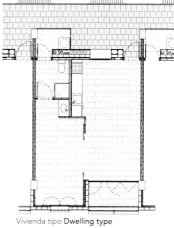

Vivienda tipo **Dwelling type**

1:200

0   1   5   10

La habitación conecta con el lavabo, que queda separado de la pasarela o calle elevada mediante un espacio amortiguador para lavar y secar la ropa. Este espacio cerrado por lamas de acero galvanizado y placas de fibrocemento, invade el ancho de la calle elevada, comprimiéndola en este punto y separando las viviendas del paso de personas. El acceso a las viviendas se da en los remansos de mayor profundidad que se generan entre lavadero y lavadero.

Estos remansos o ampliaciones de la calle pública, se convierten en pequeñas terrazas exteriores. Se encuentran adyacentes a la cocina, y pueden ser apropiados por los inquilinos como extensión del apartamento, favoreciendo la interacción social y la idea de comunidad.

The bedroom connects to the bathroom, which is buffered from the public access walkway by a space for washing and drying clothes. This space, enclosed by fibrocement panels and galvanised metal louvers, invades the width of the public access walkway, generating a recessed space where the entry door (which opens towards the outside) is located. This widening of the walkway is intended to be a small terrace-like space adjacent to the kitchen that people can appropriate as an extension of their apartment, stimulating social interaction and neighbourly communication.

1000
950
900
850
800
750
700
650
600
550
500
450
400
350
300
250
200
150
100
50
0

27 UNITS

El muro que separa la cocina de la calle pública alberga todas las conducciones verticales del edificio con el fin de ser fácilmente accesibles para mantenimiento, pero también para dar una profundidad exagerada a la ventana que comunica el interior con el exterior. El alféizar de esta ventana de guillotina se convierte en una bandeja de acero galvanizado de 60 cm de ancho, pudiéndose usar para pasar y colocar comida o bebidas directamente de la cocina a una mesa en el exterior. Se consiguió una altura mínima libre en todos los espacios de todos los apartamentos de 2,70 m.

The wall separating the kitchen and this terrace houses all utility ducts in order to make them easily accessible for maintenance, but also to give the window sill an exaggerated depth so that it becomes a 60 cm galvanised metal shelf, unobstructed when the double hung window is open, that serves to place and pass food and beverages right from the kitchen to a table outside. A 2.70 m ceiling height in all spaces of all units was accomplished.

LAYERS

EXTERNAL

CERÁMICA
BRICKWORK

HORMIGON
CONCRETE

MADERA
WOOD

CEMENTO
CEMENT

METAL
METAL

COMPUESTO
COMPOSITE

VIDRIO
GALSS

ENFOSCADO/
ESTUCO
**MORTAR/
STUCCO**

AISLAMIENTO
INSULATION

MEMBRANA
MEMBRANE

PRINCIPAL

CERÁMICA
BRICKWORK

VIDRIO
GALSS

HORMIGON
CONCRETE

MADERA
WOOD

COMPUESTO
COMPOSITE

INTERNAL

CARTÓN-YESO
PLASTER-BOARD

CERÁMICA
BRICKWORK

ENLUCIDO
PLASTER

FACHADA FACADE

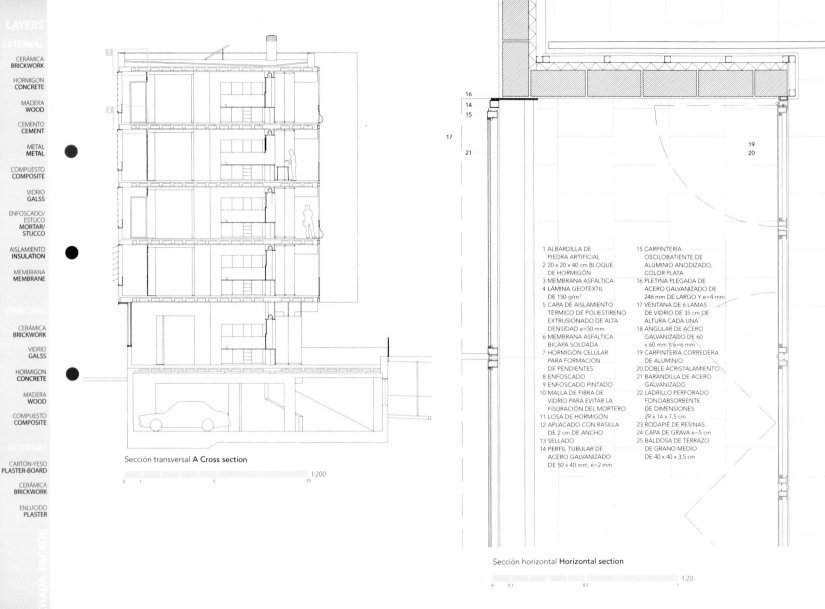

Sección transversal **A Cross section**

0 1   5   10   1:200

1 ALBARDILLA DE
  PIEDRA ARTIFICIAL
2 20 x 20 x 40 cm BLOQUE
  DE HORMIGÓN
3 MEMBRANA ASFÁLTICA
4 LÁMINA GEOTEXTIL
  DE 150 g/m²
5 CAPA DE AISLAMIENTO
  TÉRMICO DE POLIESTIRENO
  EXTRUSIONADO DE ALTA
  DENSIDAD e=50 mm
6 MEMBRANA ASFALTICA
  BICAPA SOLDADA
7 HORMIGÓN CELULAR
  PARA FORMACIÓN
  DE PENDIENTES
8 ENFOSCADO
9 ENFOSCADO PINTADO
10 MALLA DE FIBRA DE
  VIDRIO PARA EVITAR LA
  FISURACIÓN DEL MORTERO
11 LOSA DE HORMIGÓN
12 APLACADO CON RASILLA
  DE 2 cm DE ANCHO
13 SELLADO
14 PERFIL TUBULAR DE
  ACERO GALVANIZADO
  DE 50 x 40 mm, e=2 mm

15 CARPINTERÍA
  OSCILOBATIENTE DE
  ALUMINIO ANODIZADO,
  COLOR PLATA
16 PLETINA PLEGADA DE
  ACERO GALVANIZADO DE
  246 mm DE LARGO Y e=4 mm
17 VENTANA DE 6 LAMAS
  DE VIDRIO DE 35 cm DE
  ALTURA CADA UNA
18 ANGULAR DE ACERO
  GALVANIZADO DE 60
  x 60 mm Y e=6 mm
19 CARPINTERÍA CORREDERA
  DE ALUMINIO
20 DOBLE ACRISTALAMIENTO
21 BARANDILLA DE ACERO
  GALVANIZADO
22 LADRILLO PERFORADO
  FONOABSORBENTE
  DE DIMENSIONES
  29 x 14 x 7,5 cm
23 RODAPIÉ DE RESINAS
24 CAPA DE GRAVA e=5 cm
25 BALDOSA DE TERRAZO
  DE GRANO MEDIO
  DE 40 x 40 x 3,5 cm

Sección horizontal **Horizontal section**

0   0.1   0.5   1   1:20

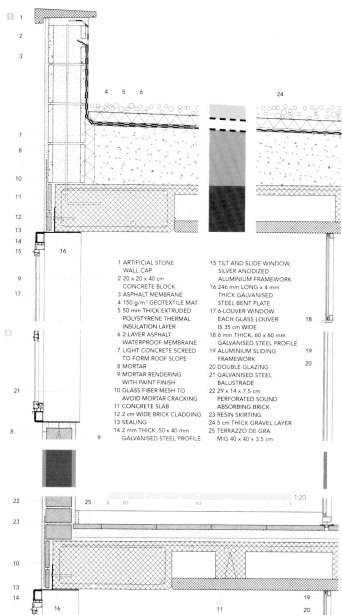

LAYERS

EXTERNAL

GRAVA
GRAVEL

CERÁMICA
TERRACOTTA

MADERA
WOOD

CEMENTO
CEMENT

VEGETACIÓN
PLANTING

METAL
METAL

AISLAMIENTO
INSULATION

MEMBRANA
MEMBRANE

PRINCIPAL

HORMIGÓN
CONCRETE

MADERA
WOOD

CERÁMICA
TERRACOTTA

INTERNAL

CARTÓN-YESO
PLASTER-BOARD

ENLUCIDO
PLASTER

METAL
METAL

CUBIERTA ROOF

1 ARTIFICIAL STONE
WALL CAP
2 20 x 20 x 40 cm
CONCRETE BLOCK
3 ASPHALT MEMBRANE
4 150 g/m² GEOTEXTILE MAT
5 50 mm THICK EXTRUDED
POLYSTYRENE THERMAL
INSULATION LAYER
6 2-LAYER ASPHALT
WATERPROOF MEMBRANE
7 LIGHT CONCRETE SCREED
TO FORM ROOF SLOPE
8 MORTAR
9 MORTAR RENDERING
WITH PAINT FINISH
10 GLASS FIBER MESH TO
AVOID MORTAR CRACKING
11 CONCRETE SLAB
12 2 cm WIDE BRICK CLADDING
13 SEALING
14 2 mm THICK, 50 x 40 mm
GALVANISED STEEL PROFILE

15 TILT AND SLIDE WINDOW,
SILVER ANODIZED
ALUMINIUM FRAMEWORK
16 246 mm LONG x 4 mm
THICK GALVANISED
STEEL BENT PLATE
17 6-LOUVER WINDOW.
EACH GLASS LOUVER
IS 35 cm WIDE
18 6 mm THICK, 60 x 60 mm
GALVANISED STEEL PROFILE
19 ALUMINIUM SLIDING
FRAMEWORK
20 DOUBLE GLAZING
21 GALVANISED STEEL
BALUSTRADE
22 29 x 14 x 7.5 cm
PERFORATED SOUND
ABSORBING BRICK
23 RESIN SKIRTING
24 5 cm THICK GRAVEL LAYER
25 TERRAZZO DE GRA
MIG 40 x 40 x 3.5 cm

1:20

3,153
mill.☺

847
☺/km²

13.710 m²
SUPERFICIE CONSTRUIDA
GROSS FLOOR AREA

7.373 m²
SUPERFICIE DE PARCELA
PLOT AREA

37,8%
OCUPACIÓN
COVERED AREA

1,60
EDIFICABILIDAD
FLOOR AREA RATIO

100%
ALQUILER
RENTAL

PROPIEDAD
OWNERSHIP

JÓVENES
YOUNG PEOPLE

MAYORES
SENIORS

ESTUDIANTES
STUDENTS

100%
CUALQUIERA
ANY

287
UNITS

73,7%
VIVIENDA
LIVING

8%
RESIDENCIA
DORM

PÚBLICA
SUBSIDISED

100%
PRIVADA
PRIVATE

14,3%
COMERCIOS
SHOPPING

393
⌂/ha

763
☺/ha

DENSIDAD DE VIVIENDAS
DWELLING DENSITY

DENSIDAD DE POBLACIÓN
RESIDENTIAL DENSITY

4%
HOTEL
HOTEL

1:5.000
0   10   50

2.631
CHY/m²

2.000

1.900

1.800

1.700

1.600

1.500

1.400

1.300

1.200

1.100

1.000

900

800

700

600

500

400

300

200

100

0

760
$/m²

09

Viviendas *tulou* construidas hace 400 años en los alrededores de Yongding
The original 400 year old *tulou* housing around Yongding

Montaje fotográfico de las nuevas viviendas *tulou* en Guangzhou
Photomontage of the new *tulou* housing in Guangzhou

Tulou es una tipología de viviendas propias del pueblo Hakka, un subgrupo de los chinos Han que vive en las provincias chinas de Guangdong, Jiangxi y Fujian y conserva su propio idioma. Se trata de un edificio de vivienda colectiva a caballo entre el campo y la ciudad que integra vivienda, almacenes, comercio, espacio espiritual y áreas públicas de ocio.

Tradicionalmente, las viviendas se distribuyen por el edificio como en una residencia de estudiantes pero con mayores posibilidades de interacción social. Esta tipología se adapta muy fácilmente a viviendas para rentas bajas, aunque la simple copia de su forma no sea solución suficiente para el diseño de vivienda de bajo coste. Lo que se puede es, sin embargo, aprender del *tulou* y preservar el espíritu comunitario entre familias de bajo poder adquisitivo.

Tulou is a dwelling type unique to the Hakka people. It is a communal residence between the city and the countryside, integrating living, storage, shopping, spiritual, and public entertainment into one single building entity.

Traditional units in tulou are evenly laid out along its perimeter, like modern slab-style dormitory buildings, but with greater opportunities for social interaction. Although this type is very much suitable for low-income housing, simply copying the form and style of the *tulou* would not be a good solution for the design of low-income housing. However, by learning from the *tulou*, one can help preserve community spirit among low-income families.

By introducing a 'new *tulou*' to modern cities and by careful experimentation of form and

La introducción de nuevos *tulou* en la ciudad moderna podría permitir la superación del urbanismo convencional. Nuestra experimentación plantea vincular el *tulou* al tejido urbano existente (áreas verdes, autopistas, puentes y zonas residuales abandonadas por la ciudad). En este sentido, el precio del suelo en las áreas residuales es muy bajo, gracias a los incentivos gubernamentales, y por tanto atractivo para la construcción de vivienda asequible. Además, la cercanía de los *tulou* entre sí permitiria aislar a sus residentes del caos y el ruido del entorno, dando lugar a un hábitat íntimo y confortable en el interior. La integración del modo de vida tradicional del pueblo Hakka con la vivienda asequible no es tan solo un asunto académico, sino también social, ya que las condiciones de vida de los pobres en China comienzan a captar la atención del público.

economy, one can transcend conventional urban design.
Our experiments explored ways to stitch the *tulou* within the existing urban fabric of the city- green areas, overpasses, expressways, and residual land left over by urbanization. The cost of residual sites is quite low due to incentives by the government, and this is an important factor in developing low-income housing. The close proximity of each *tulou* building helps insulate the users from the chaos and noise of the outside environment, while creating an intimate and comfortable environment inside.
Integrating the living culture of traditional Hakka *tulou* buildings with low-income housing is not only an academic issue- there is an important social issue too. The living condition of the poor is now gaining more public attention.

Estudio de densidad
Density study

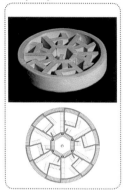

ENVOLVENTES
CONCÉNTRICAS 1
RADIO: 75 m

**CONCENTRIC
ENCLOSURE 1
RADIUS: 75 m**

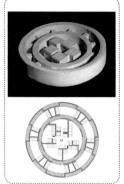

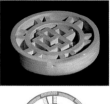

ESTRUCTURA DE
PÉTALOS
RADIO: 75 m

**PETALINE
STRUCTURE
RADIUS: 75 m**

CUADRADOS CHINOS
RADIO: 75 m

**CHINESE QUADRANGLES
RADIUS: 75 m**

ENVOLVENTES
CONCÉNTRICAS 2
RADIO: 75 m

**CONCENTRIC
ENCLOSURE 2
RADIUS: 75 m**

Viviendas *tulou* originales
Original 400 year old *tulou* housing

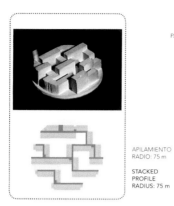

APILAMIENTO
RADIO: 75 m

STACKED
PROFILE
RADIUS: 75 m

PATIO HOMOGÉNEO
RADIO: 50 m

HOMOGENEOUS
COURTYARD
RADIUS: 50 m

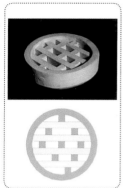

BUCLE CON FORMA DE E
(EL ELEGIDO FINALMENTE)
RADIO: 50 m

E-SHAPE LOOP
(THE CHOSEN ONE)
RADIUS: 50 m

VIVIENDA
ITINERANTE
RADIO: 50 m

MIGRANT
LIVING
RADIUS: 50 m

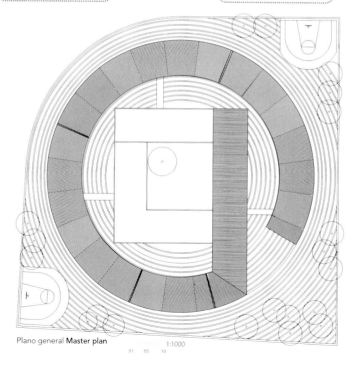

Plano general **Master plan**   1:1000
01 05 10

Viviendas *tulou* originales
Original 400 year old *tulou* housing

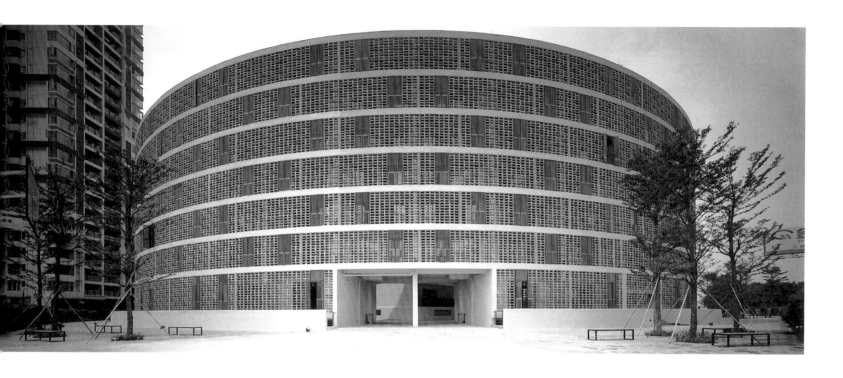

Alzado **Elevation** 1:1000

01 05 10

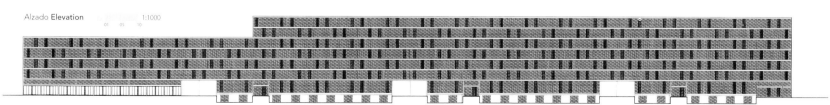

Viviendas tulou originales
Original 400 year old tulou housing

Viviendas *tulou* originales
Original 400 year old *tulou* housing

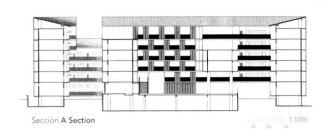

Sección A Section   1:1000
01   05   10

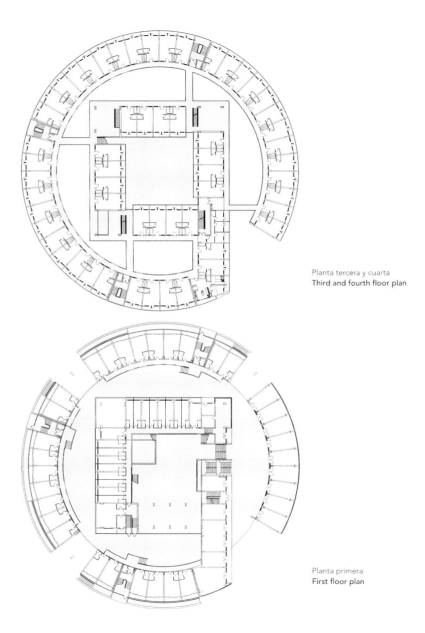

Planta tercera y cuarta
Third and fourth floor plan

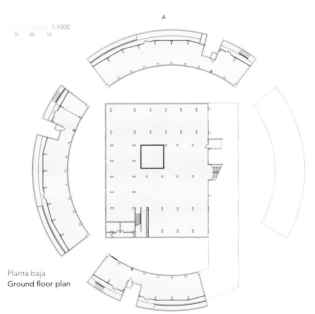

Planta baja
Ground floor plan

Planta primera
First floor plan

800
750
700
650
600
550
500
450
400
350

DORMITORIOS **BEDROOMS**

287
UNITS

300
250
200
150
100
50
0

UNITS

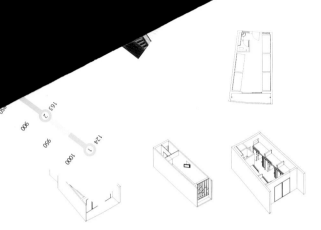

Tipos de vivienda **Dwelling types**

¿Cómo adaptar pues el *tulou* a la ciudad moderna? La investigación se basó en el análisis y la traslación a la práctica de los resultados teóricos. Este análisis se centró en el tamaño, los patrones espaciales y las funciones de los *tulou*. Asimismo, introdujimos nuevos elementos urbanos en el estilo tradicional para equilibrar la tensión entre tradición y modernidad. Al final, no sólo nos dimos cuenta de los beneficios y la utilidad del *tulou*, sino que aprendimos a entender todo un tipo de asentamiento urbano.

How can one effectively adapt the *tulou* into the modern city? Research was characterized by comprehensive analyses and continuity from the theoretical to the practical. The study has examined size, space patterns, and functions of *tulou* buildings. We also tried to inject new urban elements with the traditional style, and balance the tension between these two paradigms. In the end, we not only realized the feasibility and usefulness of the *tulou*, but we also gained experience and a deep understanding of a veritable urban form.

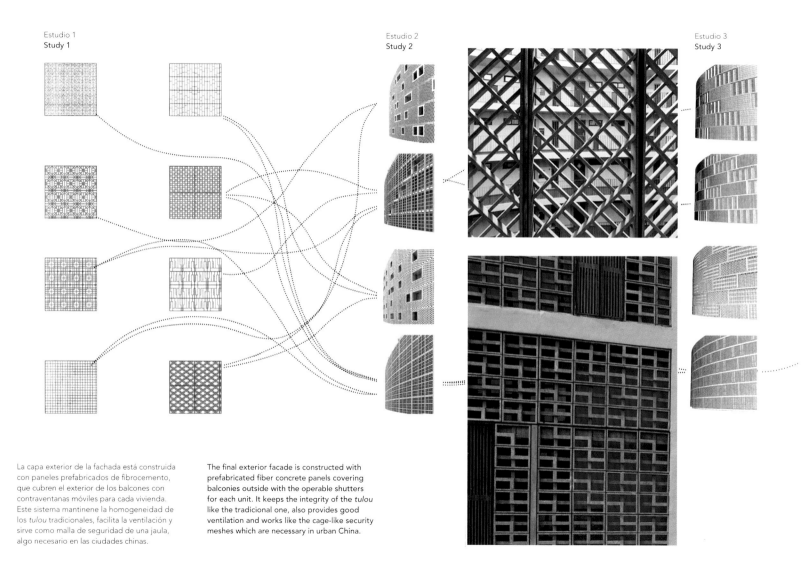

Estudio 1
Study 1

Estudio 2
Study 2

Estudio 3
Study 3

La capa exterior de la fachada está construida con paneles prefabricados de fibrocemento, que cubren el exterior de los balcones con contraventanas móviles para cada vivienda. Este sistema mantinene la homogeneidad de los *tulou* tradicionales, facilita la ventilación y sirve como malla de seguridad de una jaula, algo necesario en las ciudades chinas.

The final exterior facade is constructed with prefabricated fiber concrete panels covering balconies outside with the operable shutters for each unit. It keeps the integrity of the *tulou* like the tradicional one, also provides good ventilation and works like the cage-like security meshes which are necessary in urban China.

10 bevk perović arhitekti bevkperovic.com Maribor. SLOVENIA, 2007 Engelsova Ulica, Poljane

0,119 mill.☺ 807 ☺/km²

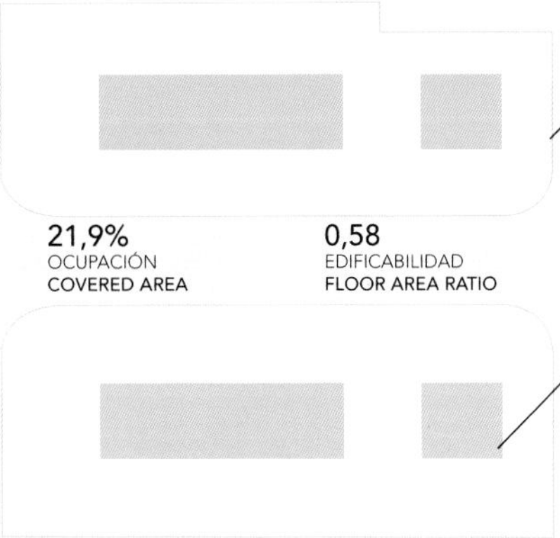

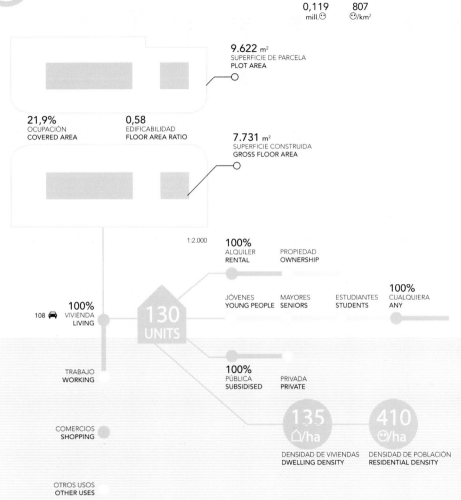

9.622 m² SUPERFICIE DE PARCELA PLOT AREA

21,9% OCUPACIÓN COVERED AREA

0,58 EDIFICABILIDAD FLOOR AREA RATIO

7.731 m² SUPERFICIE CONSTRUIDA GROSS FLOOR AREA

1:2.000

100% ALQUILER RENTAL — PROPIEDAD OWNERSHIP

JÓVENES YOUNG PEOPLE — MAYORES SENIORS — ESTUDIANTES STUDENTS — 100% CUALQUIERA ANY

108 🚗 100% VIVIENDA LIVING

130 UNITS

100% PÚBLICA SUBSIDISED — PRIVADA PRIVATE

TRABAJO WORKING

COMERCIOS SHOPPING

OTROS USOS OTHER USES

135 ⌂/ha DENSIDAD DE VIVIENDAS DWELLING DENSITY

410 ☺/ha DENSIDAD DE POBLACIÓN RESIDENTIAL DENSITY

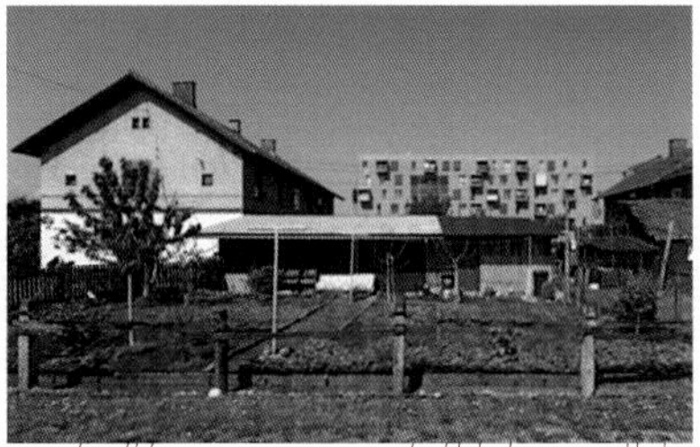

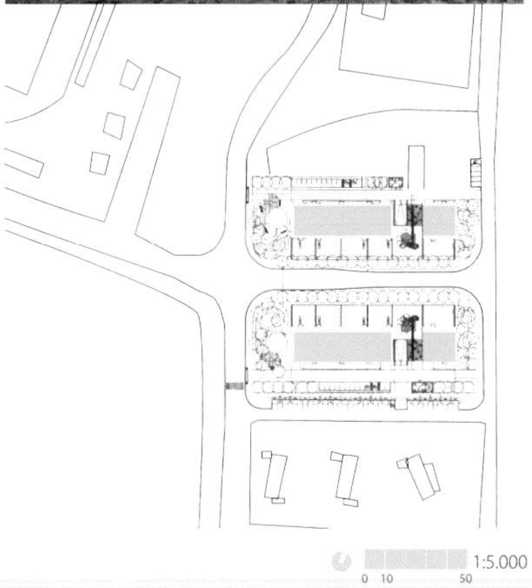

1:5.000

2.000

1.900

1.800

1.700

1.600

1.500

1.400

1.300

1.200

1.100

1.000

768
$/m²

900

800

700

550
€/m²

600

500

400

300

200

100

0

El conjunto de viviendas Poljane se encuentra a poca distancia de un importante nudo de carreteras en las afueras de Maribor. Consta de 4 edificios (dos torres y dos bloques lineales) que contienen 130 viviendas sociales. El proyecto se atiene a las estrictas limitaciones del planeamiento y sustituye el espacio público exterior inexistente por zonas comunes dentro de los edificios. Una serie de grandes espacios –estancias públicas– se excavan en el volumen y alojan los programas comunitarios. Estos espacios, unas veces están cubiertos y funcionan como zonas de juegos al aire libre, o bien se trata de cubiertas ajardinadas orientadas al sol.

Las viviendas se organizan en torno a un núcleo central de comunicación y su distribución responde a una tipología estándar. La individualidad de las viviendas se produce gracias a los balcones de colores, ubicados en diferentes lugares de la fachada para dar al conjunto un carácter dinámico. Además, es posible leer la sección del edificio en fachada. Los paneles ondulados de cemento indican los apartamentos, mientras que las bandas horizontales revelan los forjados. En este sentido, la elección de los materiales y el aspecto del edificio responden al carácter industrial de los alrededores.

Social housing settlement Poljane is located near a busy crossroads on the outskirts of Maribor. It consists of four buildings (2 slabs + 2 towers), a total of 130 social apartments. Project –limited with the existing rigid urban plan of the area, which had to be followed to a dot– replaces the missing exterior public spaces with collective areas inside the buildings. Vast empty spaces –public 'rooms'– are carved out of the volumes of the blocks and designated for public programmes. This spaces are either covered –designed as covered open-air playgrounds or open– as roof gardens oriented towards the sun. The apartments, arranged around the central communication core are of a standard typology, but their individuality is expressed with colourful balconies, inserted into the apartment plans. The balconies appear in different positions on the facade and work as accents which give the whole settlement a dynamic character.

The section of the block is also readable on the facade. The stacking fields of ondulated cement facade panels mark the apartments while the smooth horizontal belts mark the floor plates. The choice and appearance of facade materials follows the industrial character of the surroundings.

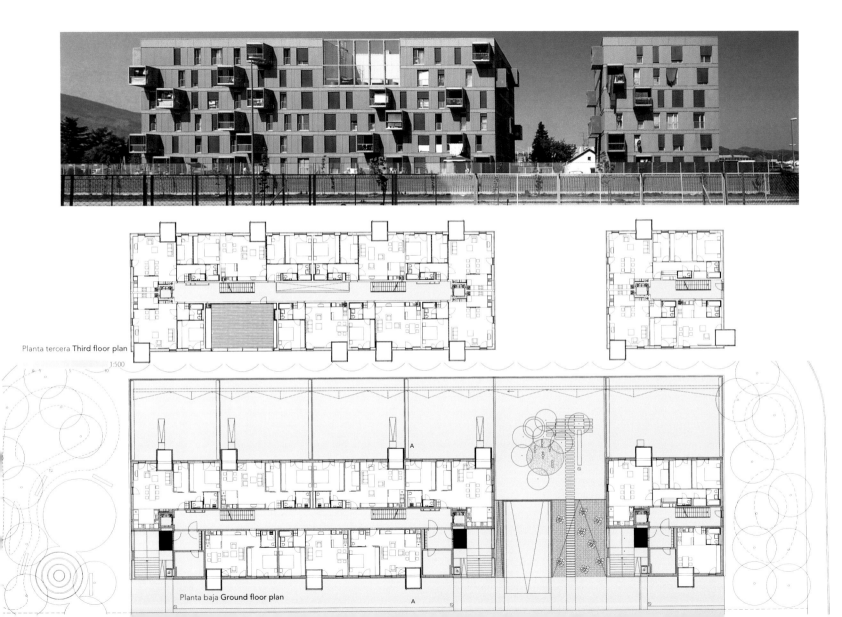

Planta tercera Third floor plan
1:500

Planta baja Ground floor plan

DORMITORIOS BEDROOMS

12 ① 1000

950

62 ② 900

850

44 ③ 800

750

12 ④ 700

650

600

550

500

450

400

350

300

250

200

130 UNITS 150

100

50

0
UNITS

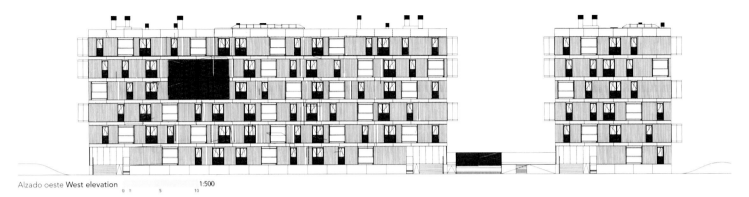

Alzado oeste West elevation 1:500

0 1 5 10

CERÁMICA
BRICKWORK

HORMIGON
CONCRETE

MADERA
WOOD

CEMENTO
CEMENT

METAL
METAL

COMPUESTO
COMPOSITE

VIDRIO
GALSS

ENFOSCADO/
ESTUCO
**MORTAR/
STUCCO**

AISLAMIENTO
INSULATION

MEMBRANA
MEMBRANE

CERÁMICA
BRICKWORK

VIDRIO
GALSS

HORMIGON
CONCRETE

MADERA
WOOD

COMPUESTO
COMPOSITE

CARTÓN-YESO
PLASTER-BOARD

CERÁMICA
BRICKWORK

ENLUCIDO
PLASTER

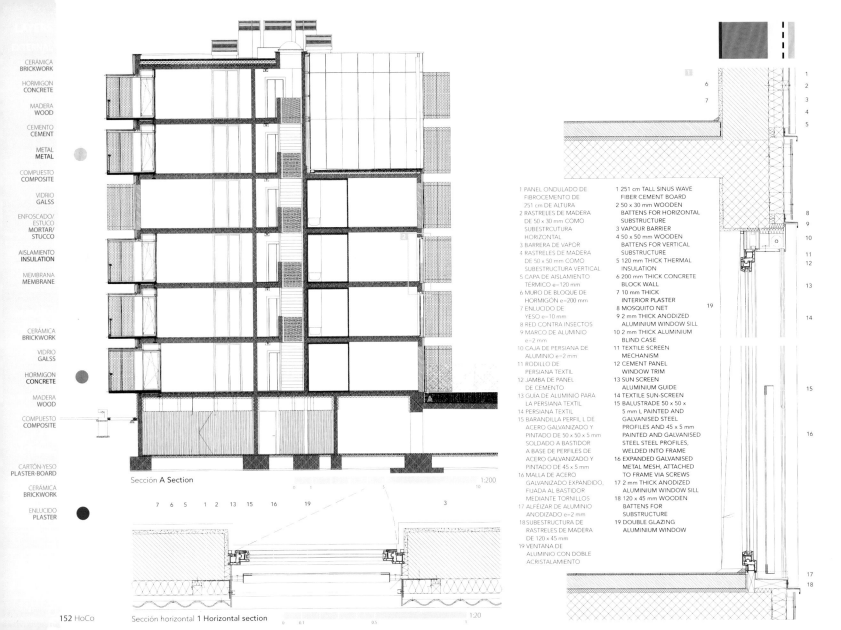

Sección **A** Section

1:200

1 PANEL ONDULADO DE
FIBROCEMENTO DE
251 cm DE ALTURA
2 RASTRELES DE MADERA
DE 50 x 30 mm COMO
SUBESTRCUTURA
HORIZONTAL
3 BARRERA DE VAPOR
4 RASTRELES DE MADERA
DE 50 x 50 mm COMO
SUBESTRUCTURA VERTICAL
5 CAPA DE AISLAMIENTO
TÉRMICO e=120 mm
6 MURO DE BLOQUE DE
HORMIGÓN e=200 mm
7 ENLUCIDO DE
YESO e=10 mm
8 RED CONTRA INSECTOS
9 MARCO DE ALUMINIO
e=2 mm
10 CAJA DE PERSIANA DE
ALUMINIO e=2 mm
11 RODILLO DE
PERSIANA TEXTIL
12 JAMBA DE PANEL
DE CEMENTO
13 GUIA DE ALUMINIO PARA
LA PERSIANA TEXTIL
14 PERSIANA TEXTIL
15 BARANDILLA PERFIL L DE
ACERO GALVANIZADO Y
PINTADO DE 50 x 50 x 5 mm
SOLDADO A BASTIDOR
A BASE DE PERFILES DE
ACERO GALVANIZADO Y
PINTADO DE 45 x 5 mm
16 MALLA DE ACERO
GALVANIZADO EXPANDIDO,
FIJADA AL BASTIDOR
MEDIANTE TORNILLOS
17 ALFÉIZAR DE ALUMINIO
ANODIZADO e=2 mm
18 SUBESTRUCTURA DE
RASTRELES DE MADERA
DE 120 x 45 mm
19 VENTANA DE
ALUMINIO CON DOBLE
ACRISTALAMIENTO

1 251 cm TALL SINUS WAVE
FIBER CEMENT BOARD
2 50 x 30 mm WOODEN
BATTENS FOR HORIZONTAL
SUBSTRUCTURE
3 VAPOUR BARRIER
4 50 x 50 mm WOODEN
BATTENS FOR VERTICAL
SUBSTRUCTURE
5 120 mm THICK THERMAL
INSULATION
6 200 mm THICK CONCRETE
BLOCK WALL
7 10 mm THICK
INTERIOR PLASTER
8 MOSQUITO NET
9 2 mm THICK ANODIZED
ALUMINIUM WINDOW SILL
10 2 mm THICK ALUMINIUM
BLIND CASE
11 TEXTILE SCREEN
MECHANISM
12 CEMENT PANEL
WINDOW TRIM
13 SUN SCREEN
ALUMINIUM GUIDE
14 TEXTILE SUN-SCREEN
15 BALUSTRADE 50 x 50 x
5 mm L PAINTED AND
GALVANISED STEEL
PROFILES AND 45 x 5 mm
PAINTED AND GALVANISED
STEEL STEEL PROFILES,
WELDED INTO FRAME
16 EXPANDED GALVANISED
METAL MESH, ATTACHED
TO FRAME VIA SCREWS
17 2 mm THICK ANODIZED
ALUMINIUM WINDOW SILL
18 120 x 45 mm WOODEN
BATTENS FOR
SUBSTRUCTURE
19 DOUBLE GLAZING
ALUMINIUM WINDOW

Sección horizontal **1** Horizontal section
1:20

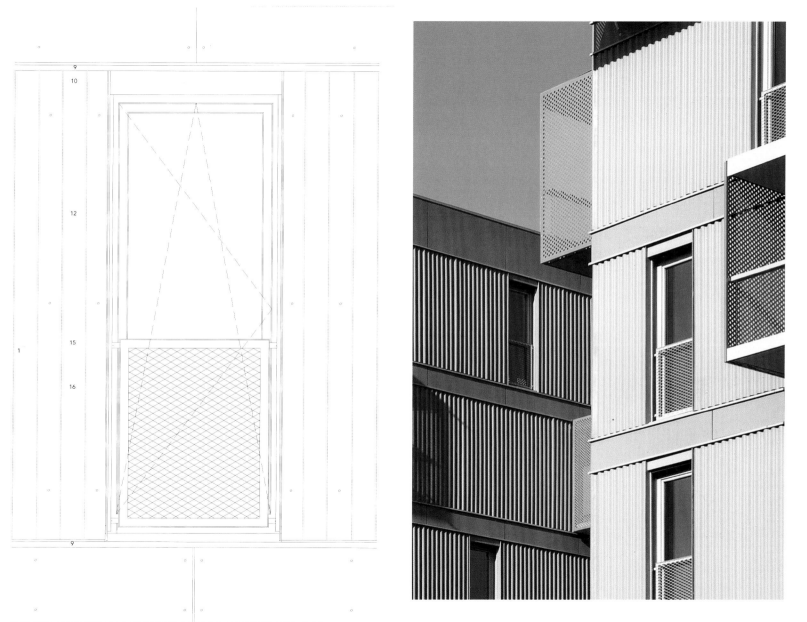

BIG+JDS big.dk, jdsarchitects.com **Copenhagen.** DENMARK, 2008 Orestads Boulevard 55, Orestad

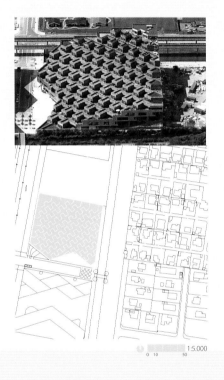

0,518
mill.☺

5.780
☺/km²

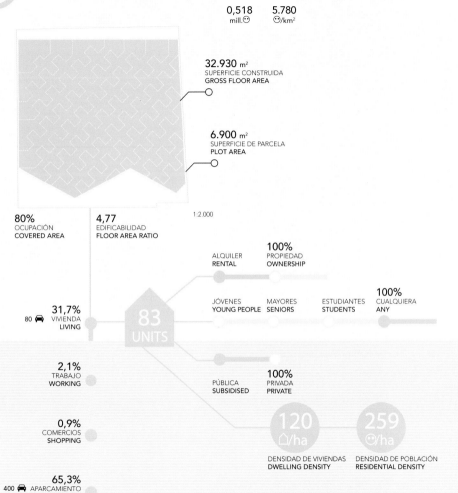

32.930 m²
SUPERFICIE CONSTRUIDA
GROSS FLOOR AREA

6.900 m²
SUPERFICIE DE PARCELA
PLOT AREA

1:2.000

80%
OCUPACIÓN
COVERED AREA

4,77
EDIFICABILIDAD
FLOOR AREA RATIO

80 🚗 31,7%
VIVIENDA
LIVING

2,1%
TRABAJO
WORKING

0,9%
COMERCIOS
SHOPPING

400 🚗 65,3%
APARCAMIENTO
CAR PARK

83
UNITS

ALQUILER
RENTAL

100%
PROPIEDAD
OWNERSHIP

JÓVENES
YOUNG PEOPLE

MAYORES
SENIORS

ESTUDIANTES
STUDENTS

100%
CUALQUIERA
ANY

PÚBLICA
SUBSIDISED

100%
PRIVADA
PRIVATE

120
🏠/ha
DENSIDAD DE VIVIENDAS
DWELLING DENSITY

259
☺/ha
DENSIDAD DE POBLACIÓN
RESIDENTIAL DENSITY

1:5.000
0 10   50

9,871
DKK/m²

2.000

1.900

1.800

1.700

1.600

1.500

1.400

1.300

1.200

1.100

1.000

900

800

700

600

500

400

300

200

100

0

773
$/m²

11

 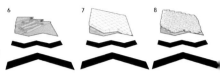

¿Cómo combinar las maravillas del jardín de tu casa en un suburbio con la intensidad social de la densidad urbana?

El proyecto Mountain Dwellings es la segunda generación tras el proyecto VM, con el mismo cliente, en la misma calle y del mismo tamaño.

El programa, sin embargo, comprende 2/3 de aparcamiento y tan solo 1/3 de viviendas. ¿Y si entonces el aparcamiento se convirtiese en la base sobre la que las viviendas se distribuyen escalonadamente, como una montaña recubierta de una capa de vivienda, desde el undécimo piso hasta la calle? En vez de proyectar dos edificios (un aparcamiento y un bloque de viviendas) decidimos integrar ambas funciones en una relación simbiótica.

El aparcamiento necesita estar conectado con la calle, mientras que las viviendas requieren iluminación natural, aire fresco y buenas vistas. De modo que todos los apartamentos tienen cubiertas ajardinadas orientadas al sol, espléndidas vistas y aparcamiento hasta el décimo piso. Mountain Dwellings es un edificio que se presenta pues como un desarrollo suburbial de viviendas con jardín que sin embargo flotan sobre una base de diez pisos: vida suburbana con densidad urbana.

How do you combine the splendours of the suburban backyard with the social intensity of urban density? The Mountain Dwellings are the 2nd generation of the VM Houses - same client, same size and same street. The program, however, is 2/3 car park and 1/3 living. What if the parking area became the base upon which to place terraced housing - like a concrete hillside covered by a thin layer of housing, cascading from the 11th floor to the street edge? Rather than doing two separate buildings next to each other - a car park and a housing block - we decided to merge the two functions into a symbiotic relationship. The car park area needs to be connected to the street, and the homes require sunlight, fresh air and views, thus all apartments have roof gardens facing the sun, amazing views and car park on the 10th floor. The Mountain Dwellings appear as a suburban neighbourhood of garden homes flowing over a 10-storey building - suburban living with urban density.

The roof gardens consist of a terrace and a garden with plants changing character according to the changing seasons. The building has a huge watering system which maintains the roof gardens. The only thing that

Las cubiertas-jardín están plantadas con una vegetación que cambia de carácter con las estaciones, y se mantienen mediante un sistema de riego integrado en el edificio. La única separación entre el jardín y el interior de las viviendas es una fachada de vidrio con puertas correderas que permiten el paso de la luz y el aire fresco.

Los habitantes de estas 80 viviendas serán los primeros en el barrio de Orestad en tener la posibilidad de aparcar justo a la puerta de su casa. El enorme aparcamiento tiene una capacidad de 480 plazas y un ascensor en ladera que recorre los muros interiores de la "montaña". En algunos puntos, donde la altura libre alcanza los 16 m, el espacio resultante se asemeja al de una catedral.

Las fachadas norte y oeste están revestidas con paneles de aluminio perforado que permiten ventilar e iluminar el aparcamiento.

Estas perforaciones reproducen una imagen del Everest. Durante el día, los orificios de los paneles aluminio se oscurecen, dejando ver una enorme imagen pixelizada de la montaña. De noche, la fachada se ilumina desde el interior ofreciendo una imagen en negativo de diferentes colores que corresponden con la iluminación de cada planta del aparcamiento.

El edificio Mountain Dwellings se encuentra en el ensanche de Orestad y ofrece lo mejor de dos mundos distintos: la cercanía la agitada vida de Copenhague y la tranquilidad propia de la vida suburbana.

separates the apartment and the garden is a glass facade with sliding doors to provide light and fresh air. The residents of the 80 apartments will be the first in Orestaden to have the possibility of parking directly outside their homes. The gigantic car park area contains 480 car park spots and a sloping elevator that moves along the mountain's inner walls. In some places the ceiling height is up to 16 meters which gives the impression of a cathedral-like space. The north and west facades are covered by perforated aluminium plates, which let in air and light to the parking area. The holes in the facade form a huge reproduction of Mount Everest. At day the holes in the aluminium plates will appear black on the bright aluminium, and the gigantic picture will resemble that of a rough rasterized photo. At night time the facade will be lit from the inside and appear as a photo negative in different colours as each floor in the parking area has different colours.

The Mountain Dwellings is located in Orestad city and offer the best of two worlds: closeness to the hectic city life in the centre of Copenhagen, and the tranquillity characteristic of suburban life.

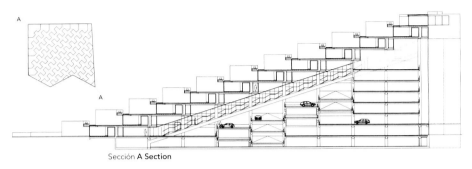

Sección **A** Section

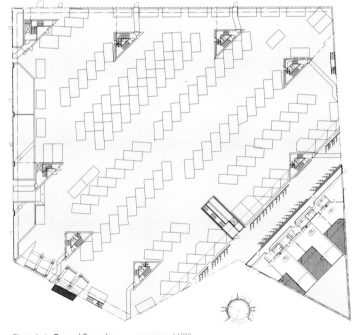

Planta baja **Ground floor plan** 1:1000

01 05 10

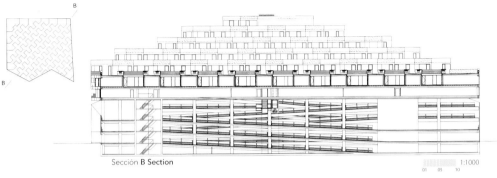

B

B

Sección B Section

1:1000
01   05   10

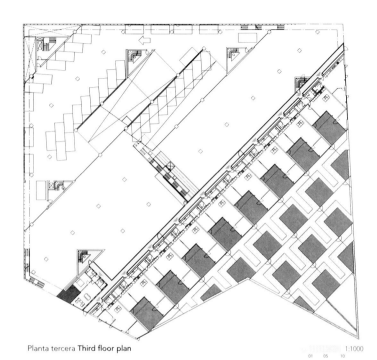

Planta tercera **Third floor plan**

1:1000
01 05 10

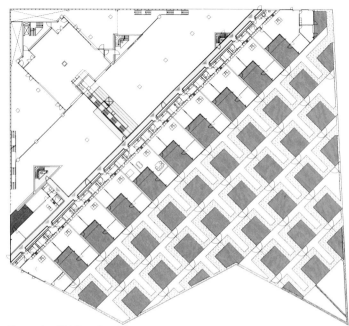

Planta quinta **Fifth floor plan**

TIPOS DE VIVIENDAS
DWELLING TYPES

Tipo **A1 Type**

Tipo **J1 Type**

1:500
0 1   5   10

Sección **A** Section ▓▓▓▓▓▓▓ 1:1000
01 05 10

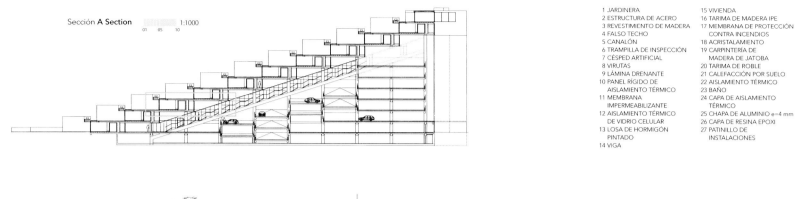

1 JARDINERA
2 ESTRUCTURA DE ACERO
3 REVESTIMIENTO DE MADERA
4 FALSO TECHO
5 CANALÓN
6 TRAMPILLA DE INSPECCIÓN
7 CÉSPED ARTIFICIAL
8 VIRUTAS
9 LÁMINA DRENANTE
10 PANEL RÍGIDO DE
   AISLAMIENTO TÉRMICO
11 MEMBRANA
   IMPERMEABILIZANTE
12 AISLAMIENTO TÉRMICO
   DE VIDRIO CELULAR
13 LOSA DE HORMIGÓN
   PINTADO
14 VIGA

15 VIVIENDA
16 TARIMA DE MADERA IPE
17 MEMBRANA DE PROTECCIÓN
   CONTRA INCENDIOS
18 ACRISTALAMIENTO
19 CARPINTERÍA DE
   MADERA DE JATOBA
20 TARIMA DE ROBLE
21 CALEFACCIÓN POR SUELO
22 AISLAMIENTO TÉRMICO
23 BAÑO
24 CAPA DE AISLAMIENTO
   TÉRMICO
25 CHAPA DE ALUMINIO e=4 mm
26 CAPA DE RESINA EPOXI
27 PATINILLO DE
   INSTALACIONES

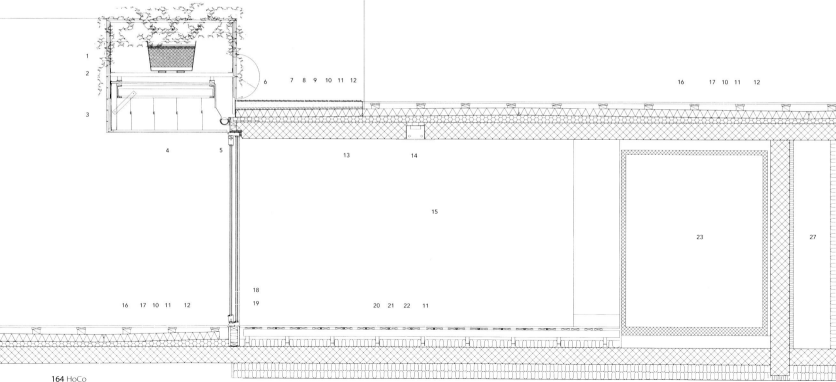

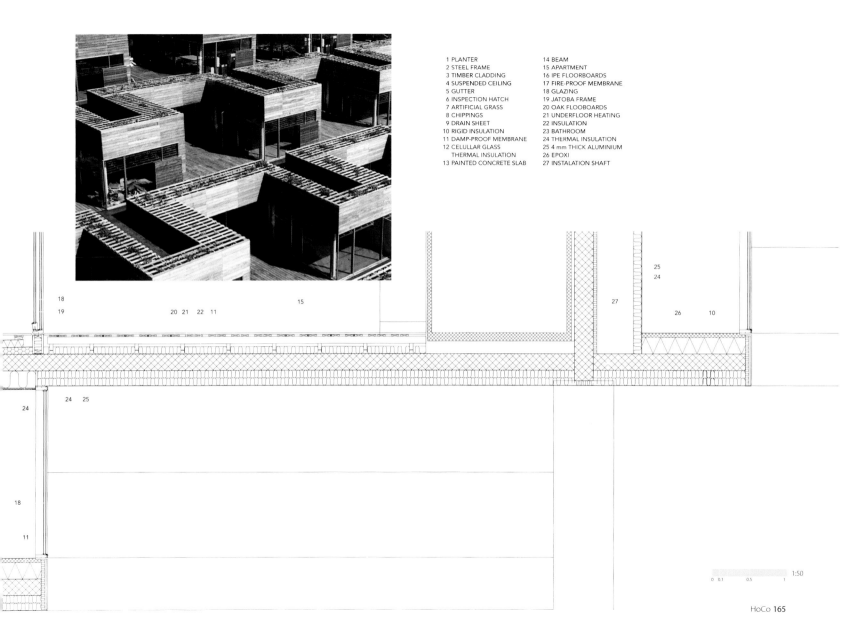

1 PLANTER
2 STEEL FRAME
3 TIMBER CLADDING
4 SUSPENDED CEILING
5 GUTTER
6 INSPECTION HATCH
7 ARTIFICIAL GRASS
8 CHIPPINGS
9 DRAIN SHEET
10 RIGID INSULATION
11 DAMP-PROOF MEMBRANE
12 CELULLAR GLASS
   THERMAL INSULATION
13 PAINTED CONCRETE SLAB

14 BEAM
15 APARTMENT
16 IPE FLOORBOARDS
17 FIRE-PROOF MEMBRANE
18 GLAZING
19 JATOBA FRAME
20 OAK FLOOBOARDS
21 UNDERFLOOR HEATING
22 INSULATION
23 BATHROOM
24 THERMAL INSULATION
25 4 mm THICK ALUMINIUM
26 EPOXI
27 INSTALATION SHAFT

18
19   20 21 22 11   15

25
24

27   26   10

24 25

24

18

11

1:50
0 0.1   0.5   1

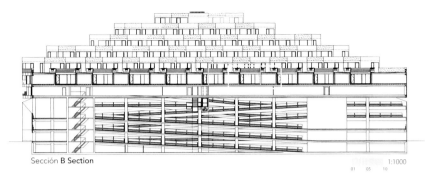

Sección B Section

1:1000

01 05 10

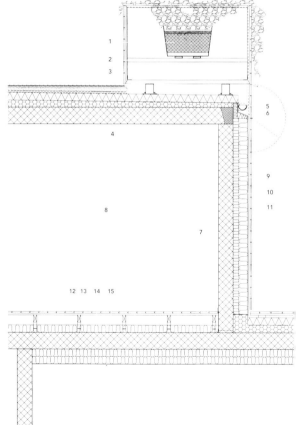

1
2
3

4

8

7

5
6

9
10
11

12 13 14 15

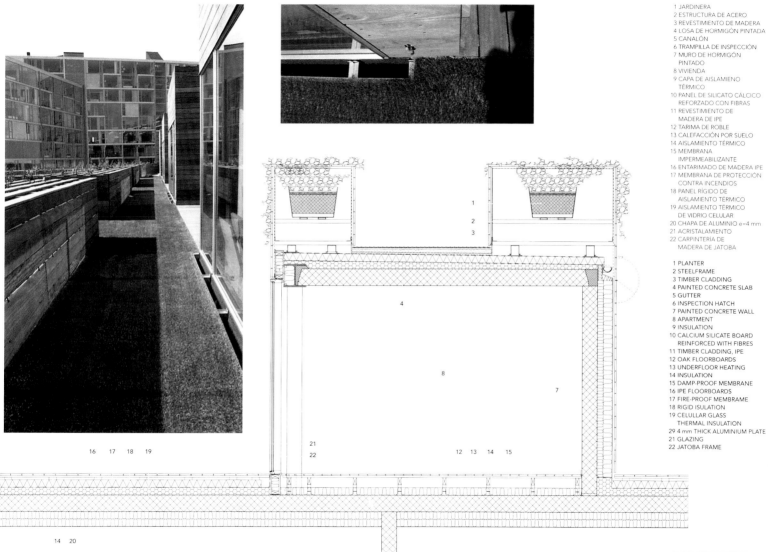

1 JARDINERA
2 ESTRUCTURA DE ACERO
3 REVESTIMIENTO DE MADERA
4 LOSA DE HORMIGÓN PINTADA
5 CANALÓN
6 TRAMPILLA DE INSPECCIÓN
7 MURO DE HORMIGÓN
   PINTADO
8 VIVIENDA
9 CAPA DE AISLAMIENO
   TÉRMICO
10 PANEL DE SILICATO CÁLCICO
   REFORZADO CON FIBRAS
11 REVESTIMIENTO DE
   MADERA DE IPE
12 TARIMA DE ROBLE
13 CALEFACCIÓN POR SUELO
14 AISLAMIENTO TÉRMICO
15 MEMBRANA
   IMPERMEABILIZANTE
16 ENTARIMADO DE MADERA IPE
17 MEMBRANA DE PROTECCIÓN
   CONTRA INCENDIOS
18 PANEL RÍGIDO DE
   AISLAMIENTO TÉRMICO
19 AISLAMIENTO TÉRMICO
   DE VIDRIO CELULAR
20 CHAPA DE ALUMINIO e=4 mm
21 ACRISTALAMIENTO
22 CARPINTERÍA DE
   MADERA DE JATOBA

1 PLANTER
2 STEELFRAME
3 TIMBER CLADDING
4 PAINTED CONCRETE SLAB
5 GUTTER
6 INSPECTION HATCH
7 PAINTED CONCRETE WALL
8 APARTMENT
9 INSULATION
10 CALCIUM SILICATE BOARD
   REINFORCED WITH FIBRES
11 TIMBER CLADDING, IPE
12 OAK FLOORBOARDS
13 UNDERFLOOR HEATING
14 INSULATION
15 DAMP-PROOF MEMBRANE
16 IPE FLOORBOARDS
17 FIRE-PROOF MEMBRAME
18 RIGID ISULATION
19 CELULLAR GLASS
   THERMAL INSULATION
29 4 mm THICK ALUMINIUM PLATE
21 GLAZING
22 JATOBA FRAME

1:50

CERÁMICA
BRICKWORK

HORMIGON
CONCRETE

MADERA
WOOD

CEMENTO
CEMENT

METAL
METAL

COMPUESTO
COMPOSITE

VIDRIO
GALSS

ENFOSCADO/
ESTUCO
**MORTAR/
STUCCO**

AISLAMIENTO
INSULATION

MEMBRANA
MEMBRANE

PRINCIPAL

CERÁMICA
BRICKWORK

VIDRIO
GALSS

HORMIGON
CONCRETE

MADERA
WOOD

COMPUESTO
COMPOSITE

CARTÓN-YESO
PLASTER-BOARD

CERÁMICA
BRICKWORK

ENLUCIDO
PLASTER

1 PERFIL DE ACERO DE
  50 x 30 x 4 mm
2 SOLADO DE LA TERRAZA
3 FACHADA EXTERIOR CON
  REVESTIMIENTO DE CHAPA
4 LOSA DE HORMIGÓN
  PINTADO
5 REVESTIMIENTO DE
  VIGAS Y SOPORTES
6 VENTANA

1 50 x 30 x 4 mm STEEL PROFILE
2 TERRACE FLOORING
3 LIGHT EXTERNAL WALL
  WITH FACADE PLATES
4 PAINTED CONCRETE SLAB
5 BEAM AND COLUMN
  EXTERIOR SHEETING
6 WINDOW

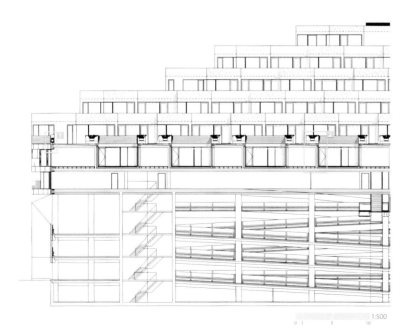

1:500
0 1   5   10

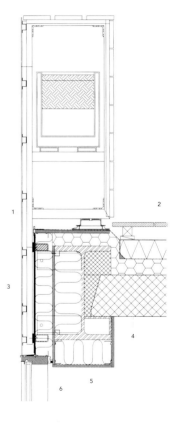

1   1:20
0 0.1   0.5   1

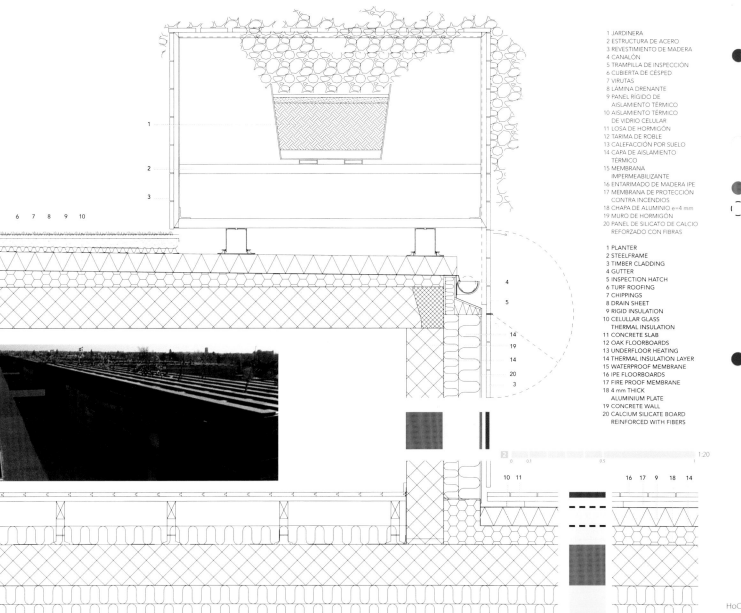

1 JARDINERA
2 ESTRUCTURA DE ACERO
3 REVESTIMIENTO DE MADERA
4 CANALÓN
5 TRAMPILLA DE INSPECCIÓN
6 CUBIERTA DE CÉSPED
7 VIRUTAS
8 LÁMINA DRENANTE
9 PANEL RÍGIDO DE
   AISLAMIENTO TÉRMICO
10 AISLAMIENTO TÉRMICO
   DE VIDRIO CELULAR
11 LOSA DE HORMIGÓN
12 TARIMA DE ROBLE
13 CALEFACCIÓN POR SUELO
14 CAPA DE AISLAMIENTO
   TÉRMICO
15 MEMBRANA
   IMPERMEABILIZANTE
16 ENTARIMADO DE MADERA IPE
17 MEMBRANA DE PROTECCIÓN
   CONTRA INCENDIOS
18 CHAPA DE ALUMINIO e=4 mm
19 MURO DE HORMIGÓN
20 PANEL DE SILICATO DE CALCIO
   REFORZADO CON FIBRAS

1 PLANTER
2 STEELFRAME
3 TIMBER CLADDING
4 GUTTER
5 INSPECTION HATCH
6 TURF ROOFING
7 CHIPPINGS
8 DRAIN SHEET
9 RIGID INSULATION
10 CELULLAR GLASS
   THERMAL INSULATION
11 CONCRETE SLAB
12 OAK FLOORBOARDS
13 UNDERFLOOR HEATING
14 THERMAL INSULATION LAYER
15 WATERPROOF MEMBRANE
16 IPE FLOORBOARDS
17 FIRE PROOF MEMBRANE
18 4 mm THICK
   ALUMINIUM PLATE
19 CONCRETE WALL
20 CALCIUM SILICATE BOARD
   REINFORCED WITH FIBERS

LAYERS

EXTERNAL

GRAVA
GRAVEL

CERÁMICA
TERRACOTTA

MADERA
WOOD

CEMENTO
CEMENT

VEGETACIÓN
PLANTING

METAL
METAL

AISLAMIENTO
INSULATION

MEMBRANA
MEMBRANE

PRINCIPAL

HORMIGÓN
CONCRETE

MADERA
WOOD

CERÁMICA
TERRACOTTA

INTERNAL

CARTÓN-YESO
PLASTER-BOARD

ENLUCIDO
PLASTER

METAL
METAL

1:20

1,603
mill.☺

15.810
☺/km²

Este proyecto para la ciudad, de Barcelona, junto al puente de Vallcarca, en la zona norte de la ciudad donde se inician las montañas, es una pieza que precipita como en una reacción química la densidad del barrio sobre el solar del proyecto.

This project for the city of Barcelona, next to the Vallcarca bridge and to the North of the city where the mountains begin, is a piece that precipitates the density of the neighbourhood on the lot of the project, as in a chemical reaction.

1.050 m²
SUPERFICIE DE PARCELA
PLOT AREA

7.035 m²
SUPERFICIE CONSTRUIDA
GROSS FLOOR AREA

1:2.000

100%
OCUPACIÓN
COVERED AREA

5,33
EDIFICABILIDAD
FLOOR AREA RATIO

ALQUILER
RENTAL

100%
PROPIEDAD
OWNERSHIP

91,6%
39 🚗 VIVIENDA
LIVING

42
UNITS

JÓVENES
YOUNG PEOPLE

MAYORES
SENIORS

ESTUDIANTES
STUDENTS

100%
CUALQUIERA
ANY

TRABAJO
WORKING

100%
PÚBLICA
SUBSIDISED

PRIVADA
PRIVATE

8,4%
COMERCIOS
SHOPPING

400
⌂/ha

1.476
☺/ha

DENSIDAD DE VIVIENDAS
DWELLING DENSITY

DENSIDAD DE POBLACIÓN
RESIDENTIAL DENSITY

OTROS USOS
OTHER USES

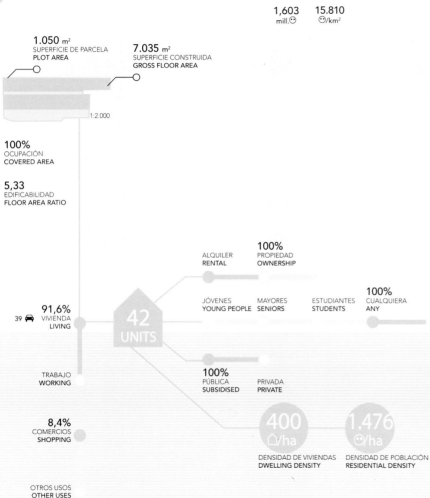

1:5.000
0 10   50

12

802
$/m²

723
€/m²

2.000

1.900

1.800

1.700

1.600

1.500

1.400

1.300

1.200

1.100

1.000

900

800

700

600

500

400

300

200

100

0

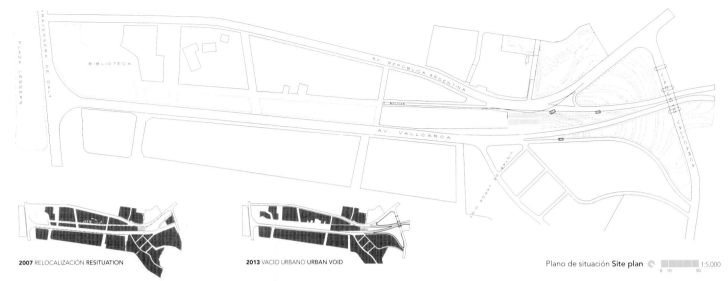

Plano de situación **Site plan** 1:5.000

0   10   50

El edificio se fragmenta en tres cuerpos, organizados horizontalmente por la planta baja de República Argentina y en profundidad por los pasillos que van de la medianera a la testera. De este modo, se disminuye el impacto visual hacia la vertiente del parque Güell y el viaducto, y se puede cambiar la volumetría total, acotando o alargando las bandas y variando su altura. Los tres cuerpos reciben un tratamiento distinto (materiales, aperturas...) que refuerza su independencia: una franja con zócalo que continúa la fachada fragmentaria de avenida Vallcarca y se vincula a la urbanización de la zona verde; una segunda franja "suspendida" sobre la anterior y separada de la medianera, y una tercera, final de la fachada continua de República Argentina

The building is fragmented into three bodies, organised horizontally by the street level at República Argentina and organised in depth by the corridors that run from the dividing wall to the main facade. In this way, visual impact toward the hill to Parc Güell and the viaduct is reduced. The total volumetry can also be changed, shortening or lengthening bands and varying height. Each of the three bodies receives a different treatment (materials, openings, etc.), which reinforces its independence. There is one strip with a base that continues the fragmentary facade of the Avenida Vallcarca and is linked to the development of the green area. A second strip is 'suspended' over the previous on and separated from the dividing wall. A third strip is the end of the continuous facade of República Argentina; the porch

(el porche enmarca las visuales actuales de República Argentina hacia el viaducto). En lo referente a las viviendas, se utilizan elementos estandarizados y repetitivos, aunque aplicados de forma flexible-opcional: (PACK) unidad constructiva apta para prefabricar; para la repetición de elementos y la claridad, el tamaño y la simplificación de los ensamblajes. El pasillo abierto ofrece versatilidad para combinar o modificar el tipo de viviendas a cada lado: de 1 a 4 dormitorios (el tamaño de la vivienda no está condicionado por el núcleo de comunicaciones vertical). La fachada, con inercia térmica, proporciona protección y posibilita el ahorro energético. Los apartamentos tienen todas las estancias exteriores y ventilación cruzada, y disponen de captadores solares para el precalentamiento del agua sanitaria y de la calefacción.

frames the current lines of sight of República Argentina towards the viaduct. Regarding the housing units, standardised and repetitive elements are used, though they are applied flexibly and optionally: PACK, a constructive unit suitable for prefabricating; for the repetition of elements and clarity, size and simplification of assembly. The open corridor offers versatility to combine or modify housing types on either side, from one to four bedrooms (the size of the housing units are not conditioned by the central staircase and lift). The facade, with its thermal inertia, provides protection and allows for energy savings. All apartment rooms face outside and have cross ventilation. They also have solar panels to heat water for lavatory and heating.

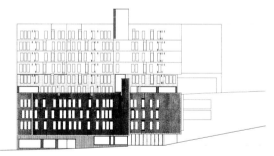

Alzado por la avenida Vallcarca **Elevation towards Vallcarca Avenue**

Alzado por la avenida República Argentina 1:1000
Elevation from towards República Argentina Avenue

01 05   10

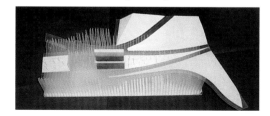

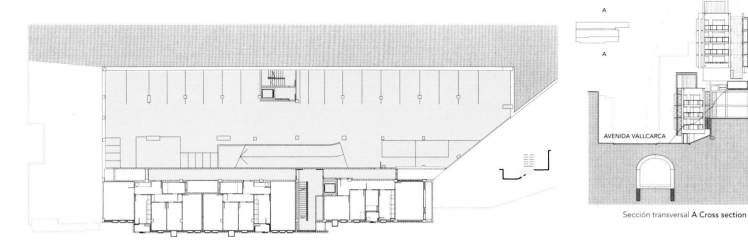

Plantas 1ª-3ª **1st-3rd floor plans**

Sección transversal **A Cross section**

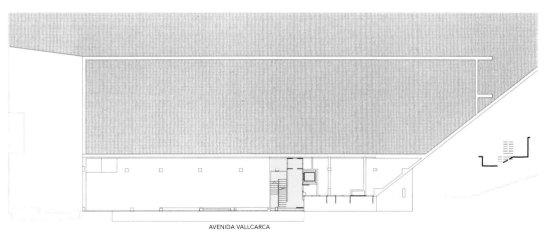

AVENIDA VALLCARCA

Planta baja **Ground floor plan** 1:500

0 1   5   10

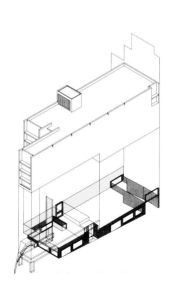

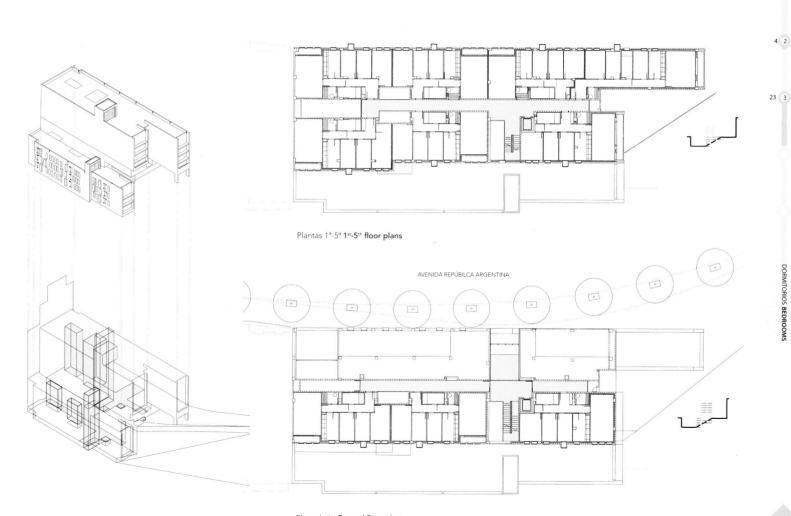

Plantas 1ª-5ª 1st-5th floor plans

AVENIDA REPÚBILCA ARGENTINA

Planta baja Ground floor plan

DORMITORIOS **BEDROOMS**

4 2
23 3

42 UNITS

1000
950
900
850
800
750
700
650
600
550
500
450
400
350
300
250
200
150
100
50
0
UNITS

Las aperturas son marcos negros de 0,8 x 2,1 m homogéneamente repartidos por los paños de fachada. Podríamos leerlos como una colección de ventanas o puertas, algunas de ellas agrupadas y otras dispersas, o como el craqueado de la pintura de un lienzo. Dependiendo del programa que estos huecos iluminan, los marcos se cierran como ventanas en el plano de fachada. Son huecos que modulan las aberturas de unas terrazas interiores, o se proyectan hacia el exterior, como cajas formando pequeñas tribunas. Los balcones los reservamos a los testeros y son habitaciones abiertas, de color blanco, independiente del color base de los tres sólidos. Las ventanas tienen unas vistas de larga distancia, inusuales en Barcelona. Desde el interior, al igual que en los buques, se compensa esta visión de la lejanía con un marco negro.

The openings are 0.8 x 2.1 m black frames evenly distributed over the facade. They could be interpreted as a collection of windows like doors, some of them grouped together and others dispersed, or like the cracking on a canvas painting. Depending on the programme that these openings illuminate, frames open up as windows on the facade, they are modulating openings of indoor terraces or they are projected out, like boxes making up small platforms. The balconies are reserved for main walls. They are open rooms and are white, regardless of the base colour of the three solids. Windows have long-distance views, unusual in Barcelona. From the inside, like port holes, this far-off view is compensated with a black frame.

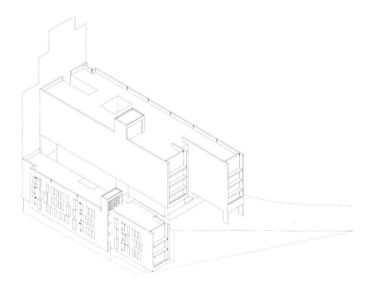

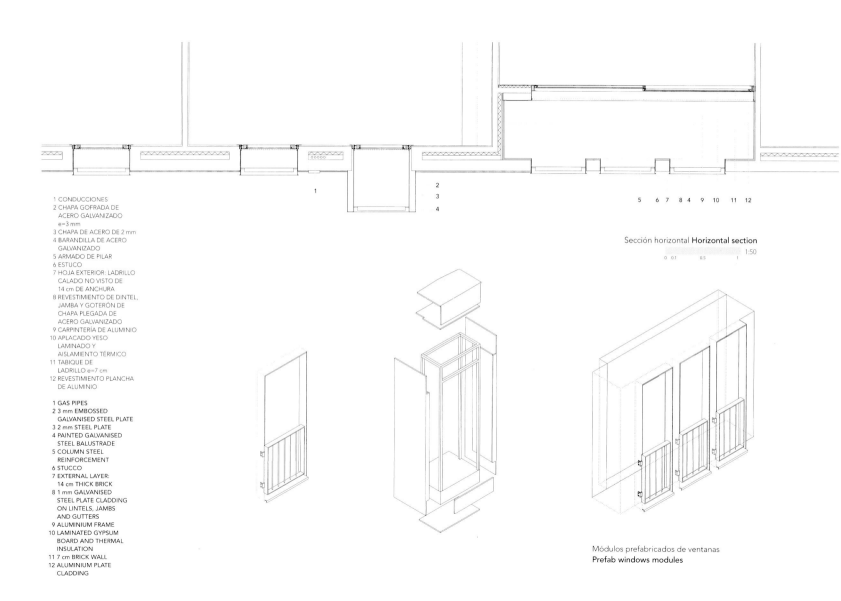

1 CONDUCCIONES
2 CHAPA GOFRADA DE
  ACERO GALVANIZADO
  e=3 mm
3 CHAPA DE ACERO DE 2 mm
4 BARANDILLA DE ACERO
  GALVANIZADO
5 ARMADO DE PILAR
6 ESTUCO
7 HOJA EXTERIOR: LADRILLO
  CALADO NO VISTO DE
  14 cm DE ANCHURA
8 REVESTIMIENTO DE DINTEL,
  JAMBA Y GOTERÓN DE
  CHAPA PLEGADA DE
  ACERO GALVANIZADO
9 CARPINTERÍA DE ALUMINIO
10 APLACADO YESO
  LAMINADO Y
  AISLAMIENTO TÉRMICO
11 TABIQUE DE
  LADRILLO e=7 cm
12 REVESTIMIENTO PLANCHA
  DE ALUMINIO

1 GAS PIPES
2 3 mm EMBOSSED
  GALVANISED STEEL PLATE
3 2 mm STEEL PLATE
4 PAINTED GALVANISED
  STEEL BALUSTRADE
5 COLUMN STEEL
  REINFORCEMENT
6 STUCCO
7 EXTERNAL LAYER:
  14 cm THICK BRICK
8 1 mm GALVANISED
  STEEL PLATE CLADDING
  ON LINTELS, JAMBS
  AND GUTTERS
9 ALUMINIUM FRAME
10 LAMINATED GYPSUM
  BOARD AND THERMAL
  INSULATION
11 7 cm BRICK WALL
12 ALUMINIUM PLATE
  CLADDING

Sección horizontal **Horizontal section**

0 0.1   0.5   1   1:50

Módulos prefabricados de ventanas
Prefab windows modules

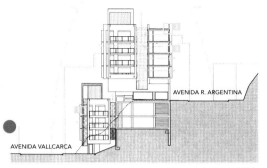

AVENIDA R. ARGENTINA

AVENIDA VALLCARCA

Sección transversal **A Cross section**

1:1000

01   05   10

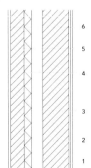

1 ESTUCO DE CAL ACABADO
 BRILLANTE e=2 cm
2 LADRILLO PERFORADO NO
 VISTO DE 14 cm DE ANCHURA
3 CÁMARA DE AIRE e=6 cm
4 CAPA DE AISLAMIENTO
 TÉRMICO e=4 cm
5 HOJA INTERIOR: LADRILLO
 DE 7 cm DE ANCHURA
6 ENYESADO Y PINTADO

1 2 cm BRIGHT FINISH
 LIME STUCCO LAYER
2 14 cm THICK
 PERFORATED BRICK
3 6 cm WIDE CAVITY
4 4 cm THERMAL
 INSULATION LAYER
5 7 cm HOLLOW BRICK
6 PAINTED PLASTER LAYER

1:20

0   0.1   0.5   1

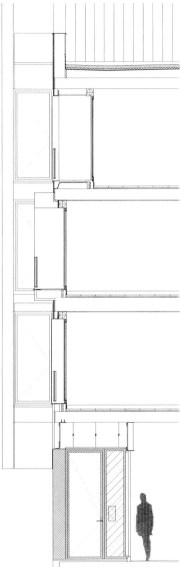

Sección **1 Section**

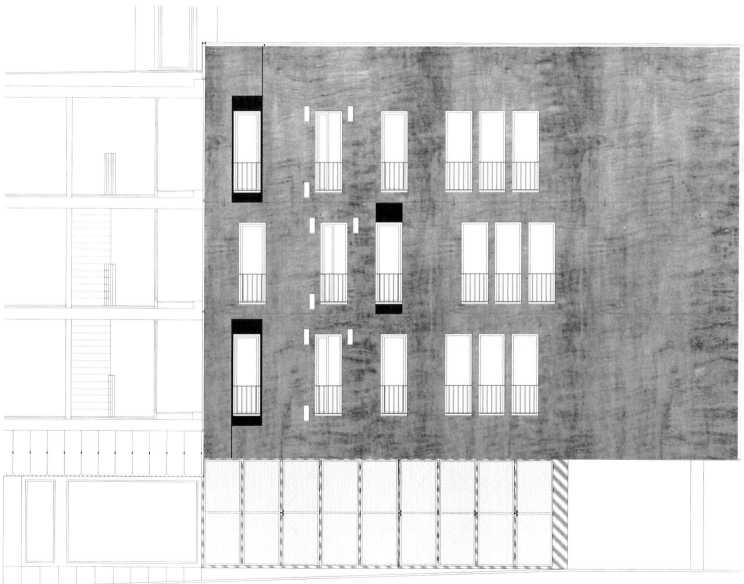

Alzado por la avenida Vallcarca **Elevation towards Vallcarca Avenue** 1:100

0   0,5   1

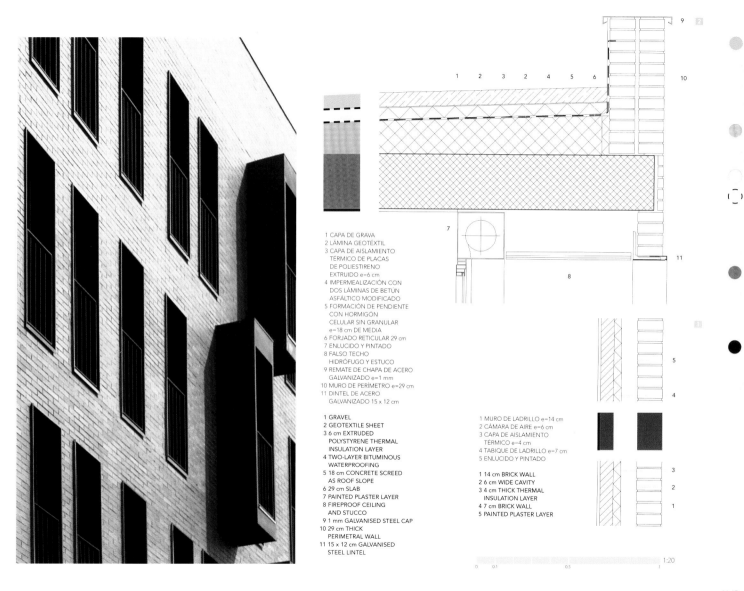

LAYERS
EXTERNAL

GRAVA
GRAVEL

CERÁMICA
TERRACOTTA

MADERA
WOOD

CEMENTO
CEMENT

VEGETACIÓN
PLANTING

METAL
METAL

AISLAMIENTO
INSULATION

MEMBRANA
MEMBRANE

HORMIGÓN
CONCRETE

MADERA
WOOD

CERÁMICA
TERRACOTTA

EXTERNAL

CARTÓN-YESO
PLASTER-BOARD

ENLUCIDO
PLASTER

METAL
METAL

1 CAPA DE GRAVA
2 LÁMINA GEOTÉXTIL
3 CAPA DE AISLAMIENTO
  TÉRMICO DE PLACAS
  DE POLIESTIRENO
  EXTRUIDO e=6 cm
4 IMPERMEALIZACIÓN CON
  DOS LÁMINAS DE BETÚN
  ASFÁLTICO MODIFICADO
5 FORMACIÓN DE PENDIENTE
  CON HORMIGÓN
  CELULAR SIN GRANULAR
  e=18 cm DE MEDIA
6 FORJADO RETICULAR 29 cm
7 ENLUCIDO Y PINTADO
8 FALSO TECHO
  HIDRÓFUGO Y ESTUCO
9 REMATE DE CHAPA DE ACERO
  GALVANIZADO e=1 mm
10 MURO DE PERÍMETRO e=29 cm
11 DINTEL DE ACERO
   GALVANIZADO 15 x 12 cm

1 GRAVEL
2 GEOTEXTILE SHEET
3 6 cm EXTRUDED
  POLYSTYRENE THERMAL
  INSULATION LAYER
4 TWO-LAYER BITUMINOUS
  WATERPROOFING
5 18 cm CONCRETE SCREED
  AS ROOF SLOPE
6 29 cm SLAB
7 PAINTED PLASTER LAYER
8 FIREPROOF CEILING
  AND STUCCO
9 1 mm GALVANISED STEEL CAP
10 29 cm THICK
   PERIMETRAL WALL
11 15 x 12 cm GALVANISED
   STEEL LINTEL

1 MURO DE LADRILLO e=14 cm
2 CÁMARA DE AIRE e=6 cm
3 CAPA DE AISLAMIENTO
  TÉRMICO e=4 cm
4 TABIQUE DE LADRILLO e=7 cm
5 ENLUCIDO Y PINTADO

1 14 cm BRICK WALL
2 6 cm WIDE CAVITY
3 4 cm THICK THERMAL
  INSULATION LAYER
4 7 cm BRICK WALL
5 PAINTED PLASTER LAYER

1:20

0   0.1   0.5   1

Poolen Architekten poolen.nl Culemborg. THE NETHERLANDS, 2008 Admiraal Vlinderlaan 1

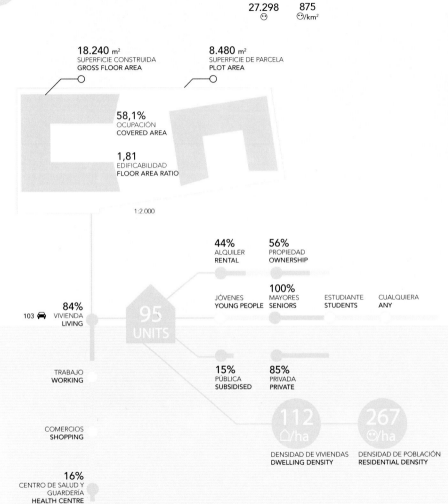

27.298 ☺

875 ☺/km²

18.240 m²
SUPERFICIE CONSTRUIDA
GROSS FLOOR AREA

8.480 m²
SUPERFICIE DE PARCELA
PLOT AREA

58,1%
OCUPACIÓN
COVERED AREA

1,81
EDIFICABILIDAD
FLOOR AREA RATIO

1:2.000

44%
ALQUILER
RENTAL

56%
PROPIEDAD
OWNERSHIP

84%
VIVIENDA
LIVING

103 🚗

95 UNITS

JÓVENES
YOUNG PEOPLE

100%
MAYORES
SENIORS

ESTUDIANTE
STUDENTS

CUALQUIERA
ANY

TRABAJO
WORKING

15%
PÚBLICA
SUBSIDISED

85%
PRIVADA
PRIVATE

COMERCIOS
SHOPPING

112 ⌂/ha

267 ☺/ha

DENSIDAD DE VIVIENDAS
DWELLING DENSITY

DENSIDAD DE POBLACIÓN
RESIDENTIAL DENSITY

16%
CENTRO DE SALUD Y
GUARDERÍA
HEALTH CENTRE
AND KINDERGARTEN

1:5.000
0 10   50

BonVie es una residencia de ancianos y centro de salud en el barrio de Parijsch-Zuid de la ciudad de Culemborg. Los edificios forman parte de un área de equipamientos y servicios y están colocados a lo largo de una ruta que de sur a norte conecta un centro comercial con una escuela primaria. BonVie consiste en dos edificios con forma de U. Decidimos proyectar dos edificios abiertos por un lado de modo que el patio que generan se integrase en la red de espacio público y el paisaje circundante. Ambos edificios están ligeramente girados hasta formar, junto al edificio Weversgilde en las proximidades, un interesante conjunto.

BonVie, a centre for living and care, is located in Parijsch-Zuid, a service centre area in Culemborg. The buildings are part of the service centre and are situated along the North –South route connecting the shopping centre and the primary school buildings. BonVie consists of two U-shaped housing blocks. We have deliberately chosen building structures with an open side to let the courtyard be part of the public square and the surrounding landscape. The blocks are turned slightly to one another by which an interesting ensemble is created together with the nearby Weversgilde building block.

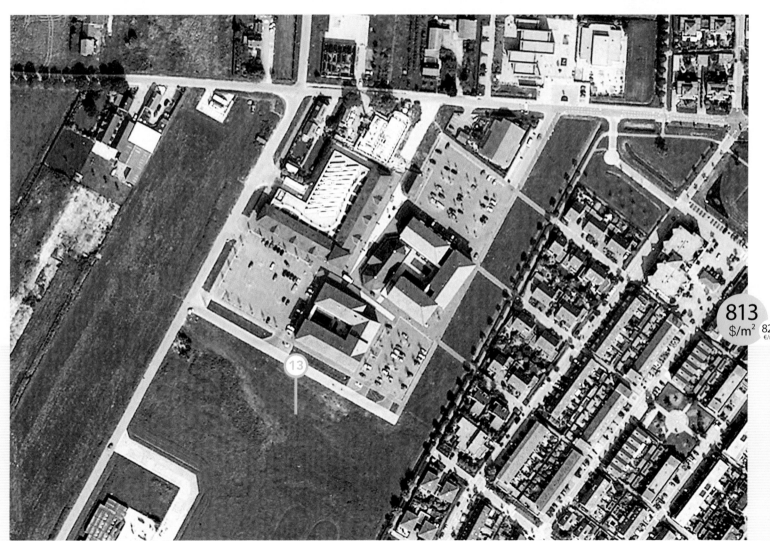

813 $/m² 821 €/m²

13

2.000

1.900

1.800

1.700

1.600

1.500

1.400

1.300

1.200

1.100

1.000

900

800

700

600

500

400

300

200

100

0

El acceso se realiza a través de los patios por los dos extremos de ambos edificios, lo cual contribuye a vitalizar la plaza. Una galería permite el acceso desde las escaleras y los ascensores hasta las viviendas. Su ubicación varía entre la fachada exterior o la interior, lo que da lugar a una animada circulación y permite ubicar viviendas sobre el patio.

El proyecto comprende varios tipos de viviendas de acuerdo a su orientación. Así, las hay con vistas orientadas al sur o bien otras con un gran salón en los lados este y oeste. Por su parte, el centro de salud se distribuye por la planta baja de uno de los edificios. La guardería y las consultas infantiles se sitúan en el ala norte, mientras que el restaurante se encuentra en el lado sur.

La arquitectura del proyecto se inspira en fundamentos tipológicos clásicos. La composición de los alzados depende de la orientación y su ubicación exterior o sobre el patio. El edificio resultante es fácil de reconocer pese a las diferencias entre fachadas. La cubierta, ligeramente inclinada hacia el interior del patio, es metálica. Las galerías y las logias se dibujan de manera clara en la fachada, articulando el edificio de manera rotunda. La fachada a la calle está revestida con ladrillo marrón/púrpura y contiene diferentes tipos de paños verticales y bandas horizontales. Sobre el patio, la fachada está enfoscada con mortero, mientras que el plano interior de las galerías se ha pintado con motivos vegetales. A través de sus materiales, el edificio tiene un interior y un exterior reconocibles, que se encuentran en el patio, cerca del camino peatonal.

Access for both buildings is provided from the courtyard, at the corners and both ends of the building, contributing to the liveliness of the square. A walkway connected to the staircases and lift is providing access to the apartments. The location of the walkway changes, shifting between the internal and external elevation of the building. This creates an interesting route and also provides for living space facing the courtyard. The location of the walkway is influenced by the orientation, preferably on the North or East-West side of the building. The building contains various types of apartments, following its orientation. For example panoramic sight apartments on the south side and apartments with a through lounge on the East/West side. The care department has a continuous service zone.The nursery, the children's clinic and the infant welfare centre are situated at the North side of the building.

The restaurant is situated in the southern side of the building.

The courtyards are carefully designed matching the square at the shopping centre.

The architecture is inspired by classical building typologies. The elevations are depended upon the orientation and location, either facing the street or the courtyard. The building is very recognizable, despite the variety in the elevations. The 4-layered U-shaped buildings are covered by a metal roof, sloping down towards the courtyard and chamfered at the head of the building. The walkway is not intended to be recognizable in the elevation, despite its changing position. The walkways and loggia's are situated within the building outline creating a strong articulated and layered building. The external elevation is constructed with rough brown/purple brickwork with changing vertical elements and horizontal layers. At the courtyard the elevation is showing a regular grid of white stucco and a set-back elevation facing the walkway showing a fresh grass pattern. Through its materialisation the building has a recognizable interior and exterior, which encounter each other at the courtyard near de pedestrian walkway.

Alzado sur de los bloques 1 y 2 **South elevation of Block 1 and Block 2**

1:1000
01   05   10

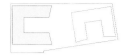

Edificio 1

En él se ubican el centro de salud y la guardería, a los que se accede desde el patio. El edificio se abre hacia la plaza pública y la ruta peatonal que une el patio con la plaza. El "zotel", un hotel dotado con servicios especiales y las viviendas para mayores se encuentran en el primer piso. Los demás niveles alojan viviendas de dos dormitorios.

Block 1

This building contains the health-care centre and kindergarten. The building structure is opened towards the public square and the pedestrian route, by which the courtyard is integrated with the public square. The health-care centre gains access from the courtyard. The *zotel*, a hotel with extra care facilities, and the special care apartments are located on the first floor of the building. At the other floors two bedroom apartments can be found, which meet the *woonkeur* (Dutch certificate for newly built houses) requirements.

Alzado este **East elevation**

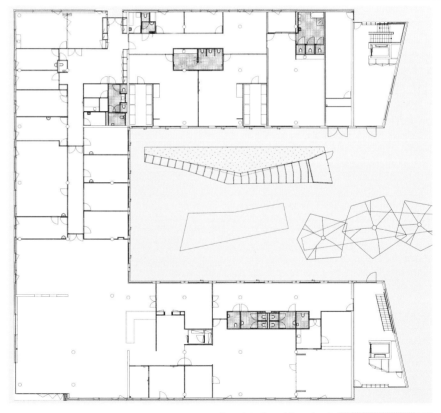

Planta baja **Ground floor plan**   1:500

Edificio 2

Se eleva 1,2 m sobre la rasante del terreno.
Por debajo se sitúa el aparcamiento con
capacidad para 95 vehículos y ocupa una
superficie superior a la huella del edificio que
da lugar a una plataforma elevada junto a la
ruta peatonal. Varios escalones y una rampa
la ponen en contacto con el nivel del terreno.
El patio se abre por el lado sur al paisaje
circundante.

Block 2

This building block is raised 1.2 metre above
ground level. The car park is situated at
basement level. It has room for about 95 cars
and its outline is greater then the outline of the
building, therefore creating a raised platform
nearby the pedestrian walkway. The raised
platform is connected to the public square
with several stairs and ramps. The U-shaped
building block is opened on the south side
creating an attractive sunny courtyard facing
the surrounding water en green landscape.
The building contains apartments also meeting
the *woonkeur* requirements.

Sección **A section**

Planta baja **Ground floor plan**

1:500
0 1   5   10

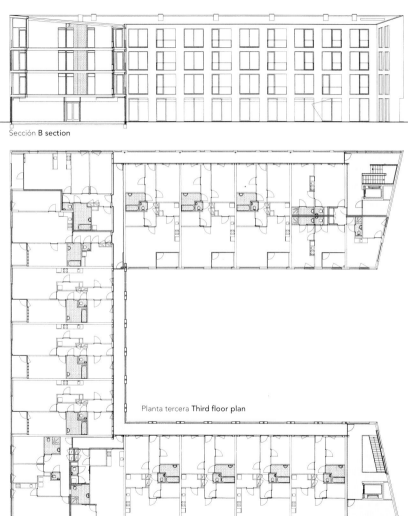

Sección B section

Planta tercera Third floor plan

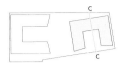

Sección **C section**

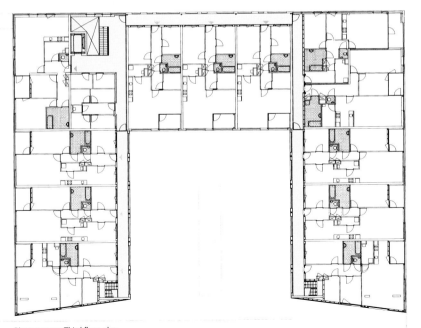

Planta tercera **Third floor plan**

9 1 1000

86 2 900
950

850

800

750

700

650

600

550

500

450

DORMITORIOS **BEDROOMS**

400

350

300

250

200

150

95
UNITS

100

50

Sección **A** section

0 1   5   10   1:500

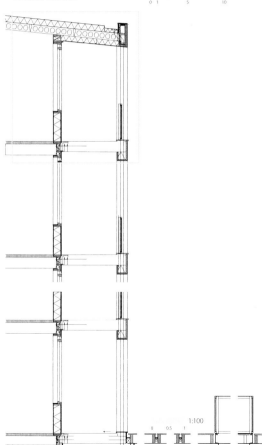

0 0.5 1   1:100

CERÁMICA
BRICKWORK

HORMIGON
CONCRETE

MADERA
WOOD

CEMENTO
CEMENT

METAL
METAL

COMPUESTO
COMPOSITE

VIDRIO
GALSS

ENFOSCADO/
ESTUCO
**MORTAR/
STUCCO**

AISLAMIENTO
INSULATION

MEMBRANA
MEMBRANE

CERÁMICA
BRICKWORK

VIDRIO
GALSS

HORMIGON
CONCRETE

MADERA
WOOD

COMPUESTO
COMPOSITE

CARTÓN-YESO
PLASTER-BOARD

CERÁMICA
BRICKWORK

ENLUCIDO
PLASTER

GRAVA
GRAVEL

CERÁMICA
TERRACOTTA

MADERA
WOOD

CEMENTO
CEMENT

VEGETACIÓN
PLANTING

METAL
METAL

AISLAMIENTO
INSULATION

MEMBRANA
MEMBRANE

HORMIGÓN
CONCRETE

MADERA
WOOD

CERÁMICA
TERRACOTTA

CARTÓN-YESO
PLASTER-BOARD

ENLUCIDO
PLASTER

METAL
METAL

1 ENLUCIDO DE YESO
2 CAPA DE AISLAMIENTO
   TÉRMICO e=50 mm
3 TABLERO DE FIBROCEMENTO
4 BASTIDOR DE MADERA
5 BAJANTE EMBEBIDA
   EN EL MURO
6 PIEZA DE HORMIGÓN
   PREFABRICADO
7 PANEL COMPUESTO CON
   IMPRESIÓN EXTERIOR
8 CÁMARA DE AIRE
9 CAPA DE AISLAMIENTO
   TÉRMICO DE LANA DE ROCA
10 PLACA DE CARTÓN YESO
11 MEMBRANA DE CAUCHO
12 MEMBRANA
   IMPERMEABILIZANTE
13 FORJADO ALVEOLAR
14 BARRERA DE VAPOR

1 PLASTER FINISHING
2 50 mm THICK THERMAL
   INSULATION
3 FIBRE CEMENT BOARD
4 TIMBER FRAME
5 DOWNPIPE IN
   CONSTRUCTION
6 PRECAST CONCRETE
   ELEMENT
7 COMPOSITE PANEL
   WITH CUSTOM PRINT
8 CAVITY
9 MINERAL WOOL THERMAL
   INSULATION LAYER
10 GYPSUM BOARD
11 RUBBER MEMBRANE
12 WATERPROOF MEMBRANE
13 HOLLOW CORE SLAB
14 VAPOUR PERMEABLE
   MEMBRANE

1:20

0   0.1   0.5   1

Sección **A** section

1:500

0   1   5   10

1:100

0   0.5   1

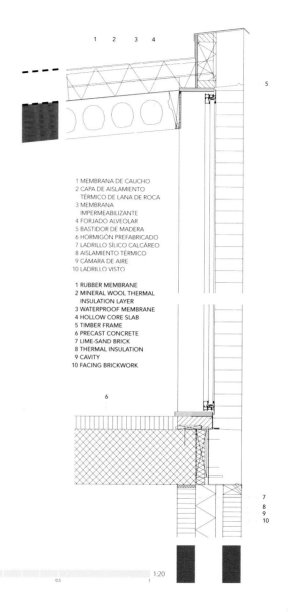

LAYERS

EXTERNAL

GRAVA
GRAVEL

CERÁMICA
TERRACOTTA

MADERA
WOOD

CEMENTO
CEMENT

VEGETACIÓN
PLANTING

METAL
METAL

AISLAMIENTO
INSULATION

MEMBRANA
MEMBRANE

PRINCIPAL

HORMIGÓN
CONCRETE

MADERA
WOOD

CERÁMICA
TERRACOTTA

INTERNAL

CARTÓN-YESO
PLASTER-BOARD

ENLUCIDO
PLASTER

METAL
METAL

1 MEMBRANA DE CAUCHO
2 CAPA DE AISLAMIENTO
   TÉRMICO DE LANA DE ROCA
3 MEMBRANA
   IMPERMEABILIZANTE
4 FORJADO ALVEOLAR
5 BASTIDOR DE MADERA
6 HORMIGÓN PREFABRICADO
7 LADRILLO SÍLICO CALCÁREO
8 AISLAMIENTO TÉRMICO
9 CÁMARA DE AIRE
10 LADRILLO VISTO

1 RUBBER MEMBRANE
2 MINERAL WOOL THERMAL
   INSULATION LAYER
3 WATERPROOF MEMBRANE
4 HOLLOW CORE SLAB
5 TIMBER FRAME
6 PRECAST CONCRETE
7 LIME-SAND BRICK
8 THERMAL INSULATION
9 CAVITY
10 FACING BRICKWORK

1:20

0   0.1   0.5   1

MVRDV, Blanca Lleó
mvrdv.nl, blancalleo.net **Madrid.** SPAIN, 2009 Francisco Pi y Margall 10, Sanchinarro

3,213 mill.☺

5.293 ☺/km²

21.550 m²
SUPERFICIE CONSTRUIDA
GROSS FLOOR AREA

35%
OCUPACIÓN
COVERED AREA

2,79
EDIFICABILIDAD
FLOOR AREA RATIO

6.021 m²
SUPERFICIE DE PARCELA
PLOT AREA

1:2.000

ALQUILER
RENTAL

100%
PROPIEDAD
OWNERSHIP

JÓVENES
YOUNG PEOPLE

MAYORES
SENIORS

ESTUDIANTES
STUDENTS

100%
CUALQUIERA
ANY

162 🚗 **92,4%**
VIVIENDA
LIVING

146
UNITS

TRABAJO
WORKING

100%
PÚBLICA
SUBSIDISED

PRIVADA
PRIVATE

7,6%
COMERCIOS
SHOPPING

242
⌂/ha

712
☺/ha

DENSIDAD DE VIVIENDAS
DWELLING DENSITY

DENSIDAD DE POBLACIÓN
RESIDENTIAL DENSITY

OTROS USOS
OTHER USES

1:5.000
0 10   50

821
$/m²

740
€/m²

2.000

1.900

1.800

1.700

1.600

1.500

1.400

1.300

1.200

1.100

1.000

900

800

700

600

500

400

300

200

100

0

Este proyecto de vivienda social es una solución alternativa a la manzana cerrada. Se plantea como un sistema edificatorio más que como un edificio singular. El conjunto en forma de celosía, intercala 30 volúmenes construidos y 30 vacíos. Dichos vacíos son espacios intermedios para la vida vecinal. Los volúmenes contienen viviendas de 1, 2 y 3 dormitorios y los patios en altura son espacios comunes abiertos a perspectivas cruzadas en todas direcciones.

Los pájaros, el viento y el sol atraviesan el edificio. El sistema de molde total ensaya la eficacia y calidad de una construcción más rápida y sostenible. La manzana se esponja permitiendo múltiples visiones cruzadas y perspectivas abiertas de dentro a fuera. Desde la calle y desde cada casa, se cruzan las vistas en múltiples direcciones; a través de los patios ajardinados suspendidos se abren insólitas perspectivas entre el interior arbolado de la manzana y el horizonte lejano de la ciudad y la sierra. Todas las viviendas tienen una habitación añadida, la habitación exterior. El sistema de molde total permite resolver en tiempo y precio esta construcción prefabricada de estructura singular. Las 146 viviendas se resuelven con una unidad base y dos variaciones. Esto permite viviendas de uno, dos y tres dormitorios con estancias versátiles y espacios especialmente generosos para el aseo, el ocio y

This social housing project is an alternative solution to the city block. It is proposed as more of a building system than as an individual building. The lattice-like set intersperses 30 built volumes and 30 empty spaces. These empty spaces are intermediate spaces for neighbourhood life.

The volumes contain one, two and three-bedroom housing units and high-rise patios are common spaces open to perceptual cross views in all directions. Birds, wind and sun go through the building.
The complete mould system tests the efficiency and quality of a faster and more sustainable construction. The city block is opened up, allowing multiple open cross and perceptual views from inside out. From the street and from each flat, views cross in several different directions.

el almacenamiento. Beneficios del sistema de moldes: Es un sistema industrializado, ágil y sencillo. Es sostenible, no necesita rozas ni produce escombros.
Es versátil, práctico y revolucionario. Permite hacer una vivienda por día.

Facilita la organización flexible y la ejecución simultánea de estructura, cerramientos e instalaciones.
El montaje del encofrado de aluminio es ligero y manejable. Produce una construcción de calidad en tiempo y coste.Los patios en altura garantizan una ventilación cruzada mediante dos o tres fachadas opuestas para todas las unidades. Se utiliza un sistema de calderas de bajo consumo para todo el edificio. Estos sistemas se combinan con paneles solares para la producción de agua caliente sanitaria.

Unusual perspectives between the green inside of the block and the far-off horizon of the city and the mountains open up through hanging garden patio. All housing units have an added room, the exterior-facing room.
The complete mould system allows the prefabricated construction of this singular structure to be solved at the right time and price.
The 146 housing units are settled into a base unit and two variations. This allows one, two and three-bedroom units with versatile rooms and especially generous spaces for bath, leisure and storage. Some of the benefits of the mould system include industrialisation, agility and simplicity. It is sustainable and does not produce on-site damage or debris. It is versatile, practical and revolutionary. It allows a house to be built in a day. It facilitates flexible organisation and the simultaneous execution of structure, cladding and installations. The assembly of the aluminium formwork is light and manageable for workers. It produces quality construction in little time and at a low cost.
The high-rise patios guarantee cross ventilation by means of two or three opposite facades for all of the units. A system of power efficient boilers is used for the entire building, reducing energy use. These systems are combined with solar panels to heat water.

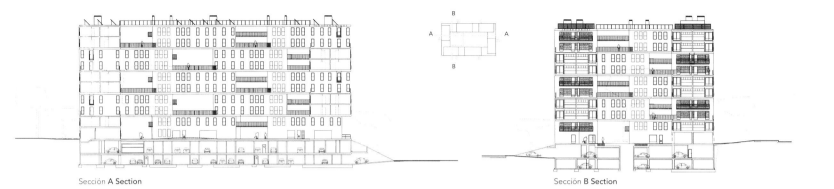

Sección **A** Section

Sección **B** Section

Planta baja **Ground floor plan**

1:1000

01 05 10 CALLE N

CALLE DEL ALCALDE DE HENCHE DE LA PLATA

CALLE FRANCISCO PI Y MARGALL

CALLE DEL ALCALDE CONDE DE MIRASOL

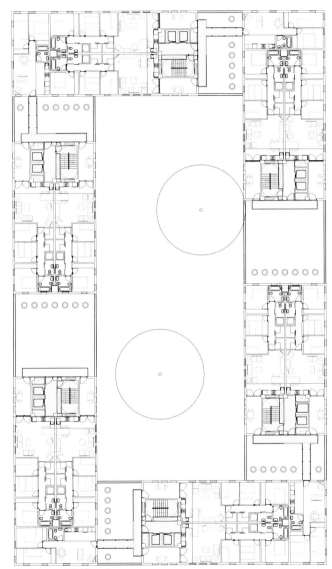

Planta tercera Third floor plan

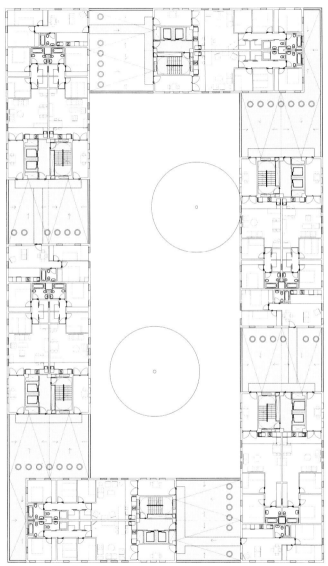

Planta cuarta Fourth floor plan

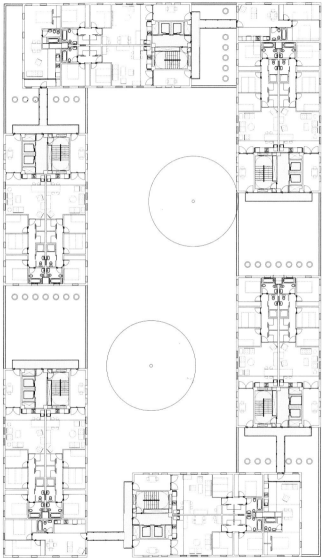

Planta Séptima **Seventh floor plan**

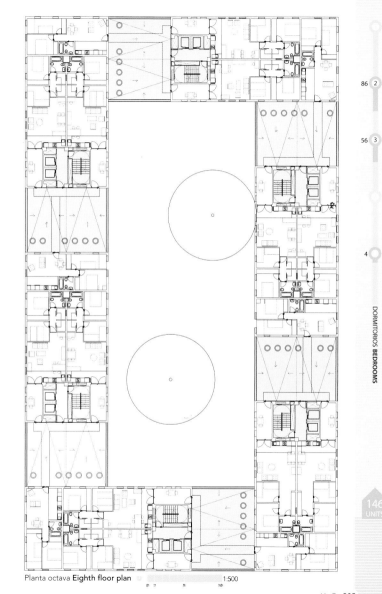

Planta octava **Eighth floor plan**   1:500

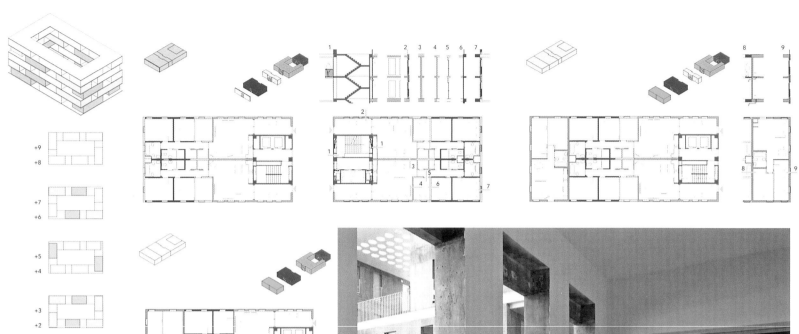

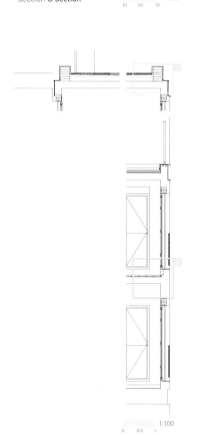

Sección **C** Section

01   05   10   1:1000

0   0.5   1   1:100

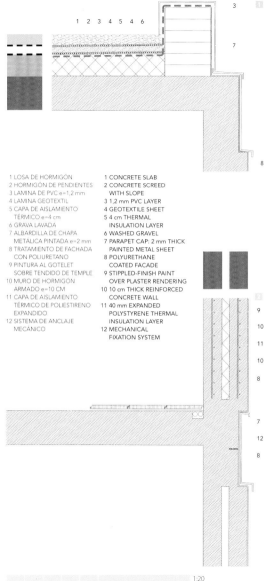

GRAVA
GRAVEL

CERÁMICA
TERRACOTTA

MADERA
WOOD

CEMENTO
CEMENT

VEGETACIÓN
PLANTING

METAL
METAL

AISLAMIENTO
INSULATION

MEMBRANA
MEMBRANE

HORMIGÓN
CONCRETE

MADERA
WOOD

CERÁMICA
TERRACOTTA

CARTÓN-YESO
PLASTER-BOARD

ENLUCIDO
PLASTER

METAL
METAL

1 LOSA DE HORMIGÓN
2 HORMIGÓN DE PENDIENTES
3 LAMINA DE PVC e=1,2 mm
4 LAMINA GEOTEXTIL
5 CAPA DE AISLAMIENTO
  TÉRMICO e=4 cm
6 GRAVA LAVADA
7 ALBARDILLA DE CHAPA
  METÁLICA PINTADA e=2 mm
8 TRATAMIENTO DE FACHADA
  CON POLIURETANO
9 PINTURA AL GOTELET
  SOBRE TENDIDO DE TEMPLE
10 MURO DE HORMIGÓN
  ARMADO e=10 CM
11 CAPA DE AISLAMIENTO
  TÉRMICO DE POLIESTIRENO
  EXPANDIDO
12 SISTEMA DE ANCLAJE
  MECÁNICO

1 CONCRETE SLAB
2 CONCRETE SCREED
  WITH SLOPE
3 1,2 mm PVC LAYER
4 GEOTEXTILE SHEET
5 4 cm THERMAL
  INSULATION LAYER
6 WASHED GRAVEL
7 PARAPET CAP: 2 mm THICK
  PAINTED METAL SHEET
8 POLYURETHANE
  COATED FACADE
9 STIPPLED-FINISH PAINT
  OVER PLASTER RENDERING
10 10 cm THICK REINFORCED
  CONCRETE WALL
11 40 mm EXPANDED
  POLYSTYRENE THERMAL
  INSULATION LAYER
12 MECHANICAL
  FIXATION SYSTEM

1:20

0   0.1   0.5   1

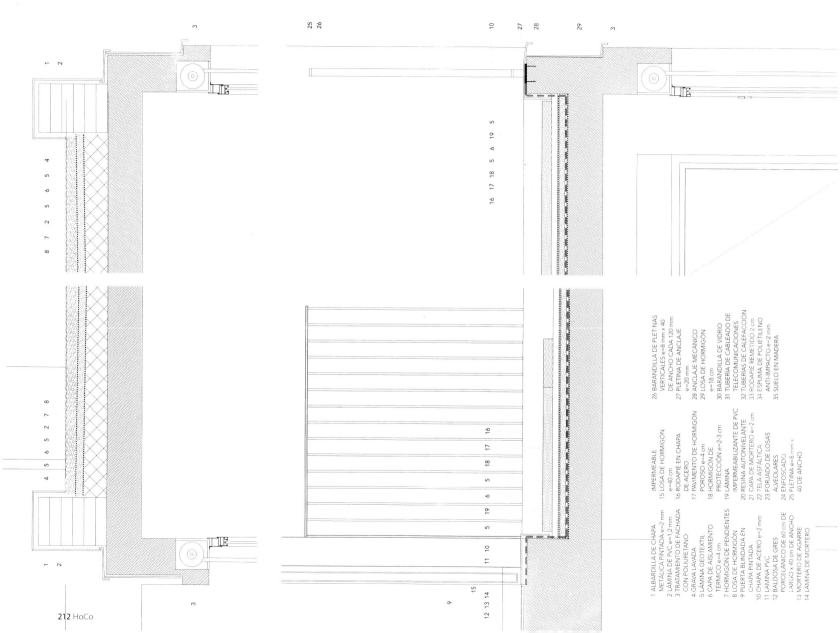

1 ALBARDILLA DE CHAPA
METÁLICA PINTADA e=2 mm
2 LÁMINA DE PVC e=1,2 mm
3 TRATAMIENTO DE FACHADA
CON POLIURETANO
4 GRAVA LAVADA
5 LÁMINA GEOTEXTIL
6 CAPA DE AISLAMIENTO
TÉRMICO e=4 cm
7 HORMIGÓN DE PENDIENTES
8 LOSA DE HORMIGÓN
9 PUERTA BLINDADA EN
CHAPA PINTADA
10 CHAPA DE ACERO e=2 mm
11 LÁMINA PVC
12 BALDOSA DE GRES
PORCELÁNICO DE 60 cm DE
LARGO ×40 cm DE ANCHO
13 MORTERO DE AGARRE
14 LÁMINA DE MORTERO

IMPERMEABLE
15 LOSA DE HORMIGÓN
e=40 cm
16 RODAPIÉ EN CHAPA
DE ACERO
17 PAVIMENTO DE HORMIGÓN
POROSO e=4 cm
18 HORMIGÓN DE
PROTECCIÓN e=2-3 cm
19 LÁMINA
IMPERMEABILIZANTE DE PVC
20 RESINA AUTONIVELANTE
21 CAPA DE MORTERO e=2 cm
22 TELA ASFÁLTICA
23 FORJADO DE LOSAS
ALVEOLARES
24 ENFOSCADO
25 PLETINA e=8 mm ×
40 DE ANCHO

26 BARANDILLA DE PLETINAS
VERTICALES e=8 mm × 40
DE ANCHO CADA 120 mm
27 PLETINA DE ANCLAJE
e=20 mm
28 ANCLAJE MECÁNICO
29 LOSA DE HORMIGÓN
e=18 cm
30 BARANDILLA DE VIDRIO
31 TUBERÍA DE CABLEADO DE
TELECOMUNICACIONES
32 TUBERÍAS DE CALEFACCIÓN
33 RODAPIÉ REMETIDO 2 cm
34 ESPUMA DE POLIETILENO
ANTI-IMPACTO e=2 mm
35 SUELO EN MADERA

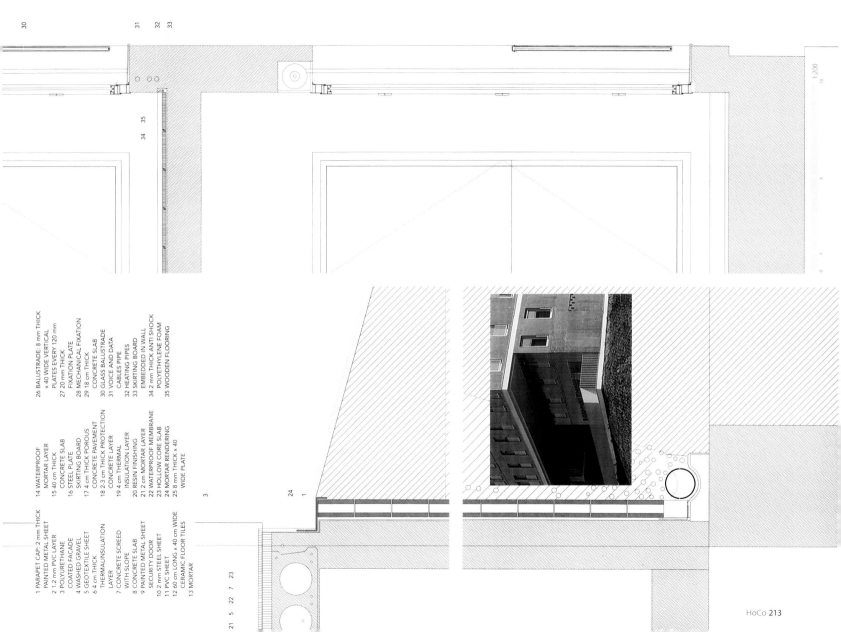

1:200

34 35

34

1 PARAPET CAP: 2 mm THICK
PAINTED METAL SHEET
2 1.2 mm PVC LAYER
3 POLYURETHANE
COATED FACADE
4 WASHED GRAVEL
5 GEOTEXTILE SHEET
6 4 cm THICK
THERMALINSULATION
LAYER
7 CONCRETE SCREED
WITH SLOPE
8 CONCRETE SLAB
9 PAINTED METAL SHEET
SECURITY DOOR
10 2 mm STEEL SHEET
11 PVC SHEET
12 60 cm LONG x 40 cm WIDE
CERAMIC FLOOR TILES
13 MORTAR

14 WATERPROOF
MORTAR LAYER
15 40 cm THICK
CONCRETE SLAB
16 STEEL PLATE
SKIRTING BOARD
17 4 cm THICK POROUS
CONCRETE PAVEMENT
18 2-3 cm THICK PROTECTION
CONCRETE LAYER
19 4 cm THERMAL
INSULATION LAYER
20 RESIN FINISHING
21 2 cm MORTAR LAYER
22 WATERPROOF MEMBRANE
23 HOLLOW CORE SLAB
24 MORTAR RENDERING
25 8 mm THICK x 40
WIDE PLATE

26 BALUSTRADE: 8 mm THICK
x 40 WIDE VERTICAL
PLATES EVERY 120 mm
27 20 mm THICK
FIXATION PLATE
28 MECHANICAL FIXATION
29 18 cm THICK
CONCRETE SLAB
30 GLASS BALUSTRADE
31 VOICE AND DATA
CABLES PIPE
32 HEATING PIPES
33 SKIRTING BOARD
34 2 mm THICK ANTI SHOCK
EMBEDDED IN WALL
POLYETHYLENE FOAM
35 WOODEN FLOORING

3

24

1

21 5 22 7 23

1 PATINILLO DE
  INSTALACIONES
2 TUBO PVC
3 SELLADO INTERIOR
  CON POLIURETANO
4 SELLADO EXTERIOR
  CON SILICONA
5 VAINA PARA PROTECCIÓN
  DE TUBERÍAS
6 TUBO PVC CON SUMINISTRO
  DE AGUA, ELECTRICIDAD
  Y CALEFACCIÓN
7 PAVIMENTO EN
  HORMIGÓN POROSO

1 INSTALLATIONS SHAFT
2 PVC PIPE
3 INTERIOR POLYURETHANE
  SEALANT
4 OUTER SILICON SEALANT
5 PIPE PROTECTION JACKET
6 PVC PIPE FOR WATER,
  ELECTRICITY OR
  HEATING SUPPLY
7 POROUS CONCRETE
  PAVEMENT

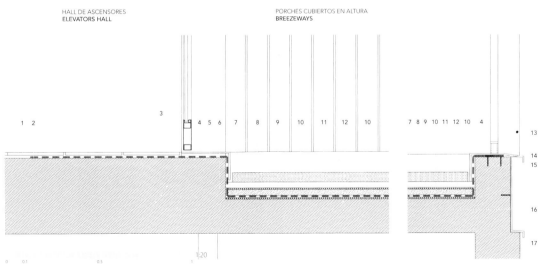

1 BALDOSA DE GRES
  PORCELÁNICO DE 60 cm DE
  LARGO x 40 cm DE ANCHO
2 MORTERO DE AGARRE
3 PUERTA EN CRISTAL Y ACERO
4 CHAPA DE ACERO e=2 mm
5 IMPERMEABILIZACIÓN
  CON PVC SOLAPE DE 1m
6 LOSA DE HORMIGÓN e=40 cm
7 RODAPIÉ EN CHAPA
  DE ACERO
8 PAVIMENTO DE HORMIGÓN
  POROSO e=4 cm
9 HORMIGÓN DE
  PROTECCIÓN e=2-3 cm
10 LAMINA GEOTEXTIL
11 CAPA DE AISLAMIENTO
  TÉRMICO e=4 cm
12 LAMINA IMPERMEABILIZANTE
  DE PVC
13 BARANDILLA EN TUBO
  CUADRADO DE 10 x 40 mm
14 PLETINA DE ANCLAJE
  e=20 mm
15 ANCLAJE MECÁNICO
16 LOSA DE HORMIGÓN e=18 cm
17 TRATAMIENTO DE FACHADA
  CON POLIURETANO

1 60 cm LONG x 40 cm WIDE
  CERAMIC FLOOR TILES
2 MORTAR
3 GLASS AND STEEL DOOR
4 2 mm STEEL SHEET
5 PVC WATERPROOF LAYER
6 40 cm CONCRETE SLAB
7 STEEL PLATE
  SKIRTING BOARD
8 4 cm THICK POROUS
  CONCRETE PAVEMENT
9 2-3 cm PROTECTION
  CONCRETE LAYER
10 GEOTEXTILE SHEETL
11 4 cm THERMAL
  INSULATION LAYER
12 PVC WATERPROOF LAYER
13 BALUSTRADE:
  10 x 40 mm TUBE
14 20 mm FIXATION PLATE
15 MECHANICAL FIXATION
16 18 cm CONCRETE SLAB
17 POLYURETHANE
  COATED FACADE

HALL DE ASCENSORES
ELEVATORS HALL

PORCHES CUBIERTOS EN ALTURA
BREEZEWAYS

1:20

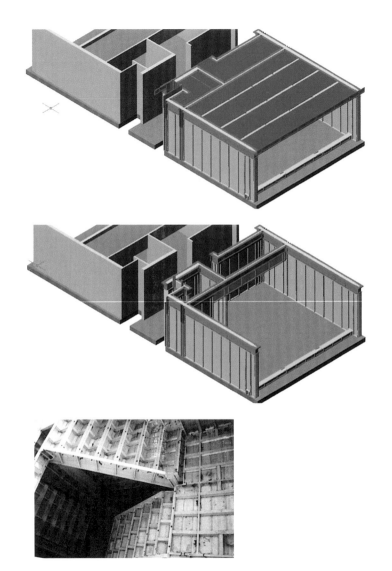

1 PANTALLA DE
  HORMIGÓN e=10 cm
2 CAJEADO PARA TUBOS
  DE CALEFACCIÓN
3 PILAR
4 RELLENO Y ACABADO
5 AISLAMIENTO

1 10 cm THICK
  CONCRETE WALL
2 HOLLOW FOR
  HEATING PIPES
3 COLUMN
4 FILLING AND FINISH
5 THERMAL INSULATION

Sección B Section

1:50

6.369

2.773 m²
SUPERFICIE DE PARCELA
PLOT AREA

5.826 m²
SUPERFICIE CONSTRUIDA
GROSS FLOOR AREA

1:2.000

35,1%
OCUPACIÓN
COVERED AREA

1,30
EDIFICABILIDAD
FLOOR AREA RATIO

59 🚗 **100%**
VIVIENDA
LIVING

TRABAJO
WORKING

COMERCIOS
SHOPPING

OTROS USOS
OTHER USES

48
UNITS

ALQUILER
RENTAL

100%
PROPIEDAD
OWNERSHIP

JÓVENES
YOUNG PEOPLE

MAYORES
SENIORS

ESTUDIANTES
STUDENTS

100%
CUALQUIERA
ANY

100%
PÚBLICA
SUBSIDISED

PRIVADA
PRIVATE

173
⌂/ha
DENSIDAD DE VIVIENDAS
DWELLING DENSITY

428
☉/ha
DENSIDAD DE POBLACIÓN
RESIDENTIAL DENSITY

El solar se encuentra en los límites de la ciudad alpina de Cerklie (cerca del aeropuerto de Liubliana) y goza de magníficas vistas del paisaje circundante y las montañas.

The site is the edge of alpine town Cerklje (near the Ljubljana Airport) with beautiful views to surrounding fields and mountains.

0 10   50   1:5.000

15

838
$/m²

600
€/m²

2.000

1.900

1.800

1.700

1.600

1.500

1.400

1.300

1.200

1.100

1.000

900

800

700

600

500

400

300

200

100

0

En la parcela había un tilo de 300 años protegido. Por este motivo, la planta tiene forma de L y abraza un patio ajardinado alrededor del árbol. Las viviendas se abren a este patio y gozan de las vistas de las montañas. Se trata de una promoción pública de vivienda vendida a familias jóvenes por 900 €/m², un precio muy bajo que obligaba a reducir los costes de construcción a 660 €/m² mediante el empleo de materiales simples y económicos.

El paisaje y las aldeas de los alrededores se han mantenido intactos y es frecuente encontrar ejemplos de arquitectura tradicional: antiguas granjas, establos y graneros. De hecho, la fachada está inspirada en estos graneros y sus vigas de madera imitan la composición de las viejas construcciones. Tradicionalmente, los agricultores almacenan hierbas o maíz sobre las vigas; en sus viviendas, los residentes pueden colocar flores o cualquier otra decoración para su balcón.

Los tipos de vivienda comprenden desde estudios de 30 m² hasta apartamentos de cuatro dormitorios y 80 m². Las viviendas de mayor tamaño se sitúan en las esquinas y disponen de mejores vistas. Los materiales son baratos pero de calidad: suelos de madera de roble, revestimiento de granito en los baños y grandes ventanas con persianas metálicas exteriores. El sistema estructural permite una distribución libre de las plantas, ya que los muros de

The site is the edge of alpine town Cerklje (near the Ljubljana Airport) with beautiful views to surrounding fields and mountains. On the site there is beautiful protected 300 year old lime-tree. The plan of the building therefore is L-shaped and embraces a green area around the tree. Also mountain views are opening from this courtyard therefore most of apartments have beautiful views. Apartments are social –they were sold to Slovenian Housing Fund for young families at price 900 €/m² that is extremely cheap. Therefore the budget had to be very limited (600 €/m²) and materials are simple and economic.

The landscape and villages in the area remained unspoiled with many examples of traditional architecture such as old farms, barns and hayracks. The concept of the facade is taken from the hayrack system –wooden beams follow traditional details and patterns. Traditionally farmers store grass and corn on beams, on the housing one can store flowers or other balcony decoration. Apartments are of different sizes –from 30 m² studio flats up to 4 room apartment of 80 m². Bigger apartments are developed on the corners of the building and have corner opened and nicer views. They are made of economic but quality materials such as wooden oak floors, granite tiled bathrooms and have large windows with external metal blinds. The concept of structure

carga son sólo los que separan unos apartamentos de otros. El resto de particiones interiores carece de función estructural.

El revestimiento exterior de la cubierta es de tejas de fibrocemento con una textura que imita la pizarra. Esta cubierta, inclinada en parte, permite esconder las instalaciones que quedan detrás: chimeneas, aire acondicionado, ventilación de las cocinas...

Por su parte, en cuanto a la fachada, el revestimiento exterior es un enlucido de yeso pintado de tres colores diferentes, las ventanas de PVC tienen color en la parte exterior y las vigas de los balcones son de abeto laminado y encolado para una mejor resistencia.

is made in a way, that floor plans are flexible, since only structural walls are those, that separate apartment shell from the rest of the building. All other inner walls are non-structural.

Roof tiling is made of grey cement tiles in atexture that copy traditional slate roof. The roof is pitched roof but cut on the ridge –there flat roof appears. The pitched roof partly functions as 1 m high blind, that covers all the installation, that is hidden behind –chimneys, external air conditioning, kitchen ventilation... Facade is plaster of three different colors. Windows are PVC, but colored from outside and wooden elements are of spruce-wood that is cut and glued for better resistance.

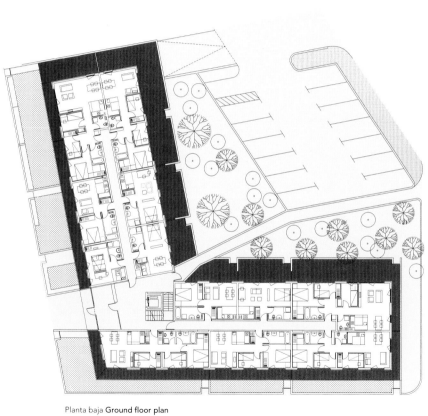

Planta baja Ground floor plan

1:500
0 1   5   10

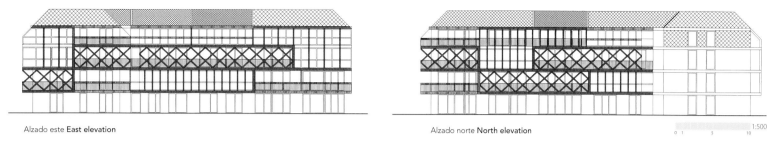

Alzado este **East elevation**

Alzado norte **North elevation**

1:500
0 1   5   10

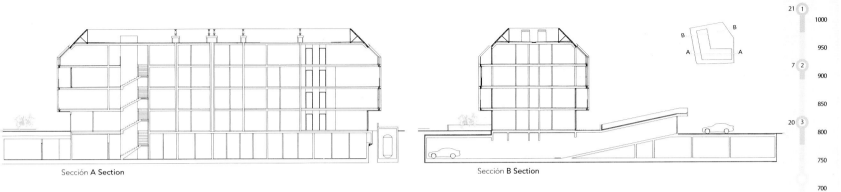

Sección **A** Section

Sección **B** Section

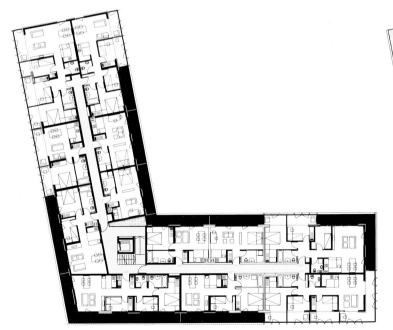

Planta primera y segunda **First and second floor plan**

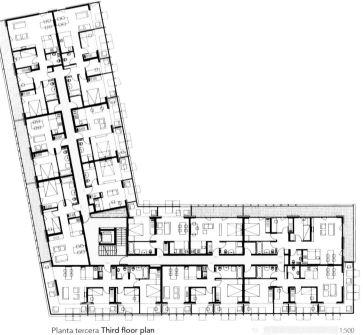

Planta tercera **Third floor plan**

1:500

0 1   5   10

DORMITORIOS **BEDROOMS**

21 **1** — 1000
      950
7 **2** — 900
      850
20 **3** — 800
      750
      700
      650
      600
      550
      500
      450
      400
      350
      300
      250
      200
      150
      100
      50

48
UNITS

0
UNITS

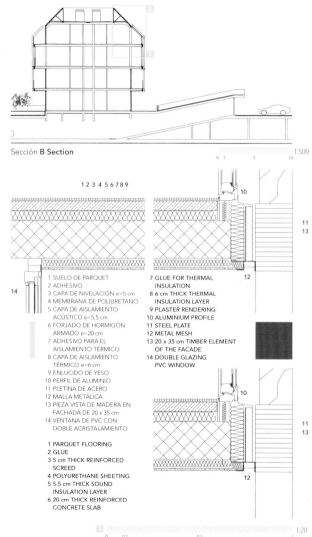

Sección **B** Section

1:500

1 2 3 4 5 6 7 8 9

1 SUELO DE PARQUET
2 ADHESIVO
3 CAPA DE NIVELACIÓN e=5 cm
4 MEMBRANA DE POLIURETANO
5 CAPA DE AISLAMIENTO
  ACÚSTICO e=5,5 cm
6 FORJADO DE HORMIGÓN
  ARMADO e=20 cm
7 ADHESIVO PARA EL
  AISLAMIENTO TÉRMICO
8 CAPA DE AISLAMIENTO
  TÉRMICO e=6 cm
9 ENLUCIDO DE YESO
10 PERFIL DE ALUMINIO
11 PLETINA DE ACERO
12 MALLA METÁLICA
13 PIEZA VISTA DE MADERA EN
  FACHADA DE 20 x 35 cm
14 VENTANA DE PVC CON
  DOBLE ACRISTALAMIENTO

7 GLUE FOR THERMAL
  INSULATION
8 6 cm THICK THERMAL
  INSULATION LAYER
9 PLASTER RENDERING
10 ALUMINIUM PROFILE
11 STEEL PLATE
12 METAL MESH
13 20 x 35 cm TIMBER ELEMENT
  OF THE FACADE
14 DOUBLE GLAZING
  PVC WINDOW

1 PARQUET FLOORING
2 GLUE
3 5 cm THICK REINFORCED
  SCREED
4 POLYURETHANE SHEETING
5 5.5 cm THICK SOUND
  INSULATION LAYER
6 20 cm THICK REINFORCED
  CONCRETE SLAB

1:20

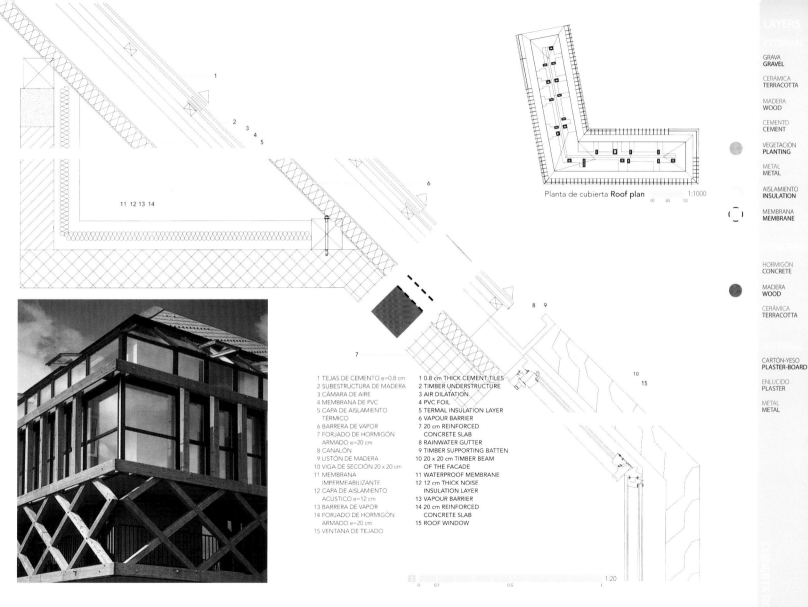

Planta de cubierta **Roof plan**   1:1000

01   05   10

1 TEJAS DE CEMENTO e=0,8 cm
2 SUBESTRUCTURA DE MADERA
3 CÁMARA DE AIRE
4 MEMBRANA DE PVC
5 CAPA DE AISLAMIENTO
   TÉRMICO
6 BARRERA DE VAPOR
7 FORJADO DE HORMIGÓN
   ARMADO e=20 cm
8 CANALÓN
9 LISTÓN DE MADERA
10 VIGA DE SECCIÓN 20 x 20 cm
11 MEMBRANA
   IMPERMEABILIZANTE
12 CAPA DE AISLAMIENTO
   ACÚSTICO e=12 cm
13 BARRERA DE VAPOR
14 FORJADO DE HORMIGÓN
   ARMADO e=20 cm
15 VENTANA DE TEJADO

1 0.8 cm THICK CEMENT TILES
2 TIMBER UNDERSTRUCTURE
3 AIR DILATATION
4 PVC FOIL
5 TERMAL INSULATION LAYER
6 VAPOUR BARRIER
7 20 cm REINFORCED
   CONCRETE SLAB
8 RAINWATER GUTTER
9 TIMBER SUPPORTING BATTEN
10 20 x 20 cm TIMBER BEAM
   OF THE FACADE
11 WATERPROOF MEMBRANE
12 12 cm THICK NOISE
   INSULATION LAYER
13 VAPOUR BARRIER
14 20 cm REINFORCED
   CONCRETE SLAB
15 ROOF WINDOW

1:20

0   0.1   0.5

LAYERS

GRAVA
GRAVEL

CERÁMICA
TERRACOTTA

MADERA
WOOD

CEMENTO
CEMENT

VEGETACIÓN
PLANTING

METAL
METAL

AISLAMIENTO
INSULATION

MEMBRANA
MEMBRANE

HORMIGÓN
CONCRETE

MADERA
WOOD

CERÁMICA
TERRACOTTA

CARTÓN-YESO
PLASTER-BOARD

ENLUCIDO
PLASTER

METAL
METAL

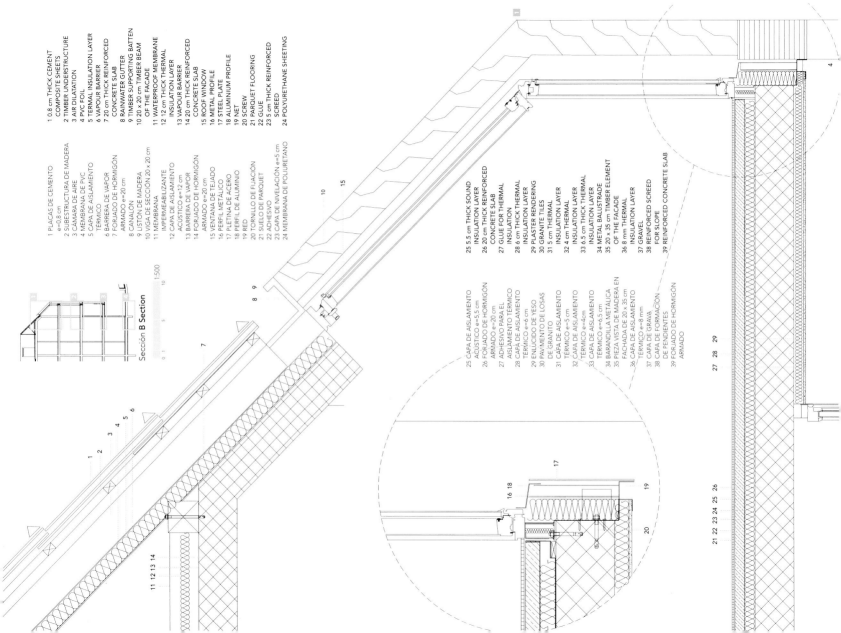

1 PLACAS DE CEMENTO e=0,8 cm
2 SUBESTRUCTURA DE MADERA
3 CÁMARA DE AIRE
4 MEMBRANA DE PVC
5 CAPA DE AISLAMIENTO TÉRMICO
6 BARRERA DE VAPOR
7 FORJADO DE HORMIGÓN ARMADO e=20 cm
8 CANALÓN
9 LISTÓN DE MADERA
10 VIGA DE SECCIÓN 20 x 20 cm
11 MEMBRANA IMPERMEABILIZANTE
12 CAPA DE AISLAMIENTO ACÚSTICO e=12 cm
13 BARRERA DE VAPOR
14 FORJADO DE HORMIGÓN ARMADO e=20 cm
15 VENTANA DE TEJADO
16 PERFIL METÁLICO
17 PLETINA DE ACERO
18 PERFIL DE ALUMINIO
19 RED
20 TORNILLO DE FIJACIÓN
21 SUELO DE PARQUET
22 ADHESIVO
23 CAPA DE NIVELACIÓN e=5 cm
24 MEMBRANA DE POLIURETANO

1 0.8 cm THICK CEMENT COMPOSITE SHEETS
2 TIMBER UNDERSTRUCTURE
3 AIR DILATATION
4 PVC FOIL
5 TERMAL INSULATION LAYER
6 VAPOUR BARRIER
7 20 cm THICK REINFORCED CONCRETE SLAB
8 RAINWATER GUTTER
9 TIMBER SUPPORTING BATTEN
10 20 x 20 cm TIMBER BEAM OF THE FACADE
11 WATERPROOF MEMBRANE
12 12 cm THICK THERMAL INSULATION LAYER
13 VAPOUR BARRIER
14 20 cm THICK REINFORCED CONCRETE SLAB
15 ROOF WINDOW
16 METAL PROFILE
17 STEEL PLATE
18 ALUMINIUM PROFILE
19 NET
20 SCREW
21 PARQUET FLOORING
22 GLUE
23 5 cm THICK REINFORCED SCREED
24 POLYURETHANE SHEETING

25 CAPA DE AISLAMIENTO ACÚSTICO e=5,5 cm
26 FORJADO DE HORMIGÓN ARMADO e=20 cm
27 ADHESIVO PARA EL AISLAMIENTO TÉRMICO
28 CAPA DE AISLAMIENTO TÉRMICO e=6 cm
29 ENLUCIDO DE YESO
30 PAVIMENTO DE LOSAS DE GRANITO
31 CAPA DE AISLAMIENTO TÉRMICO e=5 cm
32 CAPA DE AISLAMIENTO TÉRMICO e=4 cm
33 CAPA DE AISLAMIENTO TÉRMICO e=6,5 cm
34 BARANDILLA METÁLICA
35 PIEZA VISTA DE MADERA EN FACHADA DE 20 x 35 cm
36 CAPA DE AISLAMIENTO TÉRMICO e=8 mm
37 CAPA DE GRAVA
38 CAPA DE FORMACIÓN DE PENDIENTES
39 FORJADO DE HORMIGÓN ARMADO

25 5.5 cm THICK SOUND INSULATION LAYER
26 20 cm THICK REINFORCED CONCRETE SLAB
27 GLUE FOR THERMAL INSULATION
28 6 cm THICK THERMAL INSULATION LAYER
29 PLASTER RENDERING
30 GRANITE TILES
31 5 cm THERMAL INSULATION LAYER
32 4 cm THERMAL INSULATION LAYER
33 6.5 cm THICK THERMAL INSULATION LAYER
34 METAL BALUSTRADE
35 20 x 35 cm TIMBER ELEMENT OF THE FACADE
36 8 mm THERMAL INSULATION LAYER
37 GRAVEL
38 REINFORCED SCREED FOR SLOPE
39 REINFORCED CONCRETE SLAB

Sección B Section

1:500

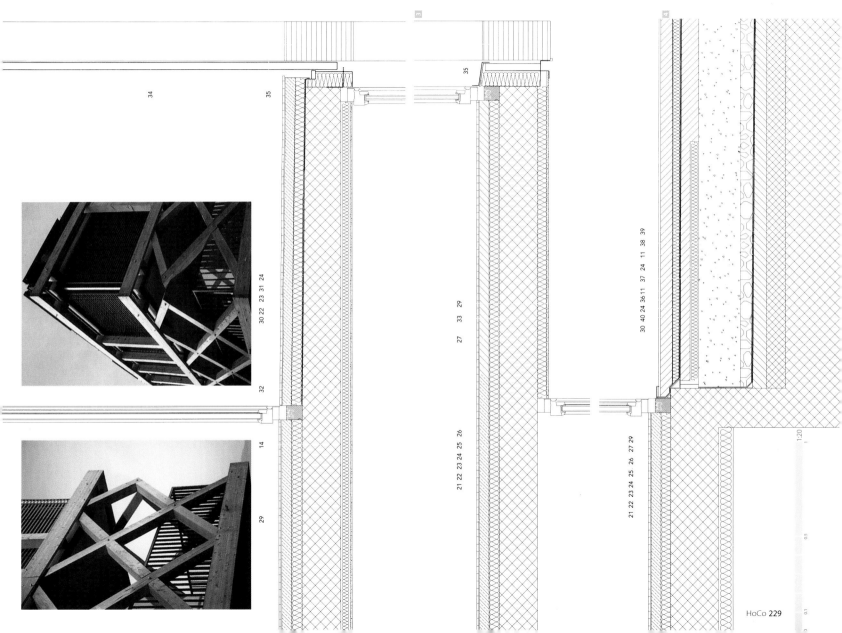

34

35

35

32

14

29

30 22 23 31 24

27 33 29

21 22 23 24 25 26

30 40 24 36 11 37 24 11 38 39

21 22 23 24 25 26 27 29

1:20

0.5

0.1

16

Atelier Kempe Thill atelierkempethill.com Amsterdam. THE NETHERLANDS, 2008 Domela Nieuwenhuisstraat 3, Osdorp

0,755 mill.☺   **3.449** ☺/km²

2.761 m²
SUPERFICIE DE PARCELA
PLOT AREA

5.104 m²
SUPERFICIE CONSTRUIDA
GROSS FLOOR AREA

1:2.000

74,3%
OCUPACIÓN
COVERED AREA

1,85
EDIFICABILIDAD
FLOOR AREA RATIO

ALQUILER
RENTAL

100%
PROPIEDAD
OWNERSHIP

JÓVENES
YOUNG PEOPLE

MAYORES
SENIORS

ESTUDIANTES
STUDENTS

100%
CUALQUIERA
ANY

23 🚗 **100%**
VIVIENDA
LIVING

23 UNITS

TRABAJO
WORKING

100%
PÚBLICA
SUBSIDISED

PRIVADA
PRIVATE

COMERCIOS
SHOPPING

83
⌂/ha

335
☺/ha

DENSIDAD DE VIVIENDAS
DWELLING DENSITY

DENSIDAD DE POBLACIÓN
RESIDENTIAL DENSITY

OTROS USOS
OTHER USES

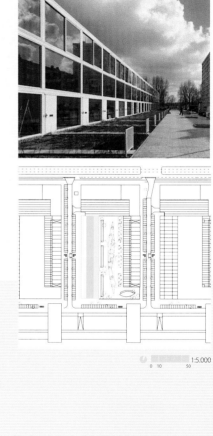

0 10   50   1:5.000

868
$/m² 877
€/m²

Comunidad frente a individualismo en el urbanismo de posguerra

El barrio de Amsterdam Osdorp fue construido en los años 60 y desde hace poco tiempo está siendo rehabilitado. El objetivo del proyecto de reforma consiste en introducir una mayor variedad de viviendas individualizadas para la clase media. Un importante número de los edificios existentes está siendo demolido y los reducidos apartamentos que contenían están siendo reemplazados por viviendas contemporáneas de mayor tamaño.

En este contexto, una de las cuestiones que afloraron durante el proceso de elaboración del proyecto fue cómo enfrentarse a la herencia urbana y arquitectónica del urbanismo posterior a la Segunda Guerra Mundial.

El edificio se encuentra en el área sur del Masterplan Zuidwest-Kwadrant, que fue elaborado por la firma De Nijl, un estudio de arquitectura y urbanismo radicado en Rotterdam. El principal objetivo de este proyecto es mantener la anchura de las calles y los patios comunes ajardinados mediante la integración de los aparcamientos bajo los nuevos edificios.

El edificio que hemos proyectado se basa en el relajado entorno urbano en que se inserta como punto de partida para la organización de las viviendas y busca la solución más convincente posible para el aparcamiento. El resultado es un

Community versus individuality: within post-war urbanism

Amsterdam Osdorp was built in the sixties and is since a few years in a process of urban renewal.

The ambition of the program is to create a bigger variety of more individual housing types serving the middle class. Big parts of the existing building structures with mostly small apartments are demolished and replaced by bigger, more contemporary homes. One of the important questions that arose during the process is how to deal with the urban and architectural heritage of post-war modernism. The building project is situated in the southern part of the 'Masterplan Zuidwest-Kwadrant'. The plan is developed and supervised by the De Nijl - a Rotterdam based firm for urban planning and architecture. Ambition of the master plan is to maintain the typical wide urban street profiles and the green collective courtyards by integrating the car parking under the new buildings.

The building project takes the very relaxed urban setting as direct starting point for the organisation of the houses and tries to find a convincing solution for the parking. The result is a prototypical housing project that supports the more collective scale of Amsterdam Osdorp without suppressing the individual expression of the single homes. Traditional values of

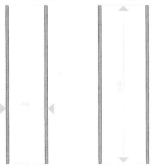

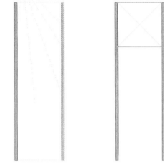

1 DISTANCIA REDUCIDA entre muros para limitar la superficie de fachada **SMALL SPAN** to reduce facade surface

2 GRAN PROFUNDIDAD de crujías para obtener m² de bajo precio **DEEP PLAN** to produce 'cheap square meters'

3 FACHADA DE VIDRIO para permitir la entrada de suficiente luz al interior y extender el espacio interior hacia afuera **GLASS FACADE** to bring in enough light and extend the inside space towards the outside

4 ESPACIO EN DOBLE ALTURA que redunda en riqueza y jerarquía espacial **VOID SPACE** to create spatial richness an hirarchy

prototipo que se adapta a la gran escala de los bloques de Osdorp sin suprimir la individualidad de la vivienda unifamiliar. De este modo, se reinterpretan los valores tradicionales del Movimiento Moderno y estimulan las formas de vida actuales.

Esta intervención es una contraoferta al movimiento del Nuevo Urbanismo que en este momento domina el panorama holandés. No es el resultado de sentimentalismos sobre la forma histórica, sino la derivación consecuente de la organización interna de los espacios en que se vive. Asimismo, el proyecto pretende demostrar que los prejuicios hacia la arquitectura contemporánea son erróneos. La arquitectura actual no es más cara que la construcción tradicional y resulta fácil de vender: todas las viviendas se vendieron en un periodo de tan solo dos semanas.

modernism get a new interpretation and more contemporary forms of living are stimulated.

This project is presenting a counter pole against the New Urbanism movement that is at the moment very dominant in the Netherlands. The project is not the result of sentimental ideas about historic forms but a consequent result of the inner organisation of the living spaces.

Also the prejudices against contemporary architecture are to prove wrong. Modern architecture has not to be more expensive than a more traditional way of building. Good modern architecture is also easy to sell –all houses have been sold within the very short period of just two weeks.

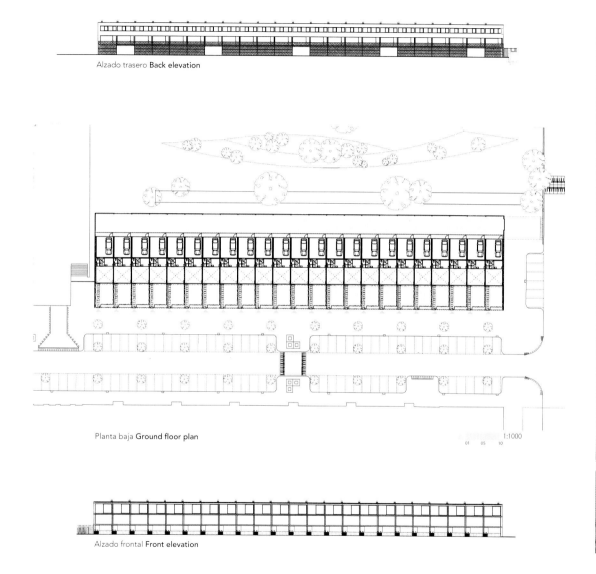

Alzado trasero **Back elevation**

Planta baja **Ground floor plan**

1:1000
01 05 10

Alzado frontal **Front elevation**

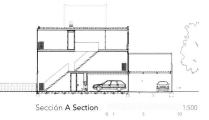

Sección **A Section**   1:500

Terraza **Roof plan**

Planta segunda **Second floor plan**

Planta primera **First floor plan**

A
B

Planta baja **Ground floor plan**

Arquitectura de a pie: estrategia económica

El presupuesto de construcción corresponde
con los estándares holandeses y es
relativamente pequeño comparado con los
precios medios en Ámsterdam. Con el fin
de mantener el equilibrio presupuestario, se
tuvieron en cuenta los siguientes principios:
el ancho entre muros de carga y por tanto, la
anchura de las viviendas, se limitó a 4,80 m. De
esta manera, se reduce un 20% la superficie de
fachada. Por su parte, la planta tiene 12,50 m de
longitud, un 30% más de lo habitual.
Así es como se construyen muchos m² baratos
en el interior de la vivienda y se obtienen
buenos niveles de eficiencia energética.
Para compensar la estrechez del volumen, se
introduce una fachada de vidrio en doble altura
sobre los salones.
El aparcamiento no se sitúa bajo tierra, sino
que se coloca en planta baja para evitar el
sobrecoste de una planta subterránea estanca
y ventilada mecánicamente. Su estructura de
acero se coloca en la fachada trasera de las
viviendas de hormigón y su cubierta sirve de
soporte a terrazas privadas.

Down-to-earth architecture: Economic strategy

The building budget corresponds to the normal
Dutch standard and is relatively limited for
Amsterdam conditions. To create a good starting
point for the materialisation the following
strategy is forming the basis for the design.
The span of the town houses is reduced to an
acceptable minimum of 4.80 m. By doing so the
facade surface is in comparison to the standard
20% less. The plan is with a size of 12.50 m ca.
30% deeper than the standard. Inside the house
a lot of 'cheap square meters' are produced
and good conditions for energy efficiency are
created. The produced spatial confinement is
compensated by introduction of a complete
glass facade and a double high living room.
The necessary parking garage is not built under
ground but at ground level to avoid waterproof
concrete constructions and mechanical
ventilation. The car park is realised as a cost-
effective steel construction and put in front of
the concrete construction of the town houses.
The roof of the garage is used for private
terraces.

LAYERS

EXTERNAL

CERÁMICA
BRICKWORK

HORMIGON
CONCRETE

MADERA
WOOD

CEMENTO
CEMENT

METAL
METAL

COMPUESTO
COMPOSITE

VIDRIO
GALSS

ENFOSCADO/
ESTUCO
**MORTAR/
STUCCO**

AISLAMIENTO
INSULATION

MEMBRANA
MEMBRANE

PRINCIPAL

CERÁMICA
BRICKWORK

VIDRIO
GALSS

HORMIGON
CONCRETE

MADERA
WOOD

COMPUESTO
COMPOSITE

INTERNAL

CARTÓN-YESO
PLASTER-BOARD

CERÁMICA
BRICKWORK

ENLUCIDO
PLASTER

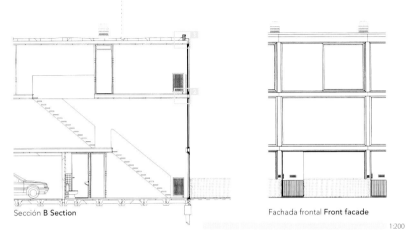

Sección **B Section**

Fachada frontal **Front facade**

1:200

1 GRAVA
2 MEMBRANA DE CUBIERTA
3 CAPA DE AISLAMIENTO
  TÉRMICO
4 FORJADO DE HORMIGÓN
5 MEMBRANA
  IMPERMEABILIZANTE
6 MEMBRANA
  IMPERMEABILIZANTE
7 PANEL DE ALUMINIO
  e=3 mm
8 VIDRIO CON
  PROTECCIÓN SOLAR
9 CARPINTERÍA DE ALUMINIO

1 GRAVEL
2 ROOFING MEMBRANE
3 INSULATION
4 CONCRETE FLOOR
5 DAMP PROOF MEMBRANE
6 WATERPROOF LAYER
7 3 mm THICK
  ALUMINIUM PLATE
8 SUN PROTECTED GLAZING
9 ALUMINIUM
  WINDOWFRAME

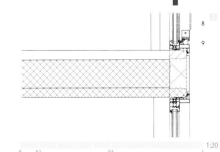

1:20

Ligereza informal y collage desmaterializado: materialización

El uso de los materiales intenta no ser pretencioso y servir de soporte a una mayor ligereza en el modo contemporáneo de habitar. Los espacios interiores se extienden hacia afuera mediante grandes ventanales de suelo a techo. De este modo, la vivienda no tiene una fachada en el sentido clásico del término, sino que se trata de un esqueleto que muestra su construcción al exterior y cuya vida interior se muestra al espacio público. La fachada se compone de vidrio con protección solar garantizando el confort a lo largo del año sin necesidad de emplear persianas. Con el fin de ahorrar espacio, la puerta de entrada es corredera.

La fachada al patio está dominada en planta baja por la presencia del aparcamiento y una malla metálica como sistema de cerramiento por la que crecerá la hiedra en el futuro. Sobre la cubierta del aparcamiento, las terrazas de cada vivienda están separadas por pantallas sintéticas que dejan pasar la luz. El muro trasero, por su parte, consta de huecos y paños opacos revestidos de chapa ondulada.

El diseño interior es muy modesto. Se han evitado los pasillos para ahorrar espacio y la escalera arranca directamente del salón. Se trata de una escalera muy económica, cuya barandilla se integra en la composición de la vivienda. Por motivos económicos, el edificio está construido a partir de diferentes materiales y tecnologías: la estructura es de acero y hormigón, las carpinterías de aluminio o madera y las puertas de acero, aluminio o madera. Mientras, otros elementos están hechos de varios materiales sintéticos.

Para conseguir un aspecto uniforme y permitir que el espacio se imponga sobre los materiales, todos los elementos constructivos están pintados con color RAL 9010. De esta forma, la promoción de viviendas se desdibuja y se presenta como una estructura clásica de color blanco que sirve de fondo perfecto a los espacios habitados. Sobre este trasfondo, la generación IKEA tiene la oportunidad de hacer realidad sus sueños de un modo de vida libre y liviano.

Informal lightness and dematerialized collage: materialisation

The use of materials is relatively unpretentious and tries to support a more contemporary lightness of living. The inside spaces are extended towards the outside by big glass windows from floor to sealing. Therefore the town house project has no facade in the classical sense but presents itself as skeleton demonstrating the construction. Within the skeleton – behind the glass – the living is exhibited towards the public space.

The glass facade is made of slightly reflecting sun protection glass guaranteeing climate comfort through the year without extra outside sunscreens. To save space the entrance door is realised as a special designed sliding door. The courtyard facade is dominated at the ground floor by the parking garage with an open metal mesh as facade system. In the future the mesh will be grown with ivy. The terraces on top of the garage are separated from each other by synthetic light-transmissive screens. The actual facade of the houses has big windows as well but is partly closed with a facade system of corrugated metal sheets. The same system is used for the head facades. The interior design is very modest. Corridors are avoided to be able to save space. The stairs are directly positioned into the living room. Very economic standard stairs are used but covered by a special designed balustrade to integrate them into the total composition of the houses.

For economic reasons the project is constructed out of an efficient collage of different building materials and technologies like concrete- and steel construction; aluminium- and wood windows; steel-, aluminium- and wooden doors and different synthetic materials. To create a quiet general impression for the building and to let dominate the space above the material all building elements are coated in RAL 9010. The housing estate gets optically dematerialized and presents itself as a classical white structure forming a perfect background for the living spaces. For this background the IKEA generation gets the opportunity to realise their dreams of a free and light way of living.

LAYERS
EXTERNAL

GRAVA
GRAVEL

CERÁMICA
TERRACOTTA

MADERA
WOOD

CEMENTO
CEMENT

VEGETACIÓN
PLANTING

METAL
METAL

AISLAMIENTO
INSULATION

MEMBRANA
MEMBRANE

HORMIGÓN
CONCRETE

MADERA
WOOD

CERÁMICA
TERRACOTTA

INTERNAL

CARTÓN-YESO
PLASTER-BOARD

ENLUCIDO
PLASTER

METAL
METAL

1 VIDRIO CON
  PROTECCIÓN SOLAR
2 CARPINTERÍA DE ALUMINIO
3 PERFIL U DE ACERO
4 MEMBRANA
  IMPERMEABILIZANTE
5 PANEL DE ALUMINIO
  e≈3 mm
6 LOSAS DE CEMENTO
7 PIEZA DE HORMIGÓN
  PREFABRICADO
8 CAPA DE AISLAMIENTO
  TÉRMICO
9 FORJADO DE HORMIGÓN
  PREFABRICADO

1 SUN PROTECTED GLAZING
2 ALUMINIUM
  WINDOW FRAME
3 STEEL U SECTION
4 WATERPROOF LAYER
5 3 mm THICK
  ALUMINIUM PLATE
6 CONCRETE TILES
7 PREFABRICATED
  CONCRETE ELEMENT
8 INSULATION
9 PREFABRICATED FLOOR

Sección B **Section**

Fachada frontal **Front facade**

1:200

0 1   5   10

1:20

0   0.1   0.5   1

1 PERFIL DE ALUMINIO
  e=3 mm
2 TIMBRE
3 MEMBRANA
  IMPERMEABILIZANTE
4 CAPA DE AISLAMIENTO
  TÉRMICO
5 MURO DE HORMIGÓN
6 TIRADOR
7 CARPINTERÍA DE ALUMINIO
8 PANEL SANDWICH
9 CHAPA DE ALUMINIO
  e=3 mm PEGADA A
  PUERTA CORREDERA

1 3 mm THICK
  ALUMINIUM PROFILE
2 DOOR BELL
3 WATERPROOF LAYER
4 INSULATION
5 CONCRETE WALL
6 DOORHANDLE
7 ALUMINIUM
  WINDOWFRAME
8 SANDWICH PANEL
9 3 mm THICK ALUMINIUM
  PLATE GLUED ONTO
  SLIDING DOOR

Detalle de la puerta corredera del acceso principal
Sliding front door detail

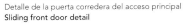

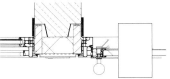

1 2 3 4 5   6   7   8   9

2,201
mill.☺

20.887
☺/km²

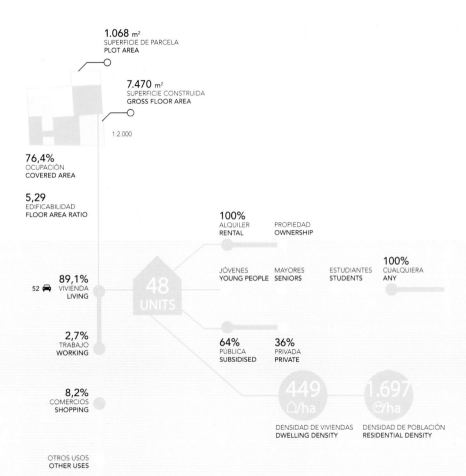

1.068 m²
SUPERFICIE DE PARCELA
PLOT AREA

7.470 m²
SUPERFICIE CONSTRUIDA
GROSS FLOOR AREA

1:2.000

76,4%
OCUPACIÓN
COVERED AREA

5,29
EDIFICABILIDAD
FLOOR AREA RATIO

100%
ALQUILER
RENTAL

PROPIEDAD
OWNERSHIP

JÓVENES
YOUNG PEOPLE

MAYORES
SENIORS

ESTUDIANTES
STUDENTS

100%
CUALQUIERA
ANY

52 🚗 89,1%
VIVIENDA
LIVING

48
UNITS

2,7%
TRABAJO
WORKING

64%
PÚBLICA
SUBSIDISED

36%
PRIVADA
PRIVATE

8,2%
COMERCIOS
SHOPPING

449
⌂/ha

1.697
☺/ha

DENSIDAD DE VIVIENDAS
DWELLING DENSITY

DENSIDAD DE POBLACIÓN
RESIDENTIAL DENSITY

OTROS USOS
OTHER USES

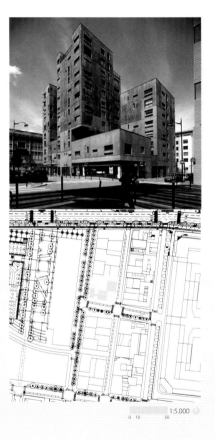

1:5.000

0 10   50

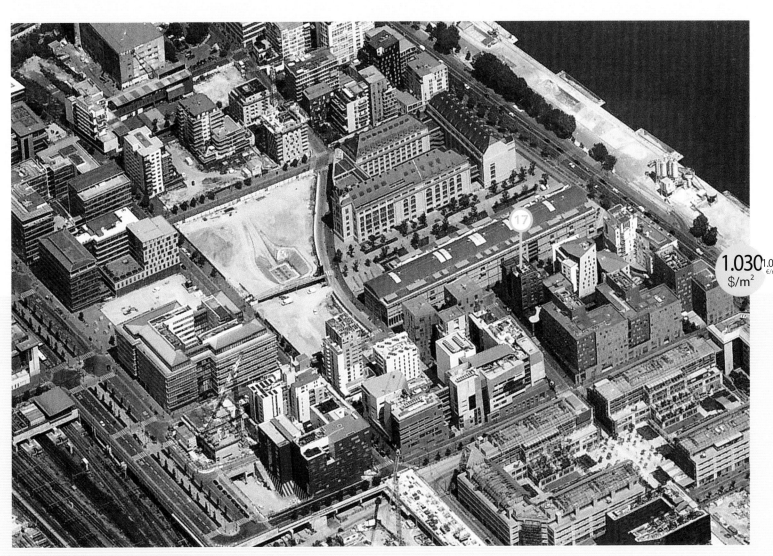

1.030 1.080
$/m² €/m² -100

2.000

1.900

1.800

1.700

1.600

1.500

1.400

1.300

1.200

1.100

1.000

900

800

700

600

500

400

300

200

100

0

El proyecto no es una intervención arquitectónica aislada, sino que forma parte del nuevo barrio Masséna en el distrito 13 de París. Basado en los criterios urbanísticos ideados por Christian de Portzamparc, el edificio emerge, se desarrolla y materializa de forma sencilla y elegante.

El volumen resultante se lleva estrictamente hasta la alineación de parcela y se recorta, dando lugar a retranqueos, vuelos, terrazas y fracturas, de acuerdo con el esquema de manzana abierta que plantea el plan urbano.

Ubicado en un cruce de calles, esta reducida estructura impone su inercia mediante un volumen profundo y sombrío.

El hormigón autocompactable de color añade un toque especial a los acabados en las esquinas y realza la belleza de la composición de los huecos, la majestuosidad del diseño y la pureza de sus líneas. Mientras, el frente de vidrio de la planta baja confiere al edificio una impresión de inmaterialidad.

Las fachadas se desarrollan en una composición gráfica, generosa y sin escala: mediante un ritmo de huecos sistemático y sorprendente, desaparece la traslación directa de los distintos niveles a fachada. Al interior, estos huecos proporcionan vistas del contexto inmediato o vistas más alejadas sobre el paisaje del este de París.

This project is not an isolated architectural mission, it contributes to the urban ambitions of the Masséna district in the 13th arrondissement of Paris. Each new construction is an additional milestone in the extension of this '3rd age' town.

Based on the principles designed by Christian de Portzamparc, the project emerges, develops, takes shape to enhance its simplicity with its own specific elegance.

The facade overlooking the street extends in strict alignment like a cheesewire. The overhangs, the recesses, the compositions of terraces and a crevasse structure the expression of the blocks forming this architectural complex, allowing the neighbouring buildings to benefit from the 'open island hub' of the development plan.

At the crossroads of the various traffic axes, this minimal structure imposes its inertia through its deep and sombre bulk. Self-compacting coloured concrete adds a finishing touch to the corners, enhances the beauty of the canvas formed by the windows, the majesty of the design and its pure lines. The large glazed facades of the ground floor confer an impression of immateriality, the structure remains absent from this composition and a large hollow joint which accommodates the solar protection of the future occupants bestows a certain sense of levitation on the various volumes.

Delicado como el ala de una mariposa, una banda metálica envuelve los distintos volúmenes del edificio creando una atmósfera especial al captar la luz y los reflejos. El edificio se refleja y refleja un tono de color, un espectro luminoso. El edificio carece de ornamentación y la naturaleza, omnipresente, surge de las cubiertas con abundantes plantas y árboles.

Los transeúntes, al mirar hacia arriba, sueñan con este nuevo París verde, cercano al Sena y a diversas infraestructuras culturales y educativas.

El edificio plantea una arquitectura crítica, rechaza las limitaciones de estilo y los arquetipos de representación. Su modernidad es esencial para una nueva urbanidad regulada en una metrópolis abierta, generosa, ecológica y social.

The facades unfold like a large graphic composition, generous and scaleless. The notion of floor levels is concealed, the rhythms of the openings are systematic and surprising. The inside is echoed by precise, nearby or far-off frames, profiting from the panoramas offered by eastern Paris.

As delicate as a butterfly wing, a metal tape running between the various volumes creates a special atmosphere catching the light, the reflections. The building is reflected and reflects a tone, a luminous spectrum. Time is on stage.

Ornamentation is banned and the omnipresent nature springs unexpectedly from the roofs of the various volumes, with an abundance of plants and trees.

Passers-by dream when looking up towards these accessible terraces which form this new 'green' Paris, close to the river Seine and large cultural and educational infrastructures.

Rejecting the limitations of style and representation archetypes, this building suggests a critical architecture, whose modernity is essential for a new regulated urbanity in an open, generous, ecological and social metropolis.

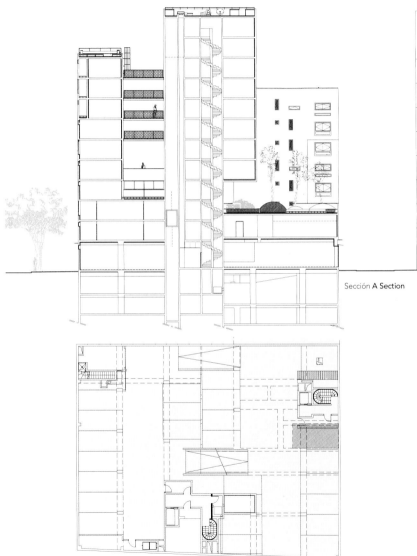

Sección **A Section**

Primera planta sótano **First basement floor plan**

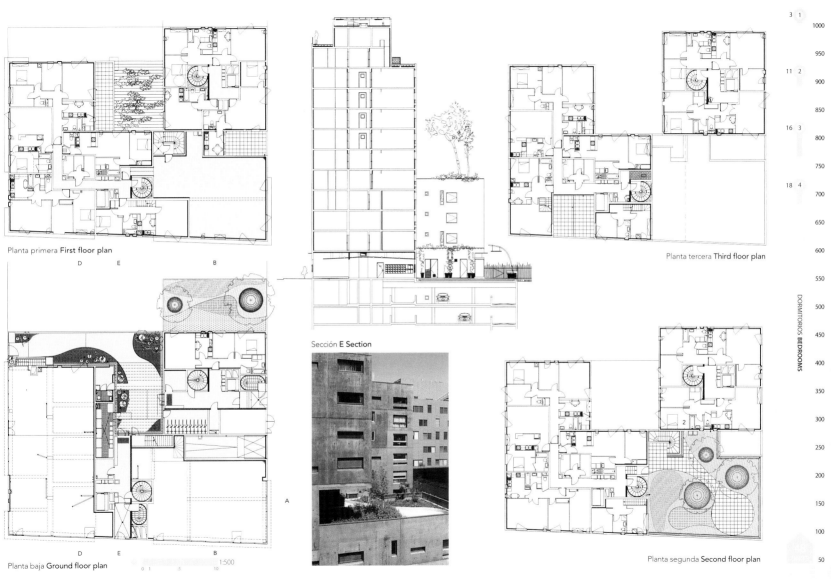

Planta primera **First floor plan**

D   E   B

Sección **E Section**

A

Planta baja **Ground floor plan**

1:500

0 1   5   10

D   E   B

Planta tercera **Third floor plan**

Planta segunda **Second floor plan**

DORMITORIOS BEDROOMS

3   1   1000

            950

11   2   900

            850

16   3   800

            750

18   4   700

650

600

550

500

450

400

350

300

250

200

150

100

50

0

UNITS

Planta quinta **Fifth floor plan**

Planta séptima **Seventh floor plan**

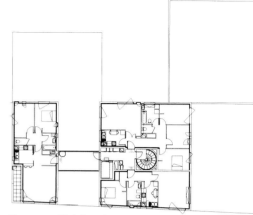

Planta novena **Ninth floor plan**

Planta cuarta **Fourth floor plan**

Planta sexta **Sixth floor plan**

Planta octava **Eighth floor plan**

0   1   5   10

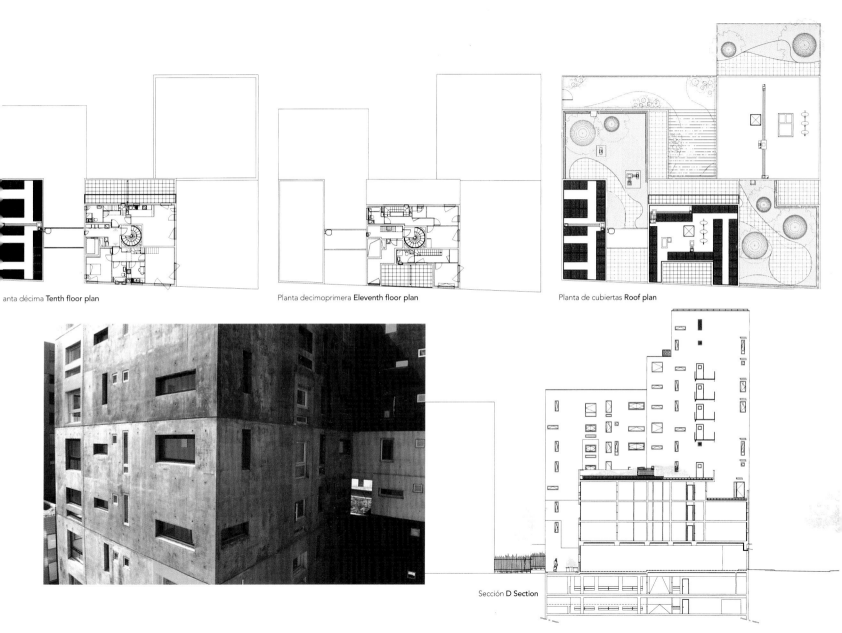

anta décima **Tenth floor plan**

Planta decimoprimera **Eleventh floor plan**

Planta de cubiertas **Roof plan**

Sección **D Section**

LAYERS

EXTERNAL

CERÁMICA
BRICKWORK

HORMIGON
CONCRETE

MADERA
WOOD

CEMENTO
CEMENT

METAL
METAL

COMPUESTO
COMPOSITE

VIDRIO
GALSS

ENFOSCADO/
ESTUCO
**MORTAR/
STUCCO**

AISLAMIENTO
INSULATION

MEMBRANA
MEMBRANE

PRINCIPAL

CERÁMICA
BRICKWORK

VIDRIO
GALSS

HORMIGON
CONCRETE

MADERA
WOOD

COMPUESTO
COMPOSITE

INTERNAL

CARTÓN-YESO
PLASTER-BOARD

CERÁMICA
BRICKWORK

ENLUCIDO
PLASTER

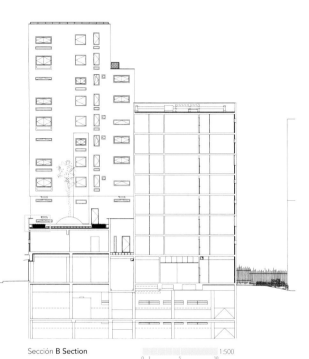

Sección **B Section**   1:500

0 1   5   10

1 ALBARDILLA DE ALUMINIO
  ANODIZADO
2 BARANDILLA
3 APOYO DE HORMIGÓN
  COLOREADO
4 LOSA REGISTRABLE
5 MURETE DE HORMIGÓN
6 PLANTACIÓN
7 TIERRA VEGETAL
8 TEJIDO FILTRANTE
9 DRENAJE
10 CAPA DE PROTECCIÓN
11 MEMBRANA
   IMPERMEABILIZANTE
12 CAPA DE AISLAMIENTO
   TÉRMICO
13 FORJADO DE HORMIGÓN
14 DRENAJE
15 MEMBRANA
   IMPERMEABILIZANTE
16 MURO DE HORMIGÓN
17 CARTÓN-YESO

1 ANODIZED ALUMINIUM
  WEATHERING TO PARAPETS
2 BALUSTRADE
3 TAINTED CONCRETE
  SUPPORT
4 RETRACTABLE TILE
5 CONCRETE WALL
6 PLANTS
7 NATURAL SOIL
8 FILTERING MAT
9 DRAIN
10 PROTECTION LAYER
11 WATERPROOF MEMBRANE
12 THERMAL INSULATION
   LAYER
13 CONCRETE SLAB
14 WATER DRAIN
15 WATERPROOF MEMBRANE
16 CONCRETE WALL
17 GYPSUM BOARD

0   0.1   0.5   1   1:20

LAYERS
EXTERNAL

GRAVA
GRAVEL

CERÁMICA
TERRACOTTA

MADERA
WOOD

CEMENTO
CEMENT

VEGETACIÓN
PLANTING

METAL
METAL

AISLAMIENTO
INSULATION

MEMBRANA
MEMBRANE

HORMIGÓN
CONCRETE

MADERA
WOOD

CERÁMICA
TERRACOTTA

INTERNAL

CARTÓN-YESO
PLASTER-BOARD

ENLUCIDO
PLASTER

METAL
METAL

CUBIERTA ROOF

Edouard François edouardfrancois.com Paris. FRANCE, 2008 Rue des Vignoles 21, Paris 20

2,201 mill.☺   20.887 ☺/km²

9.750 m²
SUPERFICIE CONSTRUIDA
GROSS FLOOR AREA

63,8%
OCUPACIÓN
COVERED AREA

1,55
EDIFICABILIDAD
FLOOR AREA RATIO

5.327 m²
SUPERFICIE DE PARCELA
PLOT AREA

1:2.000

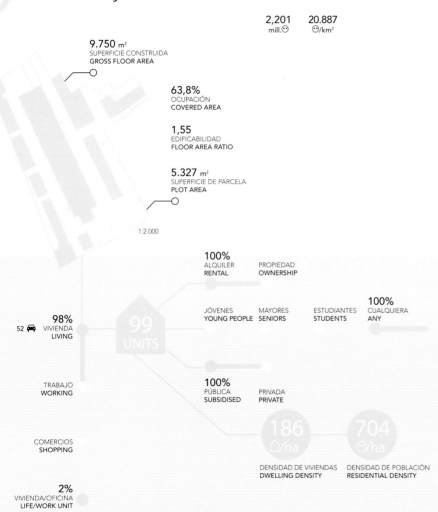

100%
ALQUILER   PROPIEDAD
RENTAL   OWNERSHIP

JÓVENES   MAYORES   ESTUDIANTES   100%
YOUNG PEOPLE SENIORS   STUDENTS   CUALQUIERA
                                          ANY

52 🚗   98%
        VIVIENDA
        LIVING

99
UNITS

TRABAJO
WORKING

100%
PÚBLICA   PRIVADA
SUBSIDISED   PRIVATE

COMERCIOS
SHOPPING

186 ⌂/ha   704 ☺/ha

DENSIDAD DE VIVIENDAS   DENSIDAD DE POBLACIÓN
DWELLING DENSITY   RESIDENTIAL DENSITY

2%
VIVIENDA/OFICINA
LIFE/WORK UNIT

El proyecto Vignoles consiste en la construcción de una manzana entera de París. Dado su tamaño, el proyecto aborda tanto la arquitectura como el urbanismo. Se sitúa en un barrio obrero, en una manzana atravesada por estrechos pasajes que proceden de la organización original del tejido urbano del barrio.

La arquitectura circundante se compone de pequeños edificios y fragmentos con mucho encanto. Se trata de una arquitectura para ser vivida y que nunca fue diseñada.

El programa incluye 100 nuevas viviendas sociales y talleres para artistas, algunos espacios comunitarios y un pequeño restaurante renovado.

Vignoles is a construction on an entire Parisian housing block. Due to its size, the project is about both urbanism and architecture.

The block of houses is not situated in Haussmannian Paris with chic boulevards as is the Fouquet's Barrière that I designed at the same time. Vignoles is situated in a picturesque and popular neighbourhood. The block is crossed by narrow alleys a couple of meters wide.

They are a relic of the bygone 'faubourg' with its fruit gardens. The surrounding architecture is of low height and is constituted of bits and pieces, little fragments that have a lot of charm. An architecture to be lived, that has never been designed.

The program comprises a hundred new social appartments and ateliers for artists, some new community rooms and a small renovated restaurant.

1:5.000
0 10   50

1.047
$/m² 1.097 €/m²

Una arquitectura específica para un contexto específico.

Las calles de la zona son estrechas y están jalonadas por edificios de diferentes alturas y vacíos por los que se accede a interiores de manzana repletos de casitas con cobertizos para conejos.

Nunca pretendimos construir nada nuevo hacia la calle, a excepción de dos invernaderos en memoria de los antiguos huertos, y que sirven como cuarto de buzones para los residentes.

El proyecto plantea un enfoque urbanístico nuevo en la ciudad, ya que mantiene la pequeña escala original del frente de la calle y densifica el interior de manzana. En este sentido, se opone a los planteamientos de Hausmann, para quien el orden y la densidad se alineaban con la calle mientras que el corazón de manzana alojaba el desorden.

El barrio cuenta con numerosas asociaciones de vecinos, cuyas opiniones fueron escuchadas a través de numerosas consultas públicas. La mayor parte del programa se sitúa en el centro, a lo largo de los pasajes originales en los que se enfrentan las viviendas adosadas con las fachadas vegetales del bloque central. Los materiales empleados son baratos, como en el resto del barrio. Así, el conjunto queda constituido por una mezcla de tejas rojas, pilares de madera, zinc, maceteros, cobre, yeso y hormigón visto.

A specific architecture for a specific context...

I love indented streets with buildings of differing heights with voids. These absences invite you to discover the interior of the housing blocks, filled with maisonettes and rabbit hutches. To demolish these rows of urban fleamarkets is not part of my job. I don't want to build anything facing the street. I leave alone the little houses worthy of a Doisneau photograph and my work is situated behind!

The only things added to the street are two greenhouses, in memory of the historic fruit gardens. They serve as mailboxes for the residents and must be the smallest street-facing constructions in all of Paris! The tenants get their mail there between banana crates and climbing vines, making bad news seem less bad.

The urbanistic approach of leaving the street frontage with its original small scale and densifying the center is new in town. It is contrary to Haussmannian belief, where order and density face the street and the wilderness is behind.

The neighbourhood has many associations whose opinions have been heard at numerous public consultations. Of course, I have been asked to favour the 'house' style over the 'apartment block' style – a phrase that makes the adjacent residents think of the atrocity of concrete... With time everything gets negociated. The density of the program is situated

Dentro de este pequeño laberinto de pasajes estrechos, no queríamos portales con ascensor sino pequeñas viviendas urbanas con jardín propio. Cada casa tiene su propia fachada y su propio material de revestimiento que lo diferencia de la fachada contigua. Mientras, una cubierta de tejas rojas unifica el conjunto. Frente a las viviendas unifamiliares, un muro vegetal disimulará las escaleras exteriores de acceso a los apartamentos que se encuentran en el bloque central de la manzana. Desde estas escaleras, numerosos puntos de vista se abren hacia el corazón del proyecto.

Las escaleras conducen a dos viviendas por nivel. Cada apartamento se abre a los lados del bloque y dispone de un balcón orientado al Sur. Este bloque central es blando en cuanto que estará recubierto por una masa vegetal y soportes de madera para el ajardinamiento. Además, su volumen longitudinal escalonado se adapta a la pendiente del terreno.

in the center, along the original alleys, where maisonettes and buildings with vegetal facades face each other. The materials used are those of the neighbourhood; poor.

The ensemble can be seen as a contextual patchwork made of prefabricated red shingles, timber pillars, zinc, flower pots, copper, whitewash plaster and coarse concrete left rough.

In this little labyrinth of narrow alleys I don't want any entry hall or elevator but little city houses with their little gardens. Every window has a cantilevered sill made of Ductal. With this device, from the inside you get the impression of thicker walls. It can also accommodate flower pots, another of my hobbies... sweet home. Every house has its own facade, its own cladding to differentiate it from the others. The ensemble is held together by a ribbon of red shingles that wraps around it.

Facing the little houses, no more apartment blocks but instead a vegetal curtain veiling oblique exterior staircases which take you gently to the sky. Thats all!

From there, numerous points of view open onto the heart of the project. The stairs lead to two appartments on each level. Each appartment has windows on both sides and a balcony oriented due South.

The central building is soft because it is wrapped with greenery and timber garden stakes. Along its length, its height is stepped in order to better embrace the sloping topography.

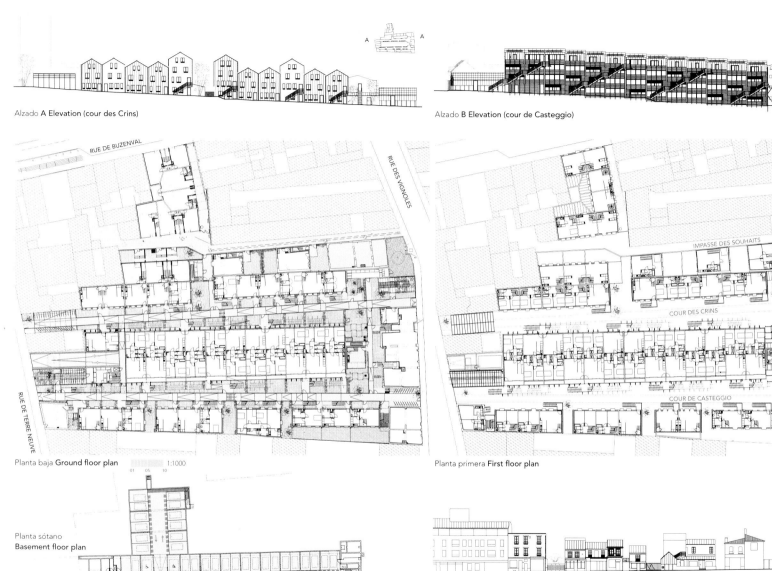

Alzado A Elevation (cour des Crins)

Alzado B Elevation (cour de Casteggio)

RUE DE BUZENVAL

RUE DES VIGNOLES

RUE DE TERRE NEUVE

IMPASSE DES SOUHAITS

COUR DES CRINS

COUR DE CASTEGGIO

Planta baja Ground floor plan   1:1000
01 05 10

Planta primera First floor plan

Planta sótano
Basement floor plan

Alzado E Elevation (rue de Vignoles)

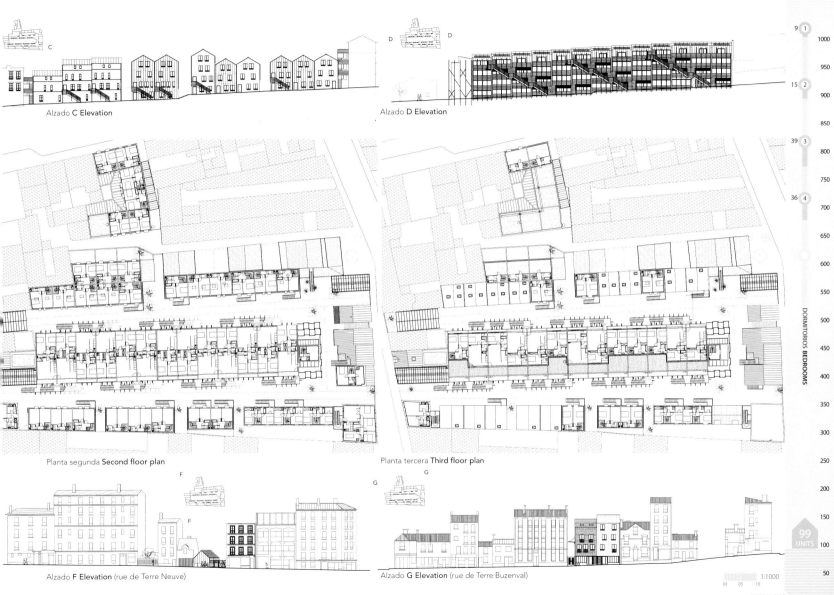

Alzado **C** Elevation

Alzado **D** Elevation

Planta segunda **Second floor plan**

Planta tercera **Third floor plan**

Alzado **F** Elevation (rue de Terre Neuve)

Alzado **G** Elevation (rue de Terre Buzenval)

DORMITORIOS **BEDROOMS**

9	1
15	2
39	3
36	4

1000
950
900
850
800
750
700
650
600
550
500
450
400
350
300
250
200
150
100
50
0
UNITS

99 UNITS

1:1000
01 05 10

Planta baja **Ground floor plan**

Planta primera **First floor plan**

Planta segunda **Second floor plan**

Planta tercera **Third floor plan**

A'
A

B'
B

C
C'

D
D'

0 1   5   10

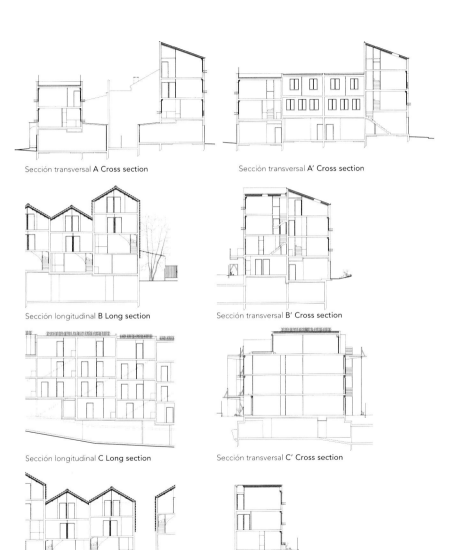

Sección transversal **A Cross section**

Sección transversal **A' Cross section**

Sección longitudinal **B Long section**

Sección transversal **B' Cross section**

Sección longitudinal **C Long section**

Sección transversal **C' Cross section**

Sección longitudinal **D Long section**

Sección transversal **D' Cross section**

LAYERS

EXTERNAL

CERÁMICA
BRICKWORK

HORMIGÓN
CONCRETE

MADERA
WOOD

CEMENTO
CEMENT

METAL
METAL

COMPUESTO
COMPOSITE

VIDRIO
GALSS

ENFOSCADO/
ESTUCO
MORTAR/
STUCCO

AISLAMIENTO
INSULATION

MEMBRANA
MEMBRANE

PRINCIPAL

CERÁMICA
BRICKWORK

VIDRIO
GALSS

HORMIGÓN
CONCRETE

MADERA
WOOD

COMPUESTO
COMPOSITE

INTERNAL

CARTÓN-YESO
PLASTER-BOARD

CERÁMICA
BRICKWORK

ENLUCIDO
PLASTER

Sección **D** Section

0 1   5   10   1:200

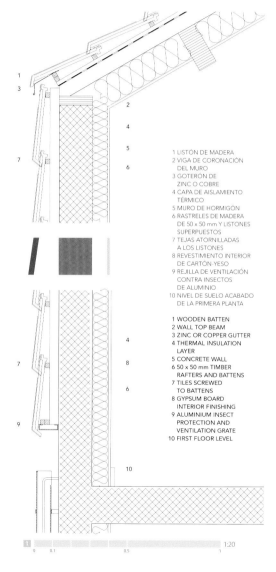

1 LISTÓN DE MADERA
2 VIGA DE CORONACIÓN
  DEL MURO
3 GOTERÓN DE
  ZINC O COBRE
4 CAPA DE AISLAMIENTO
  TÉRMICO
5 MURO DE HORMIGÓN
6 RASTRELES DE MADERA
  DE 50 x 50 mm Y LISTONES
  SUPERPUESTOS
7 TEJAS ATORNILLADAS
  A LOS LISTONES
8 REVESTIMIENTO INTERIOR
  DE CARTÓN-YESO
9 REJILLA DE VENTILACIÓN
  CONTRA INSECTOS
  DE ALUMINIO
10 NIVEL DE SUELO ACABADO
  DE LA PRIMERA PLANTA

1 WOODEN BATTEN
2 WALL TOP BEAM
3 ZINC OR COPPER GUTTER
4 THERMAL INSULATION
  LAYER
5 CONCRETE WALL
6 50 x 50 mm TIMBER
  RAFTERS AND BATTENS
7 TILES SCREWED
  TO BATTENS
8 GYPSUM BOARD
  INTERIOR FINISHING
9 ALUMINIUM INSECT
  PROTECTION AND
  VENTILATION GRATE
10 FIRST FLOOR LEVEL

0   0.1   0.5   1   1:20

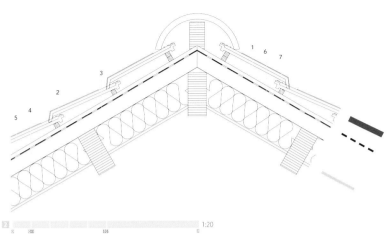

2   1:20

1 TEJA
2 ENLISTONADO DOBLE
3 VIGA DE MADERA
4 RASTREL
5 MEMBRANA
   IMPERMEABILIZANTE
6 CAPA DE AISLAMIENTO
   TÉRMICO
7 REVESTIMIENTO INTERIOR
   DE CARTÓN-YESO

1 TILE
2 WOODEN BATTENS
   (TWO LAYERS)
3 WOODEN BEAM
4 RAFTER
5 WATERPROOF MEMBRANE
6 THERMAL INSULATION
   LAYER
7 GYPSUM BOARD
   INTERIOR FINISHING

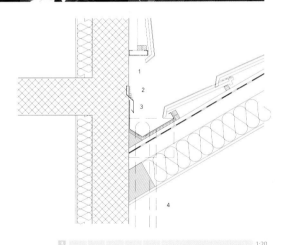

3   1:20

1 REJILLA DE VENTILACIÓN
   DE ALUMINIO CONTRA
   INSECTOS
2 TAPAJUNTAS DE MORTERO
3 CANALÓN DE ZINC
4 BAJANTE DE AGUAS
   PLUVIALES

1 ALUMINIUM INSECT
   PROTECTION AND
   VENTILATION GRATE
2 MORTAR FLASHING
3 ZINC GUTTER
4 RAIN PIPE

LAYERS

EXTERNAL

GRAVA

CERÁMICA

MADERA

CEMENTO

VEGETACIÓN

METAL

AISLAMIENTO

MEMBRANA

PRINCIPAL

HORMIGÓN

MADERA

CERÁMICA

INTERNAL

CARTÓN-YESO

ENLUCIDO

METAL

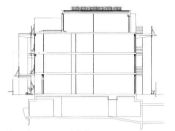

Sección transversal **C Cross section**

1:500

0   1   5   10

La fachada vegetal se planta en el terreno, desde donde miles de vides trepadoras ocuparán los postes verticales. Este andamio de madera quedará colonizado por las plantas a dos metros de la fachada.

Mientras, a ras de suelo, se plantaron plantas diminutas con certificación ecológica.

Su elección se basó en su capacidad para vivir sin necesidad de ningún fertilizante o pesticida, manteniendo sus propiedades ecológicas en el nuevo paisaje. De hecho, algunas de estas plantas poseen propiedades anti-insectos y otras tienen un tipo de hojas que funcionan como fertilizante en otoño.

Estas especies vegetales se convertirán en árboles y arbustos muy rápidamente: en tan solo tres años tendrán la robustez de cualquier planta de mayor porte que pudiera haber sido plantada desde el principio. Tanto es así que en cinco años el resultado será espectacular.

Eden Bio es un proyecto a descubrir, dentro de unos años, tras un proceso de maduración, como los buenos vinos.

The vegetal facade is planted in the ground. Thousands of wisterias will climb on as many vertically-assembled stakes. Situated every two metres between the stairs and the balconies, this scaffolding of timber pieces will be gently colonized by plants.

The ground has not been forgotten, the intersticial spaces having been carefully looked.

Watching the construction process, I realized after the excavation of the carpark that the ground was full of detritus and that it had been sprinkled with white spirit and other construction site rubbish. At the end of a project, a light coat of earth full of Monsanto chemical products is usually used to bolster plants for the handover date. This method is so anchored in the context of construction that it seems difficult to change. The result is that nothing changes. Except if... I requested that very expensive biological earth be applied in very deep coats and protected during the entire construction period. Considering the price, everyone was very careful.

At the end of construction, I planted bio-certified, very small, almost invisible plants. The choice of plants was based entirely on their capicity to live without any fertilizer or pesticides and preserve their bio caracteristics in new landscape. In fact, some plants have insect-repellent qualities and others have leaves that become fertilizer in Autumn. A real urban wilderness, self-maintained.

The smell will be bio, the fruits too.

In earth of such quality, the plants will become trees and bushes very rapidly. At the age of three, my little plants will have the strength of the most mature ones I could plant today.

In less than five years, the result will be spectacular and impossible to obtain without the extravagant soil quality we have here.

On white spirit nothing grows, it all stagnates, even with Monsanto! To be convinced, look at the new constructions next door; after 15 years after the trees have not grown one centimetre and their leaves have faded; bravo.

Two mature trunks share a single arching branch. All varieties of bio apple grow on this curiosity. Eden Bio is a project to discover, in several years, after maturation, like good wines.

1 PUERTA DE MADERA
2 PUERTA DE VIDRIO Y
CARPINTERÍA DE ALUMINIO
3 PASAMANOS DE MADERA
4 TABLERO DE MADERA
DE 144 mm DE LARGO
x 20 mm DE ANCHO
5 POSTE DE MADERA
DE 80 x 80 mm
6 DESCANSILLO
DE HORMIGÓN,
PENDIENTE 1%

1 WOODEN DOOR
2 GLASS DOOR WITH
ALUMINIUM FRAMEWORK
3 WOODEN HANDRAIL
4 140 mm LONG x 20 mm
WIDE TIMBER BOARD
5 80 x 80 mm
WOODEN POST
6 1% SLOPE CONCRETE
LANDING

1:20

0   0.1   0.5   1

0,397
mill.☺

158
☺/km²

19.400 m²
SUPERFICIE CONSTRUIDA
GROSS FLOOR AREA

5.378 m²
SUPERFICIE DE PARCELA
PLOT AREA

1:2.000

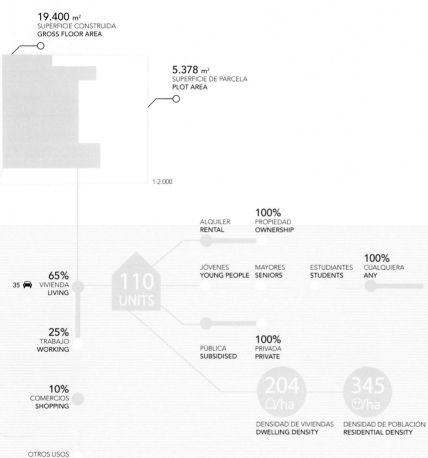

1:5.000

0   10   50

ALQUILER
RENTAL

100%
PROPIEDAD
OWNERSHIP

35 🚗 65%
VIVIENDA
LIVING

110
UNITS

JÓVENES
YOUNG PEOPLE

MAYORES
SENIORS

ESTUDIANTES
STUDENTS

100%
CUALQUIERA
ANY

25%
TRABAJO
WORKING

PÚBLICA
SUBSIDISED

100%
PRIVADA
PRIVATE

10%
COMERCIOS
SHOPPING

204
△/ha

345
☺/ha

DENSIDAD DE VIVIENDAS
DWELLING DENSITY

DENSIDAD DE POBLACIÓN
RESIDENTIAL DENSITY

OTROS USOS
OTHER USES

10.462
EEK/m²

1.050
$/m²

Edificio existente antes de la intervención
Existen building before intervantion

Hasta los años 90, el área ocupada por la antigua fábrica de celulosa de Tallinn mantuvo su carácter industrial. Esta explotación ya es mencionada en documentos históricos del año 1677. El edificio que ha sido reutilizado es obra del arquitecto E. Jacoby y se finalizó en 1926. Posteriormente, se añadieron otras construcciones durante la época soviética que en la actualidad se emplean como almacenes, viviendas modestas o simplemente están vacías.

El programa de remodelación incluye comercios y servicios en planta baja y viviendas y oficinas en las plantas superiores.

Up until the early 1990s, the entire area of the former cellulose factory in Tallinn had an industrial character. The paper factory was first mentioned in Tallinn city documents in 1677. In 1926, the cellulose factory at Tartu mnt. 84A designed by E. Jacoby was completed. Additional utilitarian factory buildings were built in the Soviet period. They are currently being used as warehouses/modest apartment space, or stand vacant. The first floor of the space to be reconstructed will house business and service areas, while higher up, there will be office space and apartments. The 9th floor of the addition is recessed slightly from the existing limestone wall, making a subtle

Una pieza nueva se añade a partir del noveno nivel, que se retranquea para permitir la transición al volumen que ocupan las plantas 10 a 14.

La nueva estructura alojará un total de 68 viviendas, 42 de ellas en el antiguo edificio de ladrillo.

La fachada de vidrio del volumen anexo es una superficie densa de varias capas. En ella, las tres variaciones de verde de los vidrios contrastan con la forma simple y rotunda del la masa existente de piedra. El resultado es una fachada pixelada que matiza la pesada fachada de piedra con nuevos detalles. Cabe destacar la rotundidad de la fachada hacia el aeropuerto, donde se ha mantenido la porción ciega que ocupa los niveles 7 y 8.

transition to the 10th through the 14th stories, which form a series of steps projecting outward from the limestone wall. The addition to the building will hold 68 apartments, 42 in the old part.

The addition's glass facade is a consistent, multi-faceted surface: three slightly different shades of green glass alternating fractally in contrast to the clear and simple form of the existing limestone mass. The resulting pixelated facade gives the heavy and visually busy limestone facades a new layeredness, rich in detail. Especially compelling is the facade on the airport side of the building, where a limestone wall—windowless in an extent of 7–8 stories—has been retained as part of the wall.

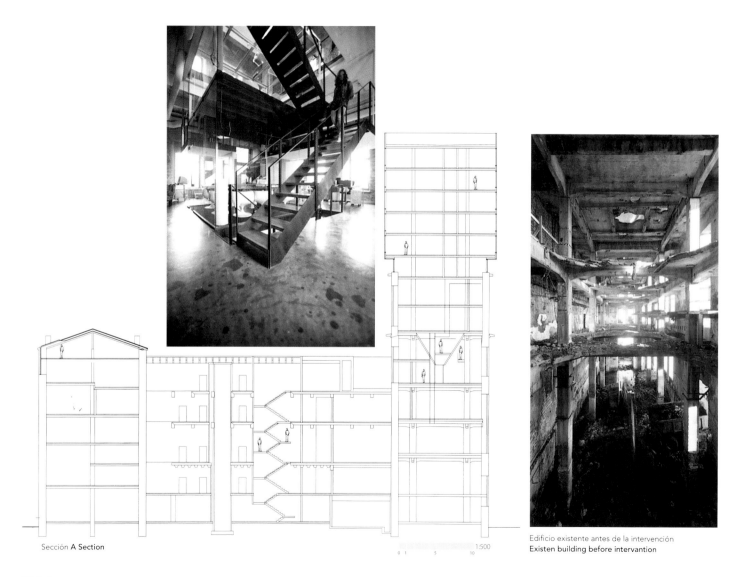

Sección **A Section**

1:500

0 1   5   10

Edificio existente antes de la intervención
Existen building before intervantion

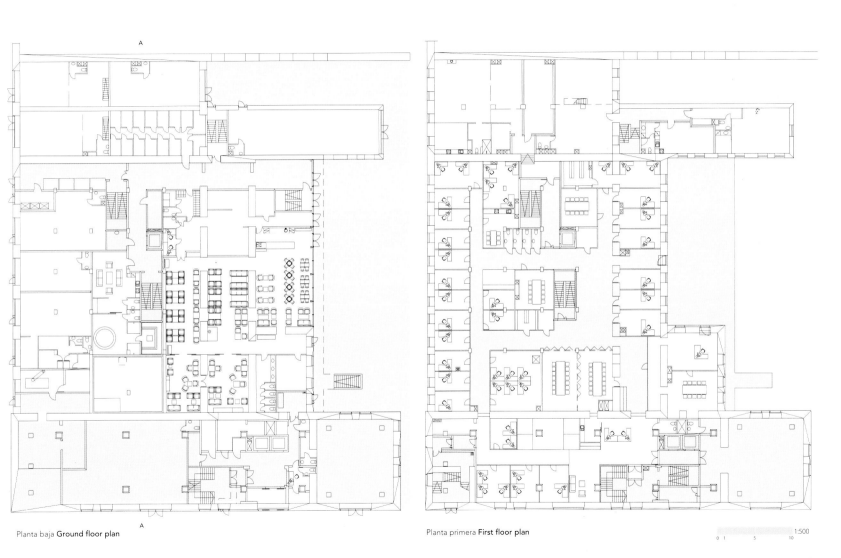

Planta baja Ground floor plan

Planta primera First floor plan

1:500

0 1   5   10

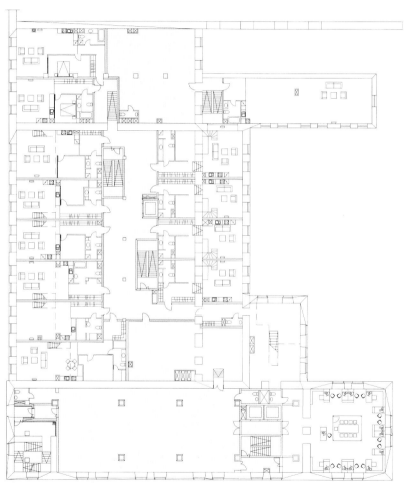

Planta segunda **Second floor plan**

Planta tercera **Third floor plan**

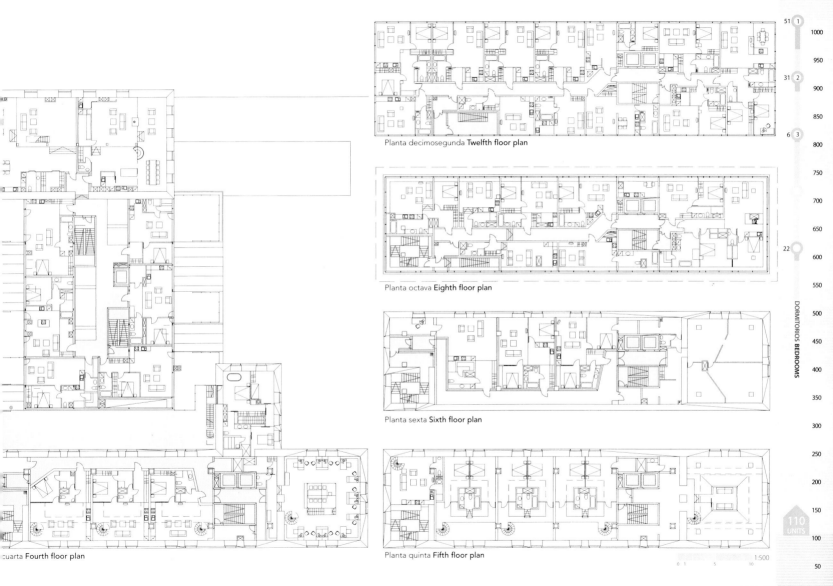

Planta decimosegunda **Twelfth floor plan**

Planta octava **Eighth floor plan**

Planta sexta **Sixth floor plan**

cuarta **Fourth floor plan**

Planta quinta **Fifth floor plan**

51 ① 1000

950

31 ② 900

850

6 ③ 800

750

700

650

22 600

550

500

450

400

350

300

250

200

150

100

DORMITORIOS **BEDROOMS**

110 UNITS

1:500

50

0 1 5 10

0

UNITS

CERÁMICA
BRICKWORK

HORMIGON
CONCRETE

MADERA
WOOD

CEMENTO
CEMENT

METAL
METAL

COMPUESTO
COMPOSITE

VIDRIO
GALSS

ENFOSCADO/
ESTUCO
**MORTAR/
STUCCO**

AISLAMIENTO
INSULATION

MEMBRANA
MEMBRANE

CERÁMICA
BRICKWORK

VIDRIO
GALSS

HORMIGON
CONCRETE

MADERA
WOOD

COMPUESTO
COMPOSITE

CARTÓN-YESO
PLASTER-BOARD

CERÁMICA
BRICKWORK

ENLUCIDO
PLASTER

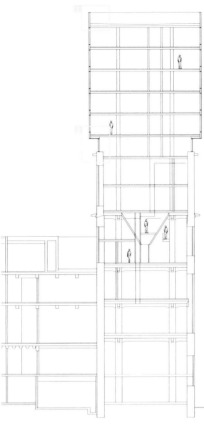

Sección **A Section**   1:500

0 1   5   10

1 MEMBRANA
  IMPERMEABILIZANTE
  DE PVC
2 TABLERO DE FIBRA
  MINERAL e=30 mm
3 CAPA DE AISLAMIENTO
  TÉRMICO e=150 mm
4 CAPA DE GRAVA
  PARA FORMACIÓN
  DE PENDIENTES
5 BARRERA DE VAPOR
6 LOSA DE HORMIGÓN
  ARMADOe=260 mm
7 DOBLE ACRISTALAMIENTO
  DE CAPA INTERIOR
  REVESTIDA CON UNA
  LAMINA DE COLOR
8 CAPA DE AISLAMIENTO
  TÉRMICO e=80 mm
9 SUBESTIMIENTO DE
  ACERO PARA LOS

PANELES DE CARTÓN
YESO CON CAPA DE
AISLAMIENTO e=35 mm
10 CARTÓN YESO e=13 mm
11 PANEL DE ESTANQUEIDAD
  e=20 mm
12 SOLADO
13 CARTÓN YESO e=15 mm
14 CAPA DE AISLAMIENTO
  ACÚSTICO e=20 mm
15 4 CAPAS DE AISLAMIENTO
  TÉRMICO e=50 mm CON
  UNA LÁMINA DE PAPEL
  ENTRE CADA CAPA
16 REVESTIMIENTO DE
  PANELES DE ALUMINIO
  ANODIZADO e=3 mm
17 ALFÉIZAR METÁLICO
18 MURO DE PIEDRA
  CALIZA DE 60 A 120
  mm DE ESPESOR

1 PVC WATERPROOFING
  LAYER
2 30 mm THICK HARD
  MINERAL-FIBRE BOARD
3 150 mm THICK THERMAL
  INSULATION LAYER
4 LIGHTWEIGHT GRAVEL
  FOR SLOPE
5 VAPOUR BARRIER
6 260 mm THICK IN
  SITU REINFORCED
  CONCRETE SLAB
7 DOUBLE-GLAZING
  FACADE WITH COLOUR-
  COATED INNER PANEL
8 80 mm THICK THERMAL
  INSULATION LAYER
9 STEEL FRAMING FOR
  PLASTER BOARD WITH
  35 mm THICK THERMAL
  INSULATION IN BETWEEN

10 13 mm THICK
  PLASTER BOARD
11 20 mm THICK WIND
  PROOFING
12 FLOORING
13 15 mm THICK
  PLASTERBOARD
14 20 mm THICK IMPACT-
  SOUND INSULATION
15 4 LAYERS OF 50 mm
  THICK THERMAL
  INSULATION WITH PAPER
  BETWEEN LAYERS
16 3 mm THICK ANODISED
  ALUMINIUM SHEETING
17 METAL WINDOWSILL
18 60-120 cm THICK
  LIMESTONE WALL

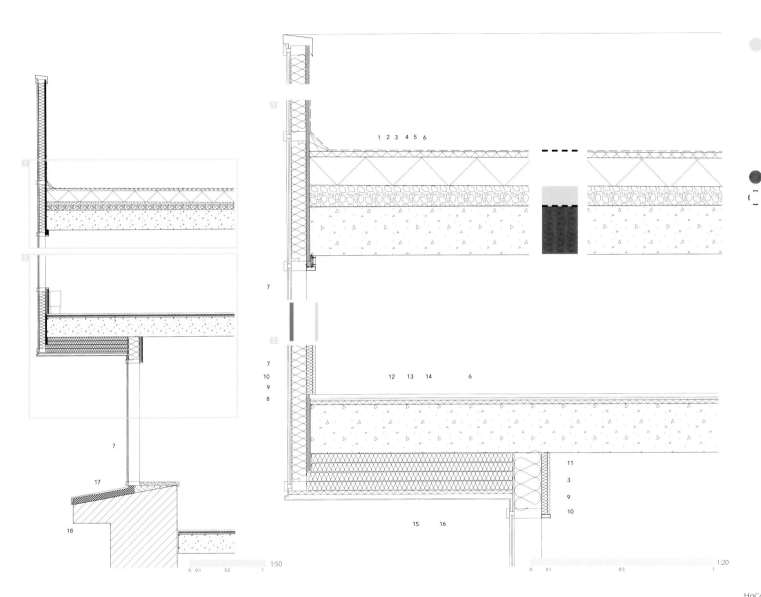

GRAVA
GRAVEL

CERÁMICA
TERRACOTTA

MADERA
WOOD

CEMENTO
CEMENT

VEGETACIÓN
PLANTING

METAL
METAL

AISLAMIENTO
INSULATION

MEMBRANA
MEMBRANE

HORMIGÓN
CONCRETE

MADERA
WOOD

CERÁMICA
TERRACOTTA

CARTÓN-YESO
PLASTER-BOARD

ENLUCIDO
PLASTER

METAL
METAL

1 2 3 4 5 6

7

7
10
9
8

12   13   14   6

11

3

9

10

15   16

7

17

18

1:50

0 0.1   0.5   1

1:20

0 0.1   0.5   1

0,755 mill.☺ **3.449** ☺/km²

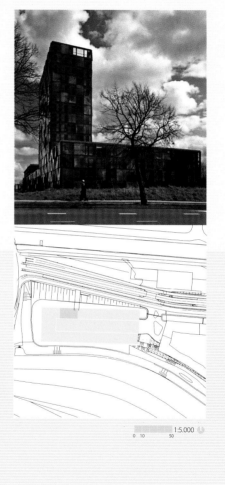

22.070 m²
SUPERFICIE CONSTRUIDA
GROSS FLOOR AREA

5.200 m²
SUPERFICIE DE PARCELA
PLOT AREA

100%
OCUPACIÓN
COVERED AREA

4,24
EDIFICABILIDAD
FLOOR AREA RATIO

1:2.000

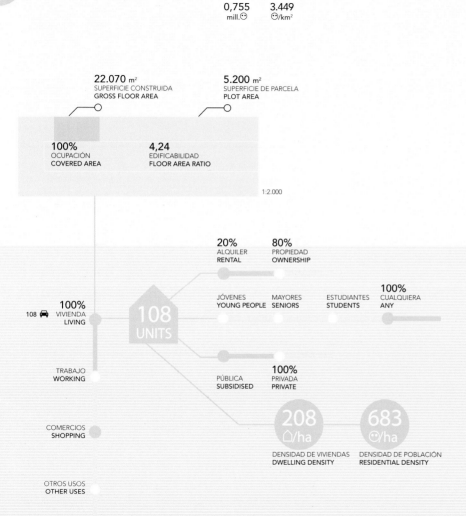

20%
ALQUILER
RENTAL

80%
PROPIEDAD
OWNERSHIP

108 🚗

100%
VIVIENDA
LIVING

108
UNITS

JÓVENES
YOUNG PEOPLE

MAYORES
SENIORS

ESTUDIANTES
STUDENTS

100%
CUALQUIERA
ANY

TRABAJO
WORKING

PÚBLICA
SUBSIDISED

100%
PRIVADA
PRIVATE

COMERCIOS
SHOPPING

208
⌂/ha

683
☺/ha

OTROS USOS
OTHER USES

DENSIDAD DE VIVIENDAS
DWELLING DENSITY

DENSIDAD DE POBLACIÓN
RESIDENTIAL DENSITY

1:5.000
0 10   50

1.089
$/m²
€/m²

20

El sector Science Park se encuentra entre el parque Flevopark, el barrio Indische y la línea férrea que une Amsterdam con Amesfoort. Hasta hace poco tiempo, la zona estaba ocupada por huertos familiares esparcidos entre centros de investigación y empresas de I+D. Sólo era accesible a través de un largo túnel bajo las vías del tren.

Sin embargo, en la actualidad, y gracias a una nueva calle, el área ha sido conectada con la ciudad. Un conjunto de cinco edificios constituye este desarrollo residencial. Uno de ellos, Het Kasteel (El Castillo), se sitúa en el extremo oeste de Science Park y ejerce el papel de tarjeta de visita de la nueva zona.

Vidrio

Las parcelas para construir nuevas viviendas son un bien escaso en Ámsterdam. En este caso, tuvimos que enfrentarnos a numerosos condicionantes relativos a la contaminación acústica, la seguridad y la calidad del aire. El proyecto se encuentra junto a un centro de mantenimiento ferroviario. Como consecuencia del ruido, fue necesario desarrollar una fachada única que lo amortiguase. El resultado es un envoltorio de paneles de vidrio con ligeras variaciones de inclinación entre unos y otros, que convierten al edificio en un gran volumen cristalográfico.

The Science Park lies between the Flevopark, the neighborhood of the Indische buurt and the Amsterdam-Amersfoort railway line. Until recently, the site was occupied by allotments alongside research institutes and science & technology companies. The Science Park was hidden in the city. It was only accessible by a long tunnel under the shunting yard. Now, by means of a new street, the area is connected to the city. An ensemble of five buildings forms a new living area on this spot. Het Kasteel (The Castle) is situated on the extreme Westside of the Science Park and functions as the calling card of the area.

Crystal

Sites where you can build dwellings have become a scarce good in Amsterdam. We deal with complex confrontations with sound outlines, security circles and air quality requirements. Het Kasteel lies in a new living area that is situated in the eastern part of Amsterdam. The building stands besides a large shunting yard. The requirement to make a sound baffle apart from the building, has conducted to a unique facade. The building is enveloped in a glazed skin of panels that are slightly angled to each other. This artifice lends the building the appearance of a gigantic crystal.

Castillo

El edificio, rodeado de agua, consta de una torre de 45 m que se levanta sobre un zócalo de 4 plantas.

Los peatones y los ciclistas acceden a través de un puente al patio interior: una plataforma de madera con aperturas al aparcamiento y entrada a todas las viviendas. El tamaño y tipología de dichas viviendas es variable: hay viviendas en planta baja, en dos plantas, apartamentos en galería y viviendas en la torre. En cada una de ellas, y pese al problema del sonido, hemos conseguido crear un espacio al aire libre con ventilación natural.

Piel

Con el fin de integrar el alto grado de aislamiento acústico necesario y los criterios estéticos, decidimos emplear un sistema de paneles de vidrio en fachada, una segunda piel que genera un espacio intermedio. Las juntas entre piezas permiten el paso del aire y por consiguiente la ventilación natural del edificio. Por su parte, y para dar una sensación de calidez al proyecto, la fachada interior ha sido revestida con madera.

Este sistema de piel exterior de vidrio encarecía notablemente los costes de construcción, y por este motivo elegimos la solución más económica para poder invertir el presupuesto en la calidad de las viviendas.

Castle

The by water surrounded building consists of a 45 m high tower standing on a four to five-storey base. Pedestrians and cyclists access the internal courtyard via a bridge. On this half-open wooden deck are the entries to all dwellings.

The dwellings vary in size and typology. There are ground-tied dwellings, upstairs-downstairs dwellings, gallery apartments and tower apartments in a two-some. Despite the sound problem we have managed to create an outdoor space for every dwelling and by developing a new system, all spaces are naturally ventilated.

Skin

To combine a high level of sound insulation with aesthetics we have chosen for glazed cassettes that can be attached to the dwellings. Through this a double facade with a cavity is generated. The joints between the cassettes enable the natural ventilation of the building. To create a warm expression, the inner (thermal) facade is covered with wood.

The extra facade contributes enormously to the costs of the building. Hence, it was chosen to design the framework as simple as possible so that the budget could be spent on the quality of the dwellings.

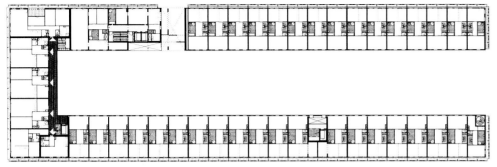

Planta primera First floor plan

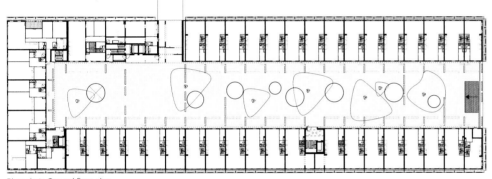

Planta baja Ground floor plan

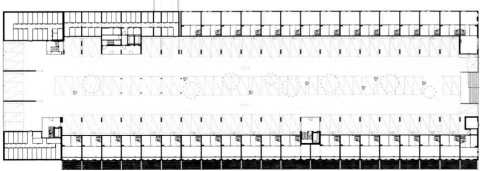

Planta sótano (nivel de aparcamiento) Basement floor plan (parking level)

1:1000
01 05 10

Llegar a casa

El diseño del edificio pretende estimular las relaciones sociales e interpersonales entre los residentes. Por este motivo pensamos en abrir un patio interior que funciona como centro del proyecto, un espacio informal y protegido para el encuentro por el que se accede a todas las viviendas.

Los portales están revestidos de vidrio de color que iluminan el patio durante la noche. Mientras, el aparcamiento se sitúa por debajo para que los coches no se vean y se ha revestido de madera como el resto de portales.

Las perforaciones en el patio permiten la entrada de luz hasta el interior y se han plantado varios árboles. En resumen, lo que desde fuera puede parecer un castillo de hielo ofrece una cálida bienvenida al interior.

El proyecto Het Kasteel demuestra así que un área residual de la ciudad puede convertirse en una ubicación óptima.

Coming home

The building's design had to stimulate social and interpersonal relationships between the inhabitants. The idea of designing an inner courtyard derived from this concept. It is the heart of the building and an informal, protected space, where people meet. All dwellings are entered through this inner court, which works as an extra invitation to social encounters.

The central entry halls are visible by coloured glazed walls that work, especially at night, as lanterns for the inner court. Underneath the wooden deck of the inner court is a car park so cars can be parked out of sight. The garage is designed like an entry hall with wooden walls, trees and daylight through the ceiling. What from the outside gives the impression of an ice castle contains a warm welcome on the inside. Het Kasteel shows in this way that it's possible to transform an apparently unusable location into a top spot.

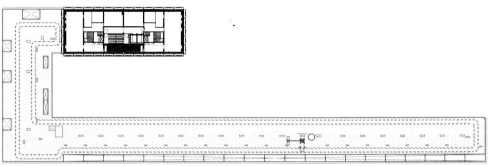

Planta 4ª-12ª **4th-12th floor plan**

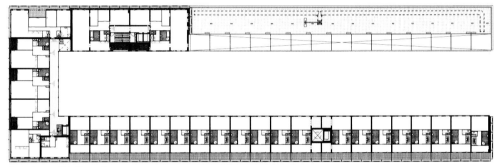

Planta tercera **Third floor plan**

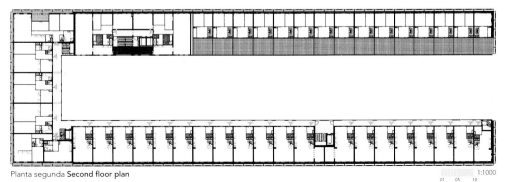

Planta segunda **Second floor plan**

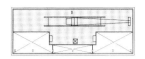

Planta de cubierta **Roof plan**

Planta 14ª **14th floor plan**

Planta 13ª **13th floor plan**

DORMITORIOS BEDROOMS

1000
950
900
850
800
750
700
650
600
550
500
450
400
350
300
250
200
150
100
50
0

UNITS

10 1
35 2
48 3
15 4

108 UNITS

1:1000
01 05 10

A

A

Sección A Section

1:1000
01   05   10

Duplex

+3

Cuadruplex

+2

+2

1:500
0 1   5   10

Torre de apartamentos
Tower apartments

+14

+13

Triplex

+1

+1

+12
+4

1:500
0 1   5   10

Vivienda en esquina
Apartment at the corner

+3
0

0

0

-1

-1

B

B

Sección B Section

1:1000
01   05   10

LAYERS

EXTERNAL

CERÁMICA
BRICKWORK

HORMIGON
CONCRETE

MADERA
WOOD

CEMENTO
CEMENT

METAL
METAL

COMPUESTO
COMPOSITE

VIDRIO
GALSS

ENFOSCADO/
ESTUCO
**MORTAR/
STUCCO**

AISLAMIENTO
INSULATION

MEMBRANA
MEMBRANE

PRINCIPAL

CERÁMICA
BRICKWORK

VIDRIO
GALSS

HORMIGON
CONCRETE

MADERA
WOOD

COMPUESTO
COMPOSITE

INTERNAL

CARTÓN-YESO
PLASTER-BOARD

CERÁMICA
BRICKWORK

ENLUCIDO
PLASTER

FACHADA FACADE

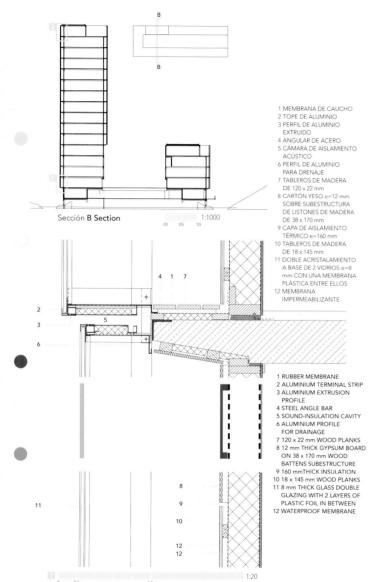

Sección B Section   1:1000

01 05 10

1 MEMBRANA DE CAUCHO
2 TOPE DE ALUMINIO
3 PERFIL DE ALUMINIO
   EXTRUIDO
4 ANGULAR DE ACERO
5 CÁMARA DE AISLAMIENTO
   ACÚSTICO
6 PERFIL DE ALUMINIO
   PARA DRENAJE
7 TABLEROS DE MADERA
   DE 120 x 22 mm
8 CARTÓN YESO e=12 mm
   SOBRE SUBESTRUCTURA
   DE LISTONES DE MADERA
   DE 38 x 170 mm
9 CAPA DE AISLAMIENTO
   TÉRMICO e=160 mm
10 TABLEROS DE MADERA
   DE 18 x 145 mm
11 DOBLE ACRISTALAMIENTO
   A BASE DE 2 VIDRIOS e=8
   mm CON UNA MEMBRANA
   PLÁSTICA ENTRE ELLOS
12 MEMBRANA
   IMPERMEABILIZANTE

1 RUBBER MEMBRANE
2 ALUMINIUM TERMINAL STRIP
3 ALUMINIUM EXTRUSION
   PROFILE
4 STEEL ANGLE BAR
5 SOUND-INSULATION CAVITY
6 ALUMINIUM PROFILE
   FOR DRAINAGE
7 120 x 22 mm WOOD PLANKS
8 12 mm THICK GYPSUM BOARD
   ON 38 x 170 mm WOOD
   BATTENS SUBESTRUCTURE
9 160 mm THICK INSULATION
10 18 x 145 mm WOOD PLANKS
11 8 mm THICK GLASS DOUBLE
   GLAZING WITH 2 LAYERS OF
   PLASTIC FOIL IN BETWEEN
12 WATERPROOF MEMBRANE

1:20

0 0.1 0.5 1

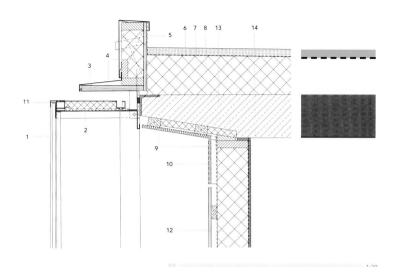

1:20

0   0.1   0.5   1

1 DOBLE ACRISTALAMIENTO
A BASE DE DOS VIDRIOS
e= 8 mm CON UNA
MEMBRANA PLÁSTICA
ENTRE ELLOS
2 CAJA DE VENTANA
CON REVESTIMIENTO
EXTERIOR DE PANELES DE
ALUMINIO PERFORADOS
e=2 mm, RELLENA DE
AISLAMIENTO ACÚSTICO
3 TABLERO CONTRACHAPADO
e=25 mm
4 REVESTIMIENTO DE CHAPA
DE ALUMINIO COLOREADA
5 TABLERO CONTRACHAPADO
e=18 mm
6 VEGETACIÓN DEL
GÉNERO SEDUM
7 MEMBRANA DE
IMPERMEABILIZACIÓN
8 CAPA DE AISLAMIENTO
TÉRMICO
9 PANEL DE CEMENTO e=8 mm
10 MEMBRANA
IMPERMEABILIZANTE,
TRANSMISORA DEL VAPOR
Y REFLECTORA DEL CALOR
11 TOPE DE ALUMINIO
12 TABLEROS DE MADERA
DE 18 x 145 mm
13 HORMIGÓN
14 ENLUCIDO

1 8 mm THICK GLASS DOUBLE
GLAZING WITH 2 LAYERS OF
PLASTIC FOIL IN BETWEEN
2 SANDWICH CASSETTE
WITH EXTERNAL CLADDING
OF 2 mm THICK PARTLY
PERFORATED ALUMINIUM
PLATE, AND ACOUSTIC
INSULATION FILLING
3 25 mm THICK PLYWOOD
4 FOLDED ALUMINIUM
COVERING, COATED
IN COLOUR
5 18 mm THICK PLYWOOD
6 MOS-SEDUM
7 WATERPROOF MEMBRANE
8 THERMAL INSULATION
LAYER
9 8 mm THICK CEMENT
BOARD
10 WATERPROOF, VAPOUR
TRANSMITTING, HEAT
REFLECTING LAYER
11 ALUMINIUM TERMINAL STRIP
12 18 x 145 mm WOOD PLANKS
13 CONCRETE
14 RENDERING

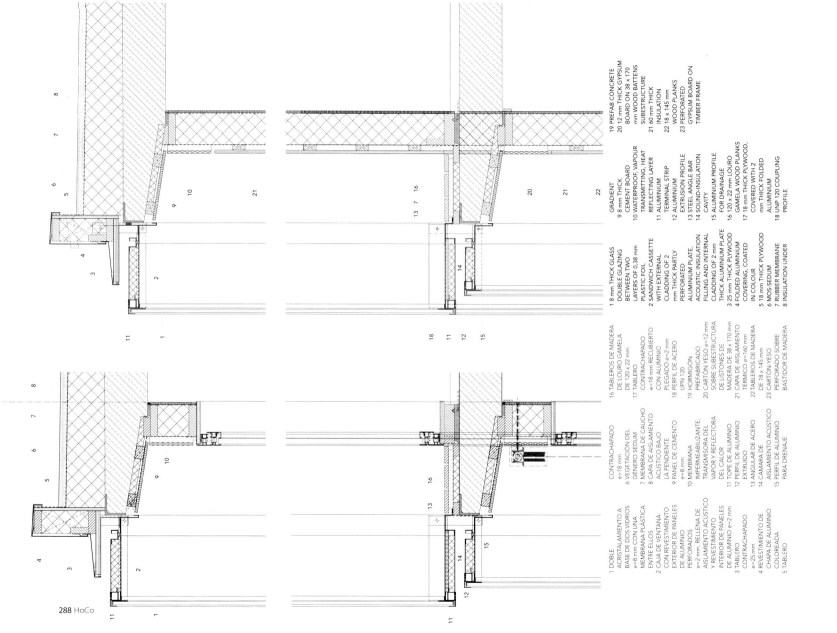

1 DOUBLE GLAZING BETWEEN TWO LAYERS OF 0.38 mm PLASTIC FOIL.
2 SANDWICH CASSETTE WITH EXTERNAL CLADDING OF 2 mm THICK PERFORATED ALUMINIUM PLATE, ACOUSTIC INSULATION FILLING AND INTERNAL CLADDING OF 2 mm THICK ALUMINIUM PLATE
3 25 mm THICK PLYWOOD
4 FOLDED ALUMINIUM COVERING, COATED IN COLOUR
5 18 mm THICK PLYWOOD
6 MOS-SEDUM
7 RUBBER MEMBRANE
8 INSULATION UNDER

9 8 mm THICK CEMENT BOARD
10 WATERPROOF VAPOUR TRANSMITTING, HEAT REFLECTING LAYER
11 ALUMINIUM TERMINAL STRIP
12 ALUMINIUM EXTRUSION PROFILE
13 STEEL ANGLE BAR
14 SOUND-INSULATION CAVITY
15 ALUMINIUM PROFILE FOR DRAINAGE
16 120 x 22 mm LOURO GAMELA WOOD PLANKS
17 18 mm THICK PLYWOOD, COVERED WITH 2 mm THICK FOLDED ALUMINIUM
18 UNP 120 COUPLING PROFILE

GRADIENT
1 8 mm THICK GLASS

19 PREFAB CONCRETE
20 12 mm THICK GYPSUM BOARD ON 38 x 170 mm WOOD BATTENS SUBSTRUCTURE
21 60 mm THICK INSULATION
22 18 x 145 mm WOOD PLANKS
23 PERFORATED GYPSUM BOARD ON TIMBER FRAME

1 DOBLE ACRISTALAMIENTO A BASE DE DOS VIDRIOS e=8 mm CON UNA MEMBRANA PLÁSTICA ENTRE ELLOS
2 CAJA DE VENTANA
3 TABLERO CONTRACHAPADO e=25 mm
4 REVESTIMIENTO DE CHAPA DE ALUMINIO COLOREADA
5 TABLERO CONTRACHAPADO e=18 mm
6 VEGETACIÓN DEL GÉNERO SEDUM
7 MEMBRANA DE CAUCHO
8 CAPA DE AISLAMIENTO ACÚSTICO BAJO
9 PANEL DE CEMENTO e=8 mm
10 MEMBRANA IMPERMEABILIZANTE, TRANSMISORA DEL VAPOR Y REFLECTORA DEL CALOR
11 TOPE DE ALUMINIO
12 PERFIL DE ALUMINIO EXTRUIDO
13 ANGULAR DE ACERO
14 CÁMARA DE AISLAMIENTO ACÚSTICO
15 PERFIL DE ALUMINIO PARA DRENAJE

16 TABLEROS DE MADERA DE LOURO GAMELA DE 120 x 22 mm
17 TABLERO CONTRACHAPADO e=18 mm RECUBIERTO CON ALUMINIO PLEGADO e=2 mm
18 PERFIL DE ACERO UPN 120
19 HORMIGÓN PREFABRICADO
20 CARTÓN YESO e=12 mm SOBRE SUBESTRUCTURA DE LISTONES DE MADERA DE 38 x 170 mm
21 CAPA DE AISLAMIENTO TÉRMICO e=160 mm
22 TABLEROS DE MADERA DE 18 x 145 mm
23 CARTÓN-YESO PERFORADO SOBRE BASTIDOR DE MADERA

CON REVESTIMIENTO EXTERIOR DE PANELES DE ALUMINIO PERFORADOS e=2 mm, RELLENA DE AISLAMIENTO ACÚSTICO Y REVESTIMIENTO INTERIOR DE PANELES DE ALUMINIO e=2 mm
LA PENDIENTE

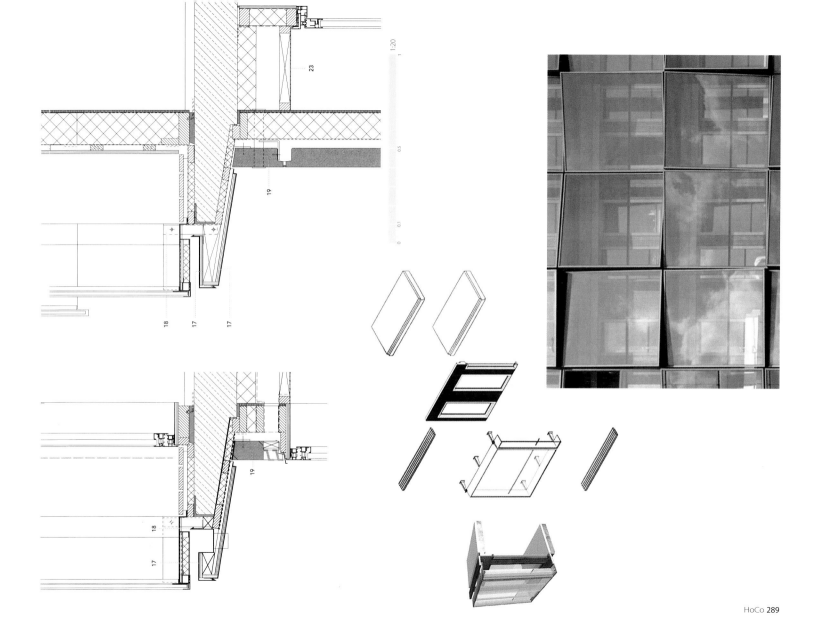

0,033
mill.☺

3.638
☺/km²

19.800 m²
SUPERFICIE CONSTRUIDA
GROSS FLOOR AREA

40,3%
OCUPACIÓN
COVERED AREA

2,34
EDIFICABILIDAD
FLOOR AREA RATIO

6.200 m²
SUPERFICIE DE PARCELA
PLOT AREA

1:2.000

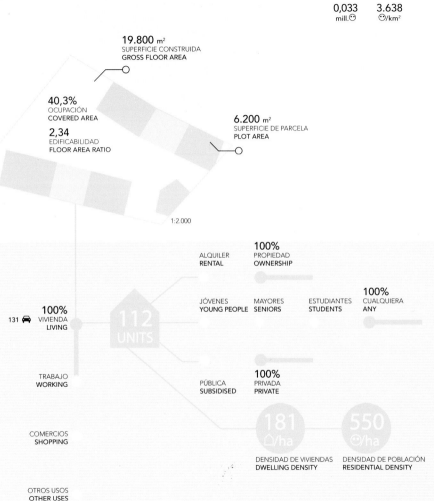

ALQUILER
RENTAL

100%
PROPIEDAD
OWNERSHIP

JÓVENES
YOUNG PEOPLE

MAYORES
SENIORS

ESTUDIANTES
STUDENTS

100%
CUALQUIERA
ANY

131 🚗 **100%**
VIVIENDA
LIVING

112 UNITS

TRABAJO
WORKING

PÚBLICA
SUBSIDISED

100%
PRIVADA
PRIVATE

COMERCIOS
SHOPPING

181 🏠/ha

550 ☺/ha

DENSIDAD DE VIVIENDAS
DWELLING DENSITY

DENSIDAD DE POBLACIÓN
RESIDENTIAL DENSITY

OTROS USOS
OTHER USES

1:5.000
0 10   50

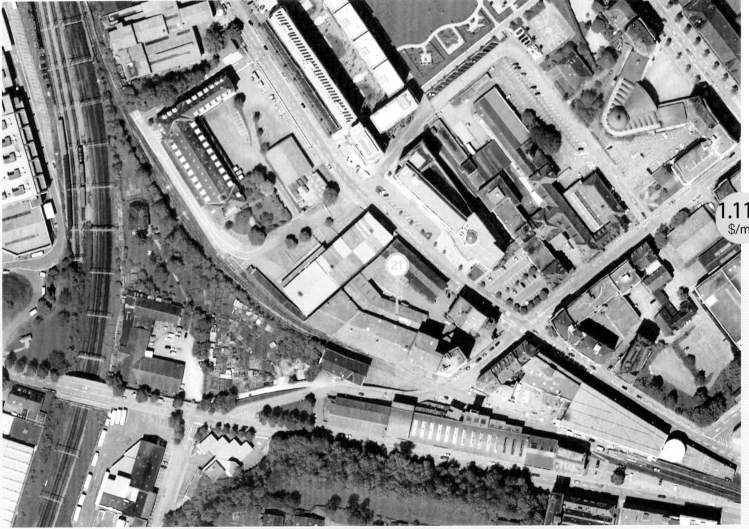

1.960
CHF/m² 2.000

1.115
$/m²

El conjunto se sitúa en una antigua zona industrial limitada por una avenida y las antiguas vías del ferrocarril.

El enfoque urbanístico del proyecto tiene básicamente dos objetivos: El primero es una reinterpretación topológica de una manzana cerrada, que se corta para abrir paisajes y vistas. Mediante estos cortes, la manzana cerrada se abre.

Esta operación tiene como resultado la aparición de dos tipos de espacios públicos al interior: uno más urbano, a nivel de la ciudad, que concentra los accesos al aparcamiento, y otro más rural situado en una cota superior.

El segundo objetivo consiste en subrayar los límites convergentes de la parcela mediante la colocación de los volúmenes sobre la alineación. La ausencia de paralelismo volverá a aparecer en la distribución en planta de los cuatro nuevos módulos y del silo.

Los 4 Módulos

La villa urbana del siglo XIX, en tanto que unidad residencial aislada, es el motivo de inspiración para los módulos. La idea tipológica básica para los cuatro parte de la intersección de los espacios principales (el salón y el pasillo de distribución). Es en la intersección de esos espacios donde se sitúa la estancia exterior, la logia.

Este principio se extiende a todos los tipos y tamaños de apartamentos (dúplex y en una planta). Aunque haya variaciones dependiendo del tipo, cuando uno entra en la vivienda, siempre es guiado hacia la logia.

El Silo

El silo es un antiguo depósito de grano construido en los años 60. Para convertirlo en edificio de viviendas fue necesario introducir un núcleo central de comunicación e instalaciones que no es paralelo a las fachadas. El resultado es que las perspectivas dentro de las viviendas van cambiando considerablemente a medida que las recorremos.

La composición de la fachada responde a un determinado algoritmo con el que un mismo hueco se abre en el alzado de forma vertical u horizontal para acabar por borrar la separación entre niveles del interior. La superposición de cuatro nuevos niveles sobre la estructura existente permite una división clásica de la fachada en basa, fuste y capitel. Por su parte, la cubierta ajardinada se ha dividido en cuatro terrazas privadas.

The urbanistic setting had basiaclly two intentions.

The first one is a topological reinterpretation of the perimeter block. The perimeter block is cutted, leading to passages and views. By cutting it, the perimeter block becomes an 'open one'.

Together with the topological situation this leads to two different squares and accesses: an 'urban' one on the level of the city including a parking lot and a 'rural' one on the higher level.

The ensemble was built on a former industrial zone that resembles the shape of a banana. The shape of the industrial zone is defined by the former course of the train tracks and the street.

The second intention of the urban setting was to follow or highlight the edges of this banana shape by assembling the volumes nonparallel on the borders of this parcel. The motive of non-parallelism reappears like a red string in different variations of the floor plans of the four modules and the silo.

The 4 Modules

The urban villa, as a free standing residential home was the reference point for the 'modules'. The urban villa dates back to the 19th century. The basic typological idea of the four 'modules' was the intersection of the main spaces (f.e. living room and the hallway).

The point of intersection is marked by the exterior room, the *loggia*. This principle stays the same throughout all the apartment sizes and apartment types (duplex and flat).

Entering the apartment one is guided towards this exterior room, with variations on level 1 and 2. In the duplex apartments the basic idea of the overlapping axis is rotated symmetrically on the second floor, so that the second *loggia* which marks the intersection point of the two axis again is oriented differently. The second *loggia* is flanked by two (bed) rooms.

The Silo

This is a former grain silo that was built in the sixties. Conversing the silo into living space, a rotated nucleus was introduced facing towards the outer walls. Through this the perspectives change considerably when walking through the rooms in one or the other direction around the nucleus.

The composition of the facade underlies an algorithm and the same window is cut out of the facade repeatedly either vertically or horizontally thereby blurring the visibility of the individual floors. Through the addition of four stories the facade receives the classical tripartite division of base, shaft and capitol. The roof is used for eight private roof-gardens.

Alzado oeste
West elevation

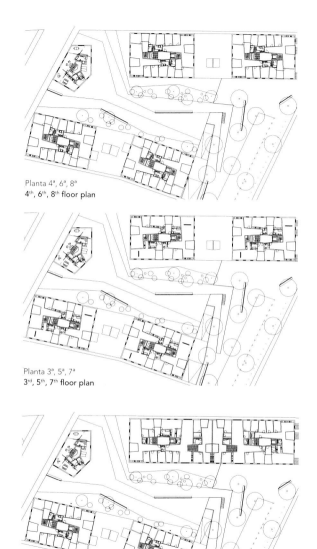

Planta 4ª, 6ª, 8ª
4th, 6th, 8th floor plan

Planta 3ª, 5ª, 7ª
3rd, 5th, 7th floor plan

Planta segunda
Second floor plan

0 5 10   1:500

Planta primera **First floor plan**

Planta baja **Ground floor plan**

0 5 10   1:500

Planta superior **Upper floor plan**

Planta inferior **Lower floor plan**   1:500

Planta tipo torre **Tower type plan**   1:500

DORMITORIOS **BEDROOMS**

		UNITS
12	1	1000
		950
22	2	900
		850
41	3	800
		750
20	4	700
		650
17		600
		550
		500
		450
		400
		350
		300
		250
		200
		150
		100
		50
		0

112 UNITS

LAYERS

EXTERNAL

CERÁMICA
BRICKWORK

HORMIGON
CONCRETE

MADERA
WOOD

CEMENTO
CEMENT

METAL
METAL

COMPUESTO
COMPOSITE

VIDRIO
GALSS

ENFOSCADO/
ESTUCO
**MORTAR/
STUCCO**

AISLAMIENTO
INSULATION

MEMBRANA
MEMBRANE

PRINCIPAL

CERÁMICA
BRICKWORK

VIDRIO
GALSS

HORMIGON
CONCRETE

MADERA
WOOD

COMPUESTO
COMPOSITE

INTERNAL

CARTÓN-YESO
PLASTER-BOARD

CERÁMICA
BRICKWORK

ENLUCIDO
PLASTER

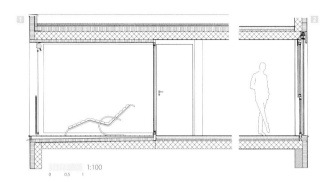

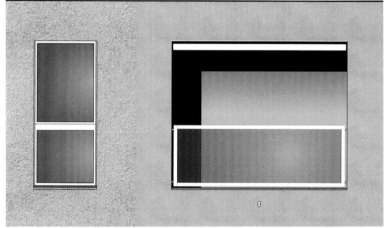

1 CAPA DE PROTECCIÓN DE GRAVA	1 GRAVEL PROTECTION LAYER
2 IMPERMEABILIZANTE	2 WATERPROOF MEMBRANE
3 CAPA DE AISLAMIENTO TÉRMICO DE POLIESTIRENO EXTRUIDO Y BARRERA DE VAPOR	3 THERMAL INSULATION LAYER AND VAPOUR BARRIER
4 FORJADO DE HORMIGÓN ARMADO	4 REINFORCED CONCRETE SLAB
5 AISLAMIENTO TÉRMICO	5 SECONDARY THERMAL INSULATION LAYER
6 ENLUCIDO DE YESO	6 PLASTER RENDERING
7 ENFOSCADO DE 1 mm A 3 mm DE ESPESOR, PINTADO	7 PAINT LAYER, 1 TO 3 mm THICK MORTAR RENDERING
8 CAPA DE AISLAMIENTO TÉRMICO DE LANA DE ROCA, CAPA DE FIJACIÓN	8 ROCKWOOL THEMAL INSULATION LAYER, FICXING LAYER
9 MURO DE LADRILLO	9 BRICKWORK WALL

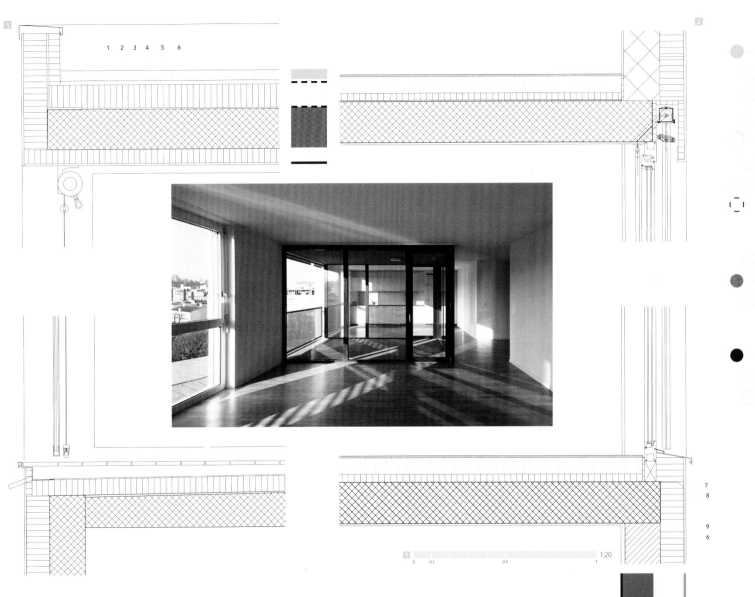

1 2 3 4 5 6

LAYERS

EXTERNAL

GRAVA
GRAVEL

CERÁMICA
TERRACOTTA

MADERA
WOOD

CEMENTO
CEMENT

VEGETACIÓN
PLANTING

METAL
METAL

AISLAMIENTO
INSULATION

MEMBRANA
MEMBRANE

PRINCIPAL

HORMIGÓN
CONCRETE

MADERA
WOOD

CERÁMICA
TERRACOTTA

INTERNAL

CARTÓN-YESO
PLASTER-BOARD

ENLUCIDO
PLASTER

METAL
METAL

CUBIERTA ROOF

7
8

9
6

0   0.1   0.5   1   1:20

ANA architecten ana.nl Amsterdam. THE NETHERLANDS, 2007 Jacob van Lennepstraat 271, Lootsbuurt

0,755
mill.☺

3.449
☺/km²

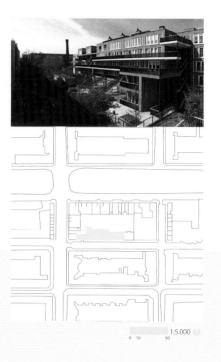

1.370 m²
SUPERFICIE DE PARCELA
PLOT AREA

4.590 m²
SUPERFICIE CONSTRUIDA
GROSS FLOOR AREA

1:2.000

58%
OCUPACIÓN
COVERED AREA

2,45
EDIFICABILIDAD
FLOOR AREA RATIO

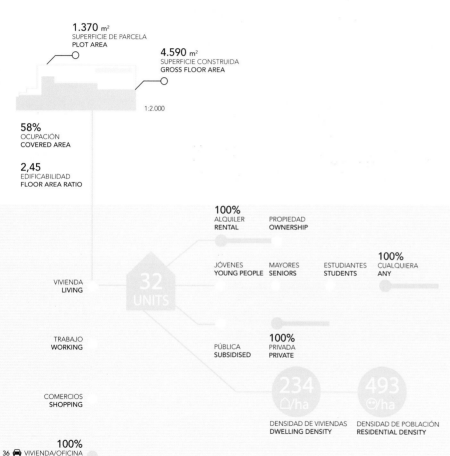

100%
ALQUILER
RENTAL

PROPIEDAD
OWNERSHIP

JÓVENES
YOUNG PEOPLE

MAYORES
SENIORS

ESTUDIANTES
STUDENTS

100%
CUALQUIERA
ANY

VIVIENDA
LIVING

32
UNITS

TRABAJO
WORKING

PÚBLICA
SUBSIDISED

100%
PRIVADA
PRIVATE

COMERCIOS
SHOPPING

234
⌂/ha

493
☺/ha

DENSIDAD DE VIVIENDAS
DWELLING DENSITY

DENSIDAD DE POBLACIÓN
RESIDENTIAL DENSITY

100%
36 🚗 VIVIENDA/OFICINA
LIVE/WORK UNITS

1:5.000
0 10   50

22

1.120
$/m² **1.132**
€/m²

2.000

1.900

1.800

1.700

1.600

1.500

1.400

1.300

1.200

1.100

1.000

900

800

700

600

500

400

300

200

100

0

TIPOS DE VIVIENDA **DWELLING TYPES**   ACCESOS **ACCESS**   FACHADA FORMAL A LA CALLE **FORMAL STREET FACADE**   MANZANA **BLOCK**

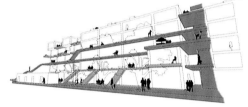

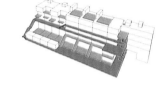

FACHADA INFORMAL AL JARDÍN **INFORMAL GARDEN SIDE**   ACESOS Y ESPACIOS EXTERIORES **ACCESS & OUTDOOR**

Catorce edificios contiguos en el barrio de Lootsbuurt de Amsterdam tenían malas cimentaciones, fueron demolidos y sustituidos por una nueva construcción de 32 viviendas sobre un aparcamiento subterráneo.

La tensión que se genera entre el tejido histórico circundante y el carácter masivo y las técnicas estandarizadas del nuevo edificio se traducen en una estructura híbrida. Por el lado del patio de manzana, la intervención reproduce el contorno recortado de los edificios antiguos. Junto a las restricciones estructurales impuestas por el aparcamiento subterráneo, este perímetro recortado determina la distribución de las viviendas, los espacios exteriores y los accesos.

Fourteen adjacent parcels in the Lootsbuurt in Amsterdam had bad foundations. These buildings are replaced by 32 modern dwellings on an underground car park. The tension between de differentiated historical fabric and the massive and standardised characteristics of contemporary building techniques is translated into a hybrid block.

On the garden side the block follows the meandering building contour of the original buildings. Together with constructional stramines determined by the underground car park this meandering building contour creates a variety of conditions for dwelling types, outdoor spaces and access typologies. In this way the contradictory aims of sun-orientation, guaranteeing privacy and providing

Por su parte, del lado de la calle, el edificio se ajusta delicadamente al tejido histórico circundante, si bien la nueva fachada refleja al exterior los distintos tipos de vivienda que hay en el interior. Así, los huecos de igual anchura se desplazan verticalmente por el alzado en función del tipo de vivienda al que sirven.

La fachada al jardín tiene un carácter informal. Galerías, balcones y terrazas proporcionan plasticidad al volumen. Esta fachada se entiende como un filtro transparente que proporciona luz a las viviendas y privacidad cuando es necesario.

access at the south facade can be solved at the same time.

On the side of the street the block fits gently in the existing urban fabric. Simultaneously the street facade reflects the hybrid block structure by showing the diversity of dwellings. A rhythm of windows with identical width is dancing up and down influenced by the different dwelling types. In this way a homogeneous and differentiated lay out of the facade is created. The garden facade has an informal character.

The presence of galleries, balconies and terraces create a strong plasticity of the volume.

The facade is treated as a transparent filter that provides daylight into the dwellings and provide privacy when needed.

Alzado frontal **Front elevation**

Alzado trasero **Back elevation**   1:1000
01 05 10

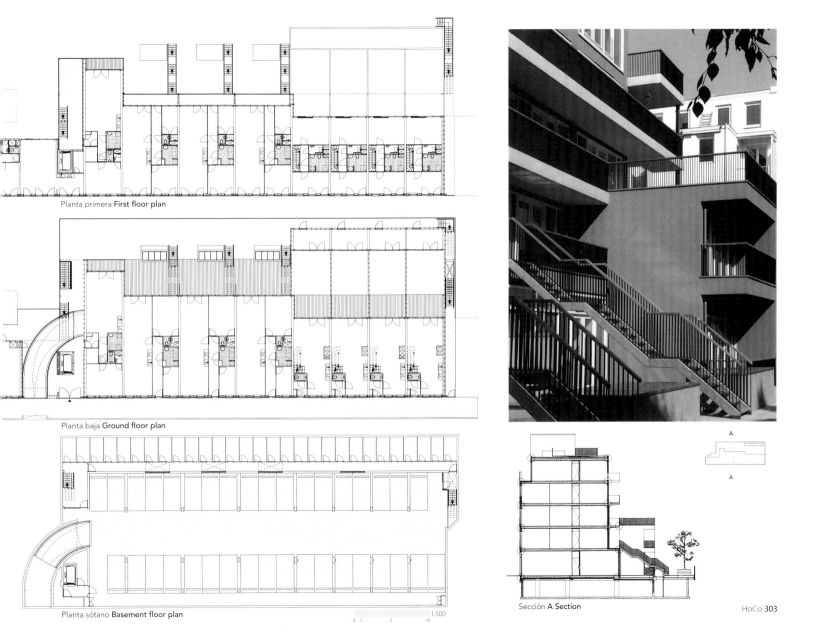

Planta primera **First floor plan**

Planta baja **Ground floor plan**

Planta sótano **Basement floor plan**

1:500
0 1   5   10

Sección **A Section**

A

A

HoCo **303**

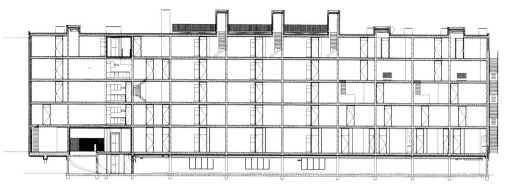

Sección B Section

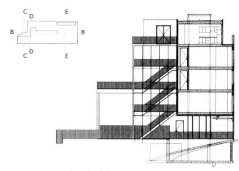

Sección C Section

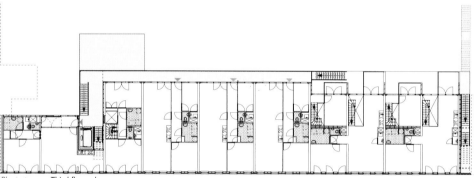

Planta tercera Third floor plan

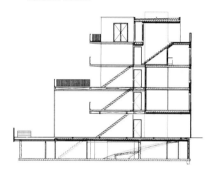

Sección D Section

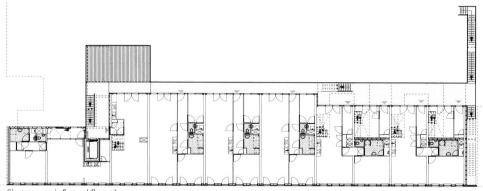

Planta segunda Second floor plan

Sección E Section   1:500

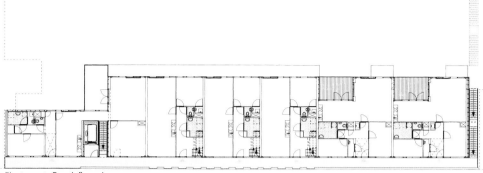

Planta cuarta **Fourth floor plan**

10 1
1000
22 2
950
900
850
800
750
700
650
600
550
500
450
400
350
300
250
200
150
100
50

DORMITORIOS **BEDROOMS**

32
UNITS

CERÁMICA
BRICKWORK

HORMIGÓN
CONCRETE

MADERA
WOOD

CEMENTO
CEMENT

METAL
METAL

COMPUESTO
COMPOSITE

VIDRIO
GALSS

ENFOSCADO/
ESTUCO
**MORTAR/
STUCCO**

AISLAMIENTO
INSULATION

MEMBRANA
MEMBRANE

CERÁMICA
BRICKWORK

VIDRIO
GALSS

HORMIGÓN
CONCRETE

MADERA
WOOD

COMPUESTO
COMPOSITE

CARTÓN-YESO
PLASTER-BOARD

CERÁMICA
BRICKWORK

ENLUCIDO
PLASTER

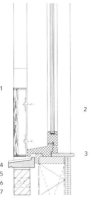

Sección F Section

0 1 5 10   1:500

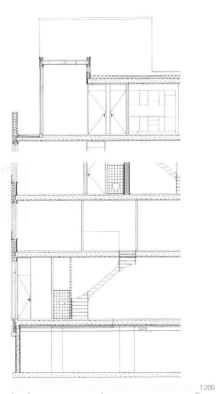

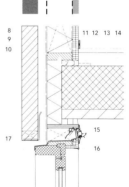

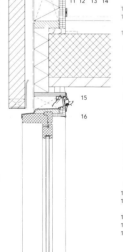

1 BARANDILLA DE ACERO GALVANIZADO RECUBIERTO DE PINTURA AL POLVO MONTADA EN BASTIDOR DE ACERO DE 70 mm DE ANCHO x 10 mm DE ESPESOR
2 VIDRIO AISLANTE MONTADO SOBRE CARPINTERÍA DE MADERA
3 ALFÉIZAR DE PIEDRA NATURAL DE 18 mm DE ANCHO Y 120 mm DE LONGITUD
4 PIEDRA COMPUESTA DE 55 mm DE ANCHO x 145 mm DE LARGO SOBRE CAPA DE MORTERO
5 MURO DE LADRILLO e=90 mm
6 CÁMARA VENTILADA DE 50 mm DE ANCHURA
7 MEMBRANA DE IMPERMEABILIZACIÓN
8 CAPA DE AISLAMIENTO TÉRMICO e=140 mm
9 BARRERA DE VAPOR
10 CARTÓN-YESO
11 ANCLAJE DE ACERO GALVANIZADO
12 SOLADO DE MADERA
13 CAPA DE NIVELACIÓN e=50 mm
14 LOSA DE HORMIGÓN PREFABRICADO e=280 mm
15 ORIFICIO DE VENTILACIÓN
16 PERFIL DE PROTECCIÓN DE LA ESQUINA
17 DINTEL DE ACERO

1 ASSEMBLED AND POWDER COATED GALVANISED STEEL BALUSTRADE IN 70 x 10 mm FRAME
2 ISOLATED GLAZING IN WOODEN WINDOW FRAME
3 18 mm WIDE x 120 mm LONG NATURAL STONE WINDOW-SILL
4 55 mm WIDE x 145 mm LONG COMPOSITE STONE ON MORTER
5 9 mm THICK BRICK WALL
6 50 mm CAVITY
7 WATERPROOF MEMBRANE
8 140 mm THICK THERMAL INSULATION LAYER
9 VAPOUR BARRIER
10 GIPSUM BOARD
11 GALVANISED STEEL ANCHORING
12 WOODEN FLOORING
13 50 mm THICK SCREED
14 280 mm THICK PREFABRICATED CONCRETE SLAB
15 AIR VENT
16 CORNER PROTECTION PROFILE
17 STEEL LINTEL

0 1 5 10   1:200

0 0.1 0.5 1   1:20

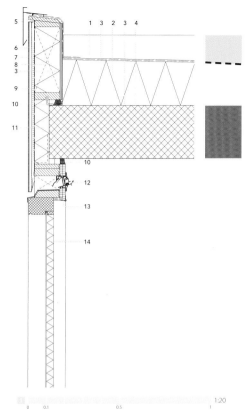

	GRAVA **GRAVEL**
	CERÁMICA **TERRACOTTA**
	MADERA **WOOD**
	CEMENTO **CEMENT**
	VEGETACIÓN **PLANTING**
	METAL **METAL**
	AISLAMIENTO **INSULATION**
	MEMBRANA **MEMBRANE**
	HORMIGÓN **CONCRETE**
	MADERA **WOOD**
	CERÁMICA **TERRACOTTA**
	CARTÓN-YESO **PLASTER-BOARD**
	ENLUCIDO **PLASTER**
	METAL **METAL**

1:20

0   0.1   0.5   1

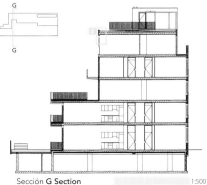

G

G

Sección **G Section**   1:500

0 1   5   10

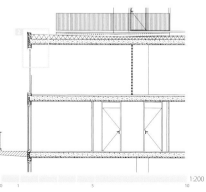

1:200

0 1   5   10

1 CAPA DE GRAVA
2 CAPA DE AISLAMIENTO
 TÉRMICO e+140 mm
3 MEMBRANA DE
 IMPERMEABILIZACIÓN
4 FORJADO DE HORMIGÓN
 PREFABRICADO e=280 mm
5 REMATE DE ALUMINIO
6 REVESTIMIENTO DE
 MORTERO e=3 mm
7 CAPA DE PROTECCIÓN
 e=3 mm
8 CAPA DE AISLAMIENTO
 TÉRMICO e=140 mm
9 CÁMARA VENTILADA
10 SELLADO
11 CAPA DE AISLAMIENTO
 TÉRMICO e=80 mm
12 ORIFICIO DE VENTILACIÓN
13 PERFIL DE PROTECCIÓN
 DE LA ESQUINA
14 PANEL SANDWICH e=50 mm

1 BALLAST LAYER
2 e+140 mm THICK THERMAL
 INSULATION LAYER
3 WATERPROOF MEMBRANE
4 280 mm THICK
 PREFABRICATED
 FLOOR SLAB
5 ALUMINIUM CAP
6 3 mm THICK MORTAR
7 3 mm PROTECTION LAYER
8 140 mm THICK THERMAL
 INSULATION LAYER
9 CAVITY
10 SEALING
11 80 mm THICK THERMAL
 INSULATION LAYER
12 AIR VENT
13 CORNER PROTECTION
 PROFILE
14 50 mm THICK
 SANDWICH PANEL

23

Emmanuel Combarel Dominique Marrec architectes combarel-marrec.com Paris. FRANCE, 2006 Rue Louis Blanc, 45, Paris 10

2,201
mill.

20.887
☺/km²

550 m²
SUPERFICIE DE PARCELA
PLOT AREA

1.537 m²
SUPERFICIE CONSTRUIDA
GROSS FLOOR AREA

1:2.000

68,2%
OCUPACIÓN
COVERED AREA

2,79
EDIFICABILIDAD
FLOOR AREA RATIO

100%
ALQUILER
RENTAL

PROPIEDAD
OWNERSHIP

13 🚗 **100%**
VIVIENDA
LIVING

17
UNITS

JÓVENES
YOUNG PEOPLE

MAYORES
SENIORS

ESTUDIANTES
STUDENTS

100%
CUALQUIERA
ANY

TRABAJO
WORKING

100%
PÚBLICA
SUBSIDISED

PRIVADA
PRIVATE

COMERCIOS
SHOPPING

309
⌂/ha

886
☺/ha

DENSIDAD DE VIVIENDAS
DWELLING DENSITY

DENSIDAD DE POBLACIÓN
RESIDENTIAL DENSITY

OTROS USOS
OTHER USES

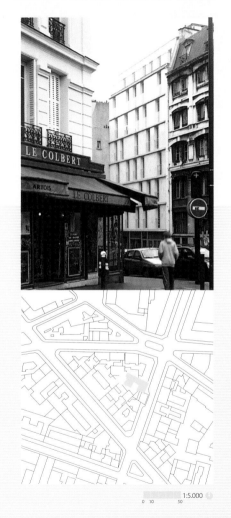

1:5.000
0 10   50

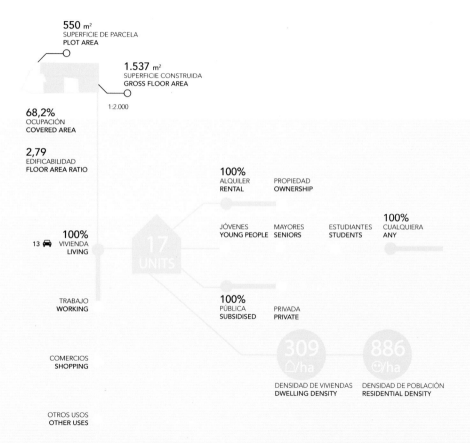

1.303 $/m² 1.366'00 €/m²

La construcción del proyecto de viviendas en el número 45 de la calle Louis Blanc, en el distrito 10 de París, es el resultado de un concurso convocado por la empresa municipal del suelo. La parcela de 550 m², ocupada por un antiguo edificio que fue demolido, debía ser ocupada por una estructura de bajo coste con 13 apartamentos y cumplir con los parámetros de la normativa de alta calidad medioambiental y que estaban siendo definidos en el momento de elaborar el proyecto. El proyecto se conforma como un puzzle, respondiendo a las limitaciones y requerimientos del contexto. Propone una tipología poco habitual respecto de los estándares parisinos al liberar la planta baja y proponer a este nivel un aparcamiento en superficie sobre el que las 17 viviendas que se construyeron finalmente parecen estar flotando. Esta decisión provocó una reacción en cadena:
· Minimización de la superficie de aparcamiento (supresión de la rampa)
· Optimización del plazo es: menos de 3 meses
· Optimización del presupuesto: 15%
· Redefinición del presupuesto...
La actitud respecto al medio ambiente ha tendido sistemáticamente a disolver las ataduras técnicas y contextuales en la arquitectura del edificio y desarrollar al máximo sus potencialidades (estructura de pórticos adaptable a cualquier reconfiguración de los volúmenes...).

The construction of the housing project located 45 Louis Blanc Street in the 10th *arrondisement* of Paris is the result of a project launched in 1998 by the Paris city real-estate authority. The property developer was expected to take a piece of land measuring 550 m² and replace an abandoned squat there which had been slotted for demolition with a low-cost building proposing 13 apartments (program specifications), that adhered to the HQE (High Quality Environmental) standards still being determined at the time. The project is sculpted like a piece of a puzzle, responding exactly to the urban constrains and solicitations of the context.
It proposes an unusual typology for the Parisian standards which frees the ground floor to propose on the ground level a landscaped parking, adequate with a small plot, above which 17 apartments seem to float.
It ensures a chain reaction
· Minimization of the car park print (suppression of the ramp)
· Optimization of the realization planning: minus 3 months
· Optimization of the budget: 15%
· Redefinition of the project economy –and so on...
The environmental attitude has systematically aimed to dissolve the technical and contextual subjections in the architecture of the building and manage maximum potentialities of the construction (Post and beam structure allowing any recomposition of the volumes...)

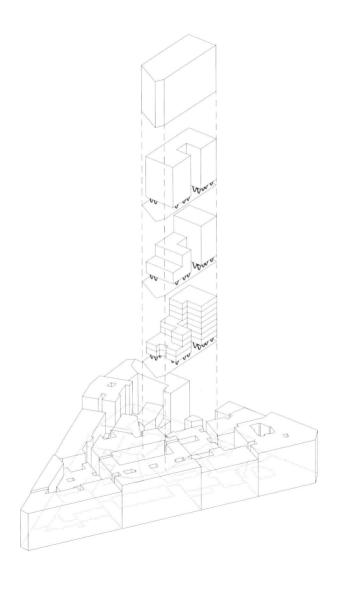

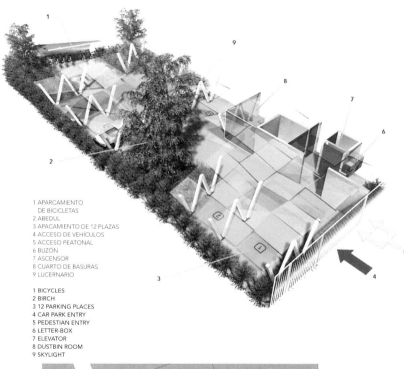

1 APARCAMIENTO
  DE BICICLETAS
2 ABEDUL
3 APARCAMIENTO DE 12 PLAZAS
4 ACCESO DE VEHÍCULOS
5 ACCESO PEATONAL
6 BUZÓN
7 ASCENSOR
8 CUARTO DE BASURAS
9 LUCERNARIO

1 BICYCLES
2 BIRCH
3 12 PARKING PLACES
4 CAR PARK ENTRY
5 PEDESTIAN ENTRY
6 LETTER-BOX
7 ELEVATOR
8 DUSTBIN ROOM
9 SKYLIGHT

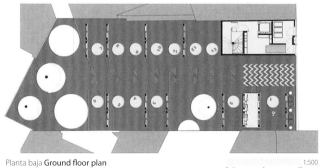

Planta baja **Ground floor plan**

1:500

Alzado desde la calle **Street elevation**

1:500
0 1   5   10

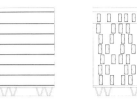 

Alzado al patio **Courtyard elevation**

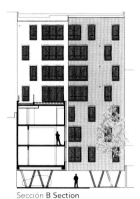

Sección B Section

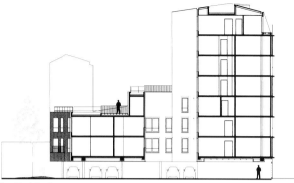

Sección A Section

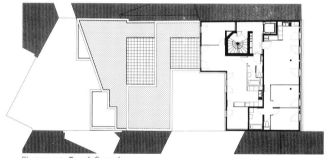

Planta quinta Fifth floor plan

Planta segunda Second floor plan

B

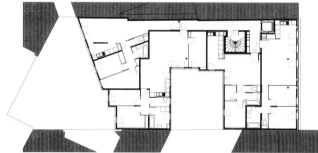

Planta cuarta Fourth floor plan

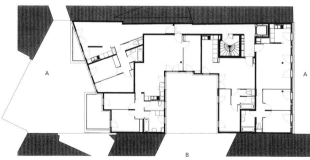

A

B

Planta primera First floor plan

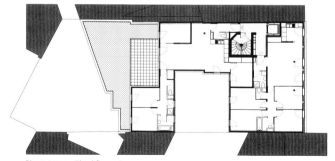

A

Planta tercera Third floor plan

1:500

0 1   5   10

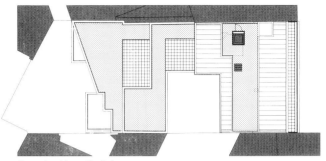

Planta de cubiertas **Roof plan**

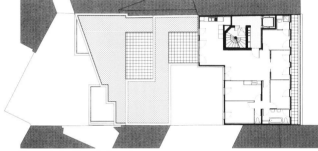

Planta séptima **Seventh floor plan**

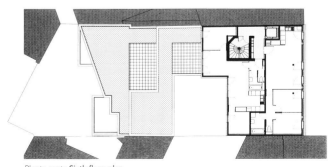

Planta sexta **Sixth floor plan**

LAYERS

EXTERNAL

CERÁMICA
BRICKWORK

HORMIGON
CONCRETE

MADERA
WOOD

CEMENTO
CEMENT

METAL
METAL

COMPUESTO
COMPOSITE

VIDRIO
GALSS

ENFOSCADO/
ESTUCO
MORTAR/
STUCCO

AISLAMIENTO
INSULATION

MEMBRANA
MEMBRANE

PRINCIPAL

CERÁMICA
BRICKWORK

VIDRIO
GALSS

HORMIGON
CONCRETE

MADERA
WOOD

COMPUESTO
COMPOSITE

INTERNAL

CARTÓN-YESO
PLASTER-BOARD

CERÁMICA
BRICKWORK

ENLUCIDO
PLASTER

FACHADA FAÇADE

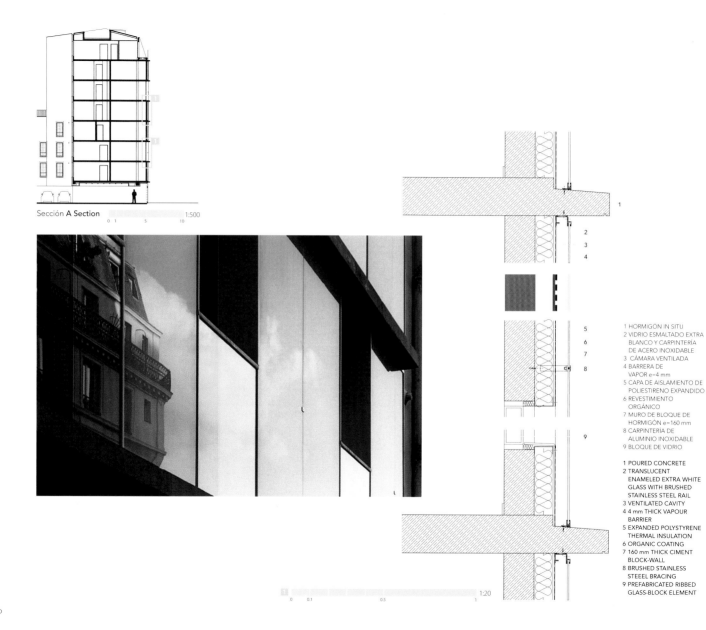

Sección **A Section**   1:500

0 1   5   10

1 HORMIGÓN IN SITU
2 VIDRIO ESMALTADO EXTRA
  BLANCO Y CARPINTERÍA
  DE ACERO INOXIDABLE
3 CÁMARA VENTILADA
4 BARRERA DE
  VAPOR e=4 mm
5 CAPA DE AISLAMIENTO DE
  POLIESTIRENO EXPANDIDO
6 REVESTIMIENTO
  ORGÁNICO
7 MURO DE BLOQUE DE
  HORMIGÓN e=160 mm
8 CARPINTERÍA DE
  ALUMINIO INOXIDABLE
9 BLOQUE DE VIDRIO

1 POURED CONCRETE
2 TRANSLUCENT
  ENAMELED EXTRA WHITE
  GLASS WITH BRUSHED
  STAINLESS STEEL RAIL
3 VENTILATED CAVITY
4 4 mm THICK VAPOUR
  BARRIER
5 EXPANDED POLYSTYRENE
  THERMAL INSULATION
6 ORGANIC COATING
7 160 mm THICK CIMENT
  BLOCK-WALL
8 BRUSHED STAINLESS
  STEEEL BRACING
9 PREFABRICATED RIBBED
  GLASS-BLOCK ELEMENT

1:20

0   0.1   0.5   1

1 HORMIGÓN IN SITU
2 BARANDILLA DE VIDRIO
   DE SEGURIDAD FIJADA
   A CANAL Y PASAMANOS
   DE ACERO INOXIDABLE
3 PUERTA DE VIDRIO Y
   CARPINTERÍA DE ALUMINIO
4 PERSIANA TEXTIL Y GUÍA

1 FLOWED IN PLACE
   CONCRETE
2 SAFETY GLASS BALUSTRADE
   FIXED TO A BRUSHED
   STAINLESS STEEL CHANNEL
   AND HANDRAIL
3 GLAZED DOOR WITH WHITE
   ALUMINIUM FRAME
4 INTERNAL TEXTILE BLIND
   WITH RAIL GUIDE

1:20

0   0.1   0.5   1

Sección **A** Section 　　　　　　　　1:500
0　1　　5　　　10

1 REVESTIMIENTO
  ORGÁNICO
2 SISTEMA DE AISLAMIENTO
  DE POLIESTIRENO
  EXPANDIDO
3 HORMIGÓN IN SITU
4 PERSIANA TEXTIL Y GUÍA
5 PUERTA DE VIDRIO Y
  CARPINTERÍA DE ALUMINIO
6 BARANDILLA Y
  BASTIDOR DE HIERRO
7 PAVIMENTO DE LOSAS
  DE HORMIGÓN
8 SELLADO ASFÁLTICO
9 CAPA DE AISLAMIENTO.
  PANELES DE ESPUMA
  RÍGIDA DE POLIESTIRENO
  EXTRUIDO
10 GRAVA

1 ORGANIC COATING
2 EXPANDED POLYSTYRENE
3 POURED CONCRETE
4 EXTERNAL TEXTILE BLIND
  WITH RAIL GUIDE
5 GLAZED DOOR WITH
  WHITE ALUMINIUM FRAME
6 IRON SAFETY HANDRAIL
  IN FLAT METAL FRAME
7 CONCRETE SLAB PAVING
8 BITUMINOUS
  SEALING LAYER
9 RIGID-FOAM INSULATION
10 GRAVEL

1:20
0　0.1　　　0.5　　　　1

FACHADA FACADE

LAYERS
EXTERNAL

GRAVA
GRAVEL

CERÁMICA
TERRACOTTA

MADERA
WOOD

CEMENTO
CEMENT

VEGETACIÓN
PLANTING

METAL
METAL

AISLAMIENTO
INSULATION

MEMBRANA
MEMBRANE

PRINCIPAL

HORMIGÓN
CONCRETE

MADERA
WOOD

CERÁMICA
TERRACOTTA

INTERNAL

CARTÓN-YESO
PLASTER-BOARD

ENLUCIDO
PLASTER

METAL
METAL

1 2 3 4 5

6 8 7

8

10

11

12

13 14 15

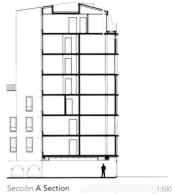

Sección **A** Section   1:500
0 1   5   10

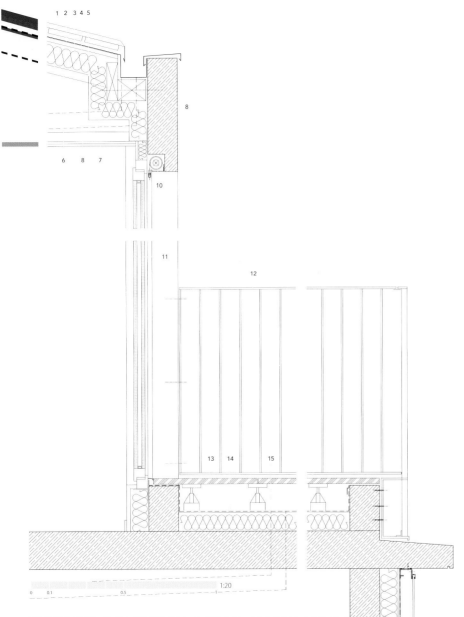

1:20
0   0.1   0.5   1

1 PLANCHA DE ZINC	1 ZINC SHEET
2 MEMBRANA IMPERMEABILIZANTE	2 WATERPROOFING MEMBRANE
3 TABLERO DE MADERA	3 WOOD BOARD
4 CAPA DE AISLAMIENTO e=120 mm	4 120 mm THICK THERMAL INSULATION
5 BARRERA DE VAPOR e=4 mm	5 4 mm THICK VAPOUR BARRIER
6 VIGA DE MADERA DE 160 mm DE CANTO	6 160 mm WOOD BEAM
7 CARTÓN-YESO	7 2 PLASTER BOARDS
8 SUBESTRUCTURA METÁLICA	8 SUSPENDED CEILING METALLIC STRUCTURE
9 HORMIGÓN IN SITU CON CAPA DE ENFOSCADO	9 POURED CONCRETE WITH COATING
10 PERSIANA TEXTIL Y GUÍA	10 EXTERNAL TEXTILE BLIND WITH RAIL GUIDE
11 PUERTA DE VIDRIO Y CARPINTERÍA DE ALUMINIO	11 GLAZED DOOR WITH WHITE ALUMINIUM FRAME
12 BARANDILLA Y BASTIDOR DE HIERRO	12 IRON SAFETY HANDRAIL IN FLAT METAL FRAME
13 PAVIMENTO DE LOSAS DE HORMIGÓN	13 CONCRETE SLAB PAVING
14 SELLADO ASFÁLTICO	14 BITUMINOUS SEALING LAYER
15 CAPA DE AISLAMIENTO PANELES DE ESPUMA RÍGIDA DE POLIESTIRENO EXTRUIDO	15 RIGID-FOAM INSULATION

1:5.000

0   10   50

0,276 mill.☺   1.003 ☺/km²

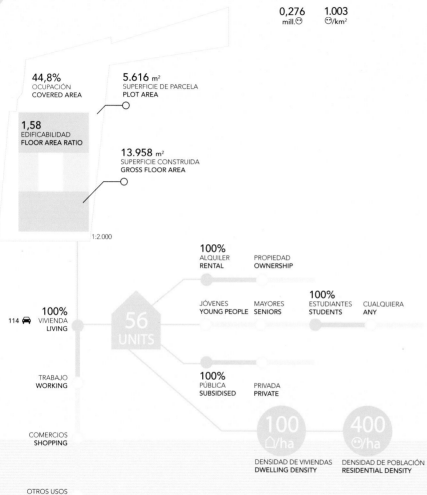

44,8%
OCUPACIÓN
COVERED AREA

5.616 m²
SUPERFICIE DE PARCELA
PLOT AREA

1,58
EDIFICABILIDAD
FLOOR AREA RATIO

13.958 m²
SUPERFICIE CONSTRUIDA
GROSS FLOOR AREA

1:2.000

100%
ALQUILER
RENTAL

PROPIEDAD
OWNERSHIP

100%
VIVIENDA
LIVING

114 🚗

56 UNITS

JÓVENES
YOUNG PEOPLE

MAYORES
SENIORS

100%
ESTUDIANTES
STUDENTS

CUALQUIERA
ANY

TRABAJO
WORKING

100%
PÚBLICA
SUBSIDISED

PRIVADA
PRIVATE

COMERCIOS
SHOPPING

100 ⌂/ha

400 ☺/ha

DENSIDAD DE VIVIENDAS
DWELLING DENSITY

DENSIDAD DE POBLACIÓN
RESIDENTIAL DENSITY

OTROS USOS
OTHER USES

2.000

1.900

1.800

1.700

1.600

1.500

1.327
$/m²

1.400

1.300

1.200

1.100

24

1.000

950
€/m²

900

800

700

600

500

400

300

200

100

0

La residencia de estudiantes se encuentra en los límites del centro histórico Liubliana, a poca distancia del río, y alberga 56 unidades de vivienda para los estudiantes de la Universidad.

El edificio goza de una gran claridad programática: los programas públicos (aulas y zonas comunes y de ocio) se concentran en una planta baja transparente, mientras que el programa residencial ocupa dos bloques apoyados sobre dicha base. Cada unidad de vivienda se organiza en torno a un núcleo central de servicios que incluye baño, cocina y comedor, y que se traduce en fachada por un gran hueco que se asoma a la calle. Por su parte, los dormitorios están protegidos del exterior mediante una serie de paneles de aluminio perforados que protegen la vida privada de los residentes del bullicio callejero.

This is a project on the edge of Ljubljana city centre, near the river bank, comprising of 56 dwelling units for students of Ljubljana University. It is a building of high programmatic clarity –a series of public programs (spaces for teaching, communal living and leisure) are concentrated in a horizontal transparent base – while series of student living units hover above in two slabs.

Student units are organized around central service cores containing bathrooms and kitchen/dining rooms, which appear on the elevation of the buildings as huge openings –windows like 'eyes', overlooking the street. Adjoining student bedrooms are, in turn, screened from the street by series of folding panels in aluminium, intricately perforated, protecting private lives of inhabitants from the street bustle.

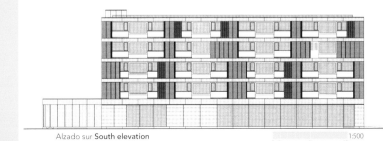

Alzado sur **South elevation**

1:500

0 1   5   10

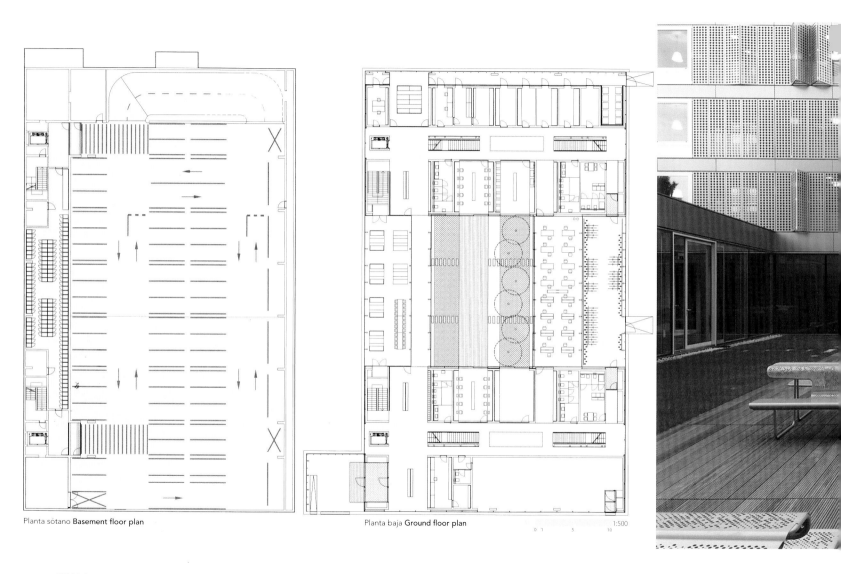

Planta sótano **Basement floor plan**

Planta baja **Ground floor plan**

1:500

0 1   5   10

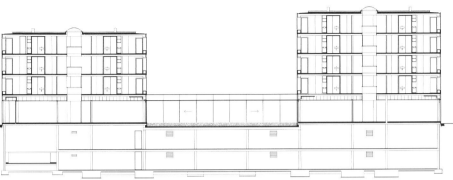

Sección **A** Section

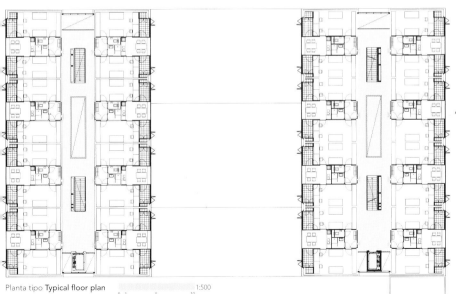

Planta tipo **Typical floor plan**   1:500

0 1   5   10

1000
950
900
850
800
750
700
650
600
550
500
450
400
350
300
250
200
150
100
50
0

56

DORMITORIOS **BEDROOMS**

A

56
UNITS

UNITS

LAYERS

CERÁMICA
BRICKWORK

HORMIGON
CONCRETE

MADERA
WOOD

CEMENTO
CEMENT

METAL
METAL

COMPUESTO
COMPOSITE

VIDRIO
GALSS

ENFOSCADO/
ESTUCO
**MORTAR/
STUCCO**

AISLAMIENTO
INSULATION

MEMBRANA
MEMBRANE

CERÁMICA
BRICKWORK

VIDRIO
GALSS

HORMIGON
CONCRETE

MADERA
WOOD

COMPUESTO
COMPOSITE

CARTÓN-YESO
PLASTER-BOARD

CERÁMICA
BRICKWORK

ENLUCIDO
PLASTER

Sección **A** Section

1:500

0 1   5   10

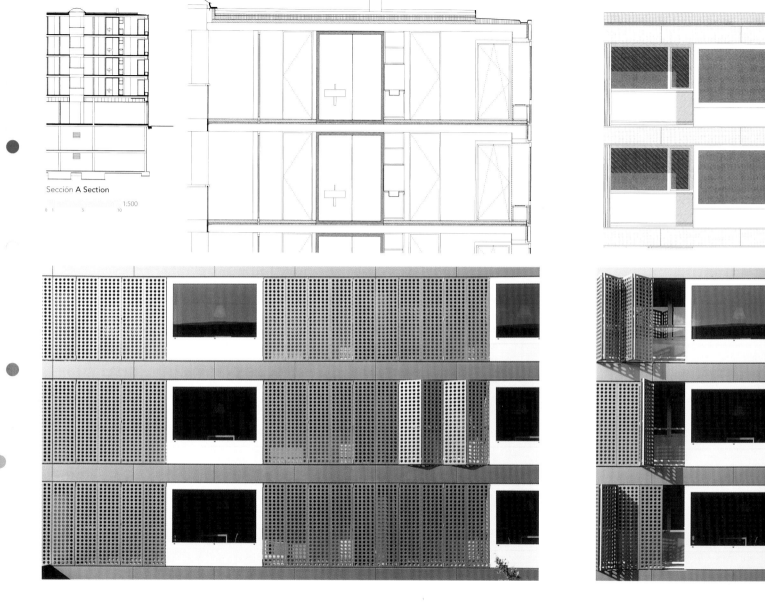

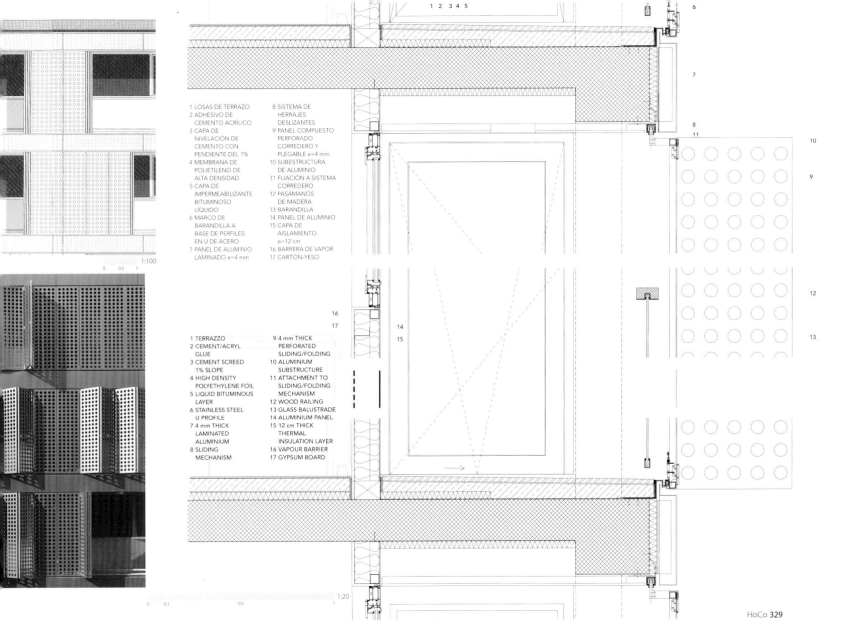

1 2 3 4 5

6

7

8
11

10

9

12

13

16
17

14
15

1 LOSAS DE TERRAZO
2 ADHESIVO DE CEMENTO ACRÍLICO
3 CAPA DE NIVELACIÓN DE CEMENTO CON PENDIENTE DEL 1%
4 MEMBRANA DE POLIETILENO DE ALTA DENSIDAD
5 CAPA DE IMPERMEABILIZANTE BITUMINOSO LÍQUIDO
6 MARCO DE BARANDILLA A BASE DE PERFILES EN U DE ACERO
7 PANEL DE ALUMINIO LAMINADO e=4 mm
8 SISTEMA DE HERRAJES DESLIZANTES
9 PANEL COMPUESTO PERFORADO CORREDERO Y PLEGABLE e=4 mm
10 SUBESTRUCTURA DE ALUMINIO
11 FIJACIÓN A SISTEMA CORREDERO
12 PASAMANOS DE MADERA
13 BARANDILLA
14 PANEL DE ALUMINIO
15 CAPA DE AISLAMIENTO e=12 cm
16 BARRERA DE VAPOR
17 CARTÓN-YESO

1:100
0   0.5   1

1 TERRAZZO
2 CEMENT/ACRYL GLUE
3 CEMENT SCREED 1% SLOPE
4 HIGH DENSITY POLYETHYLENE FOIL
5 LIQUID BITUMINOUS LAYER
6 STAINLESS STEEL U PROFILE
7 4 mm THICK LAMINATED ALUMINIUM
8 SLIDING MECHANISM
9 4 mm THICK PERFORATED SLIDING/FOLDING
10 ALUMINIUM SUBSTRUCTURE
11 ATTACHMENT TO SLIDING/FOLDING MECHANISM
12 WOOD RAILING
13 GLASS BALUSTRADE
14 ALUMINIUM PANEL
15 12 cm THICK THERMAL INSULATION LAYER
16 VAPOUR BARRIER
17 GYPSUM BOARD

1:20
0   0.1   0.5   1

2,776 mill.☺   13.679 ☺/km²

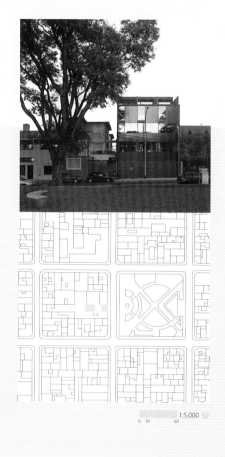

424 m²
SUPERFICIE DE PARCELA
PLOT AREA

937 m²
SUPERFICIE CONSTRUIDA
GROSS FLOOR AREA

1:2.000

69,8%
OCUPACIÓN
COVERED AREA

2,21
EDIFICABILIDAD
FLOOR AREA RATIO

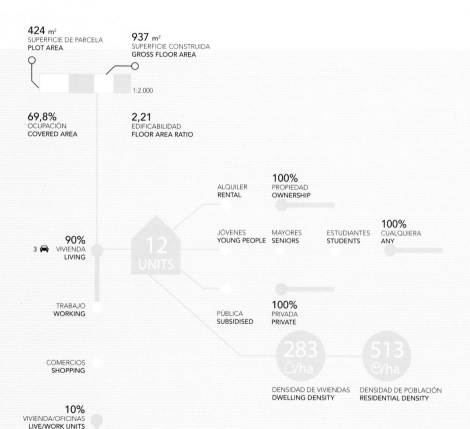

100%
ALQUILER RENTAL / PROPIEDAD OWNERSHIP

3 🚗 **90%**
VIVIENDA LIVING

JÓVENES YOUNG PEOPLE   MAYORES SENIORS   ESTUDIANTES STUDENTS

100%
CUALQUIERA ANY

TRABAJO
WORKING

PÚBLICA SUBSIDISED   **100%** PRIVADA PRIVATE

COMERCIOS
SHOPPING

283 ⌂/ha
DENSIDAD DE VIVIENDAS
DWELLING DENSITY

513 ☺/ha
DENSIDAD DE POBLACIÓN
RESIDENTIAL DENSITY

10%
VIVIENDA/OFICINAS
LIVE/WORK UNITS

12 UNITS

1:5.000   0 10 50

10.233
ARS/m²

2.000

1.900

1.800

1.700

1.547
$/m²

1.600

1.500

1.400

1.300

1.200

1.100

1.000

900

800

700

600

500

400

300

200

100

25

0

La plaza Mackenna, ubicada en el barrio de Saavedra, es el enclave elegido para la construcción de un edificio compuesto por 9 viviendas y 3 estudios. Una plaza con un centro vacío y público y un perímetro delimitado por una densa vegetación que solo se interrumpe al enfrentarse con la parcela a intervenir.
La construcción asume el protagonismo que propone esta escena barrial, apropiándose de su atmósfera como una condición estructurante del proyecto.
Un patio central vincula ambos bloques a través de un recorrido a cielo abierto que se extiende hasta la puerta de cada unidad. Las viviendas intentan continuar la tradición de las casas que históricamente definieron el carácter del barrio agrupándose hoy en un mismo terreno como consecuencia directa del aumento de densidad que se produce en esta zona de la ciudad. Cada unidad fue proyectada como una pequeña casa que incorpora a su programa una generosa expansión, posibilitando la aparición de actividades a cielo abierto tal como sucede en la plaza que el edificio tiene a sus pies.

Mackenna Plaza, located in the Saavedra neighbourhood, is the chosen location for the construction of a building made up of nine housing units and three studios. This is a plaza with an empty, public centre and a perimeter bordered by dense vegetation that is only interrupted by the lot to be built on.
The construction assumes the prominence that this neighbourhood scene proposes, supported by its atmosphere as a structuring condition of the project.
A central patio connects the two blocks by means of an open air passage that runs to the door of each unit. The houses look to continue the tradition of the houses that historically defined the neighbourhood's character by grouping together as a direct consequence of the increase in density that has occurred in this area of the city. Each unit was designed as a small house that incorporates a generous expansion to its programme, allowing open air activities, as in the plaza that stands at the foot of the building.

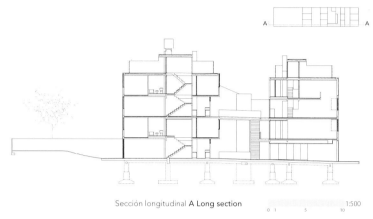

Sección longitudinal **A Long section**   0 1   5   10   1:500

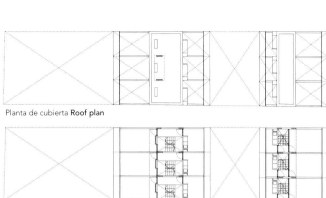

Planta de cubierta **Roof plan**

Planta cuarta **Fourth floor plan**

Planta tercera **Third floor plan**

Planta segunda **Second floor plan**

Planta primera **First floor plan**

Planta baja **Ground floor plan**

0 1   5   10   1:500

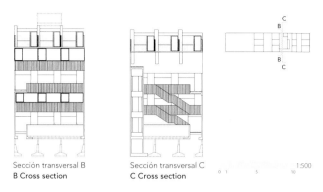

Sección transversal B
B Cross section

Sección transversal C
C Cross section

0 1   5   10   1:500

3	1	1000
	950
3	2	900
	850
	800
	750
	700
6	650
	600
	550
	500
	450
	400
	350
	300
	250
	200
	150
	100
	50

DORMITORIOS **BEDROOMS**

Sección longitudinal **A Long section**

0 1   5   10

1:500

CERÁMICA **BRICKWORK**	
HORMIGON **CONCRETE**	
MADERA **WOOD**	
CEMENTO **CEMENT**	
METAL **METAL**	●
COMPUESTO **COMPOSITE**	
VIDRIO **GALSS**	
ENFOSCADO/ ESTUCO **MORTAR/ STUCCO**	
AISLAMIENTO **INSULATION**	●
MEMBRANA **MEMBRANE**	
CERÁMICA **BRICKWORK**	
VIDRIO **GALSS**	
HORMIGON **CONCRETE**	●
MADERA **WOOD**	
COMPUESTO **COMPOSITE**	
CARTÓN-YESO **PLASTER-BOARD**	
CERÁMICA **BRICKWORK**	
ENLUCIDO **PLASTER**	●

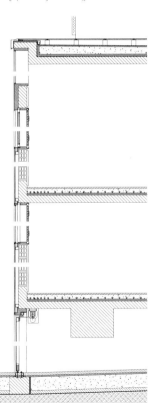

0 0.1   0.5   1

1:50

1 LOSA DE HORMIGÓN ARMADO
2 VIGA DE HORMIGÓN ARMADO
3 LADRILLO HUECO e= 12 cm
4 MEMBRANA IMPERMEABILIZANTE
5 BARRERA DE VAPOR DE FILM DE POLIETILENO
6 CAPA DE NIVELACIÓN
7 CAPA DE NIVELACIÓN DE HORMIGÓN CELULAR
8 SOLADO DE CEMENTO ANTIDESLIZANTE
9 SOLADO DE CEMENTO
10 BALDOSAS DE CEMENTO DE 60 cm DE LARGO x 40 cm DE ANCHO
11 TACO REGULABLE DE APOYO PARA BALDOSAS
12 CAPA DE AISLAMIENTO TÉRMICO DE PLACA DE POLIESTIRENO EXPANDIDO e= 3 cm
13 JUNTA DE DILATACIÓN DE PLACA DE POLIESTIRENO EXPANDIDO e= 3 cm
14 ACABADO CON IMPRIMACIÓN DE OXIDO NEGRO Y 3 MANOS DE PINTURA SINTÉTICA GRIS OSCURO
15 PINTURA EPOXI DE COLOR BLANCO
16 LÁTEX INTERIOR/EXTERIOR
17 MALLA DE ALAMBRE GALVANIZADO
18 REVOCO DE YESO PROYECTADO
19 ENFOSCADO
20 CHAPA CORRUGADA DE ALUMINIO PREPINTADA GRIS OSCURO
21 TUBO FIJACIÓN PARA PERFIL DE 30 x 30 mm
22 CHAPA DE ACERO
23 ALFÉIZAR DE CHAPA DE ACERO
24 REMATE DE CHAPA DE ZINC
25 TABLERO DE VIRUTAS DE 18 MM DE ESPESOR
26 CONDUCTO DE 20 mm DE DIÁMETRO
27 LOSA DE HORMIGÓN ARMADO e= 50 mm
28 RELLENO DE TIERRA COMPACTADA
29 SUELO NATURAL
30 POSTIGO DE CHAPA DE ACERO Y PAÑOS DE TABLERO DE VIRUTAS.

1 REINFORCED CONCRETE SLAB
2 REINFORCED CONCRETE BEAM
3 12 cm HOLLOW BRICK
4 WATERPROOF MEMBRANE
5 POLYETHYLENE FILM AS VAPOUR BARRIER
6 UPPER MORTAR LAYER
7 LIGHT CONCRETE SCREED
8 ANTI-SLIP CEMENT FLOORING
9 CEMENT FLOORING
10 60 cm LONG x 40 cm WIDE CEMENT PAVERS
11 ADJUSTABLE PAVER SUPPORT
12 3 cm THICK EXPANDED POLYSTYRENE THERMAL INSULATION LAYER
13 3 cm THICK EXPANDED POLYSTYRENE DILATATION JOINT
14 FINISHING: BLACK OXIDE COATING AND 3 LAYERS OF DARK GRAY PAINT
15 WHITE EPOXY PAINT
16 LATEX COATING
17 GALVANISED WIRE MESH
18 SPRAYED PLASTER RENDERING
19 MORTAR RENDERING
20 DARK GRAY PAINTED CORRUGATED ALUMINIUM PLATE
21 30 x 30 mm FIXATION PROFILE FOR ALUMINIUM ANGLE
22 STEEL SHEETING
23 STEEL PLATE WINDOWSILL
24 ZINC CAP
25 18 mm THICK CHIPBOARD
26 Ø 20 mm DUCT
27 50 mm THICK REINFORCED CONCRETE SLAB
28 COMPACTED SOIL FILLING
29 NATURAL SOIL
30 SHUTTER: STEEL PLATE AND CHIPBOARD

Patio interior
View of the courtyard

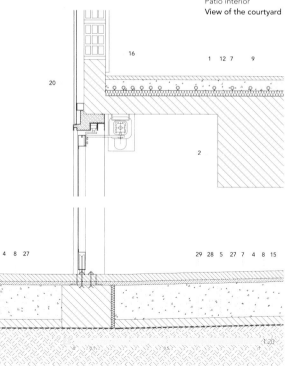

1:20

Sección horizontal **Horizontal section**

GRAVA
GRAVEL

CERÁMICA
TERRACOTTA

MADERA
WOOD

CEMENTO
CEMENT

VEGETACIÓN
PLANTING

METAL
METAL

AISLAMIENTO
INSULATION

MEMBRANA
MEMBRANE

HORMIGÓN
CONCRETE

MADERA
WOOD

CERÁMICA
TERRACOTTA

CARTÓN-YESO
PLASTER-BOARD

ENLUCIDO
PLASTER

METAL
METAL

7,56
mill.☺

4.761
☺/km²

El proyecto de viviendas en Wansey Street forma parte del plan de regeneración del distrito londinense de Elephant and Castle. En un solar rodeado por tipologías muy diferentes, la propuesta de dRMM reinterpreta la vivienda tradicional en hilera y la adapta a los requerimientos actuales de identidad, comunidad, densidad y sostenibilidad.

Wansey Street Housing is the demonstration project for Elephant and Castle Regeneration. A gap site between different typologies, dRMM's competition-winning design reinterprets the terrace with 21st century requirements for identity, community, density and sustainability.

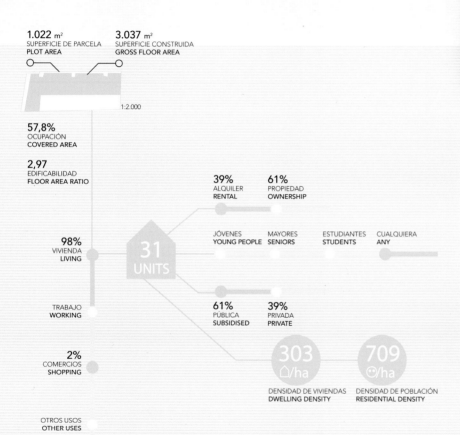

1.022 m²
SUPERFICIE DE PARCELA
PLOT AREA

3.037 m²
SUPERFICIE CONSTRUIDA
GROSS FLOOR AREA

1:2.000

57,8%
OCUPACIÓN
COVERED AREA

2,97
EDIFICABILIDAD
FLOOR AREA RATIO

39%
ALQUILER
RENTAL

61%
PROPIEDAD
OWNERSHIP

98%
VIVIENDA
LIVING

31
UNITS

JÓVENES
YOUNG PEOPLE

MAYORES
SENIORS

ESTUDIANTES
STUDENTS

CUALQUIERA
ANY

TRABAJO
WORKING

61%
PÚBLICA
SUBSIDISED

39%
PRIVADA
PRIVATE

2%
COMERCIOS
SHOPPING

303
⌂/ha

709
☺/ha

DENSIDAD DE VIVIENDAS
DWELLING DENSITY

DENSIDAD DE POBLACIÓN
RESIDENTIAL DENSITY

OTROS USOS
OTHER USES

1:5.000
0 10   50

1.562
$/m²

1.380
£/m²

26

2.000
1.900
1.800
1.700
1.600
1.500
1400
1.300
1.200
1.100
1.000
900
800
700
600
500
400
300
200
100
0

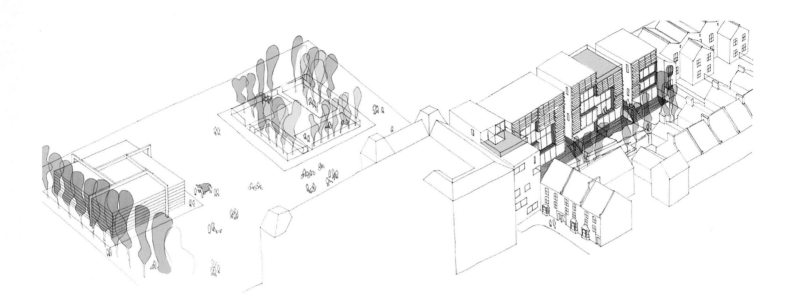

La intervención consta de cuatro bloques de apartamentos con tres accesos independientes que conducen a una circulación común al aire libre. Desde estos accesos se llega a un jardín comunitario orientado al sur al que asoman las salas de estar de las viviendas y los balcones. Sobre esta fachada, grandes huecos permiten la entrada del máximo de luz.

La fachada de color a la calle conecta los edificios vecinos (las viviendas en hilera de la época victoriana con un consistorio de estilo eduardiano) en términos de escala y proporción.

The development is divided into four apartment blocks with three separate entrances leading to communal open circulation. These entrances lead to a communal South-facing garden, towards which the living rooms open out, maximising light and views with full-height glazing, generous balconies and roof terraces.

The coloured facade connects existing neighbours –Victorian terraces with Edwardian town hall– in terms of scale and proportion.

El programa de vivienda subvencionada (61%) se mezcla aleatoriamente con el de vivienda de mercado (39%): es el logro social (invisible) del proyecto.

Una parte del plan para Elephant and Castle contempla la demolición de los bloques Heygate State de los años 60, de modo que el proyecto se convertirá en lugar de referencia del extremo sureste de una nueva plaza pública.

The 'pepper-potted' mix of accommodation is an integration without distinction of 61% affordable housing and 39% open market sale. This is the (invisible) social achievement of the design. Part of the masterplan for the Elephant and Castle is to demolish the 1960s Heygate Estate. Wansey Street Housing will then form a landmark on the south east corner of a new public square.

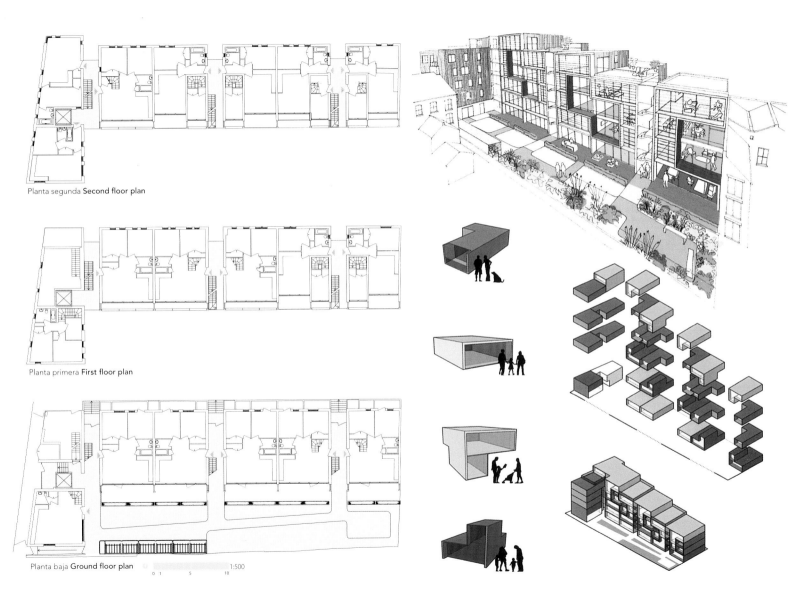

Planta segunda Second floor plan

Planta primera First floor plan

Planta baja Ground floor plan

1:500
0 1   5   10

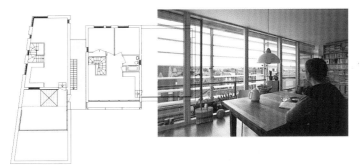

Planta quinta Fifth floor plan

Planta cuarta Fourth floor plan

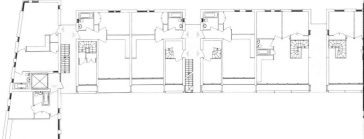

Planta tercera Third floor plan

DORMITORIOS **BEDROOMS**

UNITS

1 PANEL DE FIBROCEMENTO
2 MURO DE BLOQUE DE HORMIGÓN e=140 mm
3 PANEL DE AISLAMIENTO TÉRMICO e=75 mm FIJADO AL MURO DE BLOQUE DE HORMIGÓN
4 PERFIL Z DE ACERO GALVANIZADO DE 50 mm DE ANCHO COLOCADO CADA 600 mm Y FIJADO AL MURO DE BLOQUE DE HORMIGÓN MEDIANTE ANCLAJES DE 10 mm DE LONGITUD
5 LÁMINA IMPERMEABILIZANTE
6 PANTALLA CONTRA INSECTOS FIJADA A LISTONES DE MADERA
7 RELLENO DE MORTERO
8 CAPA DE AISLAMIENTO ACÚSTICO e=20 mm
9 ENLUCIDO DE YESO
10 CAPA DE AISLAMIENTO TÉRMICO RÍGIDO e=25 mm

1 WEATHERBOARD
2 140 mm THICK BRICKWORK
3 75 mm THICK THERMAL INSULATION PANEL FIXED TO BLOCKWORK
4 50 mm WIDE HOT DIP GALVANISED VERTICAL Z SECTION EVERY 600 mm ON 10 mm LONG PACKERS
5 WATERPROOF MEMBRANE
6 INSECT SCREEN FIXED TO TIMBER BATTENS
7 MORTAR FILLET
8 20 mm THICK MEDIUM DENSITY ROCKWOOD PACKING
9 WET PLASTER FINISH
10 25 mm THICK THERMAL INSULATION

1:20

0   0.1   0.5   1

LAYERS

CERÁMICA
BRICKWORK

HORMIGON
CONCRETE

MADERA
WOOD

CEMENTO
CEMENT

METAL
METAL

COMPUESTO
COMPOSITE

VIDRIO
GALSS

ENFOSCADO/
ESTUCO
MORTAR/
STUCCO

AISLAMIENTO
INSULATION

MEMBRANA
MEMBRANE

CERÁMICA
BRICKWORK

VIDRIO
GALSS

HORMIGON
CONCRETE

MADERA
WOOD

COMPUESTO
COMPOSITE

CARTÓN-YESO
PLASTER-BOARD

CERÁMICA
BRICKWORK

ENLUCIDO
PLASTER

Sección transversal A Cross section

1:500

0 1   5   10

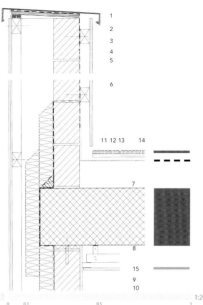

1 ALBARDILLA DE ALUMINIO
  CON FIJACIONES OCULTAS
2 CÁMARA DE VENTILACIÓN
3 LISTONES DE MADERA
  TRATADA DE 50 x 75 mm
4 RANURA DE 20 mm
  DE ANCHO
5 PANEL DE FIBROCEMENTO
6 MURO DE BLOQUE DE
  HORMIGÓN e=140 mm
7 RELLENO DE MORTERO
8 CAPA DE AISLAMIENTO
  ACÚSTICO e=20 mm
9 ENLUCIDO DE YESO
10 BARRERA DE VAPOR
11 PAVIMENTO DE MADERA
12 IMPERMEABILIZACIÓN
13 AISLAMIENTO 100-170 mm
14 LOSA DE HORMIGÓN
   e=300 mm
15 CARTÓN-YESO

1 PREFORMED ALUMINIUM
  COPING WITH SECRET,
  FASTENING CLIP
2 VENTILATION GAP
3 50 x 75 mm HORIZONTAL
  REGULARISED TREATED
  TIMBER BATTENS
4 20 mm WIDE VENTILATION/
  PACKING ZONE
5 WEATHERBOARD
6 140 mm BLOCKWORK
7 MORTAR FILLET
8 20 mm MEDIUM DENSITY
  ROCKWOOD PACKING
9 WET PLASTER FINISH
10 BREATHER MEMBRANE
11 TIMBER DECKING
   PANEL SYSTEM
12 WATERPROOF
13 ROOF INSULATION
   100-170 mm
14 300 mm CONCRETE SLAB
15 PLASTER-BOARD

1:20

Alzado sur **South elevation**

1:500

7,56 mill.☺   4.761 ☺/km²

4.237 m²
SUPERFICIE DE PARCELA
PLOT AREA

14.963 m²
SUPERFICIE CONSTRUIDA
GROSS FLOOR AREA

1:2.000

23% ALQUILER RENTAL   77% PROPIEDAD OWNERSHIP

24 🚗 95% VIVIENDA LIVING

5% TRABAJO WORKING

JÓVENES YOUNG PEOPLE   MAYORES SENIORS   ESTUDIANTES STUDENTS   100% CUALQUIERA ANY

147 UNITS

50% PÚBLICA SUBSIDISED   50% PRIVADA PRIVATE

COMERCIOS SHOPPING

347 ⌂/ha
DENSIDAD DE VIVIENDAS
DWELLING DENSITY

850 ☺/ha
DENSIDAD DE POBLACIÓN
RESIDENTIAL DENSITY

OTROS USOS
OTHER USES

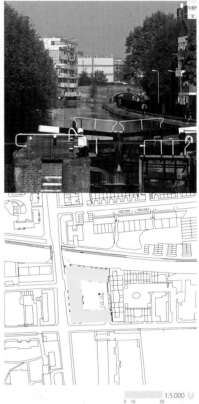

1:5.000
0 10   50

Adelaide Wharf es un ejemplo pionero de régimen mixto de vivienda. Situado junto al Regent's Canal en Hackney, un área clave para la regeneración del Este de Londres, este proyecto es el primero que entrega LWI (English Partnerships' London-Wide Initiative) con una mezcla de vivienda privada en propiedad, vivienda en alquiler suvencionada y vivienda dirigida a trabajadores de servicios esenciales. No hay diferencias visibles entre los regímenes de propiedad.

Adelaide Wharf is a pioneering mixed tenure housing scheme. Located on the Regent's Canal in Hackney, a key regeneration area of London, the scheme is the first to be delivered as part of English Partnerships' London-Wide Initiative (LWI) with a mix of privately sold, Key Worker and socially rented apartments.
There is no visible differentiation between tenures.

1.588
$/m²

1.470
£/m²

2.000
1.900
1.800
1.700
1.600
1.500
1.400
1.300
1.200
1.100
1.000
900
800
700
600
500
400
300
200
100

27

0

El edificio de seis plantas envuelve un patio ajardinado y cierra tres lados de una manzana en el centro de Londres. Los dos frentes a la calle disponen de accesos revestidos de paneles esmaltados de color intenso que comunican la calle con el patio de manzana y conducen hasta los núcleos de comunicación de las esquinas.

La planta tipo se organiza en una simetría rotacional a partir de los dos núcleos de comunicación, de los que parten los pasillos a las viviendas. Estos pasillos acaban en un hueco por el que entra la luz natural y permite orientar al usuario.

El vestíbulo principal de acceso y el hueco de escalera están decorados con un frente de 16 m de altura diseñado por el artista Richard Woods, con motivos inspirados en el anterior uso del solar y el lugar de procedencia de la madera que se emplea para revestir la fachada.

La planta baja se envuelve con una fachada de ladrillo y se ajusta a la pendiente que sube hasta el puente sobre el canal vecino. Los accesos a las viviendas desde la calle y sus puertas de color ritman la fachada y sirven de contraste al frente de ladrillo.

The six storey block wraps around three sides of a landscaped courtyard defining the edges of the city block, and the two street elevations have coloured entrance courts lined in glossy vitreous enamel cladding panels punched through between streetscape and courtyard, linking into the circulation cores in each corner.

The plan of the upper residential floors is based on a rotational symmetry about the two cores, from which the corridors radiate out.

The three blocks express this rotation externally in the way in which they turn the corners and their gable ends are clad.

The circulation is arranged in double banked corridors, each with daylight at one end to orientate the user.

The main entrance lobby and stairwell is lined with a 16 m tall printed timber pattern by local artist Richard Woods echoing the former use of the site and the external cladding.

The ground floor is a smooth engineering brick base, taking up the changes in level as the road climbs towards the canal bridge. Recesses and projections on the ground floor create a series of events on the street, with coloured doors acting as a contrast to the brick.

Por su parte, los niveles superiores poseen un carácter más ligero y matizado, y están revestidos con tableros de alerce siberiano que, fijados uno a uno, enfatizan las líneas verticales. Mientras, cada forjado, al exterior, se subraya con una banda horizontal de zinc.

Cada vivienda tiene un balcón que cuelga de las vigas que vuelan desde la cubierta, proporcionando un aspecto similar al de las grúas tradicionales en los almacenes preexistentes. Una de las barandillas de cada balcón se sustituye por un panel metálico de color y mientras todos estos se desplazan respecto al eje vertical en el alzado para limitar al máximo el exceso de sombra sobre los pisos inferiores.

El patio de manzana en el centro del proyecto es un jardín compartido por los residentes y funciona como foco de atención visto tanto desde las viviendas como desde la calle.

El simple uso de líneas relacionadas con la fachada, la circulación y el movimiento por el solar sirve para componer un jardín dotado de pequeños espacios para el uso de diferentes grupos de usuarios.

The cladding to the upper storeys is lighter and more textured in character, and consists of vertical boards of rough sawn Siberian Larch, fixed board on board to emphasise the vertical grain, set between bands of smooth zinc.

Each flat has a balcony supported from beams at roof level, cantilevering like lifting beams on warehouses. Each balcony is clad with a coloured plane with a single fold in it, and offset from the windows, cantilevering in alternate directions at each floor to produce double height gaps between them and reduce overshadowing to the living rooms below.

The courtyard at the heart of the scheme is a shared garden for use by the residents, the landscaping providing a focus when viewed from above and from the street. Simple use of geometric lines relating to the facades, circulation and lines of movement through the site create a variety of smaller spaces for the use of different groups of people.

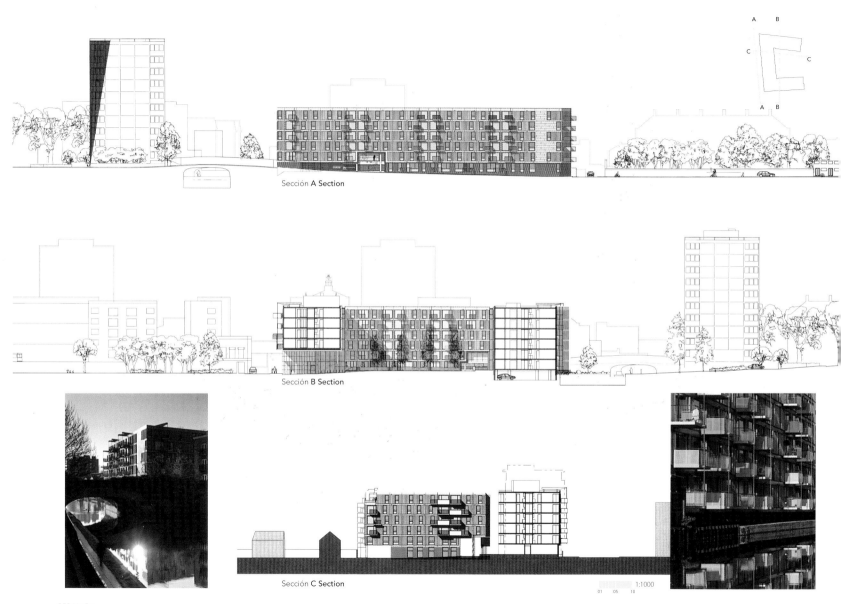

Sección A Section

Sección B Section

Sección C Section

1:1000
01 05 10

REGENT'S CANAL

WHISTON ROAD

QUEENSBRIDGE ROAD

Planta baja **Ground floor plan**

1:500

0 1   5   10

El diseño de las viviendas de 1, 2 y 3 dormitorios se basa en directrices comunes. El espacio de circulación se reduce al mínimo para maximizar los espacios vivideros y las zonas húmedas se distribuyen en una banda paralela al pasillo común. Mientras, los dormitorios y el salón se colocan junto a la fachada para aprovechar al máximo la luz. Las cocinas están abiertas al comedor y el salón. Además, los apartamentos de un dormitorio disponen de puertas dobles que lo comunican con el salón, ampliando el espacio para que sus ocupantes lo puedan utilizar de manera flexible. Las viviendas para familias se ubican en los pisos superiores y en su mayoría están orientadas hacia el sur. Sus balcones funcionan como extensiones del salón y sirven de estancia al aire libre.

The design of the 1, 2 and 3 bedroom apartments all follow a similar strategy. Circulation is kept to a minimum, so that the living area is maximised and the deep plan locates all the serviced spaces along the corridor wall, with the living/sleeping spaces making maximum use of the window walls. The layouts all have open plan living/kitchen/diners, to maximise the sense of space. Additionally, the one bedroom flats have double doors opening between the living and bedroom, extending the main space so that the occupants can use the space more flexibly. The family flats within the upper storeys are mostly located on the South facing elevations. Their enlarged balconies are extensions of the living room areas, and provide a room sized external amenity.

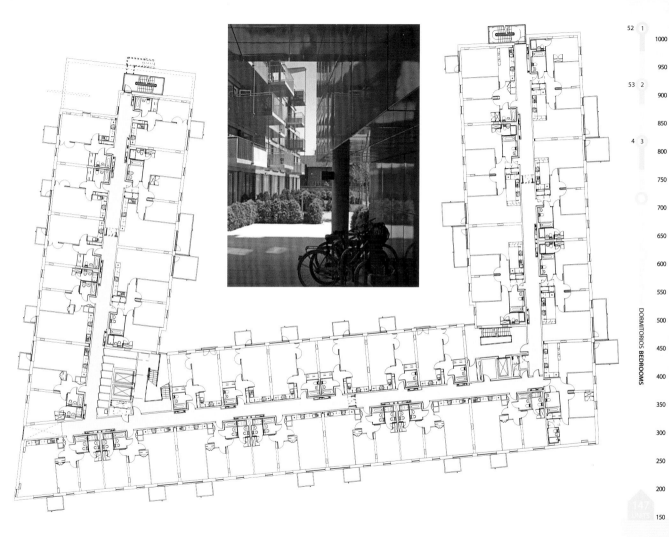

Planta cuarta **Fourth floor plan**

DORMITORIOS BEDROOMS

52	1
53	2
4	3

1000
950
900
850
800
750
700
650
600
550
500
450
400
350
300
250
200
150
100
50
0
UNITS

LAYERS

EXTERNAL

CERÁMICA
BRICKWORK

HORMIGON
CONCRETE

MADERA
WOOD

CEMENTO
CEMENT

METAL
METAL

COMPUESTO
COMPOSITE

VIDRIO
GALSS

ENFOSCADO/
ESTUCO
**MORTAR/
STUCCO**

AISLAMIENTO
INSULATION

MEMBRANA
MEMBRANE

PRINCIPAL

CERÁMICA
BRICKWORK

VIDRIO
GALSS

HORMIGON
CONCRETE

MADERA
WOOD

COMPUESTO
COMPOSITE

INTERNAL

CARTÓN-YESO
PLASTER-BOARD

CERÁMICA
BRICKWORK

ENLUCIDO
PLASTER

Sección **D** Section

1:500

0   1   5   10

Proceso y prefabricación

Adelaide Wharf es el resultado de tres años de trabajo conjunto con First Base y Bovis Lend Lease (BLL) desarrollando un sistema edificatorio que reduzca los gremios, los intermediarios y el plazo de la obra. BLL trabajó con el equipo de diseño desde el inicio, y todas las propuestas fueron discutidas en detalle con los contratistas a fin de comprobar su viabilidad y de buscar fórmulas de construcción más eficaces. El sistema resultante es un prototipo aplicado a los esquemas de vivienda First Base, que ha evolucionado y continuará haciéndolo, en función de lo aprendido a lo largo del desarrollo y construcción de Adelaide Wharf y futuros proyectos.

Los modernos métodos de construcción (MCM) empleados redujeron las subcontratas lo máximo posible, minimizando la ejecución *in situ* y haciendo un uso extensivo de la prefabricación a fin de reducir el tiempo de construcción e incrementar la calidad del edificio. Los elementos principales son una retícula de hormigón con losas y pilares prefabricados –un sistema de revestimiento prefabricado que evita el empleo de andamiaje–, cuartos húmedos y balcones prefabricados, y divisiones interiores en seco. El edificio se terminó en 18 meses, incluyendo un retraso de dos meses por obstrucciones bajo el suelo de la antigua zona industrial en la que se ubica el edificio.

A través del empleo de MCM, First Base ha reducido los costes globales de construcción en Adelaide Wharf un 20%, reduciendo a la vez el tiempo de entrega del proyecto en un 20%. Esto ha contribuido a un incremento del 10% del valor de la propiedad respecto a lo programado.

Process and Prefabrication

Adelaide Wharf is the result of three years of working closely with First Base and Bovis Lend Lease (BLL) to develop a building system that reduces trades, interfaces and construction time on site. BLL worked with the design team from the outset in putting together a fully costed bid for English Partnerships, and all proposals were discussed in detail with their trade contractors to test their buildability and find more efficient forms of construction. The resulting system is a prototype for other First Base housing schemes, which has and will continue to evolve as lessons are learnt from the procurement, construction and operation of Adelaide Wharf and future projects.

The Modern Construction Methods employed reduced trades to as few as possible, minimising wet trades on site and making extensive and pragmatic use of prefabrication to reduce time on site and improve the quality of build. The principal components are a concrete frame with flat slabs and blade columns using prefabricated reinforcement mats, a unitised cladding system avoiding the need for scaffolding, prefabricated bathroom pods, balconies and plant, and dry-lined internal partitions. The build was completed in 18 months, including for 2 months lost due to below ground obstructions in the former brownfield site.

Through the use of Modern Construction Methods, First Base has reduced overall construction costs at Adelaide Wharf by 20% whilst reducing delivery time for the project by 20%. This has also contributed to a 10% increase in property values across the schedule.

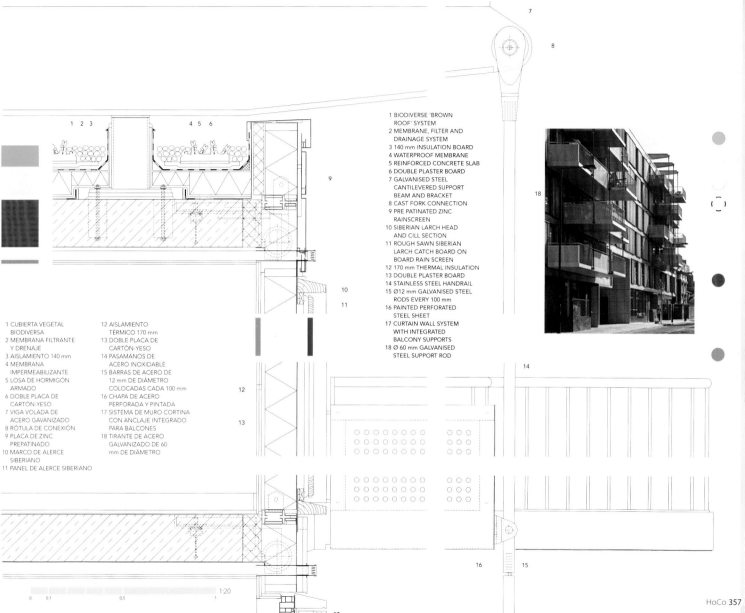

1 BIODIVERSE 'BROWN ROOF' SYSTEM
2 MEMBRANE, FILTER AND DRAINAGE SYSTEM
3 140 mm INSULATION BOARD
4 WATERPROOF MEMBRANE
5 REINFORCED CONCRETE SLAB
6 DOUBLE PLASTER BOARD
7 GALVANISED STEEL CANTILEVERED SUPPORT BEAM AND BRACKET
8 CAST FORK CONNECTION
9 PRE PATINATED ZINC RAINSCREEN
10 SIBERIAN LARCH HEAD AND CILL SECTION
11 ROUGH SAWN SIBERIAN LARCH CATCH BOARD ON BOARD RAIN SCREEN
12 170 mm THERMAL INSULATION
13 DOUBLE PLASTER BOARD
14 STAINLESS STEEL HANDRAIL
15 Ø12 mm GALVANISED STEEL RODS EVERY 100 mm
16 PAINTED PERFORATED STEEL SHEET
17 CURTAIN WALL SYSTEM WITH INTEGRATED BALCONY SUPPORTS
18 Ø 60 mm GALVANISED STEEL SUPPORT ROD

1 CUBIERTA VEGETAL BIODIVERSA
2 MEMBRANA FILTRANTE Y DRENAJE
3 AISLAMIENTO 140 mm
4 MEMBRANA IMPERMEABILIZANTE
5 LOSA DE HORMIGÓN ARMADO
6 DOBLE PLACA DE CARTÓN-YESO
7 VIGA VOLADA DE ACERO GAVANIZADO
8 RÓTULA DE CONEXIÓN
9 PLACA DE ZINC PREPATINADO
10 MARCO DE ALERCE SIBERIANO
11 PANEL DE ALERCE SIBERIANO

12 AISLAMIENTO TÉRMICO 170 mm
13 DOBLE PLACA DE CARTÓN-YESO
14 PASAMANOS DE ACERO INOXIDABLE
15 BARRAS DE ACERO DE 12 mm DE DIÁMETRO COLOCADAS CADA 100 mm
16 CHAPA DE ACERO PERFORADA Y PINTADA
17 SISTEMA DE MURO CORTINA CON ANCLAJE INTEGRADO PARA BALCONES
18 TIRANTE DE ACERO GALVANIZADO DE 60 mm DE DIÁMETRO

1:20
0   0.1   0.5   1

LAYERS

EXTERNAL

GRAVA
GRAVEL

CERÁMICA
TERRACOTTA

MADERA
WOOD

CEMENTO
CEMENT

VEGETACIÓN
PLANTING

METAL
METAL

AISLAMIENTO
INSULATION

MEMBRANA
MEMBRANE

HORMIGÓN
CONCRETE

MADERA
WOOD

CERÁMICA
TERRACOTTA

INTERNAL

CARTÓN-YESO
PLASTER-BOARD

ENLUCIDO
PLASTER

METAL
METAL

Hamonic + Masson

2,201 mill.☺   **20.887** ☺/km²

1.740 m²
SUPERFICIE CONSTRUIDA
GROSS FLOOR AREA

726 m²
SUPERFICIE DE PARCELA
PLOT AREA

1:2.000

69,7%
OCUPACIÓN
COVERED AREA

2,40
EDIFICABILIDAD
FLOOR AREA RATIO

100%
VIVIENDA
LIVING

TRABAJO
WORKING

COMERCIOS
SHOPPING

OTROS USOS
OTHER USES

100%
ALQUILER
RENTAL

PROPIEDAD
OWNERSHIP

JÓVENES
YOUNG PEOPLE

MAYORES
SENIORS

100%
ESTUDIANTES
STUDENTS

CUALQUIERA
ANY

100%
PÚBLICA
SUBSIDISED

PRIVADA
PRIVATE

65 UNITS

895 ☺/ha
DENSIDAD DE VIVIENDAS
DWELLING DENSITY

1.119 ☺/ha
DENSIDAD DE POBLACIÓN
RESIDENTIAL DENSITY

1:5.000
0 10   50

1.590 1.666 €/m²
$/m²

2.000

1900

1800

1600

1500

1400

1300

1200

1100

1000

900

800

700

600

500

400

300

200

100

0

28

Al ir remontando la calle Ménilmontant, empinada y bulliciosa, la residencia de estudiantes muestra una serie de paradojas. Así, y pese a integrarse perfectamente en el contexto del caserío de París, el edificio aparece como algo imprevisto e intrigante. La alineación exigida por el planeamiento ha sido perforada mediante un zaguán en doble altura, de color intenso, que dirige la vista del paseante hasta el interior de manzana, donde un mundo secreto le espera: dos pastillas de antiguos talleres convertidos en 16 estudios a ambos lados de una calle interior.

El espacio entre estos talleres y el zaguán, acentuado por el cambio topográfico, sirve a los estudiantes como animado lugar de encuentro al aire libre. Es además en este espacio donde se inicia un recorrido de colores e iluminación que se extiende por todo el edificio, animando los espacios de circulación. El color beige de los edificios circundantes contrasta con la fachada de la nueva residencia: un conjunto de reflejos, tonos y luces cambiantes producidos por el uso de contraventanas de acero inoxidable, lamas de aluminio y un acabado exterior reflectante. Las distintas posiciones de los sistemas de protección solar nos permite saber algo de la vida de los estudiantes: quién está en casa, quién está estudiando o quién está durmiendo.

While climbing the steep and bustling road of Ménilmontant the student residence slowly reveals itself in a series of paradoxes: deeply rooted in the context of the Parisian apartment block, it also stands out as something unexpected and intriguing.

The strict street alignment imposed by planning regulation is punctured by a two-storey porch, bursting with colour and light, begging the viewer to look deep into the heart of the Parisian block where a hidden world awaits: two rows of former workshops, rehabilitated into 16 loft apartments, a street-like space between. The spatial connection between these workshops and the porch, accentuated by a topografhical shift, provides a vibrant outdoor gathering space for the students. Here, a consistent approach to colour and lighting is established that then continues to each of the floors, giving life to the circulation zones. The beige of the surrounding buildings has been answered in the street facade by an ever-changing pattern of reflections, light and tone through the use of reflective stainless steel shutters, aluminium louvers and an iridescent render. The various forms of sun-shading devices act as a peephole into the student's lives: who is at home, who is studying, who is sleeping.

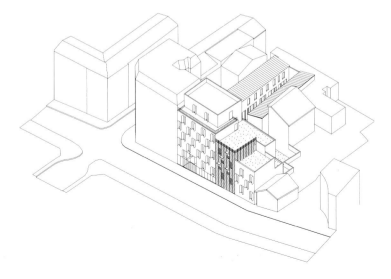

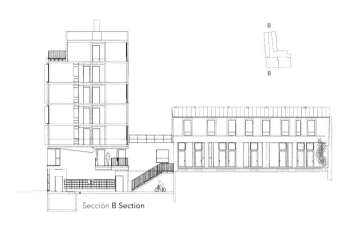

Sección B Section

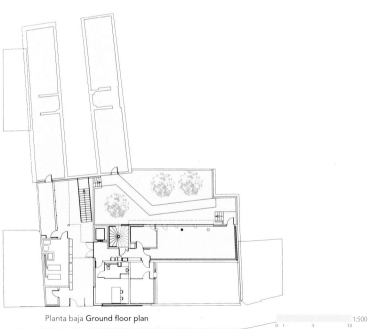

Planta baja Ground floor plan

0 1   5   10   1:500

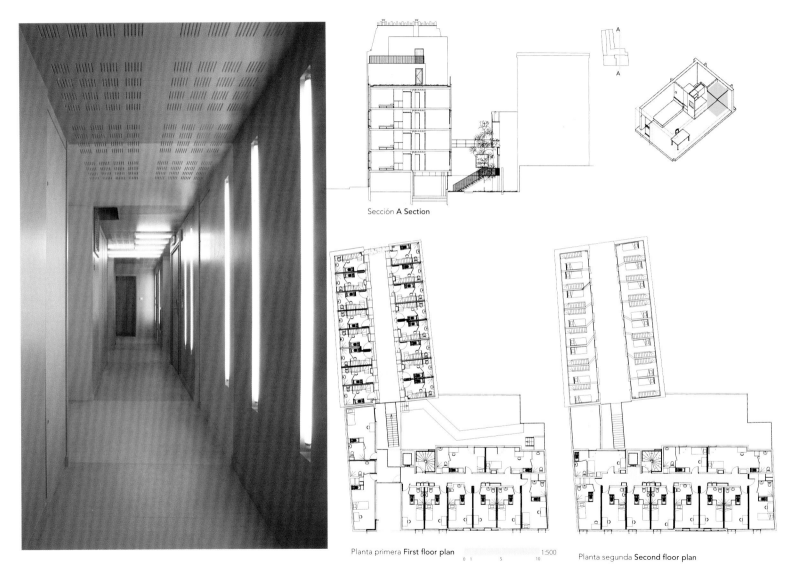

Sección **A Section**

Planta primera **First floor plan**   1:500

0 1   5   10

Planta segunda **Second floor plan**

1000

950

900

850

800

750

700

650

600

550

500

450

400

350

300

250

200

150

100

50

0

65

DORMITORIOS **BEDROOMS**

65
UNITS

UNITS

Sección **B Section**

1:500

0 1   5   10

1 ACABADO DE PINTURA ESPESA
   DE COLOR PLATA IRIDISCENTE
2 MURO DE HORMIGÓN
   e=160 mm
3 CARPINTERÍA DE
   ACERO INOXIDABLE
   TEMPLADO BRILLANTE
4 PICAPORTE DE ACERO
   INOXIDABLE
5 CONTRAVENTANA DE ACERO
   INOXIDABLE TEMPLADO
6 VENTANAS DE CARPINTERÍA
   DE ALUMINIO ANODIZADO
   Y VIDRIO DOBLE
7 CERROJO DE ACERO
   INOXIDABLE TEMPLADO
8 MARCO DE ACERO
   DE 40 x 40 mm
9 TOPE DE ACERO INOXIDABLE
10 ALFÉIZAR DE ACERO
   INOXIDABLE TEMPLADO
   BRILLANTE
11 CAPA DE AISLAMIENTO
   TÉRMICO e=100 mm

1 SILVER IRIDESCENT
   PAINT-RENDER HYBRID
2 160 CONCRETE STRUCTURE
3 BRIGHT ANNEALED
   STAINLESS STEEL FRAME
4 STAINLESS STEEL PIVOT
5 BRIGHT ANNEALED
   STAINLESS STEEL SHUTTER
6 RAW ANODISED
   WINDOW FRAMES WITH
   DOUBLE GLAZING
7 BRIGHT ANNEALED
   STAINLESS STEEL LATCH
8 40 x 40 mm STEEL FRAME
9 STAINLESS STEEL PIVOT
10 BRIGHT ANNEALED
   STAINLESS STEEL SILL
11 100 mm INSULATION

Sección horizontal **Horizontal section**

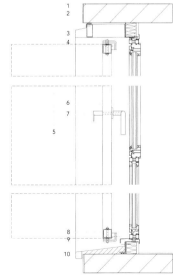

1:20

0   0.1   0.5   1

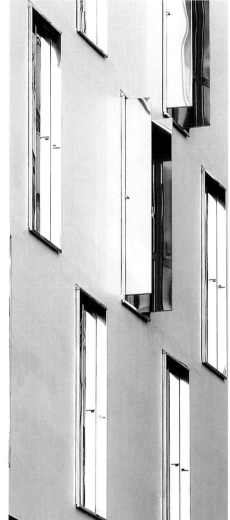

FACHADA FAÇADE

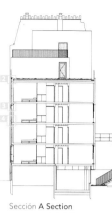

Sección **A** Section

1:500

1:50

Spanish legend:

1 ANGULAR DE ACERO DE 60 mm x 60 mm
2 LAMAS DE ALUMINIO DE 120 mm DE LARGO x 20 cm DE ANCHO
3 ESTRUCTURA DE ACERO
4 ALBARDILLA DE ALUMINIO ANODIZADO
5 CUBIERTA VERDE VEGETACIÓN, TIERRA VEGETAL, BARRERA ANTI-RAÍCES, CAPA DE DRENAJE, MEMBRANA IMPERMEABILIZANTE, CAPA DE AISLAMIENTO TÉRMICO e=100 mm, BARRERA DE VAPOR
6 REVESTIMIENTO DE LAMAS DE ALUMINIO CON SISTEMA DE FIJACIÓN OCULTO
7 SUBESTRUCTURA DE ACERO GALVANIZADO
8 MURO DE HORMIGÓN e=160 mm

9 CAPA DE AISLAMIENTO TÉRMICO e=100 mm
10 MONTANTE DE CHAPA DE ALUMINIO PLEGADA
11 ESTRUCTURA DE TUBOS DE ACERO GALVANIZADO DE 40 x 40 mm
12 POSTIGO RETRÁCTIL Y PRACTICABLE DE LAMAS DE ALUMINIO
13 POSTIGO RETRÁCTIL DE LAMAS DE ALUMINIO
14 CARPINTERÍA DE ALUMINIO ANODIZADO Y DOBLE ACRISTALAMIENTO
15 REVESTIMIENTO DE PLACAS DE ALUMINIO CON SISTEMA DE FIJACIÓN OCULTO
16 MEMBRANA
17 CARTÓN-YESO
18 LOSA DE HORMIGÓN
19 AISLAMIENTO BAJO LOSA

English legend:

1 60 x 60 STEEL ANGLE
2 120 x 20 ALUMINIUM SLATS
3 STEEL STRUCTURE
4 RAW ANODISED ALUMINIUM CAPPING
5 GREEN ROOF: 'TUNDRA' VEGETATION, GROWING MEDIUM, ROOT BARRIER, DRAINAGE LAYER, WATERPROOF MEMBRANE, 100 mm INSULATION, CONDENSATION MEMBRANE.
6 ALUMINIUM CLADDING WITH CONCEALED FASTENING SYSTEM
7 GALVANISED STEEL STRUCTURE
8 160 CONCRETE STRUCTURE
9 100 INSULATION
10 FOLDED ALUMINIUM SPINE
11 40 mm x 40 mm GALVANISED STEEL TUBE STRUCTURE
12 LOUVERED SHUTTER SYSTEM, ALUMINIUM SLATS, ROTATABLE AND OPERABLE
13 LOUVRED SHUTTER SYSTEM, ALUMINIUM SLATS, ROTATABLE
14 RAW ANODISED WINDOW FRAMES WITH DOUBLE GLAZING
15 ALUMINIUM CLADDING WITH CONCEALED FASTENING SYSTEM
16 MEMBRANE
17 PLASTER BOARD
18 CONCRETE SLAB
19 HIGH DENSITY INSULATION

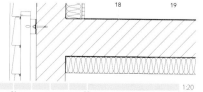

1:20

LAYERS
EXTERNAL

GRAVA
GRAVEL

CERÁMICA
TERRACOTTA

MADERA
WOOD

CEMENTO
CEMENT

VEGETACIÓN
PLANTING

METAL
METAL

AISLAMIENTO
INSULATION

MEMBRANA
MEMBRANE

HORMIGÓN
CONCRETE

MADERA
WOOD

CERÁMICA
TERRACOTTA

INTERNAL

CARTÓN-YESO
PLASTER-BOARD

ENLUCIDO
PLASTER

METAL
METAL

CUBIERTA ROOF

Kasper Danielsen Architects / Future Systems kd-arkitekter.dk, future-systems.com Copenhagen. DENMARK, 2008 Ben Websters vej 23

1:5.000

0 10   50

0,518
mill.☺

5.780
☺/km²

13.800 m²
SUPERFICIE CONSTRUIDA
GROSS FLOOR AREA

9.200 m²
SUPERFICIE DE PARCELA
PLOT AREA

1:2.000

11,1%
OCUPACIÓN
COVERED AREA

1,13
EDIFICABILIDAD
FLOOR AREA RATIO

ALQUILER
RENTAL

100%
PROPIEDAD
OWNERSHIP

JÓVENES
YOUNG PEOPLE

MAYORES
SENIORS

ESTUDIANTES
STUDENTS

100%
CUALQUIERA
ANY

105 🚗

100%
VIVIENDA
LIVING

81
UNITS

TRABAJO
WORKING

PÚBLICA
SUBSIDISED

100%
PRIVADA
PRIVATE

COMERCIOS
SHOPPING

88
⌂/ha

253
☺/ha

DENSIDAD DE VIVIENDAS
DWELLING DENSITY

DENSIDAD DE POBLACIÓN
RESIDENTIAL DENSITY

OTROS USOS
OTHER USES

16.315
DDK/m²

2.000

1900

1.688
$/m²

1800

1700

1600

1500

1400

1300

1200

1100

1000

900

800

700

600

500

400

300

200

100

0

La torre de viviendas Metropolis se encuentra sobre una pequeña península del puerto de Copenhague, Sluseholmen, que en el pasado formó parte del sistema de esclusas que lo regulaban. La esclusa fue cerrada en 1995 y reabierta en 2004, permitiendo la navegación hasta el acceso al edificio Metropolis. Las industrias que ocupaban la zona han dejado paso a un nuevo tejido residencial de gran desarrollo que en la actualidad comprende unas 1100 nuevas viviendas.

Cabe destacar en los alrededores el área de Kanalbyen (Ciudad del Canal) al sur del edificio Metropolis, una zona que se inspira en los barrios que jalonan los canales de Amsterdam. En ella, la llegada de nuevos residentes ha impulsado la aparición de comercios, cafés y oficinas. El edificio consta de 10 plantas que alojan 81 viviendas de entre 90 y 210 m² con al menos dos balcones cada una.

Los puentes históricos del puerto de Copenhague solían tener alguna torre con una cubierta de cobre verde. Junto al paisaje de silos industriales, estas torres han servido como motivo de inspiración para el diseño del edificio. Las fachadas curvas de este edificio están revestidas de paneles de hormigón aligerado de color verde o azulado en función de la climatología. Dichos paneles están fabricados con cemento blanco, polvo de mármol y fibra de vidrio de color.

La orientación del edificio busca el máximo de iluminación a través de los grandes ventanales panorámicos en los salones. Además, los áticos tienen acceso directo a terrazas sobre la cubierta. En cualquier caso, las viviendas del primer piso también poseen estupendas vistas, ya que se levantan sobre un zócalo de 4 m de altura que aloja el aparcamiento. Alrededor de la península, un muelle de madera, de acceso enteramente público, permite el amarre temporal de embarcaciones.

El proyecto está meticulosamente pensado para mantener el diseño original de las piezas de hormigón prefabricado. En este sentido, la obra se mantuvo dentro del presupuesto gracias al uso extensivo de módulos que se repiten.

The residential tower Metropolis is located on a small peninsula in the Copenhagen Harbour.
The peninsula called Sluseholmen has in the past been part of the locks regulating Copenhagen Harbour. The lock was closed in 1995, only to be re-opened in 2004, so today it is possible to sail right to the front door of Metropolis. The area has historically been one of primarily industry and factories, but today the area is one of the most progressive residential developments in central Copenhagen. In the last decade about 1100 dwellings has been build on and around Sluseholmen.
Of particular interest is 'Kanalbyen' (The Canal City) just south of Metropolis. An area inspired by residential neighbourhoods along the canals in Amsterdam.
The gentrification of the area has meant that a wide array of new shops and cafes as well as many multinational companies has established themselves in this part of the city.
Metropolis is a 10 story all residential development.

The 81 condominiums vary between 90 and 210 square meters and all units feature minimum two balconies. Traditionally the bridges in the harbour have featured green copper clad towers. Together with the industrial silos these towers has served as an inspirational motive for the design of Metropolis.
The projects curved forms is clad in fiber-concrete shells in a blueish-green colour, all depending on the weather. The shells are made from white cement concrete, marble dust and coloured glasfibre.
The building is oriented to take maximum advantage of daylight and is featuring large panoramic windows in the living rooms. The penthouse units have access to private roof terraces.
Even the ground level units enjoy the spectacular views due to a 4-meter high plinth, which conceals the parking garage. Surrounding most of the peninsula is a wooden bridge/marina allowing for temporary mooring.
The facility is open to the public just as the peninsula itself.
The project is meticulously thought through in order to keep the original design intend intact with the rational, pre-cast concrete element construction type. Because of the extensive use of repetitive modular components, Metropolis was build within budget.

Alzado oeste **West elevation**

Alzado este **East elevation**

1:500

0 1   5   10

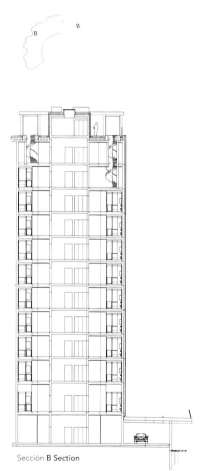

Sección B Section

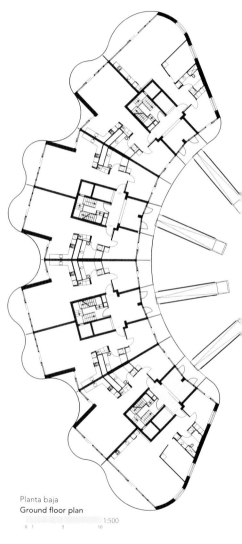

Planta baja
Ground floor plan

1:500

0 1   5   10

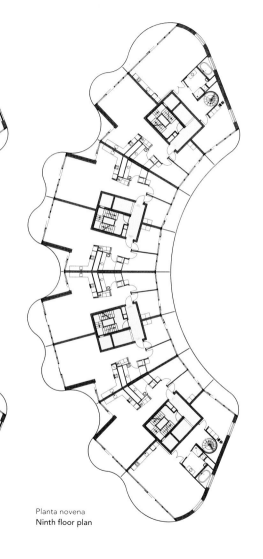

Planta cuarta
Fourth floor plan

Planta novena
Ninth floor plan

Planta décima
Tenth floor plan

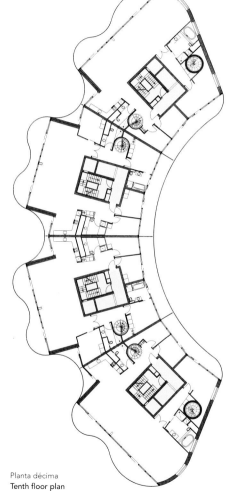

LAYERS

EXTERNAL

CERÁMICA
BRICKWORK

HORMIGON
CONCRETE

MADERA
WOOD

CEMENTO
CEMENT

METAL
METAL

COMPUESTO
COMPOSITE

VIDRIO
GALSS

ENFOSCADO/
ESTUCO
**MORTAR/
STUCCO**

AISLAMIENTO
INSULATION

MEMBRANA
MEMBRANE

PRINCIPAL

CERÁMICA
BRICKWORK

VIDRIO
GALSS

HORMIGON
CONCRETE

MADERA
WOOD

COMPUESTO
COMPOSITE

INTERNAL

CARTÓN-YESO
PLASTER-BOARD

CERÁMICA
BRICKWORK

ENLUCIDO
PLASTER

FACHADA FAÇADE

1:500   Sección **A** Section

0 1   5   10

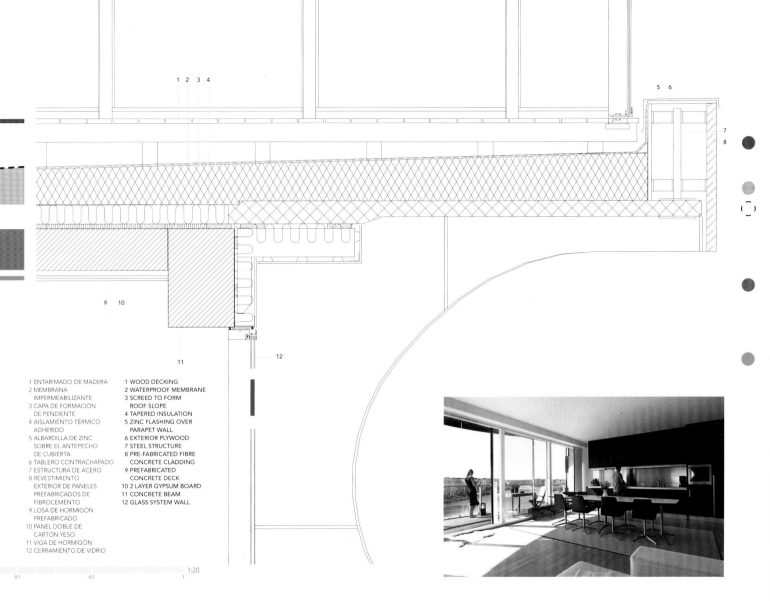

1 2 3 4

5 6

7
8

9 10

11

12

LAYERS

EXTERNAL

GRAVA
GRAVEL

CERÁMICA
TERRACOTTA

MADERA
WOOD

CEMENTO
CEMENT

VEGETACIÓN
PLANTING

METAL
METAL

AISLAMIENTO
INSULATION

MEMBRANA
MEMBRANE

HORMIGÓN
CONCRETE

MADERA
WOOD

CERÁMICA
TERRACOTTA

INTERNAL

CARTÓN-YESO
PLASTER-BOARD

ENLUCIDO
PLASTER

METAL
METAL

1 ENTARIMADO DE MADERA	1 WOOD DECKING
2 MEMBRANA IMPERMEABILIZANTE	2 WATERPROOF MEMBRANE
3 CAPA DE FORMACIÓN DE PENDIENTE	3 SCREED TO FORM ROOF SLOPE
4 AISLAMIENTO TÉRMICO ADHERIDO	4 TAPERED INSULATION
5 ALBARDILLA DE ZINC SOBRE EL ANTEPECHO DE CUBIERTA	5 ZINC FLASHING OVER PARAPET WALL
6 TABLERO CONTRACHAPADO	6 EXTERIOR PLYWOOD
7 ESTRUCTURA DE ACERO	7 STEEL STRUCTURE
8 REVESTIMIENTO EXTERIOR DE PANELES PREFABRICADOS DE FIBROCEMENTO	8 PRE-FABRICATED FIBRE CONCRETE CLADDING
9 LOSA DE HORMIGÓN PREFABRICADO	9 PREFABRICATED CONCRETE DECK
10 PANEL DOBLE DE CARTÓN YESO	10 2 LAYER GYPSUM BOARD
11 VIGA DE HORMIGÓN	11 CONCRETE BEAM
12 CERRAMIENTO DE VIDRIO	12 GLASS SYSTEM WALL

1:20

0   0.1   0.5   1

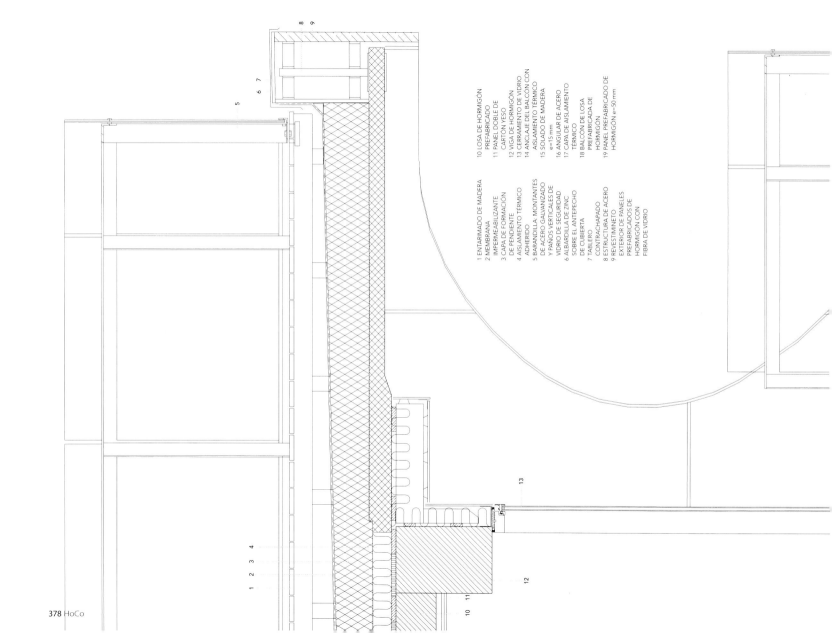

1 ENTARIMADO DE MADERA
2 MEMBRANA IMPERMEABILIZANTE
3 CAPA DE FORMACIÓN DE PENDIENTE
4 AISLAMIENTO TÉRMICO ADHERIDO
5 BARANDILLA. MONTANTES DE ACERO GALVANIZADO Y PAÑOS VERTICALES DE VIDRIO DE SEGURIDAD
6 ALBARDILLA DE ZINC SOBRE EL ANTEPECHO DE CUBIERTA
7 TABLERO CONTRACHAPADO
8 ESTRUCTURA DE ACERO
9 REVESTIMINETO EXTERIOR DE PANELES PREFABRICADOS DE HORMIGÓN CON FIBRA DE VIDRIO

10 LOSA DE HORMIGÓN PREFABRICADO
11 PANEL DOBLE DE CARTÓN YESO
12 VIGA DE HORMIGÓN
13 CERRAMIENTO DE VIDRIO
14 ANCLAJE DEL BALCÓN CON AISLAMIENTO TÉRMICO
15 SOLADO DE MADERA e=15mm
16 ANGULAR DE ACERO
17 CAPA DE AISLAMIENTO TÉRMICO
18 BALCÓN DE LOSA PREFABRICADA DE HORMIGÓN
19 PANEL PREFABRICADO DE HORMIGÓN e=50 mm

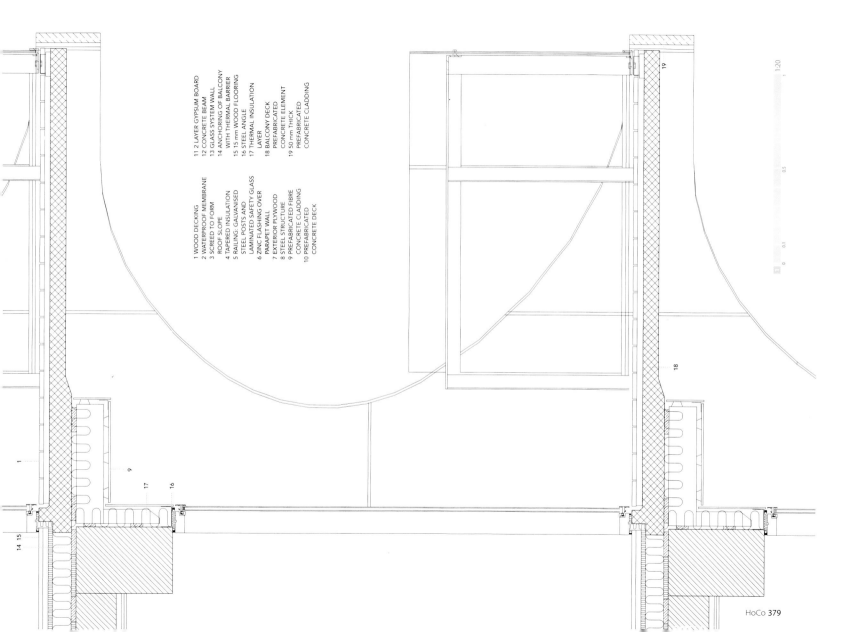

1 WOOD DECKING
2 WATERPROOF MEMBRANE
3 SCREED TO FORM
  ROOF SLOPE
4 TAPERED INSULATION
5 RAILING; GALVANISED
  STEEL POSTS AND
  LAMINATED SAFETY GLASS
6 ZINC FLASHING OVER
  PARAPET WALL
7 EXTERIOR PLYWOOD
8 STEEL STRUCTURE
9 PREFABRICATED FIBRE
  CONCRETE CLADDING
10 PREFABRICATED
   CONCRETE DECK

11 2 LAYER GYPSUM BOARD
12 CONCRETE BEAM
13 GLASS SYSTEM WALL
14 ANCHORING OF BALCONY
   WITH THERMAL BARRIER
15 15 mm WOOD FLOORING
16 STEEL ANGLE
17 THERMAL INSULATION
   LAYER
18 BALCONY DECK
   PREFABRICATED
   CONCRETE ELEMENT
19 50 mm THICK
   PREFABRICATED
   CONCRETE CLADDING

1:20

Gigon / Guyer gigon-guyer.ch Zurich. SWITZERLAND, 2007 Hofwiesenstrasse 140, Brunnenhofstrasse 6

0,358
mill.☺

4.083
☺/km²

8.519 m²
SUPERFICIE DE PARCELA
PLOT AREA

18.437 m²
SUPERFICIE CONSTRUIDA
GROSS FLOOR AREA

1:2.000

36,5%
OCUPACIÓN
COVERED AREA

1,66
EDIFICABILIDAD
FLOOR AREA RATIO

100%
ALQUILER
RENTAL

PROPIEDAD
OWNERSHIP

75 🚗

95%
VIVIENDA
LIVING

78 UNITS

JÓVENES
YOUNG PEOPLE

MAYORES
SENIORS

ESTUDIANTES
STUDENTS

100%
FAMILIAS NUMEROSAS
LARGE FAMILIES

TRABAJO
WORKING

100%
PÚBLICA
SUBSIDISED

PRIVADA
PRIVATE

COMERCIOS
SHOPPING

92 ⌂/ha

458 ☺/ha

DENSIDAD DE VIVIENDAS
DWELLING DENSITY

DENSIDAD DE POBLACIÓN
RESIDENTIAL DENSITY

5%
EDUCACIÓN
EDUCATION

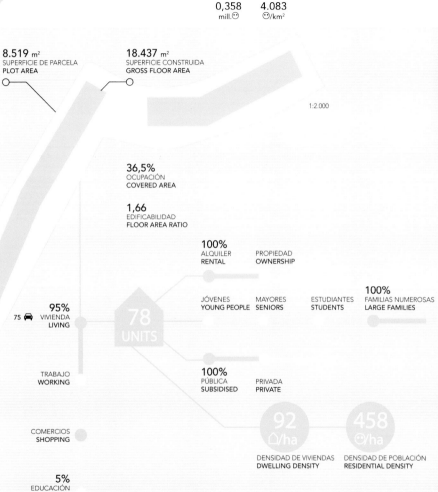

1:5.000

0 10   50

Los dos volúmenes alargados y ligeramente quebrados sirven para reestructurar el parque Buchegg. El edificio de seis niveles en la calle Hofwiesen se orienta hacia la calle y el parque, bordeándolo y protegiéndolo del ruido del tráfico. Por su parte, el bloque de cuatro a seis niveles sobre la calle Brunnenhof está rodeado por vegetación a ambos lados, situación que lo convierte en un edificio dentro del parque, y se ajusta a la altura de las construcciones próximas.

Two lightly bent, elongated volumes of different heights restructure Buchegg Park. The six-storey building on Hofwiesenstrasse is oriented towards the park as well as to the street. It borders off the park from the street and protects it from the street noise. The four to five-storey building on Brunnenhofstrasse is surrounded by green on both sides, making it a 'house within the park' and it corresponds to the height development of the neighbouring buildings.

3.224
CHF/m²

1.838
$/m²

2.000

1.900

1.800

1.700

1.600

1.500

1.400

1.300

1.200

1.100

1.000

900

800

700

600

500

400

300

200

100

0

Ambos edificios se conciben como apilamientos de planos horizontales volados en mayor o menor medida. En el lado del parque, estos vuelos sirven de soporte a generosos balcones, mientras que del lado de la calle se sitúan los núcleos de escaleras y logias. Así, el acceso al edificio sobre la calle Hofwiesen se realiza a través de escaleras longitudinales y logias exteriores junto a las cocinas que sirven de espacio protegido al aire libre orientadas a poniente. Los salones tienen doble orientación a poniente y a levante, desde donde se accede a una gran terraza. Mientras, los dormitorios miran al lado más tranquilo del parque.

En el edificio de la calle Brunnenhof los salones están orientados hacia la fachada sur-sureste del parque, con el que se conectan mediante un balcón. En el volumen de cuatro niveles, con orientación norte-sur, la cocina comunica con el salón sobre la fachada sur. En el resto del bloque, las cocinas miran al noroeste.

Los espacios de las viviendas son generosos y su distribución beneficia la flexibilidad de usos y la libertad de movimientos. Esta flexibilidad se ve además favorecida en planta baja por una serie de espacios intermedios entre viviendas compartidos por todos los residentes. Los portales se comportan como estancias que conectan la calle con el parque.

Both buildings are conceived as 'stacks' of horizontal plates that cantilever to different degrees. Facing the park they form generous balconies and towards the street they provide stairways with *loggias*. For the noise-polluted building on Hofwiesenstrasse access to the apartments is via longitudinally arranged stairways and *loggias* that adjoin to the eat-in kitchens and serve as protected exterior spaces oriented towards the evening sun.

All bedrooms are organised towards the quiet park side. The living rooms are oriented towards both the East and the West, and towards the park side they lead onto a deep balcony. Within the Brunnenhofstrasse building the living rooms are positioned along the facade and are oriented towards the park to the South and Southeast via the balcony area. In the four-storey, purely North or South oriented part of the building the eat-in kitchen is connected to the living room on the south side. In the averted parts of the building the eat-in kitchens are directed towards the evening sun and provide the apartment with a two-sided orientation.

A circuit-like layout lends all apartment types spatial generosity, freedom of movement and enhanced flexibility of use. The latter is further enhanced within the ground floor apartments by means of anterooms between apartments that can be shared by residents and each with their own access.

En ellos se pueden almacenar carritos de niños, motocicletas, triciclos o juguetes.

Mientras, el sótano aloja salas de lavado y secado de ropa con iluminación natural y conectadas directamente con la escalera. La guardería y la escuela infantil se encuentran a pie de calle, en los extremos de ambos edificios y con salida al parque. En ellos, la sala de juego ocupa un lugar prominente frente a la calle y el parque.

A los dos edificios se accede por patios que comunican con la calle y que están delimitados por setos que protegen la privacidad de las viviendas en planta baja que se elevan ligeramente del plano del terreno. Entre el edificio y el parque, una porción de este terreno sirve como área de juegos y vivero de plantas y está delimitada por una línea de seto. La fachada se compone de balcones y de las bandas horizontales de los forjados que rodean el edificio. Entre estos forjados, se platea un sistema de ventanas de suelo a techo que alterna con paneles de vidrio de color, más un plano externo de paneles deslizantes de vidrio reflectante o mate para proteger del sol.

The entrance lobbies on the ground floor are connecting rooms that link to the park and are where pushchairs, scooters, children's bikes and toys can be stored. The illuminated laundry rooms and drying rooms are located in the basement directly next to the stairs.

The double kindergarten and nursery are housed at the top ends of both buildings at the pathway to the park. The recreation room takes the most prominent position at the corner of the street and the pathway. Both residential buildings are accessed from the street via forecourts. A continuous hedgerow along the street creates a green zone that provides the necessary privacy for the lightly elevated ground floor apartments.

The park-facing apartments are staggered by half a storey to allow the incorporation of recreational and play areas as well as seedling nurseries between the park and the building. Hedges connecting to the extended building approaches form the border between these zones and the park.

The facades are formed by the protracting balconies and the concrete bands that wrap horizontally around the building. Between them storey-height windows and alternately coloured glass panels form together with sliding anti-sun and screening glass panels an interplay of reflecting and matt, translucent and transparent coloured surfaces.

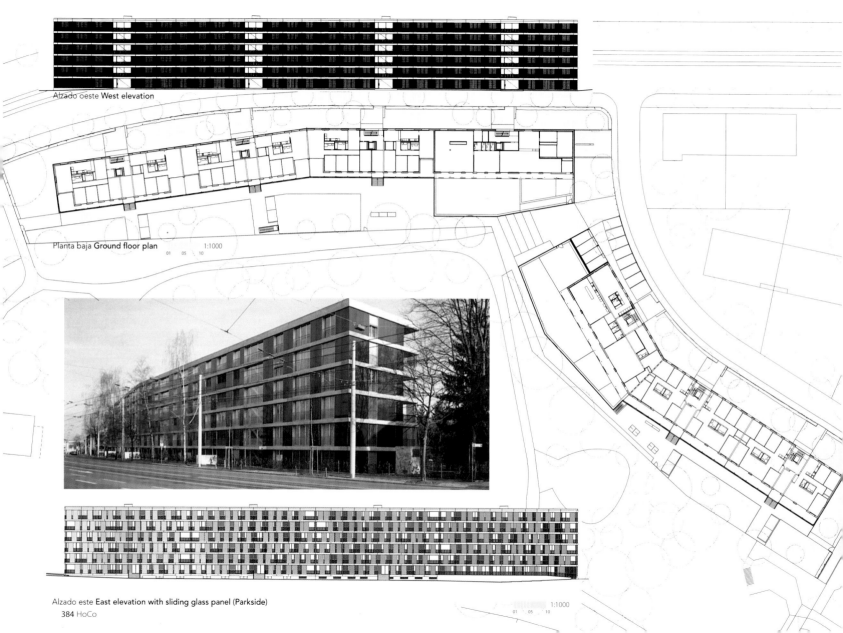

Alzado oeste West elevation

Planta baja Ground floor plan   1:1000
01   05   10

Alzado este East elevation with sliding glass panel (Parkside)

1:1000
01   05   10

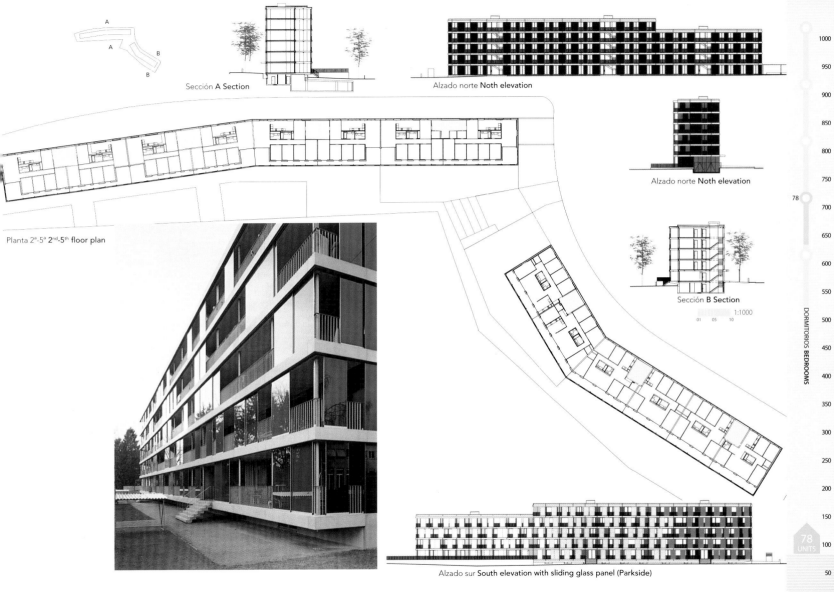

Sección **A** Section

Alzado norte **Noth elevation**

Alzado norte **Noth elevation**

Planta 2ª-5ª **2ⁿᵈ-5ᵗʰ floor plan**

Sección **B** Section

1:1000

01   05   10

Alzado sur **South elevation with sliding glass panel (Parkside)**

78

DORMITORIOS BEDROOMS

78
UNITS

1000
950
900
850
800
750
700
650
600
550
500
450
400
350
300
250
200
150
100
50
0
UNITS

Planta **B6 plan, 6 1/2 Rooms**

Planta **H2 plan, 5 1/2 Rooms**

Planta **H4 plan, 5 1/2 Rooms**

1:500

0 1   5   10

PLANTAS TIPO **TYPE PLANS**

La combinación de colores es producto de la colaboración con el artista Adrian Schiess. Hacia la calle, los vidrios son de color azul oscuro y violeta, mientras que hacia el parque los colores pasan de los tonos azulados al verde y luego al rojo.

El aspecto fluido y cambiante de los colores se ve además favorecido por la posición variable de los paneles deslizantes, hasta el punto que son los residentes quienes en última instancia componen la gama de colores cada día.

The colour concept was developed together with the artist Adrian Schiess. Facing the street the glazing is dark blue and violet while facing the park the colour tones progress over large spaces from blue tones to green and then red. The impression of the fluent, changing play of colours is enhanced by the varying positions of the sliding elements – ultimately the residents amend and create new colour compositions every day, even every hour.

LAYERS

EXTERNAL

CERÁMICA
BRICKWORK

HORMIGON
CONCRETE

MADERA
WOOD

CEMENTO
CEMENT

METAL
METAL

COMPUESTO
COMPOSITE

VIDRIO
GALSS

ENFOSCADO/
ESTUCO
MORTAR/
STUCCO

AISLAMIENTO
INSULATION

MEMBRANA
MEMBRANE

PRINCIPAL

CERÁMICA
BRICKWORK

VIDRIO
GALSS

HORMIGON
CONCRETE

MADERA
WOOD

COMPUESTO
COMPOSITE

INTERNAL

CARTÓN-YESO
PLASTER-BOARD

CERÁMICA
BRICKWORK

ENLUCIDO
PLASTER

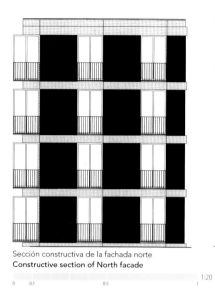

Sección constructiva de la fachada norte
Constructive section of North facade

0   0.1   0.5   1   1:20

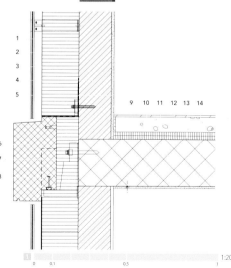

1 2 VIDRIOS DE SEGURIDAD
  LAMINADOS e=6 mm DE
  COLOR ACORDE CON
  DISEÑO DE FACHADA
2 CÁMARA DE AIRE e=4,4 cm
3 CAPA DE AISLAMIENTO
  TÉRMICO DE LANA
  DE ROCA e=20 cm
4 MURO DE LADRILLO
  e=17,5 cm
5 ENLUCIDO DE
  YESO e=1,5 cm
6 PIEZA DE HORMIGÓN
  PREFABRICADO
7 CAPA DE AISLAMIENTO
  TÉRMICO e=12 cm
8 PIEZA DE ANCLAJE
9 SOLADO DE PARQUÉ e=1 cm
10 CAPA DE NIVELACIÓN
   DE CEMENTO e=8 cm
11 LÁMINA PLÁSTICA
12 CAPA DE AISLAMIENTO
   ACÚSTICO e=2 cm
13 CAPA DE AISLAMINETO
   TÉRMICO e=2 cm
14 FORJADO DE
   HORMIGÓN e=25 cm

1 2 x 6 mm THICK LAMINATED
  SAFETY GLASS, COLOUR
  ACCORDING TO
  COLOUR SCHEME
2 4.4 cm THICK AIR CAVITY
3 20 cm THICK MINERAL
  WOLL INSULATION LAYER
4 17.5 cm THICK BRICK WALL
5 1.5 cm THICK
  PLASTER LAYER
6 PREFABRICATED
  CONCRETE ELEMENT
7 12 cm THICK THERMAL
  INSULATION LAYER
8 FASTENING PIECE
9 1 cm THICK PARQUET
  FLOORING
10 8 cm THICK CEMENT
   SCREED
11 PLASTIC SHEET
12 2 cm THICK ACOUSTIC
   INSULATION LAYER
13 2 cm THICK THERMAL
   INSULATION LAYER
14 25 cm THICK
   CONCRETE SLAB

1   1:20

0   0.1   0.5   1

LAYERS

EXTERNAL

GRAVA
GRAVEL

CERÁMICA
TERRACOTTA

MADERA
WOOD

CEMENTO
CEMENT

VEGETACIÓN
PLANTING

METAL
METAL

AISLAMIENTO
INSULATION

MEMBRANA
MEMBRANE

PRINCIPAL

HORMIGÓN
CONCRETE

MADERA
WOOD

CERÁMICA
TERRACOTTA

INTERNAL

CARTÓN-YESO
PLASTER-BOARD

ENLUCIDO
PLASTER

METAL
METAL

1 2 3 4 5 6 7 8 9

10

11

1:20

0   0.1   0.5   1

1 VEGETACIÓN	1 VEGETATION
2 CAPA DE TIERRA NATURAL e=8 cm	2 8 cm THICK NATURAL SOIL LAYER
3 LÁMINA GEOTEXTIL	3 GEOTEXTILE MAT
4 BARRERA DE VAPOR	4 VAPOUR BARRIER
5 LÁMINA GEOTEXTIL	5 GEOTEXTILE MAT
6 CAPA DE AISLAMIENTO TÉRMICO e=20 cm	6 20 cm THICK THERMAL INSULATION LAYER
7 MEMBRANA IMPERMEABILIZANTE	7 WATERPROOF MEMBRANE
8 FORJADO DE HORMIGÓN DE ESPESOR VARIABLE (24-35 cm)	8 24-35 cm THICK CONCRETE SLAB
9 ENLUCIDO DE YESO	9 WITHE PLASTER LAYER
10 PIEZA DE HORMIGÓN PREFABRICADO	10 PREFABRICATED CONCRETE ELEMENT
11 CAPA DE AISLAMIENTO TÉRMICO e=12 cm	11 12 cm THICK THERMAL INSULATION LAYER

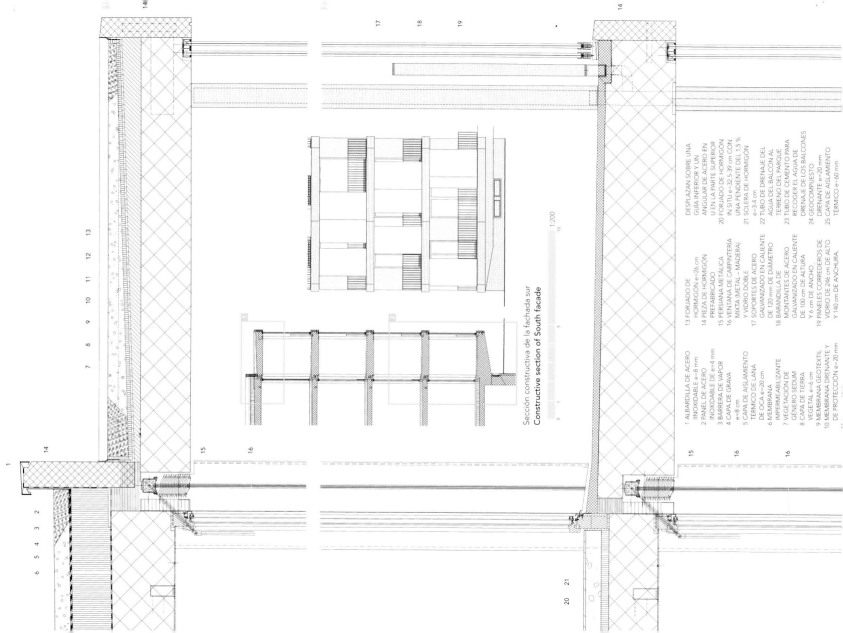

Sección constructiva de la fachada sur
Constructive section of South facade

1:200

1 ALBARDILLA DE ACERO
INOXIDABLE e=8 mm
2 PANEL DE ACERO
INOXIDABLE DE e=4 mm
3 BARRERA DE VAPOR
4 CAPA DE GRAVA
e=8 cm
5 CAPA DE AISLAMIENTO
TÉRMICO DE LANA
DE OCA e=20 cm
6 MEMBRANA
IMPERMEABILIZANTE
7 VEGETACIÓN DE
GÉNERO SEDUM
VEGETAL e=6 cm
8 CAPA DE TIERRA
VEGETAL e=6 cm
9 MEMBRANA GEOTEXTIL
10 MEMBRANA DRENANTE Y
DE PROTECCIÓN e=20 mm

13 FORJADO DE
HORMIGÓN e=26 cm
14 PIEZA DE HORMIGÓN
PREFABRICADO
15 PERSIANA METÁLICA
16 VENTANA DE CARPINTERÍA
MIXTA (METAL – MADERA)
Y VIDRIO DOBLE
17 SOPORTES DE ACERO
GALVANIZADO EN CALIENTE
DE 120 mm DE DIÁMETRO
18 BARANDILLA DE
MONTANTES DE ACERO
GALVANIZADO EN CALIENTE
DE 100 cm DE ALTURA
Y 6 cm DE ANCHO
19 PANELES CORREDEROS DE
VIDRIO DE 246 cm DE ALTO
Y 140 cm DE ANCHURA.

DESPLAZAN SOBRE UNA
GUÍA INFERIOR Y UN
ANGULAR DE ACERO EN
U EN LA PARTE SUPERIOR
20 FORJADO DE HORMIGÓN
IN SITU e=32,5-39 cm CON
UNA PENDIENTE DEL 1,5 %
21 SOLERA DE HORMIGÓN
e=3-4 cm
22 TUBO DE DRENAJE DEL
AGUA DEL BALCÓN AL
TERRENO DEL PARQUE
23 TUBO DE CEMENTO PARA
RECOGER EL AGUA DE
DRENAJE DE LOS BALCONES
24 GEOCOMPUESTO
DRENANTE e=20 mm
25 CAPA DE AISLAMIENTO
TÉRMICO e=60 mm

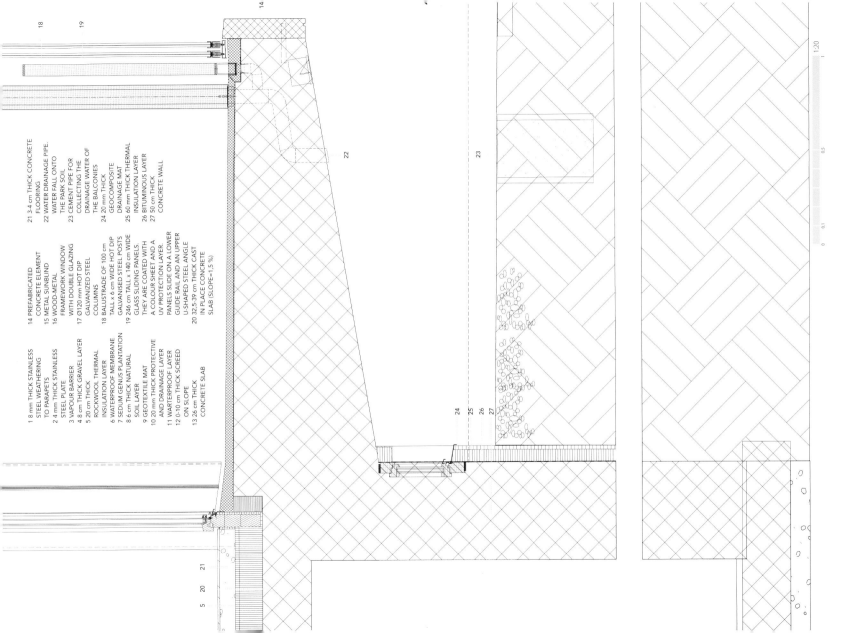

1 8 mm THICK STAINLESS STEEL WEATHERING TO PARAPETS
2 4 mm THICK STAINLESS STEEL PLATE
3 VAPOUR BARRIER
4 8 cm THICK GRAVEL LAYER
5 20 cm THICK ROCKWOOL THERMAL INSULATION LAYER
6 WATERPROOF MEMBRANE
7 SEDUM GENUS PLANTATION
8 6 cm THICK NATURAL SOIL LAYER
9 GEOTEXTILE MAT
10 20 mm THICK PROTECTIVE AND DRAINAGE LAYER
11 WATERPROOF LAYER
12 0-10 cm THICK SCREED ON SLOPE
13 26 cm THICK CONCRETE SLAB

14 PREFABRICATED CONCRETE ELEMENT
15 METAL SUNBLIND
16 WOOD-METAL FRAMEWORK WINDOW WITH DOUBLE GLAZING
17 Ø120 mm HOT DIP GALVANIZED STEEL COLUMNS
18 BALUSTRADE OF 100 cm TALL x 6 cm WIDE HOT DIP GALVANISED STEEL POSTS
19 246 cm TALL x 140 cm WIDE GLASS SLIDING PANELS. THEY ARE COATED WITH A COLOUR SHEET AND A UV PROTECTION LAYER. PANELS SLIDE ON A LOWER GUIDE RAIL AND AN UPPER U-SHAPED STEEL ANGLE
20 32.5-39 cm THICK CAST IN PLACE CONCRETE SLAB (SLOPE=1,5 %)

21 3-4 cm THICK CONCRETE FLOORING
22 WATER DRAINAGE PIPE. WATER FALL ONTO THE PARK SOIL
23 CEMENT PIPE FOR COLLECTING THE DRAINAGE WATER OF THE BALCONIES
24 20 mm THICK GEOCOMPOSITE DRAINAGE MAT
25 60 mm THICK THERMAL INSULATION LAYER
26 BITUMINOUS LAYER
27 50 cm THICK CONCRETE WALL

1:20

1,450
mill.☺

4.141
☺/km²

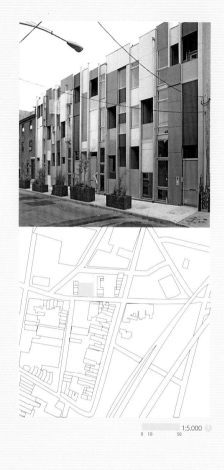

1:5.000

0 10   50

2,26
EDIFICABILIDAD
FLOOR AREA RATIO

698 m²
SUPERFICIE DE PARCELA
PLOT AREA

1.577 m²
SUPERFICIE CONSTRUIDA
GROSS FLOOR AREA

1:2.000

59,6%
OCUPACIÓN
COVERED AREA

8 🚗

100%
VIVIENDA
LIVING

TRABAJO
WORKING

COMERCIOS
SHOPPING

OTROS USOS
OTHER USES

ALQUILER
RENTAL

100%
PROPIEDAD
OWNERSHIP

8
UNITS

JÓVENES
YOUNG PEOPLE

MAYORES
SENIORS

ESTUDIANTES
STUDENTS

100%
CUALQUIERA
ANY

100%
PÚBLICA
SUBSIDISED

PRIVADA
PRIVATE

115
⌂/ha
DENSIDAD DE VIVIENDAS
DWELLING DENSITY

430
☺/ha
DENSIDAD DE POBLACIÓN
RESIDENTIAL DENSITY

2.248 $/m²

2.248 $/m²

2.000

1.900

1.800

1.700

1.600

1.500

1.400

1.300

1.200

1.100

1.000

900

800

700

600

500

400

300

200

100

31

El proyecto explora el potencial latente que se esconde en el ritmo vertical y la regularidad de la vivienda en hilera de Filadelfia. La composición de bandas verticales estrechas de las fachadas a las calles Laurel y Pollard sirve para cuestionar las líneas tradicionales de demarcación entre elementos contiguos. En el proceso, un cierto nivel de densidad e incluso expansividad programática surge a partir del estrecho margen de la vivienda en hilera.

Se ha puesto especial cuidado en iluminar el espacio resultante, estrecho y alargado, con gran cantidad de luz natural. Los muros y los puentes de vidrio traslúcido filtran la luz desde arriba a todas las estancias en las viviendas superiores. En las unidades inferiores, un baño dispuesto en el centro funciona como linterna para distribuir la luz a través de esos puentes y tabiques traslúcidos.

El proyecto es el primero en los EEUU en obtener la clasificación LEED-Homes Platinum: Thin Flats consume

This project explores the latent potentials hidden within the vertical rhythm and regularity of the Philadelphia row home. Thin faces fronting both Laurel and Pollard St. mask and question conventional lines of demarcation between neighboring parties. In the process, a degree of density yet expansiveness uncommon to the thin space of the single family and duplex Row home emerges both programmatically and experientially. Great care was taken to flood the center of these long thin spaces with light. Translucent glass bridges and walls filter light from above and into all adjacent rooms in the upper units. In the lower units a centralized bathroom acts as a 'lantern' to distribute light through the same glass bridge and walls to all rooms below.

Destined to be the first LEED-Homes Platinum duplexes in the country, Thin Flats units use on average 60% less energy than typical new construction, 50% less water and comes with an electric NEV

un 60% de energía y un 50% de agua menos que cualquier obra nueva tradicional, y las viviendas se entregan con un automóvil eléctrico.

El proyecto ofrece además, una estrecha relación entre el interior y el exterior ya que todas las viviendas tienen balcones, la vivienda superior tiene una terraza sobre la cubierta y la de la planta baja un jardín trasero. El agua caliente se obtiene mediante paneles solares y se almacena en depósitos, mientras que la calefacción por suelo radiante se obtiene de calentadores de gas de alta eficiencia energética. Toda el agua de lluvia es recogida sobre la cubierta vegetal y enviada a un depósito subterráneo de 23.000 litros de capacidad. Un sistema electrónico controla la iluminación, audio, vídeo, seguridad, calefacción, ventilación y aire acondicionado de la vivienda.

Thin Flats pretende convertirse en un modelo de vivienda contemporánea y sostenible al tiempo que se integra en la tipología de vivienda más tradicional de Filadelfia.

(Neighborhood Electric Vehicle). An intimate relationship between outside and inside is created as all rooms have balconies, the upper unit has an extensive green roof garden and the lower unit has a garden at grade. All the domestic hot water is provided by dedicated solar thermal panels and storage tanks while the units are heated with a 96% efficient condensing boiler and radiant flooring. All water that falls on the site is captured by a combination of green roofs and a 6,000 gallon storage tank below the parking area. A centralized 'home automation system' controls all lights, audio, video, security and HVAC in the home. Thin Flats strives to be a model of contemporary and sustainable dwelling while working with the most traditional building typology common in Philadelphia, the Row.

Sección longitudinal **A Long Section**   1:500

0 1   5   10

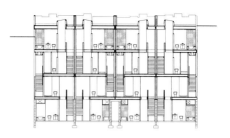

Sección transversal **B Cross section**

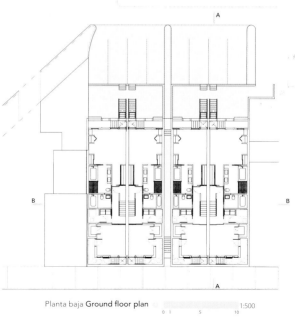

Planta baja **Ground floor plan**   1:500

0 1   5   10

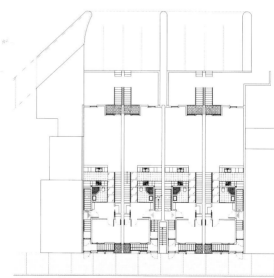

Planta primera **First floor plan**

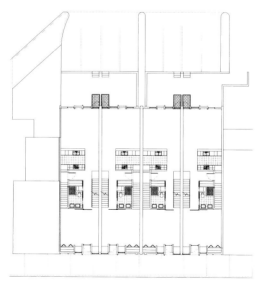

Planta segunda **Second floor plan**

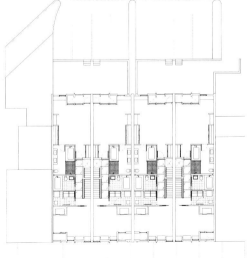

Planta tercera Third floor plan

DORMITORIOS **BEDROOMS**

1000
950
900
850
800
750
700
650
600
550
500
450
400
350
300
250
200
150
100
50
0

UNITS

8 3

CERÁMICA
BRICKWORK

HORMIGON
CONCRETE

MADERA
WOOD

CEMENTO
CEMENT

METAL
METAL

COMPUESTO
COMPOSITE

VIDRIO
GALSS

ENFOSCADO/
ESTUCO
**MORTAR/
STUCCO**

AISLAMIENTO
INSULATION

MEMBRANA
MEMBRANE

PRINCIPAL

CERÁMICA
BRICKWORK

VIDRIO
GALSS

HORMIGON
CONCRETE

MADERA
WOOD

COMPUESTO
COMPOSITE

INTERNAL

CARTÓN-YESO
PLASTER-BOARD

CERÁMICA
BRICKWORK

ENLUCIDO
PLASTER

FACHADA FACADE

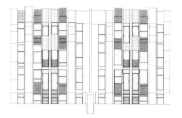

Alzado desde el jardín **Garden elevation**

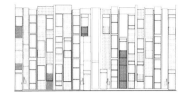

Alzado desde la calle **Street elevation**

1:500

0 1   5   10

1:100

0   0.5   1

Fachada a la calle **Street facade**

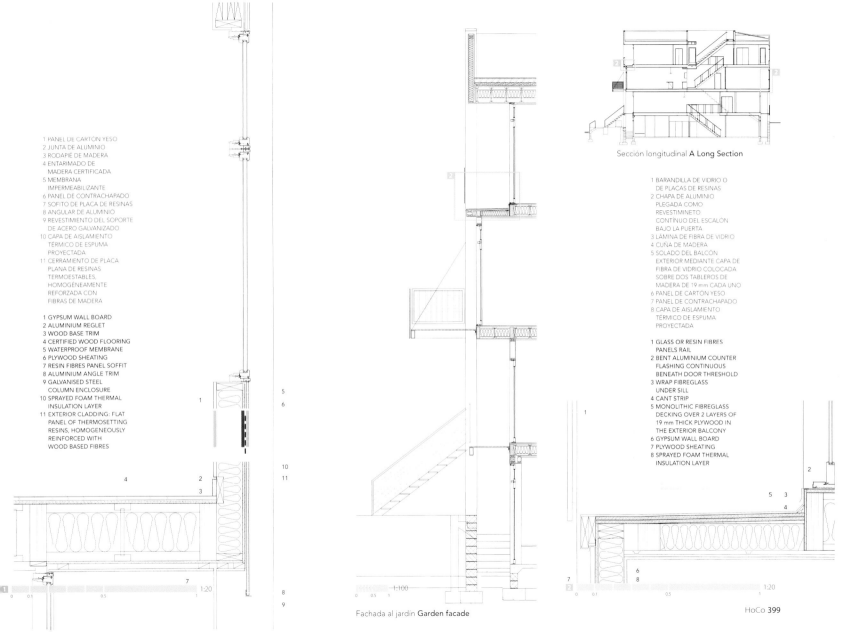

1 PANEL DE CARTÓN YESO
2 JUNTA DE ALUMINIO
3 RODAPIÉ DE MADERA
4 ENTARIMADO DE
  MADERA CERTIFICADA
5 MEMBRANA
  IMPERMEABILIZANTE
6 PANEL DE CONTRACHAPADO
7 SOFITO DE PLACA DE RESINAS
8 ANGULAR DE ALUMINIO
9 REVESTIMIENTO DEL SOPORTE
  DE ACERO GALVANIZADO
10 CAPA DE AISLAMIENTO
  TÉRMICO DE ESPUMA
  PROYECTADA
11 CERRAMIENTO DE PLACA
  PLANA DE RESINAS
  TERMOESTABLES,
  HOMOGÉNEAMENTE
  REFORZADA CON
  FIBRAS DE MADERA

1 GYPSUM WALL BOARD
2 ALUMINIUM REGLET
3 WOOD BASE TRIM
4 CERTIFIED WOOD FLOORING
5 WATERPROOF MEMBRANE
6 PLYWOOD SHEATING
7 RESIN FIBRES PANEL SOFFIT
8 ALUMINIUM ANGLE TRIM
9 GALVANISED STEEL
  COLUMN ENCLOSURE
10 SPRAYED FOAM THERMAL
  INSULATION LAYER
11 EXTERIOR CLADDING: FLAT
  PANEL OF THERMOSETTING
  RESINS, HOMOGENEOUSLY
  REINFORCED WITH
  WOOD BASED FIBRES

Sección longitudinal **A Long Section**

1 BARANDILLA DE VIDRIO O
  DE PLACAS DE RESINAS
2 CHAPA DE ALUMINIO
  PLEGADA COMO
  REVESTIMINETO
  CONTÍNUO DEL ESCALON
  BAJO LA PUERTA
3 LÁMINA DE FIBRA DE VIDRIO
4 CUÑA DE MADERA
5 SOLADO DEL BALCÓN
  EXTERIOR MEDIANTE CAPA DE
  FIBRA DE VIDRIO COLOCADA
  SOBRE DOS TABLEROS DE
  MADERA DE 19 mm CADA UNO
6 PANEL DE CARTÓN YESO
7 PANEL DE CONTRACHAPADO
8 CAPA DE AISLAMIENTO
  TÉRMICO DE ESPUMA
  PROYECTADA

1 GLASS OR RESIN FIBRES
  PANELS RAIL
2 BENT ALUMINIUM COUNTER
  FLASHING CONTINUOUS
  BENEATH DOOR THRESHOLD
3 WRAP FIBREGLASS
  UNDER SILL
4 CANT STRIP
5 MONOLITHIC FIBREGLASS
  DECKING OVER 2 LAYERS OF
  19 mm THICK PLYWOOD IN
  THE EXTERIOR BALCONY
6 GYPSUM WALL BOARD
7 PLYWOOD SHEATING
8 SPRAYED FOAM THERMAL
  INSULATION LAYER

Fachada al jardín **Garden facade**

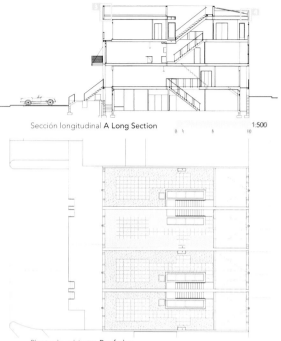

Sección longitudinal **A Long Section**　　　1:500

Planta de cubiertas **Roof plan**

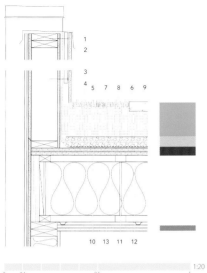

LAYERS

EXTERNAL

GRAVA
GRAVEL

CERÁMICA
TERRACOTTA

MADERA
WOOD

CEMENTO
CEMENT

VEGETACIÓN
PLANTING

METAL
METAL

AISLAMIENTO
INSULATION

MEMBRANA
MEMBRANE

PRINCIPAL

HORMIGÓN
CONCRETE

MADERA
WOOD

CERÁMICA
TERRACOTTA

INTERNAL

CARTÓN-YESO
PLASTER-BOARD

ENLUCIDO
PLASTER

METAL
METAL

1 ALBARDILLA DE ALUMINIO
2 PANEL DE CEMENTO
3 LISTÓN DE MADERA
   TRATADA
4 MEMBRANA
   IMPERMEABILIZANTE
5 PLANTACIÓN SEMI-
   INTENSIVA SOBRE CUBIERTA
6 LOSA DE CEMENTO
7 LÁMINA SEPARADORA
8 CAPA DE AGREGADO
   LIGERO DE GRAVA
9 BARRERA ANTIRRAÍCES
10 2 CAPAS DE
   CONTRACHAPADO
   DE 19 mm
11 VIGA DE MADERA
12 CAPA DE AISLAMIENTO
   TÉRMICO
13 2 CAPAS DE CARTÓN
   YESO COLGADO DE
   SUBESTRUCTURA METÁLICA

1 PREFINISHED ALUMINIUM
2 CEMENT BOARD
3 TREATED WOOD BATTEN
4 ICE AND WEATHER SEAL
5 ROOFMEADOW SEMI-
   INTENSIVE GROWTH MEDIA
6 CONCRETE PAVER
7 SEPARATION FABRIC
8 GRAVEL LIGHT WEIGHT
   AGGREGATE LAYER
9 ROOT BARRIER
10 2 LAYERS OF 19 mm
   THICK PLYWOOD
11 TIMBER ROOF JOIST
12 THERMAL INSULATION
   LAYER
13 2 GYPSUM BOARD LAYERS
   WITH DEEP METAL
   FURRING CHANNEL

3   0   0.1   0.5   1   1:20

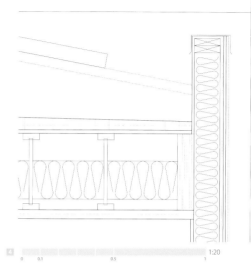

4   0   0.1   0.5   1   1:20

0,599 mill.☺   **2.581** ☺/km²

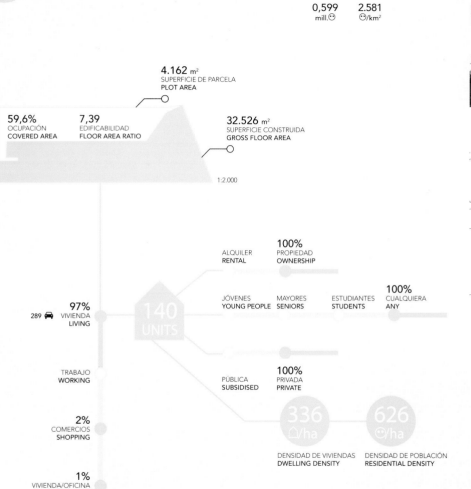

4.162 m²
SUPERFICIE DE PARCELA
PLOT AREA

59,6%
OCUPACIÓN
COVERED AREA

7,39
EDIFICABILIDAD
FLOOR AREA RATIO

32.526 m²
SUPERFICIE CONSTRUIDA
GROSS FLOOR AREA

1:2.000

ALQUILER
RENTAL

100%
PROPIEDAD
OWNERSHIP

JÓVENES
YOUNG PEOPLE

MAYORES
SENIORS

ESTUDIANTES
STUDENTS

100%
CUALQUIERA
ANY

97%
289 🚗 VIVIENDA
LIVING

140 UNITS

TRABAJO
WORKING

PÚBLICA
SUBSIDISED

100%
PRIVADA
PRIVATE

2%
COMERCIOS
SHOPPING

336 ⌂/ha

626 ☺/ha

1%
VIVIENDA/OFICINA
LIFE/WORK UNIT

DENSIDAD DE VIVIENDAS
DWELLING DENSITY

DENSIDAD DE POBLACIÓN
RESIDENTIAL DENSITY

1:5.000
0 10   50

$/m²

2.000

1.900

1.800

1.700

1.600

1.500

1.400

1.300

1.200

1.100

1.000

900

800

700

600

500

400

300

200

100

0

El edificio Macallen es una pieza fundamental en la revitalización del barrio de South Boston. Su diseño requirió una revisión de las tipologías convencionales de vivienda para dar lugar a un edificio innovador que se mantuviese dentro de las restricciones presupuestarias del promotor. El edificio se encuentra en un lugar de transición entre las rampas de acceso a la autopista elevada, un tejido residencial vetusto y una zona industrial abandonada. El proyecto responde a dos escalas diferentes y a la condición de frontera entre tejidos en que se encuentra la parcela. Para ello se plantean varias respuestas espaciales y reacciones a la esfera pública que vienen acompañadas de cambios en los materiales y en las fachadas que refuerzan las escalas de interacción. En el lado oeste, el edificio responde a la autopista con un muro cortina que proporciona vistas panorámicas a los residentes

As a pivotal building in the urban revitalization of South Boston, the Macallen Building's design requires a reassessment of conventional residential typologies to produce an innovative building that works within a developer's financially competitive budget. Occupying a transitional site that mediates between highway off-ramps, an old residential fabric, and an industrial zone, the building negotiates different scales and urban configurations. The design addresses two scales and the different edge conditions of the surrounding context through varied spatial conditions, various ways of reacting to the public sphere, and accompanying material and facade articulations to reinforce the scales of interaction. On the western end, the building responds to the highway with a curtain wall yielding panoramic views for the residents inside the building.

On the eastern end, brickwork mirrors that of the residential building fabric, extending the logic of the storefront and pedestrian scale elements on that facade. On the north and south facades, bronzed aluminum panels reflect the industrial neighborhood component and express the structural system organization. Additionally, the Macallen building was designed from the ground up to take advantage of 'green' building techniques and materials. It is the first LEED certified building of its type in Boston.

Diagram de volúmenes **Diagram mass**

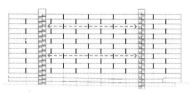

Diagramas de secciones **Diagrams sections**

En el lado este, la fábrica de ladrillo refleja la construcción tradicional en la zona y la fachada mantiene el escaparate comercial a pie de calle y los elementos a escala del peatón. Mientras, en las fachadas norte y sur los paneles de bronce reflejan el carácter industrial del barrio y su sistema de organización estructural. Además, el edificio Macallen fue proyectado desde el principio teniendo en cuenta técnicas constructivas y materiales que fueran sostenibles. Se trata del primer edifico de este tipo en Boston que obtiene la clasificación americana LEED.

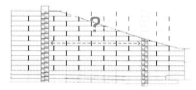

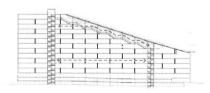

Alzado norte **North elevation**

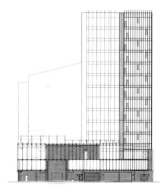

Alzado oeste **West elevation** 1:1000

01 05 10

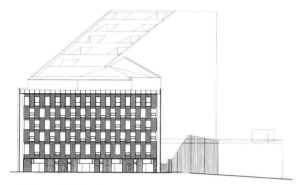

Alzado este **East elevation**

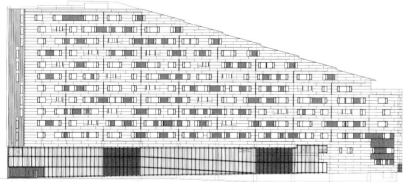

Alzado sur **South elevation**

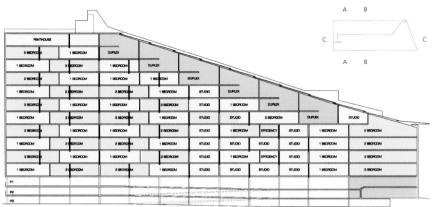

Esquema de tipos de vivienda en Sección C Dwelling types in Section C

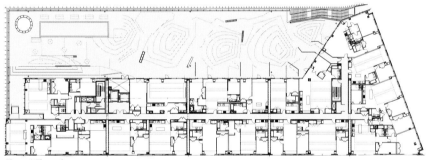

Planta 1 Floor plan

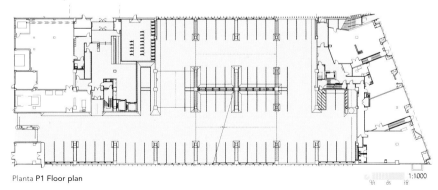

Planta P1 Floor plan

1:1000

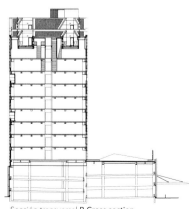

Sección transversal A Cross section

Sección transversal B Cross section

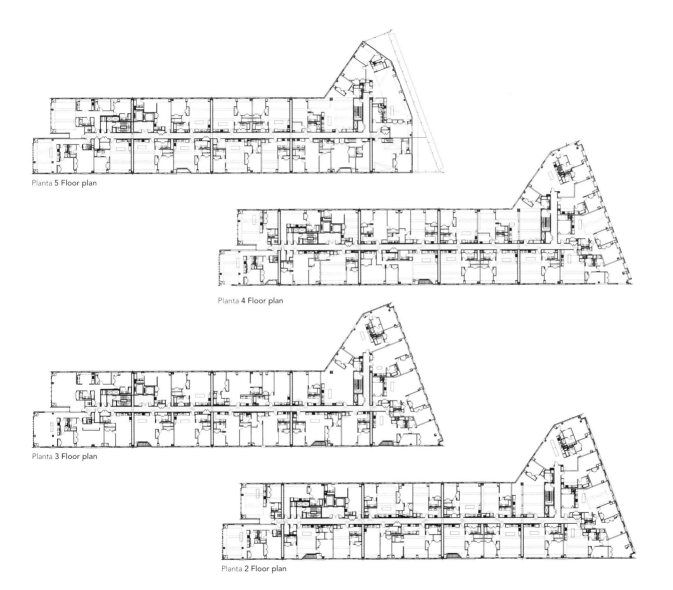

Planta 5 Floor plan

Planta 4 Floor plan

Planta 3 Floor plan

Planta 2 Floor plan

DORMITORIOS BEDROOMS

42 1 1000

950

66 2 900

850

4 3 800

750

700

650

28 600

550

500

450

400

350

300

250

200

140 UNITS 150

100

50

0 UNITS

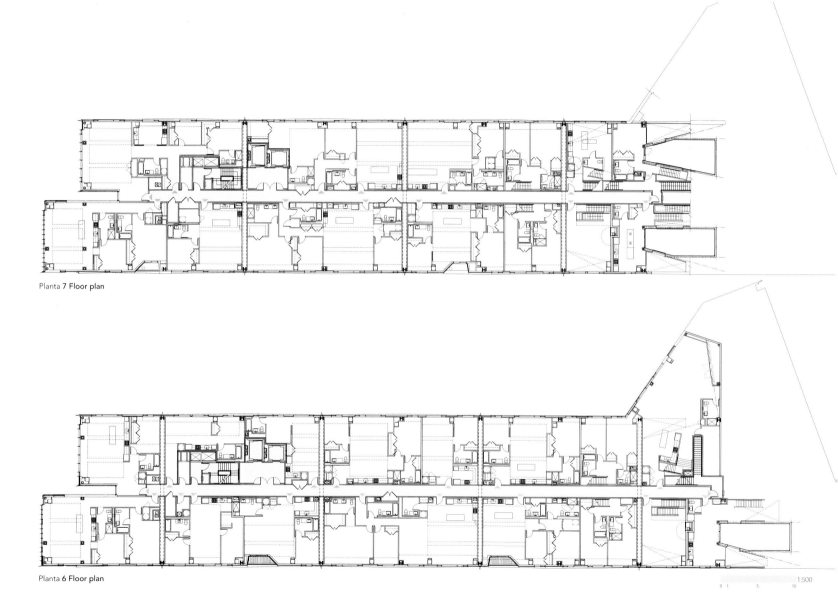

Planta 7 Floor plan

Planta 6 Floor plan

1:500

0 1   5   10

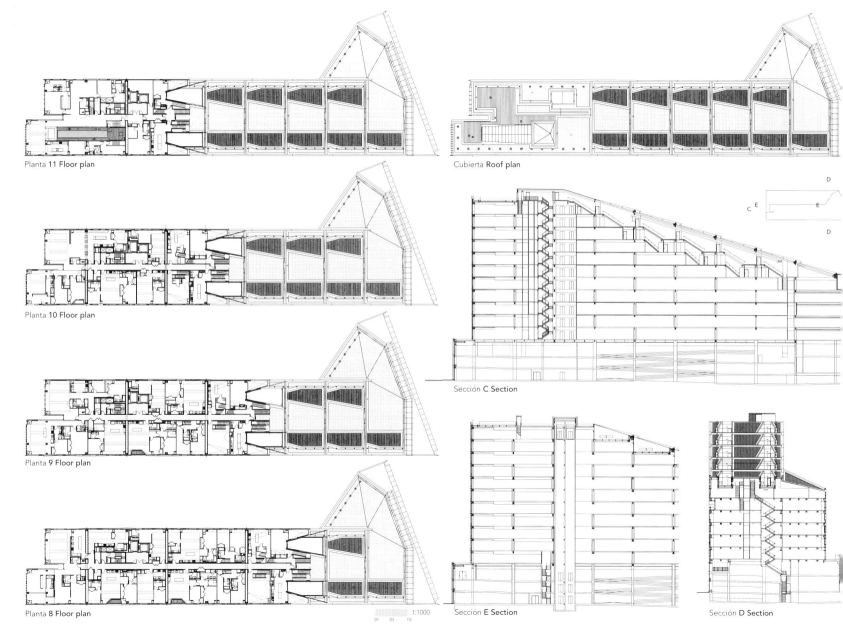

Planta 11 Floor plan

Cubierta Roof plan

Planta 10 Floor plan

Sección C Section

Planta 9 Floor plan

Planta 8 Floor plan

1:1000

01 05 10

Sección E Section

Sección D Section

LAYERS

EXTERNAL

CERÁMICA
BRICKWORK

HORMIGON
CONCRETE

MADERA
WOOD

CEMENTO
CEMENT

METAL
METAL

COMPUESTO
COMPOSITE

VIDRIO
GALSS

ENFOSCADO/
ESTUCO
**MORTAR/
STUCCO**

AISLAMIENTO
INSULATION

MEMBRANA
MEMBRANE

PRINCIPAL

CERÁMICA
BRICKWORK

VIDRIO
GALSS

HORMIGON
CONCRETE

MADERA
WOOD

COMPUESTO
COMPOSITE

INTERNAL

CARTÓN-YESO
PLASTER-BOARD

CERÁMICA
BRICKWORK

ENLUCIDO
PLASTER

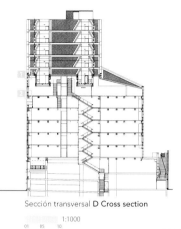

Sección transversal **D Cross section**

1:1000

01   05   10

1:200

0   1   5   10

1 SISTEMA DE MURO CORTINA CON VENTANAS FIJAS
2 MARCO DE MADERA DE 10 x 1,3 cm ALREDEDOR DEL HUECO DE VENTANA
3 1 AJUSTE DEL PANEL COMPUESTO DE FACHADA A LA CARPINTERÍA
4 PERFIL DE AJUSTE
5 SISTEMA DE FACHADA DE PANELES COMPUESTOS DE ALUMINIO
6 PANEL RÍGIDO DE AISLAMIENTO TÉRMICO e=5 cm
7 BARRERA DE VAPOR ADHERIDA
8 PANEL COMPUESTO DE YESO Y FIBRA DE VIDRIO e=1,6 cm
9 CAPA DE AISLAMIENTO ACÚSTICO e=7,6 cm EN LA FACHADA SUR
10 CARTÓN YESO e=1,6 cm
11 SUBESTRUCTURA METÁLICA PARA EL MONTAJE DE LOS PANELES DE CARTÓN-YESO
12 RODAPIE DE MADERA DE 1,6 x 7,6 cm
13 FORJADO A BASE DE ENCOFRADO METÁLICO PERMANENTE e=12,7 cm
14 VIGA DE ACERO CON CAPA DE PROTECCIÓN CONTRA INCENDIOS e=5 cm

1 FIXED CURTAIN WALL WINDOW SYSTEM
2 10 x 1,3 cm WOODEN TRIM AROUND WINDOW
3 1 RETURN COMPOSITE PANEL INTO GLAZING CHANNEL
4 REVEAL STRIP
5 HOOK & PIN RAIN SCREEN COMPOSITE ALUMINIUM PANEL SYSTEM
6 5 cm THICK RIGID THERMAL INSULATION
7 FULLY ADHERED AIR & VAPOUR BARRIER
8 1.6 cm THICK GYPSUM AND GLASS FIBER COMPOSITE PANEL
9 7.6 cm THICK SOUND INSULATION AT SOUTH WALLS
10 1.6 cm THICK GYPSUM BOARD
11 LIGHT GAUGE METAL FRAMING
12 1.6 x 7.6 cm WOODEN SKIRTING BOARD
13 12.7 cm THICK CONCRETE FILLED METAL DECK
14 STEEL BEAM WITH 5 cm THICK FIREPROOFING

1:20

0   0.1   0.5   1

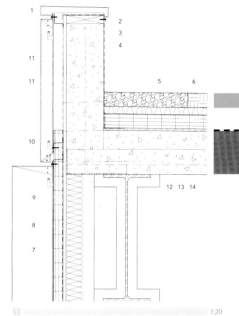

LAYERS

EXTERNAL

GRAVA
GRAVEL

CERÁMICA
TERRACOTTA

MADERA
WOOD

CEMENTO
CEMENT

VEGETACIÓN
PLANTING

METAL
METAL

AISLAMIENTO
INSULATION

MEMBRANA
MEMBRANE

HORMIGÓN
CONCRETE

MADERA
WOOD

CERÁMICA
TERRACOTTA

INTERNAL

CARTÓN-YESO
PLASTER-BOARD

ENLUCIDO
PLASTER

METAL
METAL

1:20

0   0.1   0.5   1

1 ALBARDILLA DE PANEL
  METÁLICO COMPUESTO
  Y REFORZADO
2 TOPE DE MADERA
3 MURETE DE HORMIGÓN
  e=20,3 cm
4 REVESTIMIENTO DEL MURETE
  CON PANEL DE ALUMINIO
5 BANDA SIN PLANTACIONES
  DE 45 cm DE ANCHURA
6 SISTEMA DE CUBIERTA
  VEGETAL CON CAPA
  DRENANTE
7 CAPA DE AISLAMIENTO
  ACÚSTICO DE e=7,6 cm EN LA
  FACHADA SUR ÚNICAMENTE
8 PANEL COMPUESTO DE YESO
  Y FIBRA DE VIDRIO e=1,6 cm
9 PANEL RÍGIDO
  DE AISLAMIENTO
  TÉRMICO e=5 cm
10 SISTEMA DE FACHADA DE
  PANELES COMPUESTOS
  DE ALUMINIO
11 BARRERA DE VAPOR
12 AISLAMIENTO TÉRMICO
  RÍGIDO e=7,6 cm
13 LÁMINA IMPERMEABILIZANTE
14 LOSA DE HORMIGÓN
  ARMADO

1 REINFORCED COMPOSITE
  METAL PANEL PARAPET CAP
2 WOODEN BLOCKING
3 20.3 cm THICK
  CONCRETE CURB
4 ALUMINIUM FLASHING
  OVER TOP OF CURB
5 45 cm WIDE NON-
  VEGETATION ZONE
6 GARDEN ROOF SYSTEM
  WITH DRAINAGE
7 7.6 cm THICK SOUND
  INSULATION AT SOUTH
  WALLS ONLY
8 1.6 cm THICK GYPSUM
  AND GLASS FIBER
  COMPOSITE PANEL
9 5 cm THICK RIGID
  THERMAL INSULATION
10 HOOK & PIN RAIN SCREEN
  COMPOSITE ALUMINIUM
  PANEL SYSTEM
11 WRAP AIR & VAPOUR
  BARRIER
12 7.6 cm THICK RIGID
  THERMAL INSULATION
13 WATERPROOF MEMBRANE
14 CONCRETE DECK

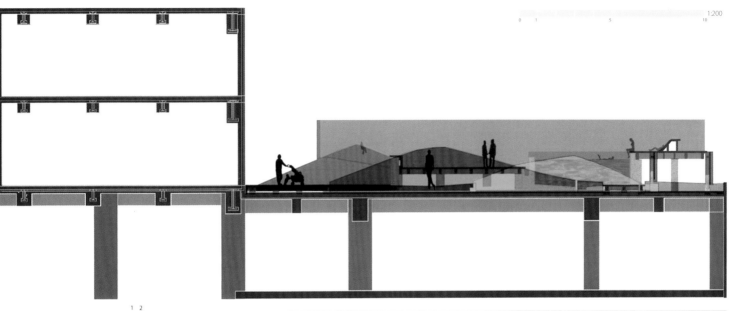

1:200

0 1   5   10

GRAVA
GRAVEL

CERÁMICA
TERRACOTTA

MADERA
WOOD

CEMENTO
CEMENT

VEGETACIÓN
PLANTING

METAL
METAL

AISLAMIENTO
INSULATION

MEMBRANA
MEMBRANE

HORMIGÓN
CONCRETE

MADERA
WOOD

CERÁMICA
TERRACOTTA

CARTÓN-YESO
PLASTER-BOARD

ENLUCIDO
PLASTER

METAL
METAL

1 2

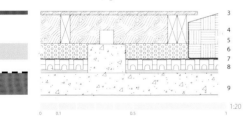

1:20

0   0.1   0.5   1

1 ELEMENTO DE UNIÓN
2 DADO DE HORMIGÓN
3 ENTARIMADO DE
  MADERA DE 3 cm
4 VIGA DE 5 x 15 cm
5 VIGUETA DE 5 x 15 cm
6 RELLENO DE ÁRIDOS
  COMPACTADOS
7 FIELTRO
8 SISTEMA DE
  IMPERMEABILIZACIÓN
  Y DRENAJE
9 LOSA DE HORMIGÓN

1 SIMPSON CLIP
2 CONCRETE PIER
3 3 cm WOOD DECKING
4 2 x 6 BEAM
5 2 x 6 JOIST
6 COARSE AGGREGATE FILL
7 FELT MAT
8 WATERPROOF AND
  DRAINAGE SYSTEM
9 CONCRETE ROOF DECK

Aspectos destacados

Highlighted features

Se emplean tratamientos superficiales y especializados de fachada como el poliuretano alifático o mezclas de colorantes incluidas en la masa del hormigón, con lo que se obtienen veladuras y colores no homogéneos. En otros casos, los revestimientos superficiales presentan tonos metalizados, como pinturas doradas o acabados iridiscentes en plata brillante.

14, 17, 18

Façade surfaces are treated with specific processes like aliphatic polyurethane coatings or concrete colouring in order to obtain glazes and non homogeneous colours. Superficial coatings with metallic colours, such golden paint or bright silver iridescent renderings.

Los productos derivados del cemento, bien sean tablas de fibrocemento coloreado, o paneles compuestos de resinas son predominantes como acabados de fachada. Se utilizan también en cubierta, como reconversión de tejas y pizarras. Aparecen bajo diversas formalizaciones: placa ondulada, placa lisa y constituyen una alternativa de media tecnología a los revestimientos más tradicionales como el ladrillo.

01, 07, 24, 25, 26

Products derived from cement, such us coloured fibre cement boards and composite resin panels are a major facade cladding system. Besides, they are used for roof cladding, instead of ceramic and slate tiles. Their formalization ranges from undulated to flat boards, and they have become a medium-tech alternative to the traditional brick revetment.

Las chapas de acero y de aluminio se utilizan en variedades estiradas, corrugadas, lisas y plegadas. Se repiten en numerosos proyectos por su economía, facilidad de montaje y durabilidad.

15, 27, 29

Steel or aluminium plates range from stretched to corrugated, flat or bent. They are commonly used due their low price, easy installation and durability.

La prefabricación aparece en algunas losas de hormigón de galerías exteriores de acceso y en módulos de baño de carcasa de acero, fabricados en taller y montados en obra. La fabricación industrializada se aprecia también en paneles curvos de hormigón, coloreados con polvo de mármol y reforzados con fibra de vidrio, realizados con un número limitado de moldes.

Prefabricated elements include some concrete slabs of the exterior entrance galleries and steel bathroom pods, which are built off site and mounted on site. Industrialised fabrication systems also include curved concrete panels, coloured with marble powder and reinforced with glass fibre. They are made-up out of a limited number of moulds.

En algunas localizaciones, los *Structural Insulated Panels*, SIP, formados por dos capas de tablero de madera, OSB, con núcleo de poliestireno expandido, EPS, son habituales como alternativa al ladrillo o al bloque.

31

Structural insulated panels are often used as an alternative to brick or concrete block walls. They consist of a core of molded expanded polystyrene (EPS) insulation with engineered oriented strand board (OSB) laminated to the top and bottom faces.

El enfoscado tradicional ha mutado en forma de mono-capa, o de morteros que dan acabado a aislamientos colocados por el exterior.

02, 05, 12

The traditional mortar rendering of walls has evolved to one-coat plasters or mortars applied over external wall insulation systems.

Ordenados por el material de la capa exterior
Arranged by the external layer material

0   0.1   0.5   1   1:20

CERÁMICA
BRICKWORK

HORMIGON
CONCRETE

MADERA
WOOD

CEMENTO
CEMENT

METAL
METAL

COMPUESTO
COMPOSITE

VIDRIO
GALSS

ENFOSCADO/
ESTUCO
**MORTAR/
STUCCO**

AISLAMIENTO
INSULATION

MEMBRANA
MEMBRANE

PRINCIPAL

CERÁMICA
BRICKWORK

VIDRIO
GALSS

HORMIGON
CONCRETE

MADERA
WOOD

COMPUESTO
COMPOSITE

INTERNAL

CARTÓN-YESO
PLASTER-BOARD

CERÁMICA
BRICKWORK

ENLUCIDO
PLASTER

1 REVESTIMIENTO
EXTERIOR DE LADRILLO
VITRIFICADO BLANCO
2 CAPA DE AISLAMIENTO
TÉRMICO DE LANA DE ROCA
3 MURO DE HORMIGÓN
IN SITU

1 MASONRY, WHITE
GLAZED BRICK
2 MINERAL WOOL THERMAL
INSULATION LAYER
3 IN-SITU CONCRETE WALL

1 MURO DE LADRILLO 14 cm
2 CAPA DE AISLAMIENTO
TÉRMICO 4 cm
3 TABIQUE DE LADRILLO 7 cm
4 ENLUCIDO Y PINTADO

1 14 cm THICK BRICK WALL
2 4 cm THICK THERMAL
INSULATION LAYER
3 7 cm THICK BRICK
4 PAINTED PLASTER LAYER

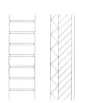

1 LADRILLO VISTO
2 AISLAMIENTO TÉRMICO
3 LADRILLO SÍLICO CALCÁREO

1 FACING BRICKWORK
2 THERMAL INSULATION
3 LIME-SAND BRICK

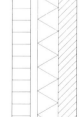

ARONS EN GELAUFF ARCHITECTEN
GRONINGEN.NL 2007

ROLDÁN + BERENGUÉ
BARCELONA.ES 2009

POOLEN ARCHITEKTEN
CULEMBORG.NL 2008

1 TEJAS ATORNILLADAS
2 MURO DE HORMIGÓN
3 CAPA DE AISLAMIENTO
  TÉRMICO
4 REVESTIMIENTO INTERIOR
  DE CARTÓN-YESO

1 SCREWED TILES
2 CONCRETE WALL
3 THERMAL INSULATION
  LAYER
4 GYPSUM BOARD
  INTERIOR FINISHING

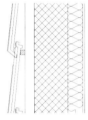

1
2
3
4

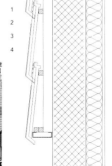

EDOUARD FRANÇOIS
PARIS.FR 2008

....252-265

1 MURO DE LADRILLO 9 cm
2 MEMBRANA DE
  IMPERMEABILIZACIÓN
3 CAPA DE AISLAMIENTO
  TÉRMICO 140 mm
4 BARRERA DE VAPOR
5 CARTÓN-YESO

1 9 cm THICK BRICK WALL
2 WATERPROOF MEMBRANE
3 140 mm THICK THERMAL
  INSULATION LAYER
4 VAPOUR BARRIER
5 GIPSUM BOARD

1
2

3
4
5

ANA ARCHITECTEN
AMSTERDAM.NL 2007

....298-307

1 TRATAMIENTO DE FACHADA
  DE POLIURETANO ALIFÁTICO
  BASE DE IMPRIMACIÓN
  CAPA BLANCA TRASLUCIDA
  CAPA DE COLOR Y BRILLO
2 MURO DE HORMIGÓN
  ARMADO 10 cm
3 CAPA DE AISLAMIENTO
  TÉRMICO DE POLIESTIRENO
  EXPANDIDO 40 mm
4 PINTURA AL GOTELET SOBRE
  TENDIDO DE TEMPLE

1 ALIPHATIC POLYURETHANE
  COATING:
  PRIMER LAYER,
  TRANSLUCENT WHITE LAYER,
  COLOUR AND
  BRIGHTNESS LAYER
2 10 cm THICK REINFORCED
  CONCRETE WALL
3 40 mm THICK EXPANDED
  POLYSTYRENE THERMAL
  INSULATION LAYER
4 STIPPLED-FINISH PAINT
  OVER PLASTER RENDERING

1
2
3
2
4

MVRDV, BLANCA LLEÓ
MADRID.ES 2009

....198-217

LAYERS
EXTERNAL

CERÁMICA
BRICKWORK

HORMIGON
CONCRETE

MADERA
WOOD

CEMENTO
CEMENT

METAL
METAL

COMPUESTO
COMPOSITE

VIDRIO
GALSS

ENFOSCADO/
ESTUCO
**MORTAR/
STUCCO**

AISLAMIENTO
INSULATION

MEMBRANA
MEMBRANE

CERÁMICA
BRICKWORK

VIDRIO
GALSS

HORMIGON
CONCRETE

MADERA
WOOD

COMPUESTO
COMPOSITE

INTERNAL

CARTÓN-YESO
PLASTER-BOARD

CERÁMICA
BRICKWORK

ENLUCIDO
PLASTER

Ordenados por el material de la capa exterior
Arranged by the external layer material

1:20

0   0.1   0.5   1

CERÁMICA
BRICKWORK

HORMIGON
CONCRETE

MADERA
WOOD

CEMENTO
CEMENT

METAL
METAL

COMPUESTO
COMPOSITE

VIDRIO
GALSS

ENFOSCADO/
ESTUCO
MORTAR/
STUCCO

AISLAMIENTO
INSULATION

MEMBRANA
MEMBRANE

PRINCIPAL

CERÁMICA
BRICKWORK

VIDRIO
GALSS

HORMIGON
CONCRETE

MADERA
WOOD

COMPUESTO
COMPOSITE

INTERNAL

CARTÓN-YESO
PLASTER-BOARD

CERÁMICA
BRICKWORK

ENLUCIDO
PLASTER

1 MURO DE HORMIGÓN
2 CAPA DE AISLAMIENTO
  TÉRMICO
3 CARTON-YESO

1 CONCRETE WALL
2 THERMAL INSULATION
  LAYER
3 GYPSUM BOARD

1 VIGA DE HORMIGÓN ARMADO
  CON ENCOFRADO DE CHAPA
  ACANALADA ZINCADA
2 BARRERA DE VAPOR DE
  FILM DE POLIETILENO
3 LADRILLO HUECO e=12 cm
4 REVOCO DE YESO
  PROYECTADO

1 REINFORCED CONCRETE
  BEAM WITH CORRUGATED
  FORMWORK
2 POLYETHYLENE FILM
  AS VAPOUR BARRIER
3 12 cm HOLLOW BRICK
4 SPRAYED PLASTER RENDERING

1 TABLERO DE ABETO
  IMPERMEABILIZADO 1.8 cm
2 PANEL DE MADERA DE 1.5 cm
3 CAPA DE AISLAMIENTO
  TÉRMICO DE LANA
  MINERAL 18 cm
4 PANEL DE CARTÓN-YESO
  1,5 cm PARA RECIBIDO
  DEL REVOCO LISO

1 1.8 cm FIR WOOD PANEL WITH
  WATERPROOF FINISHING
2 1.5 cm THICK WOODEN PANEL
3 18 cm THICK MINERAL
  WOOL INSULATION LAYER
4 1.5 cm THICK GYPSUM FIBRE
  PANEL TO BE COATED WITH A
  LAYER OF LIME RENDERING

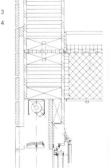

BECKMANN-N'THÉPÉ ARCHITECTES
PARIS.FR 2007

ADAMO-FAIDEN ARQUITECTOS
BUENOS AIRES.AR 2008

FREI ARCHITEKTEN
ROHR.CH 2007

1 REVESTIMIENTO DE MADERA
2 PANEL DE SILICATO DE
CALCIO REFORZADO
CON FIBRAS
3 CAPA DE AISLAMIENTO
TÉRMICO
4 MURO DE HORMIGÓN

1 TIMBER CLADDING
2 CALCIUM SILICATE BOARD
REINFORCED WITH FIBERS
3 THERMAL INSULATION
LAYER
4 CONCRETE WALL

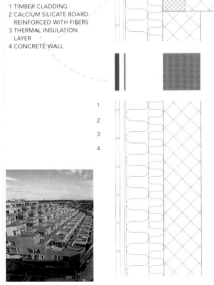

BIG+JDS
COPENHAGEN.DK 2008

1 PIEZA VISTA DE MADERA EN
FACHADA DE 20 x 35 cm
2 VENTANA DE PVC CON
DOBLE ACRISTALAMIENTO

1 20 x 35 cm TIMBER
ELEMENT OF THE FACADE
2 DOUBLE GLAZING
PVC WINDOW

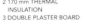

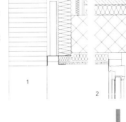

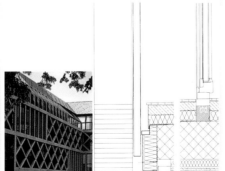

OFIS ARHITEKTI
CERKLJE.SI 2007

1 PANEL DE ALERCE
SIBERIANO SOBRE
TABLERO ANTIHUMEDAD
2 AISLAMIENTO
TÉRMICO 170 mm
3 DOBLE PLACA DE
CARTÓN-YESO

1 ROUGH SAWN SIBERIAN
LARCH CATCH BOARD ON
BOARD RAINSCREEN
2 170 mm THERMAL
INSULATION
3 DOUBLE PLASTER BOARD

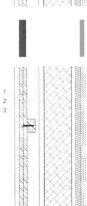

ALLFORD HALL MONAGHAN MORRIS
LONDON.UK 2007

EXTERNAL

CERÁMICA
BRICKWORK

HORMIGON
CONCRETE

MADERA
WOOD

CEMENTO
CEMENT

METAL
METAL

COMPUESTO
COMPOSITE

VIDRIO
GALSS

ENFOSCADO/
ESTUCO
MORTAR/
STUCCO

AISLAMIENTO
INSULATION

MEMBRANA
MEMBRANE

CERÁMICA
BRICKWORK

VIDRIO
GALSS

HORMIGON
CONCRETE

MADERA
WOOD

COMPUESTO
COMPOSITE

INTERNAL

CARTÓN-YESO
PLASTER-BOARD

CERÁMICA
BRICKWORK

ENLUCIDO
PLASTER

Ordenados por el material de la capa exterior
Arranged by the external layer material

1:20
0   0.1   0.5   1

CERÁMICA
BRICKWORK

HORMIGON
CONCRETE

MADERA
WOOD

CEMENTO
CEMENT

METAL
METAL

COMPUESTO
COMPOSITE

VIDRIO
GALSS

ENFOSCADO/
ESTUCO
**MORTAR/
STUCCO**

AISLAMIENTO
INSULATION

MEMBRANA
MEMBRANE

PRINCIPAL

CERÁMICA
BRICKWORK

VIDRIO
GALSS

HORMIGON
CONCRETE

MADERA
WOOD

COMPUESTO
COMPOSITE

INTERNAL

CARTÓN-YESO
PLASTER-BOARD

CERÁMICA
BRICKWORK

ENLUCIDO
PLASTER

FACHADA FACADE

1 PANEL ONDULADO DE
  FIBROCEMENTO DE
  251 cm DE ALTURA
2 BARRERA DE VAPOR
3 CAPA DE AISLAMIENTO
  TÉRMICO 120 mm
4 MURO DE BLOQUE DE
  HORMIGÓN 200 mm
5 ENLUCIDO DE YESO 10 mm

1 251 cm TALL SINUS WAVE
  FIBER CEMENT BOARD
2 VAPOUR BARRIER
3 120 mm THICK THERMAL
  INSULATION
4 200 mm THICK CONCRETE
  BLOCK WALL
5 10 mm THICK INTERIOR PLASTER

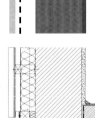

1
2
3
4
5

BEVK PEROVIC ARHITEKTI
MARIBOR.SI 2007

.... 144-153

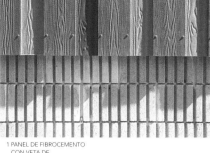

1 PANEL DE FIBROCEMENTO
  CON VETA DE
  MADERA
2 PANEL DE AISLAMIENTO
  TÉRMICO 75 mm FIJADO
  AL MURO DE BLOQUE
  DE HORMIGÓN
3 LÁMINA
  IMPERMEABILIZANTE
4 MURO DE BLOQUE DE
  HORMIGÓN 140 mm
5 ENLUCIDO DE YESO

1 WEATHERBOARD
2 75 mm THICK THERMAL
  INSULATION PANEL
  FIXED TO BLOCKWORK
3 WATERPROOF MEMBRANE
4 140 mm THICK BRICKWORK
5 WET PLASTER FINISH

1
2
3
4
5

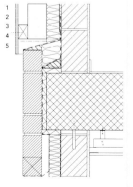

dRMM
LONDON.UK 2006

....................................340-347

1 CHAPA ESTIRADA DE
  ACERO POSGALVANIZADA
  Y LACADA
2 MURO DE HORMIGÓN
  ARMADO 10 cm
3 POLIESTIRENO
  EXTRUIDO 4 cm

1 LACQUERED GALVANISED
  STRETCHED STEEL PLATE
2 10 cm THICK REINFORCED
  CONCRETE WALL
3 4 cm THICK EXTRUDED
  POLYSTYRENE

1
2
3
2

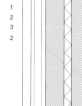

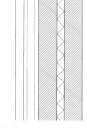

DOSMASUNO ARQUITECTOS
MADRID.ES 2006

.... 38-55

CERÁMICA
BRICKWORK

HORMIGON
CONCRETE

MADERA
WOOD

CEMENTO
CEMENT

METAL
METAL

COMPUESTO
COMPOSITE

VIDRIO
GALSS

ENFOSCADO/
ESTUCO
MORTAR/
STUCCO

AISLAMIENTO
INSULATION

MEMBRANA
MEMBRANE

1 CHAPA DE ALUMINIO
  MICRO PERFORADA
2 LANA DE VIDRIO
  HIDROFUGADA
  CON VELO 5 cm
3 MURO DE FÁBRICA DE 1/2 PIE
4 CARTÓN YESO
5 ENFOSCADO

1 PERFORATED
  ALUMINIUM PLATE
2 5 cm THICK FIREPROOF
  GLASS WOOL
3 BRICKWORK WALL
4 PLASTER BOARD
5 MORTAR RENDERING

1 CHAPA ONDULADA
2 CAPA DE AISLAMIENTO
  TÉRMICO DE POLIURETANO
  PROYECTADO 40 mm
3 LADRILLO DE 15 cm
  DE PROFUNDIDAD
4 PANELES DE CARTÓN
  YESO 13 mm APOYADOS
  SOBRE PERFILES OMEGA
  DE 16 mm CADA 400 mm

1 CORRUGATED STEEL SHEET
2 40 mm THICK SPRAYED
  POLYURETHANE THERMAL
  INSULATIONLAYER
3 15 cm BRICK WALL
4 13 mm THICK GYPSUM
  BOARD PANELS ON 16
  mm OMEGA PROFILES
  POSITIONED EVERY 400 mm

1 CHAPA CORRUGADA DE
  ALUMINIO PREPINTADA
  GRIS OSCURO
2 ENFOSCADO
3 LADRILLO HUECO 12 cm
4 REVOCO DE YESO
  PROYECTADO

1 DARK GRAY PAINTED
  CORRUGATED
  ALUMINIUM PLATE
2 MORTAR RENDERING
3 12 cm WIDE HOLLOW BRICK
4 SPRAYED PLASTER
  RENDERING

CERÁMICA
BRICKWORK

VIDRIO
GALSS

HORMIGON
CONCRETE

MADERA
WOOD

COMPUESTO
COMPOSITE

CARTÓN-YESO
PLASTER-BOARD

CERÁMICA
BRICKWORK

ENLUCIDO
PLASTER

DOSMASUNO ARQUITECTOS
MADRID.ES 2006

COLL-LECLERC ARQUITECTOS
LLEIDA.ES 2008

ADAMO-FAIDEN ARQUITECTOS
BUENOS AIRES.AR 2008

Ordenados por el material de la capa exterior
Arranged by the external layer material

1:20

0   0.1   0.5   1

CERÁMICA
BRICKWORK

HORMIGON
CONCRETE

MADERA
WOOD

CEMENTO
CEMENT

METAL
METAL

COMPUESTO
COMPOSITE

VIDRIO
GALSS

ENFOSCADO/
ESTUCO
**MORTAR/
STUCCO**

AISLAMIENTO
INSULATION

MEMBRANA
MEMBRANE

PRINCIPAL

CERÁMICA
BRICKWORK

VIDRIO
GALSS

HORMIGON
CONCRETE

MADERA
WOOD

COMPUESTO
COMPOSITE

INTERNAL

CARTÓN-YESO
PLASTER-BOARD

CERÁMICA
BRICKWORK

ENLUCIDO
PLASTER

1 REVESTIMIENTO DE LAMAS
  DE ALUMINIO CON SISTEMA
  DE FIJACIÓN OCULTO
2 MURO DE HORMIGÓN 160 mm
3 CAPA DE AISLAMIENTO
  TÉRMICO 100 mm
4 CARTÓN-YESO

1 ALUMINIUM CLADDING
  WITH CONCEALED
  FASTENING SYSTEM
2 160 mm CONCRETE WALL
3 100 mm THERMAL INSULATION
4 PLASTER BOARD

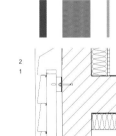

HAMONIC + MASSON
PARIS.FR 2008

1 PANEL COMPUESTO CON
  IMPRESIÓN EXTERIOR
2 BARRERA DE VAPOR
3 CAPA DE AISLAMIENTO
  TÉRMICO DE LANA DE ROCA
4 CARTÓN-YESO

1 COMPOSITE PANEL
  WITH CUSTOM PRINT
2 VAPOUR PERMEABLE
  MEMBRANE
3 MINERAL WOOL THERMAL
  INSULATION LAYER
4 PLASTER BOARD

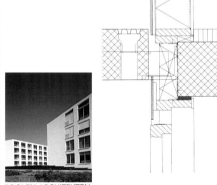

POOLEN ARCHITEKTEN
CULEMBORG.NL 2008

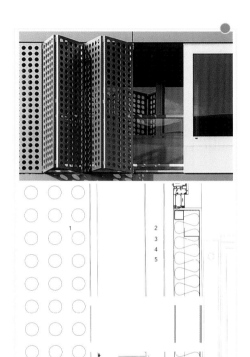

1 PANEL COMPUESTO DE
  ALUMINIO PERFORADO
  CORREDERO Y
  PLEGABLE 4 mm
2 PANEL DE ALUMINIO
3 CAPA DE AISLAMIENTO
  12 cm
4 BARRERA DE VAPOR
5 CARTÓN-YESO

1 4 mm THICK PERFORATED
  SLIDING/FOLDING
  COMPOSITE
  ALUMINIUM PANEL
2 ALUMINIUM PANEL
3 12 cm THICK THERMAL
  INSULATION LAYER
4 VAPOUR BARRIER
5 GYPSUM BOARD

BEVK PEROVIC ARHITEKTI
LJUBLJANA.SI 2006

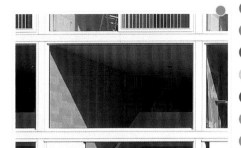

CERÁMICA
BRICKWORK

HORMIGON
CONCRETE

MADERA
WOOD

CEMENTO
CEMENT

METAL
METAL

COMPUESTO
COMPOSITE

VIDRIO
GALSS

ENFOSCADO/
ESTUCO
MORTAR/
STUCCO

AISLAMIENTO
INSULATION

MEMBRANA
MEMBRANE

CERÁMICA
BRICKWORK

VIDRIO
GALSS

HORMIGON
CONCRETE

MADERA
WOOD

COMPUESTO
COMPOSITE

CARTÓN-YESO
PLASTER-BOARD

CERÁMICA
BRICKWORK

ENLUCIDO
PLASTER

1 CERRAMIENTO DE PLACA
PLANA DE RESINAS
TERMOESTABLES,
HOMOGÉNEAMENTE
REFORZADA CON
FIBRAS DE MADERA
2 MEMBRANA
IMPERMEABILIZANTE
3 PANEL DE CONTRACHAPADO
4 CAPA DE AISLAMIENTO
TÉRMICO DE ESPUMA
PROYECTADA
5 PANEL DE CARTÓN-YESO

1 EXTERIOR CLADDING: FLAT
PANEL OF THERMOSETTING
RESINS, HOMOGENEOUSLY
REINFORCED WITH
WOOD BASED FIBRES
2 WATERPROOF MEMBRANE
3 PLYWOOD SHEATING
4 SPRAYED FOAM THERMAL
INSULATION LAYER
5 GYPSUM BOARD

1
2
3
4
5

1 SISTEMA DE FACHADA DE
PANELES COMPUESTOS
DE ALUMINIO
2 PANEL RÍGIDO
DE AISLAMIENTO
TÉRMICO e=5 cm
3 BARRERA DE VAPOR
ADHERIDA
4 PANEL COMPUESTO DE YESO
Y FIBRA DE VIDRIO 1,6 cm
5 CAPA DE AISLAMIENTO
ACÚSTICO 7,6 cm
6 CARTÓN-YESO 1,6 cm

1 HOOK & PIN RAIN SCREEN
COMPOSITE ALUMINIUM
PANEL SYSTEM
2 5 cm THICK RIGID
THERMAL INSULATION
3 FULLY ADHERED AIR
& VAPOUR BARRIER
4 1.6 cm THICK GYPSUM
EXTERIOR SHEATHING
5 7.6 cm THICK SOUND
INSULATION AT
SOUTH WALLS
6 1.6 cm GYPSUM BOARD

1
2
3

4
5
6

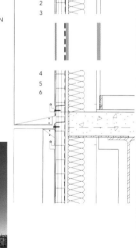

1 VIDRIO CON
PROTECCIÓN SOLAR

1 SUN PROTECTED GLAZING

1

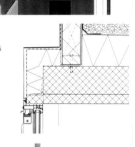

ONION FLATS
PHILADELPHIA.US 2009

OFFICE dA, BURT HILL
BOSTON.US 2007

ATELIER KEMPE THILL
AMSTERDAM.NL 2007

1:20

0   0.1   0.5   1

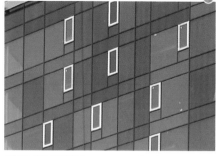

1 DOBLE ACRISTALAMIENTO
A BASE DE 2 VIDRIOS DE 8
mm CON UNA MEMBRANA
PLÁSTICA ENTRE ELLOS
2 TABLEROS DE MADERA
DE 18 x 145 mm
3 MEMBRANA
IMPERMEABILIZANTE
4 CAPA DE AISLAMIENTO
TÉRMICO 160 mm
5 CARTÓN-YESO 12 mm

1 8 mm THICK GLASS DOUBLE
GLAZING WITH 2 LAYERS OF
PLASTIC FOIL IN BETWEEN
2 18 x 145 mm WOOD PLANKS
3 WATERPROOF MEMBRANE
4 160 mmTHICK INSULATION
5 12 mm THICK GYPSUM BOARD

HVDN ARCHITECTEN
AMSTERDAM.NL 2008

1 DOBLE ACRISTALAMIENTO
DE CAPA INTERIOR
REVESTIDA CON UNA
LÁMINA DE COLOR
2 CAPA DE AISLAMIENTO
TÉRMICO 80 mm
3 CARTÓN-YESO 13 mm

1 DOUBLE-GLAZING
FACADE WITH COLOUR-
COATED INNER PANEL
2 80 mm THICK THERMAL
INSULATION LAYER
3 13 mm THICK
PLASTERBOARD

KOKO ARCHITEKTID
TALLINN.EE 2007

1 VIDRIO ESMALTADO EXTRA
BLANCO Y CARPINTERÍA
DE ACERO INOXIDABLE
2 BARRERA DE VAPOR 4 mm
3 REVESTIMIENTO ORGÁNICO
4 CAPA DE AISLAMIENTO DE
POLIESTIRENO EXPANDIDO
5 MURO DE BLOQUE DE
HORMIGÓN 160 mm

1 TRANSLUCENT
ENAMELED EXTRA WHITE
GLASS WITH BRUSHED
STAINLESS STEEL RAIL
2 4 mm THICK VAPOUR
BARRIER
3 ORGANIC COATING
4 EXPANDED
POLYSTYRENE THERMAL
INSULATION LAYER
5 160 mm THICK CEMENT
BLOCK-WALL

**EMMANUEL COMBAREL DOMINIQUE MARREC
ARCHITECTES** PARIS.FR 2006

1 2 VIDRIOS DE SEGURIDAD LAMINADOS 6 mm DE COLOR ACORDE CON DISEÑO DE FACHADA
2 CAPA DE AISLAMIENTO TÉRMICO DE LANA DE ROCA 20 cm
3 MURO DE LADRILLO 17,5 cm
4 ENLUCIDO DE YESO 1,5 cm

1 2 x 6 mm THICK LAMINATED SAFETY GLASS, COLOUR ACCORDING TO COLOUR SCHEME
2 20 cm THICK MINERAL WOLL INSULATION LAYER
3 17.5 cm THICK BRICK WALL
4 1.5 cm THICK PLASTER LAYER

1 CERRAMIENTO DE VIDRIO

1 GLASS SYSTEM WALL

1 ENFOSCADO
2 LADRILLO DE 15 cm
3 CAPA DE AISLAMIENTO TÉRMICO
4 CARTÓN-YESO 13 mm DOBLE PLACA

1 MORTAR RENDERING
2 15 cm BRICK WALL
3 THERMAL INSULATION
4 13 mm THICK DOUBLE GYPSUM BOARD

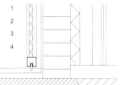

1
2
3
4

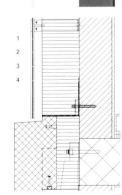

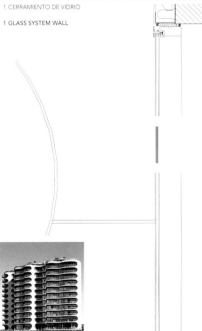

GIGON / GUYER
ZURICH.CH 2007

KASPER DANIELSEN ARCHITECTS / FUTURE SYSTEMS
COPENHAGEN.DK 2008

COLL-LECLERC ARQUITECTOS
LLEIDA.ES 2008

CERÁMICA **BRICKWORK**
HORMIGON **CONCRETE**
MADERA **WOOD**
CEMENTO **CEMENT**
METAL **METAL**
COMPUESTO **COMPOSITE**
VIDRIO **GALSS**
ENFOSCADO/ ESTUCO **MORTAR/ STUCCO**
AISLAMIENTO **INSULATION**
MEMBRANA **MEMBRANE**

CERÁMICA **BRICKWORK**
VIDRIO **GALSS**
HORMIGON **CONCRETE**
MADERA **WOOD**
COMPUESTO **COMPOSITE**

CARTÓN-YESO **PLASTER-BOARD**
CERÁMICA **BRICKWORK**
ENLUCIDO **PLASTER**

1:20

0   0.1   0.5   1

EXTERNAL

- CERÁMICA **BRICKWORK**
- HORMIGON **CONCRETE**
- MADERA **WOOD**
- CEMENTO **CEMENT**
- METAL **METAL**
- COMPUESTO **COMPOSITE**
- VIDRIO **GALSS**
- ENFOSCADO/ ESTUCO **MORTAR/ STUCCO**
- AISLAMIENTO **INSULATION**
- MEMBRANA **MEMBRANE**

PRINCIPAL

- CERÁMICA **BRICKWORK**
- VIDRIO **GALSS**
- HORMIGON **CONCRETE**
- MADERA **WOOD**
- COMPUESTO **COMPOSITE**

INTERNAL

- CARTÓN-YESO **PLASTER-BOARD**
- CERÁMICA **BRICKWORK**
- ENLUCIDO **PLASTER**

1 SISTEMA DE ENFOSCADO
2 MEMBRANA DE FIBRA DE VIDRIO
3 CAPA DE AISLAMIENTO TÉRMICO 4 cm
4 MURO DE LADRILLO
5 ENLUCIDO DE YESO

1 MORTAR RENDERING
2 GLASS FIBER MEMBRANE
3 4 cm THICK THERMAL INSULATION LAYER
4 BRICK WALL
5 PLASTER LAYER

1
2
3
4
5

AVA ARCHITECTS
PORTO.PT 2008
...............56-65

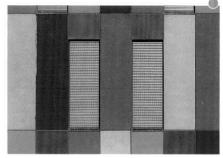

1 ENFOSCADO DE CEMENTO COLOREADO SEGÚN CÓDIGO DE COLORES DEL ALZADO
2 MURO DE LADRILLO 12 cm
3 CAPA DE AISLAMIENTO TÉRMICO 40 mm
4 MURO DE LADRILLO HUECO 4 cm
5 ENLUCIDO

1 CEMENT RENDERING, TAINTED ACCORDING TO THE COLOUR CODE ESTABLISHED FOR THE FACADES
2 12 cm BRICK WALL
3 40 mm THICK THERMAL INSULATION LAYER
4 4 cm HOLLOW BRICK WALL
5 PLASTER

1

2
3

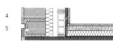

4
5

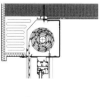

AGUINAGA Y ASOCIADOS ARQUITECTOS
MADRID.ES 2008
...............88-95

1 ENFOSCADO
2 LADRILLO PERFORADO FONOABSORBENTE DE DIMENSIONES 29 x 14 x 7,5 cm
3 ENFOSCADO PINTADO

1 MORTAR
2 29 x 14 x 7.5 cm PERFORATED SOUND ABSORBING BRICK
3 MORTAR RENDERING WITH PAINT FINISH

1
2
3

LÓPEZ-RIVERA ARQUITECTOS
BARCELONA.ES 2007
...............118-127

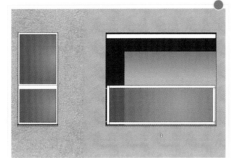

LAYERS

EXTERNAL

CERÁMICA
BRICKWORK

HORMIGON
CONCRETE

MADERA
WOOD

CEMENTO
CEMENT

METAL
METAL

COMPUESTO
COMPOSITE

VIDRIO
GALSS

ENFOSCADO/
ESTUCO
**MORTAR/
STUCCO**

AISLAMIENTO
INSULATION

MEMBRANA
MEMBRANE

PRINCIPAL

CERÁMICA
BRICKWORK

VIDRIO
GALSS

HORMIGON
CONCRETE

MADERA
WOOD

COMPUESTO
COMPOSITE

INTERNAL

CARTÓN-YESO
PLASTER-BOARD

CERÁMICA
BRICKWORK

ENLUCIDO
PLASTER

1 ESTUCO DE CAL ACABADO
   BRILLANTE 2 cm
2 LADRILLO PERFORADO
   NO VISTO 14 cm
3 CAPA DE AISLAMIENTO
   TÉRMICO 4 cm
4 LADRILLO 7 cm
5 ENYESADO Y PINTADO

1 2 cm THICK BRIGHT FINISH
   LIME STUCCO LAYER
2 14 cm THICK PERFORATED
   BRICK WALL
3 4 cm THICK THERMAL
   INSULATION LAYER
4 7 cm HOLLOW BRICK WALL
5 PAINTED PLASTER LAYER

1 ENFOSCADO e=1-3 mm
   PINTADO
2 CAPA DE AISLAMIENTO
   TÉRMICO DE LANA DE
   ROCA, CAPA DE FIJACIÓN
3 MURO DE LADRILLO
4 ENLUCIDO DE YESO

1 PAINT LAYER, 1-3 mm THICK
   MORTAR RENDERING
2 ROCKWOOL THEMAL
   INSULATION LAYER,
   FIXING LAYER
3 BRICK WALL
4 PLASTER RENDERING

1 REVESTIMIENTO ORGÁNICO
2 SISTEMA DE AISLAMIENTO
   DE POLIESTIRENO
   EXPANDIDO
3 HORMIGÓN IN SITU

1 ORGANIC COATING
2 EXPANDED POLYSTYRENE
   THERMAL INSULATION
3 POURED CONCRETE

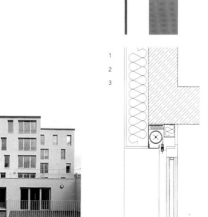

1
2
3
4
5

1
2
3
4

1
2
3

ROLDÁN + BERENGUÉ
BARCELONA.ES 2009

LEHMANN FIDANZA & ASSOCIÉS
FRIBOURG.CH 2009

EMMANUEL COMBAREL DOMINIQUE MARREC
ARCHITECTES PARIS.FR 2006

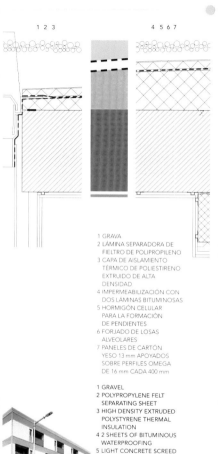

Ordenados por el material de la capa exterior
Arranged by the external layer material

1:20

0   0.1   0.5   1

GRAVA
GRAVEL

CERÁMICA
TERRACOTTA

MADERA
WOOD

CEMENTO
CEMENT

VEGETACIÓN
PLANTING

METAL
METAL

AISLAMIENTO
INSULATION

MEMBRANA
MEMBRANE

HORMIGÓN
CONCRETE

MADERA
WOOD

CERÁMICA
TERRACOTTA

CARTÓN-YESO
PLASTER-BOARD

ENLUCIDO
PLASTER

METAL
METAL

1 2 3   4 5 6

1 GRAVA
2 DOBLE LÁMINA ASFÁLTICA
3 MORTERO DE PENDIENTES
4 POLIESTIRENO
  EXTRUIDO 4 cm
5 FORJADO DE CHAPA
  COLABORANTE
6 FALSO TECHO DE ESCAYOLA

1 GRAVEL
2 DOUBLE BITUMINOUS
  LAYER
3 SLOPE FORMING MORTAR
4 4 cm THICK EXTRUDED
  POLYSTYRENE
5 STEEL PLATE AND
  CONCRETE SLAB
6 PLASTER CEILING

DOSMASUNO ARQUITECTOS
MADRID.ES 2006

1 2 3 4 5 6 7

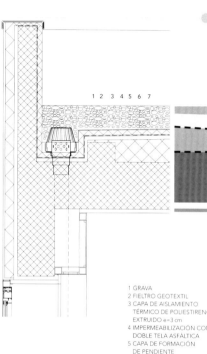

1 GRAVA
2 FIELTRO GEOTEXTIL
3 CAPA DE AISLAMIENTO
  TÉRMICO DE POLIESTIRENO
  EXTRUIDO e=3 cm
4 IMPERMEABILIZACIÓN CON
  DOBLE TELA ASFÁLTICA
5 CAPA DE FORMACIÓN
  DE PENDIENTE
6 LOSA DE HORMIGÓN
7 CARTÓN-YESO

1 GRAVEL
2 GEOTEXTILE FELT
3 3 cm THICK EXTRUDED
  POLYSTYRENE THERMAL
  INSULATION LAYER
4 2-SHEETS ASPHALT
  WATERPROOF LAYER
5 SCREED TO FORM
  ROOF SLOPE
6 CONCRETE SLAB
7 GYPSUM BOARD

AVA ARCHITECTS
PORTO.PT 2008

1 2 3   4 5 6 7

1 GRAVA
2 LÁMINA SEPARADORA DE
  FIELTRO DE POLIPROPILENO
3 CAPA DE AISLAMIENTO
  TÉRMICO DE POLIESTIRENO
  EXTRUIDO DE ALTA
  DENSIDAD
4 IMPERMEABILIZACIÓN CON
  DOS LÁMINAS BITUMINOSAS
5 HORMIGÓN CELULAR
  PARA LA FORMACIÓN
  DE PENDIENTES
6 FORJADO DE LOSAS
  ALVEOLARES
7 PANELES DE CARTÓN
  YESO 13 mm APOYADOS
  SOBRE PERFILES OMEGA
  DE 16 mm CADA 400 mm

1 GRAVEL
2 POLYPROPYLENE FELT
  SEPARATING SHEET
3 HIGH DENSITY EXTRUDED
  POLYSTYRENE THERMAL
  INSULATION
4 2 SHEETS OF BITUMINOUS
  WATERPROOFING
5 LIGHT CONCRETE SCREED
  AS ROOF SLOPE
6 HOLLOW CORE SLAB
7 13 mm THICK GYPSUM
  BOARD PANELS ON 16
  mm OMEGA PROFILES
  POSITIONED EVERY 400 mm

COLL-LECLERC ARQUITECTOS
LLEIDA.ES 2008

GRAVA
GRAVEL

CERÁMICA
TERRACOTTA

MADERA
WOOD

CEMENTO
CEMENT

VEGETACIÓN
PLANTING

METAL
METAL

AISLAMIENTO
INSULATION

MEMBRANA
MEMBRANE

PRINCIPAL

HORMIGÓN
CONCRETE

MADERA
WOOD

CERÁMICA
TERRACOTTA

INTERNAL

CARTÓN-YESO
PLASTER-BOARD

ENLUCIDO
PLASTER

METAL
METAL

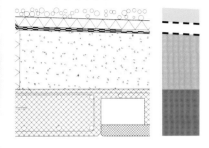

1 2 3 4 5 6

1 2 3 4 5 6 7

1 2 3 4 5 6

1 GRAVA 5 cm
2 LÁMINA GEOTEXTIL
  DE 150 g/m²
3 CAPA DE AISLAMEINTO
  TÉRMICO DE
  POLIESTIRENO
  EXTRUSIONADO DE
  ALTA DENSIDAD 50 mm
4 MEMBRANA ASFÁLTICA
  BICAPA SOLDADAS
5 HORMIGÓN CELULAR
  PARA FORMACIÓN
  DE PENDIENTES
6 LOSA DE HORMIGÓN

1 5 cm GRAVEL
2 150 g/m²
  GEOTEXTILE MAT
3 50 mm THICK EXTRUDED
  POLYSTYRENE THERMAL
  INSULATION LAYER
4 2-LAYER ASPHALT
  WATERPROOF
  MEMBRANE
5 LIGHT CONCRETE
  SCREED TO FORM
  ROOF SLOPE
6 CONCRETE SLAB

1 CAPA DE GRAVA
2 LÁMINA GEOTÉXTIL
3 CAPA DE AISLAMIENTO
  TÉRMICO DE PLACAS
  DE POLIESTIRENO
  EXTRUIDO 6 cm
4 IMPERMEABILIZACIÓN CON
  DOS LÁMINAS DE BETÚN
  ASFÁLTICO MODIFICADO
5 FORMACIÓN DE PENDIENTE
  CON HORMIGÓN
  CELULAR SIN GRANULAR
  18 cm DE MEDIA
6 FORJADO RETICULAR 29 cm
7 ENYESADO Y PINTADO

1 GRAVEL
2 GEOTEXTILE SHEET
3 6 cm THICK EXTRUDED
  POLYSTYRENE THERMAL
  INSULATION LAYER
4 TWO-LAYER BITUMINOUS
  WATERPROOFING
5 18 cm THICK CONCRETE
  SCREED AS ROOF SLOPE
6 29 cm THICK SLAB
7 PAINTED PLASTER LAYER

1 GRAVA LAVADA
2 LÁMINA GEOTEXTIL
3 CAPA DE AISLAMIENTO
  TÉRMICO 4 cm
4 LÁMINA DE PVC 1,2 mm
5 HORMIGÓN DE PENDIENTES
6 LOSA DE HORMIGÓN

1 WASHED GRAVEL
2 GEOTEXTILE SHEET
3 4 cm THICK THERMAL
  INSULATION LAYER
4 1,2 mm THICK PVC LAYER
5 CONCRETE SCREED
  WITH SLOPE
6 CONCRETE SLAB

LÓPEZ-RIVERA ARQUITECTOS
BARCELONA.ES 2007

ROLDÁN + BERENGUÉ
BARCELONA.ES 2009

MVRDV, BLANCA
LLEÓ MADRID.ES 2009

08 118-127

12 170-183

14 198-217

Ordenados por el material de la capa exterior
Arranged by the external layer material

1:20
0   0.1   0.5   1

GRAVA
GRAVEL

CERÁMICA
TERRACOTTA

MADERA
WOOD

CEMENTO
CEMENT

VEGETACIÓN
PLANTING

METAL
METAL

AISLAMIENTO
INSULATION

MEMBRANA
MEMBRANE

PRINCIPAL

HORMIGÓN
CONCRETE

MADERA
WOOD

CERÁMICA
TERRACOTTA

INTERNAL

CARTÓN-YESO
PLASTER-BOARD

ENLUCIDO
PLASTER

METAL
METAL

CUBIERTA ROOF

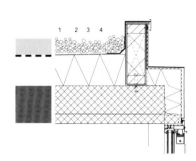

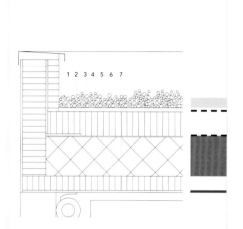

1 GRAVA
2 MEMBRANA DE CUBIERTA
3 CAPA DE AISLAMIENTO
  TÉRMICO
4 FORJADO DE HORMIGÓN

1 GRAVEL
2 ROOFING MEMBRANE
3 INSULATION
4 CONCRETE FLOOR

1 CAPA DE PROTECCIÓN
  DE GRAVA
2 IMPERMEABILIZANTE
3 CAPA DE AISLAMIENTO
  TÉRMICO DE POLIESTIRENO
  EXTRUIDO
4 BARRERA DE VAPOR
5 FORJADO DE
  HORMIGÓN ARMADO
6 AISLAMIENTO TÉRMICO
7 ENLUCIDO DE YESO

1 GRAVEL PROTECTION LAYER
2 WATERPROOF MEMBRANE
3 THERMAL INSULATION
  LAYER
4 VAPOUR BARRIER
5 REINFORCED
  CONCRETE SLAB
6 SECONDARY THERMAL
  INSULATION LAYER
7 PLASTER RENDERING

1 CAPA DE GRAVA
2 MEMBRANA DE
  IMPERMEABILIZACIÓN
3 CAPA DE AISLAMIENTO
  TÉRMICO 140 mm
4 BARRERA DE VAPOR
5 FORJADO DE HORMIGÓN
  PREFABRICADO 280 mm

1 BALLAST LAYER
2 WATERPROOF MEMBRANE
3 140 mm THICK THERMAL
  INSULATION LAYER
4 VAPOUR MEMBRANE
5 280 mm THICK
  PREFABRICATED
  FLOOR SLAB

ATELIER KEMPE THILL
AMSTERDAM.NL 2007

⑯ 230-239

LEHMANN FIDANZA & ASSOCIÉS
FRIBOURG.CH 2009

㉑ 290-297

ANA ARCHITECTEN
AMSTERDAM.NL 2007

㉒ 298-307

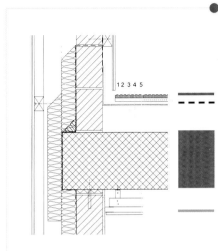

1 TEJA
2 MEMBRANA
  IMPERMEABILIZANTE
3 CAPA DE AISLAMIENTO
  TÉRMICO
4 REVESTIMIENTO INTERIOR
  DE CARTÓN-YESO

1 CERAMIC TILE
2 WATERPROOF MEMBRANE
3 THERMAL INSULATION
  LAYER
4 GYPSUM BOARD
  INTERIOR FINISHING

EDOUARD FRANÇOIS
PARIS.FR 2008

⑱ 252-265

1 REVESTIMIENTO DE MADERA
2 LÁMINA DRENANTE
3 PANEL RÍGIDO DE
  AISLAMIENTO TÉRMICO
4 MEMBRANA
  IMPERMEABILIZANTE
5 AISLAMIENTO TÉRMICO
  DE VIDRIO CELULAR
6 LOSA DE HORMIGÓN ARMADO
7 CAPA DE AISLAMIENTO
  TÉRMICO
8 CHAPA DE ALUMINIO 4 mm

1 TIMBER CLADDING
2 DRAIN SHEET
3 RIGID INSULATION
4 DAMP-PROOF MEMBRANE
5 CELLULAR GLASS
  THERMAL INSULATION
6 CONCRETE SLAB
7 THERMAL INSULATION LAYER
8 4 mm THICK
  ALUMINIUM PLATE

BIG+JDS
COPENHAGEN.DK 2008

⑪ 154-169

1 PAVIMENTO DE MADERA
2 IMPERMEABILIZACIÓN
3 AISLAMIENTO 100-170 mm
4 LOSA DE HORMIGÓN
5 CARTÓN-YESO

1 TIMBER DECKING
  PANEL SYSTEM
2 WATERPROOF MEMBRANE
3 ROOF INSULATION
  100-170 mm
4 CONCRETE SLAB
5 GYPSUM BOARD

dRMM
LONDON.UK 2006

㉖ 340-347

GRAVA
GRAVEL

CERÁMICA
TERRACOTTA

MADERA
WOOD

CEMENTO
CEMENT

VEGETACIÓN
PLANTING

METAL
METAL

AISLAMIENTO
INSULATION

MEMBRANA
MEMBRANE

PRINCIPAL

HORMIGÓN
CONCRETE

MADERA
WOOD

CERÁMICA
TERRACOTTA

INTERNAL

CARTÓN-YESO
PLASTER-BOARD

ENLUCIDO
PLASTER

METAL
METAL

CUBIERTA ROOF

1:20

0   0.1   0.5   1

GRAVA
GRAVEL

CERÁMICA
TERRACOTTA

MADERA
WOOD

CEMENTO
CEMENT

VEGETACIÓN
PLANTING

METAL
METAL

AISLAMIENTO
INSULATION

MEMBRANA
MEMBRANE

PRINCIPAL

HORMIGÓN
CONCRETE

MADERA
WOOD

CERÁMICA
TERRACOTTA

INTERNAL

CARTÓN-YESO
PLASTER-BOARD

ENLUCIDO
PLASTER

METAL
METAL

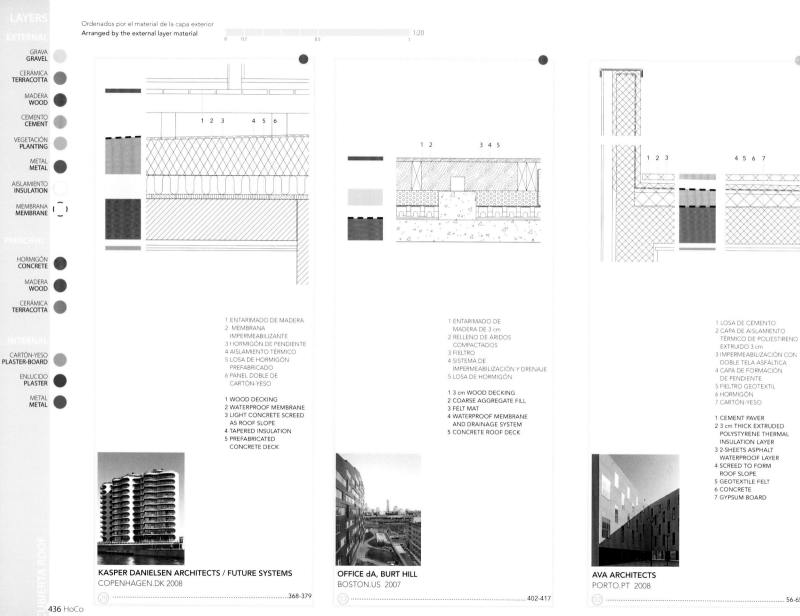

1 ENTARIMADO DE MADERA
2 MEMBRANA
   IMPERMEABILIZANTE
3 HORMIGÓN DE PENDIENTE
4 AISLAMIENTO TÉRMICO
5 LOSA DE HORMIGÓN
   PREFABRICADO
6 PANEL DOBLE DE
   CARTÓN-YESO

1 WOOD DECKING
2 WATERPROOF MEMBRANE
3 LIGHT CONCRETE SCREED
   AS ROOF SLOPE
4 TAPERED INSULATION
5 PREFABRICATED
   CONCRETE DECK

1 ENTARIMADO DE
   MADERA DE 3 cm
2 RELLENO DE ÁRIDOS
   COMPACTADOS
3 FIELTRO
4 SISTEMA DE
   IMPERMEABILIZACIÓN Y DRENAJE
5 LOSA DE HORMIGÓN

1 3 cm WOOD DECKING
2 COARSE AGGREGATE FILL
3 FELT MAT
4 WATERPROOF MEMBRANE
   AND DRAINAGE SYSTEM
5 CONCRETE ROOF DECK

1 LOSA DE CEMENTO
2 CAPA DE AISLAMIENTO
   TÉRMICO DE POLIESTIRENO
   EXTRUIDO 3 cm
3 IMPERMEABILIZACIÓN CON
   DOBLE TELA ASFÁLTICA
4 CAPA DE FORMACIÓN
   DE PENDIENTE
5 FIELTRO GEOTEXTIL
6 HORMIGÓN
7 CARTÓN-YESO

1 CEMENT PAVER
2 3 cm THICK EXTRUDED
   POLYSTYRENE THERMAL
   INSULATION LAYER
3 2-SHEETS ASPHALT
   WATERPROOF LAYER
4 SCREED TO FORM
   ROOF SLOPE
5 GEOTEXTILE FELT
6 CONCRETE
7 GYPSUM BOARD

KASPER DANIELSEN ARCHITECTS / FUTURE SYSTEMS
COPENHAGEN.DK 2008

OFFICE dA, BURT HILL
BOSTON.US 2007

AVA ARCHITECTS
PORTO.PT 2008

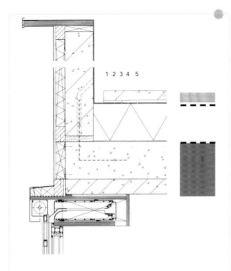

1 LOSA COMPUESTA DE
  CEMENTO Y CAPA DE
  AISLAMIENTO TÉRMICO
2 FIELTRO SEPARADOR
3 LAMINA IMPERMEBILIZANTE
4 MORTERO DE
  REGULARIZACIÓN
5 FORJADO DE HORMIGÓN
6 GUARNECIDO Y
  ENLUCIDO DE YESO

1 FLOOR SLAB CONSISTING
  OF A CEMENT LAYER
  OVER A THERMAL
  INSULATION LAYER
2 FELT
3 WATERPROOF MEMBRANE
4 SCREED MORTAR
5 CONCRETE SLAB
6 PLASTER FINISHING

AGUINAGA Y ASOCIADOS ARQUITECTOS
MADRID.ES 2008

05 88-95

1 ÁREA TRANSITABLE DE
  LOSAS DE CEMENTO
2 MEMBRANA ASFÁLTICA
3 AISLAMIENTO TÉRMICO
  RESISTENTE A LA PRESIÓN
4 BARRERA DE VAPOR
5 FORJADO DE
  HORMIGÓN IN SITU

1 TILES INSPECTION
  PATH, CONCRETE
2 BITUMINOUS ROOF
  COVERING
3 PRESSURE RESISTENT
  INSULATION
4 VAPOUR BARRIER
5 IN-SITU CONCRETE FLOOR

ARONS EN GELAUFF ARCHITECTEN
GRONINGEN.NL 2007

06 96-103

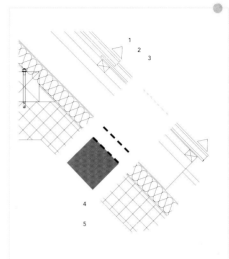

1 PANELES DE CEMENTO 8 mm
2 MEMBRANA DE PVC
3 CAPA DE AISLAMIENTO
  TÉRMICO
4 BARRERA DE VAPOR
5 FORJADO DE HORMIGÓN
  ARMADO 20 cm

1 8 mm THICK CEMENT
  COMPOSITE SHEETS
2 PVC FOIL
3 THERMAL INSULATION
  LAYER
4 VAPOUR BARRIER
5 20 cm THICK REINFORCED
  CONCRETE SLAB

OFIS ARHITEKTI
CERKLJE.SI 2007

15 218-229

LAYERS

EXTERNAL

GRAVA
GRAVEL

CERÁMICA
TERRACOTTA

MADERA
WOOD

CEMENTO
CEMENT

VEGETACIÓN
PLANTING

METAL
METAL

AISLAMIENTO
INSULATION

MEMBRANA
MEMBRANE

PRINCIPAL

HORMIGÓN
CONCRETE

MADERA
WOOD

CERÁMICA
TERRACOTTA

INTERNAL

CARTÓN-YESO
PLASTER-BOARD

ENLUCIDO
PLASTER

METAL
METAL

CUBIERTA ROOF

Ordenados por el material de la capa exterior
Arranged by the external layer material

1:20

0   0.1   0.5   1

GRAVA
GRAVEL

CERÁMICA
TERRACOTTA

MADERA
WOOD

CEMENTO
CEMENT

VEGETACIÓN
PLANTING

METAL
METAL

AISLAMIENTO
INSULATION

MEMBRANA
MEMBRANE

PRINCIPAL

HORMIGÓN
CONCRETE

MADERA
WOOD

CERÁMICA
TERRACOTTA

INTERNAL

CARTÓN-YESO
PLASTER-BOARD

ENLUCIDO
PLASTER

METAL
METAL

1 2 3 4   5 6

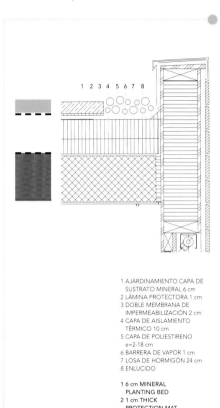

1 2 3 4 5 6 7 8

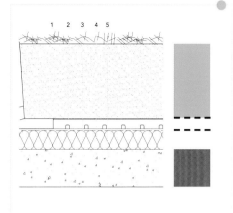

1 2 3 4 5

1 BALDOSAS DE CEMENTO
DE 60 x 40 cm
2 MEMBRANA
IMPERMEABILIZANTE
3 CAPA DE NIVELACIÓN DE
HORMIGÓN CELULAR
4 CAPA DE AISLAMIENTO
TÉRMICO DE PLACA
DE POLIESTIRENO
EXPANDIDO 3 cm
5 BARRERA DE VAPOR DE
FILM DE POLIETILENO
6 LOSA DE HORMIGÓN
ARMADO

1 60 x 40 cm CEMENT PAVERS
2 WATERPROOF MEMBRANE
3 LIGHT CONCRETE SCREED
4 3 cm THICK EXPANDED
POLYSTYRENE THERMAL
INSULATION LAYER
5 POLYETHYLENE FILM
AS VAPOUR BARRIER
6 REINFORCED
CONCRETE SLAB

1 AJARDINAMIENTO CAPA DE
SUSTRATO MINERAL 6 cm
2 LÁMINA PROTECTORA 1 cm
3 DOBLE MEMBRANA DE
IMPERMEABILIZACIÓN 2 cm
4 CAPA DE AISLAMIENTO
TÉRMICO 10 cm
5 CAPA DE POLIESTIRENO
e=2-18 cm
6 BARRERA DE VAPOR 1 cm
7 LOSA DE HORMIGÓN 24 cm
8 ENLUCIDO

1 6 cm MINERAL
PLANTING BED
2 1 cm THICK
PROTECTION MAT
3 2 cm THICK DOUBLE
WATERPROOF MEMBRANE
4 10 cm THICK THERMAL
INSULATION LAYER
5 2-18 cm THICK
POLYESTYRENE LAYER
6 1 cm THICK VAPOUR
BARRIER
7 24 cm THICK
CONCRETE SLAB
8 PLASTER

1 PLANTACIÓN Y
TIERRA VEGETAL
2 TEJIDO FILTRANTE, DRENAJE
Y CAPA DE PROTECCIÓN
3 MEMBRANA
IMPERMEABILIZANTE
4 CAPA DE AISLAMIENTO
TÉRMICO
5 FORJADO DE HORMIGÓN

1 PLANTS AND NATURAL SOIL
2 FILTERING MAT,
PROTECTION AND
DRAINAGE SYSTEM
3 WATERPROOF MEMBRANE
4 THERMAL INSULATION
LAYER
5 CONCRETE SLAB

ADAMO-FAIDEN ARQUITECTOS
BUENOS AIRES.AR 2008

FREI ARCHITEKTEN
ROHR.CH 2007

BECKMANN-N'THÉPÉ ARCHITECTES
PARIS.FR 2007

GRAVA
GRAVEL

CERÁMICA
TERRACOTTA

MADERA
WOOD

CEMENTO
CEMENT

VEGETACIÓN
PLANTING

METAL
METAL

AISLAMIENTO
INSULATION

MEMBRANA
MEMBRANE

PRINCIPAL

HORMIGÓN
CONCRETE

MADERA
WOOD

CERÁMICA
TERRACOTTA

INTERNAL

CARTÓN-YESO
PLASTER-BOARD

ENLUCIDO
PLASTER

METAL
METAL

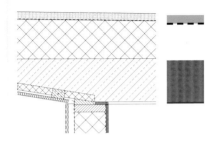

1 2 3 4 5

1 VEGETACIÓN DEL
  GÉNERO SEDUM
2 MEMBRANA DE
  IMPERMEABILIZACIÓN
3 CAPA DE AISLAMIENTO
  TÉRMICO
4 HORMIGÓN
5 ENLUCIDO

1 MOS-SEDUM
2 WATERPROOF MEMBRANE
3 THERMAL INSULATION
  LAYER
4 CONCRETE
5 PLASTER

HVDN ARCHITECTEN
AMSTERDAM.NL 2008

20 276-289

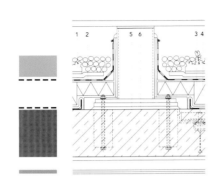

1 2   5 6   3 4

1 CUBIERTA VEGETAL
  BIODIVERSA
2 MEMBRANA FILTRANTE
  Y DRENAJE
3 AISLAMIENTO 140 mm
4 MEMBRANA
  IMPERMEABILIZANTE
5 LOSA DE HORMIGÓN
  ARMADO
6 DOBLE PLACA DE
  CARTÓN-YESO

1 BIODIVERSE 'BROWN
  ROOF' SYSTEM
2 MEMBRANE, FILTER AND
  DRAINAGE SYSTEM
3 140 mm INSULATION BOARD
4 WATERPROOF MEMBRANE
5 REINFORCED
  CONCRETE SLAB
6 DOUBLE GYPSUM BOARD

ALLFORD HALL MONAGHAN MORRIS
LONDON.UK 2007

27 348-357

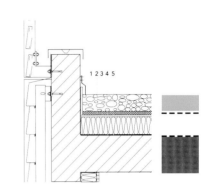

1 2 3 4 5

1 CUBIERTA VERDE Y
  SISTEMA DE DRENAJE
2 MEMBRANA
  IMPERMEABILIZANTE,
3 CAPA DE AISLAMIENTO
  TÉRMICO 100 mm
4 BARRERA DE VAPOR
5 LOSA DE HORMIGÓN

1 GREEN ROOF AND
  DRAINAGE SYSTEM
2 WATERPROOF MEMBRANE
3 100 mm INSULATION
4 VAPOUR MEMBRANE
5 CONCRETE SLAB

HAMONIC + MASSON
PARIS.FR 2008

28 358-367

LAYERS
EXTERNAL

GRAVA
GRAVEL

CERÁMICA
TERRACOTTA

MADERA
WOOD

CEMENTO
CEMENT

VEGETACIÓN
PLANTING

METAL
METAL

AISLAMIENTO
INSULATION

MEMBRANA
MEMBRANE

PRINCIPAL

HORMIGÓN
CONCRETE

MADERA
WOOD

CERÁMICA
TERRACOTTA

INTERNAL

CARTÓN-YESO
PLASTER-BOARD

ENLUCIDO
PLASTER

METAL
METAL

Ordenados por el material de la capa exterior
Arranged by the external layer material

1:20

0   .1   .5

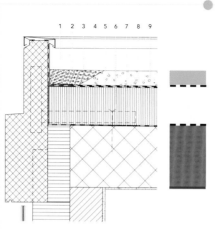
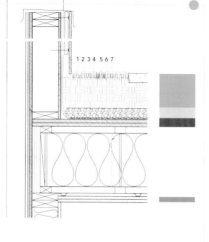
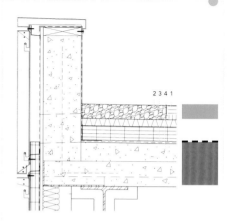

1 VEGETACIÓN
2 CAPA DE TIERRA
  NATURAL 8 cm
3 LÁMINA GEOTEXTIL
4 BARRERA DE VAPOR
5 LÁMINA GEOTEXTIL
6 CAPA DE AISLAMIENTO
  TÉRMICO 20 cm
7 MEMBRANA
  IMPERMEABILIZANTE
8 FORJADO DE
  HORMIGÓN DE ESPESOR
  VARIABLE (24-35 cm)
9 ENLUCIDO DE YESO

1 VEGETATION
2 8 cm THICK NATURAL
  SOIL LAYER
3 GEOTEXTILE MAT
4 VAPOUR BARRIER
5 GEOTEXTILE MAT
6 20 cm THICK THERMAL
  INSULATION LAYER
7 WATERPROOF MEMBRANE
8 24-35 cm THICK
  CONCRETE SLAB
9 PLASTER LAYER

1 PLANTACIÓN SEMI-
  INTENSIVA SOBRE CUBIERTA
2 LÁMINA SEPARADORA
3 CAPA DE AGREGADO
  LIGERO DE GRAVA
4 BARRERA ANTIRRAÍCES
5 2 CAPAS DE
  CONTRACHAPADO
  DE 19 mm
6 CAPA DE AISLAMIENTO
  TÉRMICO
7 2 CAPAS DE CARTÓN
  YESO COLGADO DE
  SUBESTRUCTURA METÁLICA

1 ROOFMEADOW SEMI-
  INTENSIVE GROWTH MEDIA
2 SEPARATION FABRIC
3 GRAVEL LIGHT WEIGHT
  AGGREGATE LAYER
4 ROOT BARRIER
5 2 LAYERS OF 19 mm
  THICK PLYWOOD
6 THERMAL INSULATION
  LAYER
7 2 GYPSUM BOARD LAYERS
  WITH DEEP METAL
  FURRING CHANNEL

1 SISTEMA DE CUBIERTA
  VEGETAL CON CAPA
  DRENANTE
2 AISLAMIENTO TÉRMICO
  RÍGIDO DE 7,6 cm
3 LÁMINA
  IMPERMEABILIZANTE
4 LOSA DE HORMIGÓN
  ARMADO

1 GARDEN ROOF SYSTEM
  WITH DRAINAGE
2 7.6 cm RIGID INSULATION
3 WATERPROOF MEMBRANE
4 CONCRETE DECK

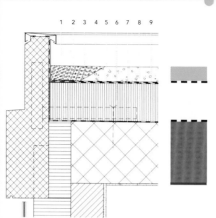

GIGON / GUYER
ZURICH.CH 2007

ONION FLATS
PHILADELPHIA.US 2009

OFFICE dA, BURT HILL
BOSTON.US 2007

440 HoCo

CUBIERTA ROOF

LAYERS

EXTERNAL

GRAVA
GRAVEL

CERÁMICA
TERRACOTTA

MADERA
WOOD

CEMENTO
CEMENT

VEGETACIÓN
PLANTING

METAL
METAL

AISLAMIENTO
INSULATION

MEMBRANA
MEMBRANE

HORMIGÓN
CONCRETE

MADERA
WOOD

CERÁMICA
TERRACOTTA

INTERNAL

CARTÓN-YESO
PLASTER-BOARD

ENLUCIDO
PLASTER

METAL
METAL

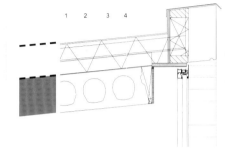

1 PLANCHA DE ZINC SOBRE
  ENLISTONADO DE MADERA
2 MEMBRANA
  IMPERMEABILIZANTE
3 TABLERO DE MADERA
4 CAPA DE AISLAMIENTO
  120 mm
5 BARRERA DE VAPOR 4 mm
6 DOBLE PLACA DE CARTÓN-
  YESO

1 ZINC SHEET ON
  WOOD BRACKET
2 WATERPROOFING
  MEMBRANE
3 PLYWOOD
4 120 mm THICK THERMAL
  INSULATION
5 4 mm THICK VAPOUR
  BARRIER
6 DOUBLE PLASTER BOARD

1 MEMBRANA DE CAUCHO
2 CAPA DE AISLAMIENTO
  TÉRMICO DE LANA DE ROCA
3 MEMBRANA
  IMPERMEABILIZANTE
4 FORJADO ALVEOLAR

1 RUBBER MEMBRANE
2 MINERAL WOOL THERMAL
  INSULATION LAYER
3 WATERPROOF MEMBRANE
4 HOLLOW CORE SLAB

1 MEMBRANA
  IMPERMEABILIZANTE DE PVC
2 TABLERO DE FIBRA
  MINERAL 30 mm
3 CAPA DE AISLAMIENTO
  TÉRMICO 150 mm
4 CAPA DE GRAVA PARA
  FORMACIÓN DE PENDIENTES
5 BARRERA DE VAPOR
6 LOSA DE HORMIGÓN
  ARMADO 260 mm

1 PVC WATERPROOFING LAYER
2 30 mm THICK HARD
  MINERAL-FIBRE BOARD
3 150 mm THICK THERMAL
  INSULATION LAYER
4 LIGHTWEIGHT GRAVEL
  FOR INCLINATION
5 VAPOUR BARRIER
6 260 mm THICK IN SITU
  REINFORCED CONCRETE SLAB

EMMANUEL COMBAREL DOMINIQUE MARREC
ARCHITECTES PARIS.FR 2006

POOLEN ARCHITEKTEN
CULEMBORG.NL 2008

KOKO ARCHITEKTID
TALLINN.EE 2007

Aspectos destacados	Número de proyecto Project number	Highlighted features
Sistema industrializado de construcción mediante encofrados integrales de aluminio: acelera los plazos de ejecución y anula la aparición de escombros.	01, 14	Industrial construction system throughout the use of custom integral aluminium formworks: speeds-up execution time and eliminates debris in the construction process.
Recogida y almacenaje del agua de lluvia para su uso posterior en el riego de jardines.	13, 17, 26, 27, 31, 32	Rainwater collection and re-use for irrigation.
Cubierta ajardinada que mejora el aislamiento térmico del interior y la emisión de calor a la atmósfera.	17, 20, 27, 28, 31, 32	Green roof allowing for better thermal insulation and prevents the heat island effect.
Empleo de maderas procedentes de plantaciones social y medioambientalmente responsables.	22, 26, 27, 31	Use of timber products coming from socially and environmentally responsible forestry.
Preocupación por el aislamiento acústico y no sólo térmico de los edificios, para proteger tanto del ruido exterior como del ruido entre viviendas.	20, 26, 27, 28, 30, 32	Use of sound insulation systems besides thermal insulation, in order to protect from outdoor noise as well as to protect from noise originated in other dwellings.
Empleo de materiales reciclados o con algún componente reciclado o bien empleo de materiales posteriormente reciclables.	22, 26, 31, 32	Use of entirely recycled materials, materials with recycled components, or subsequently recyclable materials.
Sistema de ventilación con recuperación de calor mediante el cual, el calor desprendido durante el proceso de ventilación mecánica es devuelto a las viviendas.	30, 32	Heat recovery ventilator: the heat given off in the mechanical ventilation process goes back to the housing units.
Aparcamiento en la planta baja y no en el sótano: emplea luz artificial sólo de noche y no necesita de ventilación mecánica.	6	The car park is located above grade and not underground: it makes use of daylight and natural ventilation.
Aparcamiento provisto de puntos de recarga para vehículos eléctricos.	31, 32	Private parking with electric car charging port.
Presencia de un vehículo comunitario en el aparcamiento a disposición de los residentes.	32	Zip car located in the garage for resident use.
Espacio destinado específicamente al aparcamiento de bicicletas.	21, 26, 32, 27	Storage space meant specifically for bikes.

Los encofrados integrales realizados a medida ya han sido utilizados en otras ocasiones, incluso por la propia Empresa Municipal de la Vivienda de Madrid, que ya ha comprobado sus resultados. En este proyecto se introduce una novedad bastante importante desde el punto de vista de la puesta en obra, que consiste en la fabricación de los encofrados con aluminio. Esto supone un aligeramiento considerable que permite a los operarios manipular las piezas con seguridad, sin la asistencia de grúas.

Estas innovaciones han exigido una especial dedicación desde el proyecto de ejecución hasta la dirección de obra para resolver cuestiones poco convencionales en cuanto a espesores de hormigón, tiempos de fraguado y desencofrado, disposición de instalaciones, y métodos de control de la calidad de la ejecución, que una vez resueltos, han dado unos resultados muy competitivos.

El proyecto de 102 viviendas de protección pública en Carabanchel, comprende 52 viviendas de un dormitorio, 35 de dos dormitorios, y 15 de tres dormitorios. Se ha diseñado una célula común que constituye la vivienda de un dormitorio, la cual se transforma en los otros dos tipos mediante la adición de los dormitorios adosados a la fachada.

De esta manera, el proyecto presenta un núcleo invariable que se repite 102 veces y que justifica el uso de este sistema industrializado. Los encofrados de aluminio conforman la distribución del núcleo (vivienda de un dormitorio) incluyendo fachadas, muros medianeros, tabiques, e incluso armarios. Estos muros contienen, una vez hormigonados, el aislamiento en los muros perimetrales, y todas las instalaciones.

Los dormitorios extra, que se añaden para obtener las viviendas más grandes, son unos módulos ligeros de estructura metálica que se anclan en la fachada de hormigón y se fijan en unos puntos previstos.

Su construcción responde a esta necesidad de optimización industria. Así el cuerpo principal se construye en hormigón a partir de un único molde de alta precisión, mientras las variaciones, excepciones que posibilitan el sistema, son ligeros esqueletos metálicos.

El proceso se asemeja a la industria automovilística de manera que cada trabajador se especializa en una parte del montaje, y tras varias puestas, la eficiencia se optimiza. Comienza con el replanteo de los muros de la vivienda sobre la losa inferior. Después se disponen las mallazos de armadura vertical que se mantienen en pie por sí solos ayudada por las vueltas en las esquinas.

Sobre ellos, se colocan separadores para mantenerlos en la posición centrada y los paneles de aislamiento (cuando es fachada) que se alojan en el centro de dos mallas. En este proyecto hemos simplificado todos los muros de hormigón a dos tipos: los de fachada, de 24 cm (10 cm + 4 cm de aislamiento + 10 cm), y todos los demás; medianeros, tabiques y armarios, de 10 cm. Todos ellos son portantes.

Una vez instalados los mallazos y el aislamiento, se disponen todas las instalaciones en el espesor de los muros de 10cm, a excepción de la calefacción que se distribuye perimetralmente en el canto de la losa.

El siguiente paso es la colocación del encofrado de aluminio, proveniente, pieza por pieza, de la vivienda contigua, y su hormigonado.

Para terminar falta recibir ventanas, pintar, e instalar una tarima flotante sobre una losa autonivelada, y alicatar baño y cocina.

El ritmo de ejecución es diario, ya que se puede desencofrar, encofrar, y hormigonar en el mismo día, y trabajar en el resto de la cadena de montaje. De esta manera se obtiene un ritmo de una vivienda por día.

Las ventajas de este sistema industrializado son la rapidez de la puesta en obra, que acelera los plazos de ejecución y anula la aparición de escombros en el proceso constructivo. Por contra, hay que tener en cuenta el encarecimiento material de la ejecución al emplear una cantidad de hormigón superior al habitual.

El sistema conlleva una desventaja de cara al usuario que consiste en la dificultad de acometer futuras reformas en la vivienda, ya que todo es estructura. Sin embargo, esta posibilidad no se contempló en este proyecto por dos razones: la primera es que, al tratarse de viviendas muy reducidas (entre 42 y 66 m²), las posibilidades espaciales están muy limitadas a la distribución propuesta, y la segunda, razón fundamental, es que se trata de viviendas en régimen de alquiler, por lo que en cualquier caso estas reformas no estarían permitidas.

El acabado final exterior está sujeto a las diferentes orientaciones para ofrecer una respuesta climática adecuada y fomentar un comportamiento energético más sostenible.

Las estancias principales (estar y dormitorio) de todas las viviendas se encuentran orientadas a sureste, y suroeste, y las cocinas, aseos, y dormitorios secundarios a noreste y noroeste.

El aislamiento alberga la mayor parte de la masa en el interior, para aumentar la inercia térmica de estas viviendas de uso permanente, y permitir que el calor acumulado en su interior en invierno no se disipe rápidamente, y que el calor recibido exteriormente en verano no se acumule innecesariamente.

Aparte del aislamiento integral, se dispone de una fachada metálica de chapa estirada galvanizada y lacada en blanco (el color más reflectante, y por lo tanto menos absorbente de las radiaciones solares) en la fachada sur. Esta chapa conforma una doble piel ventilada que se dispone en horizontal en la fachada sureste, y vertical en la fachada suroeste. De esta manera, se permite en mayor medida, el paso de la radiación rasante invernal, y se protege de la radiación más vertical estival. En la fachada suroeste se dispone verticalmente para proteger mejor los rayos del fuerte poniente de verano de Madrid,

que se ocultarán más cuanto más se acerque su puesta al noroeste (21 de junio).

En la fachada norte el hormigón esta únicamente regularizado con una pintura blanca, y los dormitorios en voladizo van revestidos por una chapa galvanizada y blanca, en este caso simplemente perforada, ya que suponen una fachada ventilada, que además protege el aislamiento proyectado.

Las instalaciones son centralizadas y distribuidas a cada vivienda a través de las pasarelas de acceso sin interferir de esta manera con el cuerpo principal de hormigón. Existe un apoyo energético solar en cubierta, también centralizado, y una preinstalación de aire acondicionado, que se prevé en la terraza-tendedero, oculta de las vistas desde el exterior.

La centralización de las instalaciones se organiza en la planta sótano, la cual se abre al exterior a través de grandes patios de los que nacerán los árboles, y entre los cuales aparcarán los coches.

En general se optó por organizar la vivienda y la distribución de los espacios teniendo en cuenta la orientación solar predominante, condicionada por la configuración del terreno disponible para la construcción del edificio. Se optó por un revestimiento exterior denominado por sistema "ETICS" para funcionar en simultáneo con el conjunto de la estructura de las ventanas permitiendo llenar todo el perímetro del edificio.

la limpieza periódica de la fachada cada 5 ó 10 años dependiendo de la polución ambiental que se produzca en su momento. Las carpinterías de las ventanas tampoco necesitan de un mantenimiento especial.

La producción de energía del edificio se encuentra centralizada. Aprovecha la aportación energética de los paneles solares situados en cubierta. La misma empresa que ha realizado la instalación gestionará su mantenimiento y su uso.

El proyecto se ciñó desde sus comienzos a criterios de economía, viabilidad y sostenibilidad. Se han utilizado unas luces entorno a los 5,50 m, se ha resuelto la fachada con módulos de mortero monocapa de diferentes colores que, además de aportar economía en su ejecución, no necesitan labores de repintado: será suficiente

Los desniveles del patio central de acceso a los portales, aunque incluyen gradas en diversas zonas, cuentan también con rampas de muy suave pendiente que permiten el acceso a los portales y a los jardines a personas de movilidad reducida de modo totalmente independiente.

Se ha tomado un gran número de medidas orientadas a la sostenibilidad, que conducen a la categoría más alta en lo que a ésta se refiere: Groninger Housing Quality II.
Medidas clave:
· Fácil adaptación de la planta baja de los apartamentos (además de los tres tipos base) a las necesidades cambiantes de sus habitantes, a medida que éstos envejecen o sufren alguna discapacidad.
· Ventilación: ventilación natural y mecánica.

Pese a que el edificio tiene 63 m de altura, logramos prescindir de la ventilación equilibrada (gracias a una distribución de 4 apartamentos por planta, en sección transversal).
· Calefacción: suelo radiante a baja temperatura, graduable en cada apartamento y en cada habitación.
· La huella del edificio en la parcela es relativamente pequeña. Apenas fue necesaria la tala de árboles. Circuito cerrado para el suelo durante la construcción.
· Persianas verticales como protección contra el sol estival.
· Con la ubicación del aparcamiento en la planta baja, el empleo de luz artificial se limita a la noche, y puede prescindirse de la ventilación mecánica, costosa en términos de energía y no siempre eficiente.
· Empleo de materiales prefabricados siempre que sea posible (miradores, ventanas circulares, refuerzos de acero) reduciendo así el material sobrante del montaje.

El criterio más importante y de obligado cumplimiento para vivienda social en Cataluña es disponer de una hora de sol entre las 10 y las 12 horas solares en el solscíticio de invierno en las salas de estar de al menos el 80% de las viviendas. El bloque obtiene el 91%, mientras que el 9% restante al menos recibe 45 minutos.

Además hay que demostrar que las soluciones constructivas cumplen unos parámetros de ecoeficiencia, cuya suma de puntos ha de superar 10. El proyecto obtuvo 30 puntos:
1. Fachada ventilada a orientacion sur-oeste +- 90° (5 puntos).
2. Una hora de sol en el solsticio de invierno (5 puntos).
3. Ventilación cruzada natural (6 puntos).
4. Sistemas pre-industrializados en el 80% de la estructura (placas alveolares) (6 puntos).
5. Reducir el coeficiente medio de transmitancia térmica K_m de los cerramientos verticales en un 30% de 0,70 w/m^2K ; $K_m = 0,49$ w/m^2K. (8 puntos).

Ventilación cruzada

Tanto la ventilación natural, como la abundante luz natural en todos los espacios, están garantizadas por la distribución interior y por disponer todas las unidades de dos fachadas opuestas abiertas.

Aprovechando el clima mediterráneo, la entrada a los apartamentos se realiza mediante una calle elevada en la parte posterior del edificio que mira hacia un típico patio interior de manzana barcelonés.

Luz y ventilación natural: Orientación

La cocina y el lavabo se colocan adyacentes a esta fachada, mientras que la zona principal de estar se encuentra en la fachada sureste opuesta, con el fin de cumplir con el decreto local de eco-eficiencia. Este decreto pide que el 80% de las viviendas dispongan de al menos una hora de sol directo en la sala de estar de 10:00 a 14:00 en el solsticio de invierno.

Las ventanas a sur y oeste cuentan con protección solar por el exterior regulable.

La ventana de la cocina y el espacio de terraza de verano se orientan a noroeste estando siempre en sombra.

Galería como captador solar pasivo

Funcionando como amortiguador entre la calle y el estar y recuperando una tradición barcelonesa, colocamos una pequeña galería en el extremo sur del estar. Ésta galería se genera entre dos superficies vidriadas y funciona como captador solar pasivo en el invierno. En verano, debido a la verticalidad de la incidencia solar, abriendo las lamas vidriadas exteriores y cerrando las puertas plegables interiores, la galería se transforma en un balcón.

El edificio también cuenta con:

Placas solares para producción de agua caliente sanitaria

Fachada ventilada a orientación noroeste.

· Orientación de las viviendas a Este y Oeste. Fachada con inercia térmica que proporciona protección y posibilita el ahorro energético.
Los apartamentos tienen todas las estancias exteriores y ventilación cruzada.

· Cubierta: captadores solares (energía fototérmica) para el precalentamiento de agua sanitaria y de calefacción. La otra parte de la cubierta es ecológica-solarium.

· Tratamiento de los caudales de agua en todos los puntos de suministro. Aparatos sanitarios de bajo consumo.

· Ascensores de bajo gasto energético.
Uso de pinturas ecológicas interiores y exteriores, y de maderas de origen controlado.

La arquitectura sostenible es una parte esencial de nuestro proceso de diseño. Esto no solo se refiere a la técnica y materialización del edificio, donde se presta especial atención al medio ambiente y al consumo de energía. La sostenibilidad también hace referencia a la durabilidad y flexibilidad del diseño a lo largo del tiempo.

El edificio debe ser fácilmente manejable, de bajo mantenimiento y bajo consumo de energía. En la medida de lo posible, el agua de lluvia ha de ser recogida y almacenada, o reconducida a una corriente de agua próxima. BonVie es un edificio de bajo consumo energético con un aislamiento de alto nivel, y construido con materiales respetuosos con el medio ambiente. Además, la planta flexible y el programa variado, se traducen en un sistema constructivo modular y flexible.

El sistema de molde total permite resolver en tiempo y precio esta construcción prefabricada de estructura singular. Las 146 viviendas se resuelven con una unidad base y dos variaciones. Esto permite viviendas de uno, dos y tres dormitorios con estancias versátiles y espacios especialmente generosos para el aseo, el ocio y el almacenamiento. El sistema de moldes industrializados, es ágil, sencillo y sostenible, pues no produce rozas ni escombros en obra. Es versátil, práctico y revolucionario. Permite hacer una vivienda por día. Facilita la organización flexible y la ejecución simultánea de estructura, cerramientos e instalaciones. El montaje del encofrado de aluminio es ligero y manejable para los operarios. Produce una construcción de calidad en tiempo y coste.

Los patios en altura garantizan una ventilación cruzada mediante dos o tres fachadas opuestas para todas las unidades. Se utiliza un sistema de calderas de bajo consumo para todo el edificio reduciendo el gasto energético. Estos sistemas se combinan con paneles solares para la producción de agua caliente sanitaria.

HoCo **ESTRATEGIAS SOSTENIBLES** especificadas por los autores

OFIS ARHITEKTI CERKLJE.SI 2007

La galería recorre todo el bloque. Los elementos ornamentales de madera, en el frente de las galerías y logias, han sido diseñados con un sen-

tido similar al de los estantes para el heno (elementos de madera cuya función era almacenar y dejar secar la hierba). Estos elementos crean una zona térmica previa al estar principal y a los dormitorios, y dan sombra en las galerías.

En la cara exterior de las logias de invierno y de las galerías, se han dispuesto paneles de aluminio para dar sombra.

Los espacios de comunicación y servicio se han reducido al mínimo. De este modo, la luz del día procede de los ejes. Los gastos mensuales en energía y servicios son muy bajos, lo cual es bueno para los residentes, ya que se trata de vivienda social.

ATELIER KEMPE THILL AMSTERDAM.NL 2007

· Eje de pequeñas medidas y reducida superficie de alzado (ratio superficie/superficie de alzado efectivo).

· Bajo consumo de energía por medio del "sistema de ventilación equilibrada en toda la casa" (ventilación mecánica).

BECKMANN-N'THÉPÉ ARCHITECTES PARÍS.FR 2007

· Se disponen paneles fotovoltaicos en la cubierta de los edificios R+9 y R+11 para reducir los gastos en electricidad.

Paneles de tipo monocristalino.
Dimensiones de los paneles: 1 x 1,30 m.
Número de paneles: 63.
Superficie total: en torno a 82 m².
Producción: 11, 6 Kw.

· En el sótano se ubica un depósito de agua, para el riego de las plantas de la terraza y la limpieza del edificio.

· En el centro del edificio se sitúan los jardines colgantes, que moderan los cambios térmicos bruscos.

· Empleo de hormigón autocompactante in situ coloreado. Este material ha resultado efectivo de cara a reducir los niveles de ruido durante la fase de construcción.

HVDN ARCHITECTEN AMSTERDAM.NL 2008

Tala sostenible
La cubierta de madera del patio del Het Kasteel tiene certificado FSC.
Hemos optado por hacer la cubierta con seis tipos distintos de madera. Así se favorecerá la tala sostenible. Junto con el suministrador de madera buscamos la combinación más adecuada para el medio ambiente.

Además de usar una mezcla de maderas, el hecho de que tengan distintas dimensiones beneficia a la tala.

Ingeniería de lo natural
Het Kasteel está dotado de muros acústicos.
La fachada era uno de los condicionantes a los que el proyecto debía obedecer, y se usa también en planta como cámara de aire.
La fachada, que ha sido especialmente desarrollada para este proyecto, permite la ventilación natural y la entrada de aire fresco. Al usar la fuerza natural del aire calefactado, las casas se mantienen también fácilmente frescas en verano.

Almacenamiento de agua
Las cubiertas del edificio están cubiertas de musgo, que retiene el agua de lluvia durante largo tiempo. El musgo no es sólo más duradero que las cubiertas bituminosas, sino que presenta mejor aspecto.

Norma base : SIA 112/1 2004

Ámbito social

Vida en común:

· Integración, mestizaje: creación de condiciones óptimas para una integración y mezcolanza social, cultural e intergeneracional (centro de la ciudad, mantener a las familias en la ciudad).

· Relaciones sociales: creación de lugares de encuentro que favorezcan el intercambio y la comunicación (espacios semipúblicos, patios y lugares de juego).

Ordenación:

· Identidad del lugar, pertenencia: potenciación de la orientación y de la identidad del lugar (sentimiento de seguridad y de pertenencia, responsabilidad de cara al medio ambiente).

Explotación, viabilidad:

· Proximidad a los puntos de aprovisionamiento, mixicidad: reducción de las distancias, creación de una mezcla atractiva dentro del barrio (promoción de la vida de barrio, densidad urbana).

· Movilidad suave: garantía de disponibilidad de una red satisfactoria (vías peatonales seguras y bien iluminadas, aparcamiento para bicicletas, buena conexión con la red de transporte público).

· Accesibilidad y utilización para todos: concepción y adaptación de los edificios para los minusválidos.

Confort, salud:

· Seguridad: incremento de la sensación de seguridad, reducción de los peligros potenciales.

· Luz: optimizar la utilización de la luz del día, garantizar una iluminación adecuada.

· Protección contra el sol estival: alto confort gracias a una buena protección solar en verano.

· Ruido, vibraciones: reducción de las molestias derivadas.

Ámbito económico

Respecto al edificio:

· Emplazamiento: garantía de una explotación económica a largo plazo adaptada al lugar (buena accesibilidad, elevada densidad).

· Objeto construido: obtención de un valor duradero y de una buena calidad en relación a la vida útil (construcción en conformidad con la técnica)

Gastos de inversión:

· Costes y vida útil: invertir en función de los costes aplicados sobre el total de la vida útil (reducir los costes de explotación).

· Financiación: optar por un sistema de financiación que garantice a largo plazo los costes de inversión, de renovación y de demolición (amortización de las inversiones en función de la duración de su utilización).

· Costes externos: reducir al mínimo e internalizar los costes externos (efectos externos de la polución del aire, del ruido, y de los residuos especiales procedentes de la construcción, la explotación, el mantenimiento y la demolición).

Gastos de explotación y mantenimiento:

· Explotación y mantenimiento: reducir los gastos de mantenimiento por medio de una planificación previa y de la adopción de medidas continuas (disminución del coste de explotación a través de las inversiones iniciales valoradas).

· Renovación: reducción de gastos de renovación velando por una buena accesibilidad y calidad óptima.

Ámbito medioambiental

Materiales de construcción:

· Contaminantes: reducción de los contaminantes en los elementos de construcción.

Energía de explotación:

· Necesidades de calor o frío: reducción del consumo de energía necesaria para calefactar, adoptando medidas constructivas y técnicas (buena calidad de la envolvente y de la producción de calor).

· Necesidades de energía para la producción de agua caliente: disminución del consumo de energía adoptando medidas constructivas y técnicas.

· Electricidad: reducir el consumo eléctrico adoptando medidas constructivas y técnicas.

Sol, paisaje:

· Superficie de los terrenos: reducir el consumo de suelo (recalificación de terrenos industriales, incitación a la creación de nuevas zonas en la ciudad).

Infraestructura:

· Movilidad: puesta en marcha de una movilidad compatible con el medio ambiente (solar bien comunicado con los medios de transporte y ubicado en las proximidades de comercios, escuelas, oficinas, lugares de ocio...).

Sostenibilidad

En el proyecto Lootsbuurt tratamos el tema de la sostenibilidad de tres modos. La ley holandesa de la Edificación dicta diversas medidas a adoptar a fin de alcanzar un alto nivel de sostenibilidad en cada proyecto construido en los Países Bajos.

Naturalmente, el proyecto Lootsbuurt está construido atendiendo enteramente a estas normas edificatorias. Por otra parte, presenta algunos rasgos relativos a la sostenibilidad que no están escritos en ninguna ley o norma, y que realzan las cualidades sostenibles del proyecto.

Vida del edificio

Estamos muy concienciados con la pregunta de cómo los edificios pueden adaptarse a las nuevas demandas y necesidades futuras del alojamiento. Pensamos que hay dos respuestas principales a esta pregunta: flexibilidad o especificidad.

La flexibilidad ofrece la posibilidad de cambiar la distribución en planta de la vivienda en función de las necesidades futuras. La especificidad trata de crear distribuciones únicas con cualidades extraordinarias, en virtud de las cuales, dicha planta resultará siempre atractiva (estúdiese nuestro proyecto Multifunk, un edificio totalmente flexible y multifuncional a lo largo del tiempo, cuya fachada está hecha de plástico reciclable).

En el presente proyecto, la respuesta es la especificidad. El proyecto aboga por una reducción de los modelos de vivienda, incluyendo únicamente y como máximo tres viviendas del mismo tipo. Al mismo tiempo, cada una de ellas ofrece unas cualidades espaciales o programáticas específicas (por ejemplo, un gran espacio exterior, un porche, una cubierta vegetal, un vacío, un lugar de trabajo...), de modo que su singularidad queda garantizada, lo que hace que tanto la vivienda como el edificio mantengan su atractivo en el futuro.

Además de esto, se ha prestado especial atención a otorgar a la estructura del edificio valores sostenibles. El "casco" de hormigón está sobredimensionado. Suelos y paredes son más gruesas de lo legalmente requerido, lo que aumenta las cualidades constructivas así como la insonorización entre viviendas, hecho que mejora tanto la calidad de vida en el edificio como su faceta sostenible.

Respeto al medioambiente

En la medida de lo posible, en el edificio se emplean materiales duraderos. La estructura es de hormigón. Los muros exteriores paralelos a la calle son de ladrillo. El ladrillo es un material duradero, más hermoso a medida que pasa el tiempo. La fachada sur es de madera con certificado FSC (Forest Stewardship Council).

Esta organización propone potenciar el bosque duradero, en concreto la selva tropical, teniendo como objetivo la explotación responsable desde un punto de vista social, medioambiental y económico. El interior es de vidrio (incluso los paneles cerrados son vidrio) y estuco.

Ahorro de energía

El edificio presenta un valor Rc muy bajo, gracias a la adopción de diversas medidas de ahorro de energía. A ello ayuda en gran medida la orientación sur de las viviendas. Todos los estares están orientados al sol, mientras que los dormitorios se orientan al noroeste. El vidrio tiene las más altas prestaciones relativas al ahorro de energía.

La parcela escogida para construir este edificio estaba ocupada por una vivienda de tres dormitorios habitada por una familia conformada por una señora mayor y su hija. Una vez adquirida dicha parcela, se prosiguió con la demolición de la antigua casa y la construcción del edificio, multiplicando exponencialmente la densidad de habitantes por metro cuadrado. Confiamos en que el aumento de densidad habitacional haga más sostenible nuestras ciudades.

EcoHomes con calificación Excellent; empleo de materiales certificados y de bajo impacto ambiental; excelente aislamiento acústico; buena iluminación natural; espacios exteriores comunes; facilidades de reciclaje completo; comunidades mixtas a fin de facilitar la integración social; pisos con ventilación cruzada; recogida del agua para riego de plantas y jardín comunal; desarrollo libre de coches con espacio destinado al almacenaje de bicicletas.

Adelaide Wharf está actualmente en trámites para lograr el certificado BREEAM, teniendo como meta la obtención de la calificación *Excellent* (sujeta a los resultados de los informes acústicos y de iluminación natural). Puntos clave han sido la búsqueda de lo asequible y de la eficiencia, con la instalación de una central de planta en la cubierta que calefacta todas las plantas, y que es fácilmente sustituible, caso de que fuera necesario cambiar la fuente de energía.

La producción de agua caliente sanitaria también corre a cargo de dicha central de planta, por medio de intercambiadores de calor que evitan las pérdidas de energía propias del almacenaje centralizado del agua caliente.

En todo el edificio, la iluminación es de bajo consumo. Todos los pisos tienen en torno al 50-60% de mecanismos de bajo consumo y hay

detectores de presencia en las zonas comunes. Se ha colocado grifería con válvulas reductoras de caudal, duchas de bajo consumo y cisternas con fluxor de dos descargas, a fin de reducir los consumos.

Ubicado en las proximidades del corredor Wildlife del Regent's Canal, el bloque norte tiene una cubierta vegetal que, con el paso del tiempo, será colonizada por la flora local, y que cuenta además con 40 jaulas para pájaros diseñadas para alojar a varias especies distintas. El agua de lluvia procedente de la cubierta se recoge, almacena y emplea para riego del jardín, y se ha dispuesto una franja de terreno entre el edificio y el canal para que en ella crezca una pradera y flores silvestres.

Toda la madera empleada en Adelaide Wharf cuenta con el certificado FSC, incluso los revestimientos de madera de alerce, los suelos, puertas, carpintería y madera empleada en los trabajos de montaje. El conjunto tiene 183 espacios seguros para bicicletas, y un área de juegos para niños.

Adelaide Wharf es un conjunto sostenible, cuya base es una comunidad de propietarios genuina y mixta que aporta una nueva densidad urbana, escala y cualidad arquitectónica al área, conformando un innovador prototipo para futuros desarrollos de viviendas.

HPE 2000 Cref −8% Label: aislamiento térmico, protección exterior contra el sol (a través de contraventanas, lamas o persianas) para todas las ventanas del nuevo edificio, cubiertas vegetales, calefacción central por gas, ventanas con doble acristalamiento con alto nivel de aislamiento acústico (42 DbA), aireadores.

En lo que a salud y ecología se refiere, la urbanización Brunnenhof es modélica, y la primera en Zúrich que cuenta con el certificado *Minergie-Eco* (un grado más que el *Minergie-Standard*). Los criterios de salubridad y ecología del Standard hacen referencia al aprovechamiento de la luz natural, la protección contra el ruido, la exposición a las radiaciones y sustancias contaminantes, el empleo de buenas materias primas, los gastos a lo largo del proceso constructivo así como la retirada de escombros respetuosa con el medioambiente.

En términos energéticos, Brunnenhof también sale airosa. Ambos cuerpos edificados apenas pierden calor gracias a su forma compacta y a los 20 cm de lana de roca que aíslan sus fachadas. Los residuos se tratan y reciclan en la planta de incineración Hagenholz. Tanto el agua caliente sanitaria como la calefacción emplean al 100% el sistema de "calor a distancia".

Queda aún otro factor relevante de la calidad energética del conjunto: la instalación de ventilación, típica de las construcciones con certificado *Minergie*. Ésta no se preocupa sólo de la buena calidad del aire interior en el edificio, sino que además presenta ventajas en términos de energía. El calor desprendido durante el proceso de ventilación vuelve, a través del propio sistema, a las viviendas (sistema de ventilación con recuperación de calor).

Costes

"Adecuado para familias" significa también precios razonables. En la urbanización Brunnenhof hasta las viviendas no subvencionadas son económicas. Una vivienda de 5,5 habitaciones y 140 m² cuesta alrededor de 2000 CHF (neto), más costes de mantenimiento. Estos precios de alquiler sólo son posibles gracias a que la propiedad estableció desde el principio un claro tope presupuestario: 37 millones CHF, correspondientes a 3600 CHF por metro cuadrado de superficie útil.

El patronato de viviendas para familias numerosas estableció también como requisito inicial, en el pliego de condiciones del proyecto, la obtención de la calificación *Minergie-Standard*.
Para el jefe de proyecto Markus Seiller, de la oficina de arquitectura Gigon-Guyer, el estricto presupuesto no constituyó una limitación, sino una motivación adicional. "Queríamos mostrar que, con el dinero disponible, era absolutamente posible hacer algo especial, por ejemplo, una fachada de vidrio".

Superficie de referencia para datos relativos a la energía: 13904 m².
Envolvente del edificio: 0,96.
Necesidades de calor:
Requerido por *Minergie* (hasta 2007): 36 Kwh/m².
Edificio: 31,4 Kwh/m².
Indicador ponderado de energía:
Requerido por *Minergie* (hasta 2007): 42 Kwh/m².
Edificio: 32,8 Kwh/m²

Thin Flats es una comunidad urbana sostenible de ocho unidades. Ubicada en el corazón de Northern Liberties, Filadelfia, Thin Flats será el primer proyecto residencial de dúplex que obtenga, a nivel nacional, la certificación *Leed Homes Platinum*.

Rasgos ecológicos

· Paneles solares térmicos para suelo radiante y agua caliente sanitaria.
· Cubierta vegetal que reduce las ganancias de calor, mejora la vida útil de la cubierta y emplea el agua de lluvia.
· Depósitos de agua procedente de la lluvia para riego del jardín.
· Parquet con certificado FSC *White Tiger*.
· Válvulas reductoras del caudal para reducir el consumo de agua.
· Hormigón con contenido de al menos un 25% de ceniza reciclada.
· Ventanas y puertas de aluminio revestidas de madera con doble acristalamiento, baja emisividad, aislamiento de argón y rotura de puente térmico.
· Tecnología domótica: luz centralizada y programable; los sistemas de calefacción, climatización, seguridad y audio/video maximizan la con-

veniencia y minimizan el consumo de energía.
· Paquete de aislamiento Grado 1, incluyendo espuma sellante en las juntas para minimizar las filtraciones de aire y aislamiento de espuma proyectada en los muros exteriores.
· Máxima utilización de materiales sostenibles.
· Máxima utilización de materiales locales.
· Suelo radiante hidrónico.
· Sistema de climatización diseñado conforme a las recomendaciones del manual ACCA.
· Sistema de ventilación con recuperación de calor.
· Tuberías de suministro de agua caliente aisladas.
· Pinturas, adhesivos y sellantes de nula o baja emisividad (Compuestos Orgánicos Volátiles).
· Situado a una manzana del transporte público.
· Aparcamiento privado con cargador para coche eléctrico.
· Libro del edificio especificando los tiempos de uso y disfrute de las dotaciones de la casa.

Acabados

· Electrodomésticos de bajo consumo.
· Puertas y ventanas *Energy Star Rated*.
· Azulejo cerámico en baños.
· Válvulas reductoras de caudal.
· Inodoros con fluxor de doble descarga.
· Bañera.
· Mobiliario a medida.
· Pila a medida.
· Escalera y puente de acero y vidrio.

Jardín/espacio exterior

· Jardín o patio privado.
· Terrazas exteriores privadas.
· Urbanización exterior permeable.
· Ajardinamiento tolerante a la sequía.

Emplazamiento sostenible

· Reducir el efecto "isla de calor" con cubiertas vegetales.
· Reducir la contaminación lumínica.
· Empleo del agua de lluvia (reducir la evacuación a la red municipal disponiendo cubiertas vegetales).
· Zonas de aparcamiento previstas e integradas en el edificio (reduce el efecto "isla de calor").

Transporte alternativo

· El solar está próximo a la red de transporte público: proximidad a metro y autobuses.
· Vehículo compartido en garaje para los residentes.
· Dotación de cuatro cargadores para coches eléctricos en el garaje, y espacio de almacenaje para bicicletas.

Eficiencia en el uso del agua

· Recogida y almacenaje del agua de lluvia y de la torre de refrigeración para riego.
· Mecanismos para reducir el consumo de agua: fluxores de doble descarga en inodoros.

Materiales/Recursos

· Gestión de residuos y reciclaje *in situ* para los residentes.
· Reciclaje de escombros de la construcción.
· Materiales que contienen elementos reciclados:
  Hormigón (en masa y estructural).
  Acero estructural.
  Forjado de chapa colaborante.
  Exterior: tablero de tabicar.
  Interior: tabique de cartón yeso.
  Paneles correderos de aluminio.
  Aislamiento rígido.
  Aislamiento de fibra de algodón.
  Perfiles de aluminio.
  Alfombra.
  Formación de suelo.
  Almacenaje de bicicletas.

· Materiales rápidamente renovables:
  Bambú.
  Papel de pared de corcho.
  Papel de pared de fibra vegetal.
  Falso techo acústico de fibra de madera.
  Suelo de linóleo.
  Tablero de fibra de trigo.
  Aislamiento de fibra de algodón.
· Empleo de materiales locales y regionales obtenidos dentro de un radio de 800 Km.
· Madera certificada de crecimiento sostenible:
  Suelo en bruto y acabado.
  Chapado.
  Cubierta y mobiliario de jardín.

Energía/Atmósfera

· Optimizar el rendimiento energetico al 15% (ingeniería de fachadas, control lumínico):
  Los sistemas de climatización no emplean hidro-cloroflurocarburos ni halon.
  Se recurre a un evaluador independiente que verifique la operación.
  Todos los aparatos de bajo consumo de agua y energía (incluyendo secadoras). Etiqueta *Energy Star*.

Calidad del aire interior

· Control de la calidad del aire.
· Control del humo de tabaco, agentes químicos y polución.
· Monitorización de los niveles de CO_2.
· Sistema de ventilación natural con unidades de recuperación de energía.
· Pinturas de baja emisividad (Compuestos Orgánicos Volátiles).
· Adhesivos y sellantes de baja emisividad (Compuestos Orgánicos Volátiles).
· Alfombra de baja emisividad (Compuestos Orgánicos Volátiles).
· Compuesto de madera de baja emisividad (Compuestos Orgánicos Volátiles).
· Incremento de la luz solar y vistas al exterior.
· Control individual de las condiciones térmicas, ventilación e iluminación (incluyendo ventanas practicables).

Innovaciones

· Sistema de tratamiento y procesamiento del agua sin agentes químicos.
· Reducción del ruido en la fachada sur.
· Sistema de tuberías silenciosas.
· Programa de educación en colaboración con las escuelas de diseño locales.

Custom integral formwork has already been used on other occasions, even by the Madrid's Municipal Housing Trust. The public company has been able to confirm its results. In this project an important constructions systems novelty has been introduced. This novelty involves the fabrication with aluminium formworks. This provides considerable lightening that allows workers to manipulate pieces safely, without the need for cranes.

These innovations required special dedication from the project completion period to project management to solve unconventional issues regarding concrete thickness, setting and form removal, installation distribution and quality control methods. Once solved, results were very competitive.

The project of 102 public housing units in Carabanchel includes 52 one-bedroom flats, 35 two-bedroom flats and 15 three-bedroom flats. A common cell was designed to make up the one-bedroom flat, the cell also used for the other two types with the addition of adjoining bedrooms against the facade.

In this way, the project presents an invariable nucleus which is repeated 102 times and which justifies the use of this industrialised system. Aluminium formwork makes up the layout of the nucleus (one-bedroom flat), including facades, dividing walls, partition walls and even cabinets. Once concrete is poured, these walls contain insulation in the perimetre walls and installations.

The extra bedrooms, which are added to create larger housing units, are light modules with metal structures that are anchored to the concrete facade and attached to specific anchors.

The construction responds to the need for industrial optimisation, thus the main section is done in concrete from one single high precision mould. The variations, exceptions that make the system possible, are light metal skeletons.

The process is similar to that of the automobile industry in that each worker specialises in a specific part of assembly and after several tries, efficiency is optimised. It begins with the redesigning of the house's walls on the lower slab. Then, wire meshes of vertical reinforcement framework stand on their own, helped by folds on the corners.

Over them, separators are placed to keep them in the centred position and that of the insulation panels (when it is the facade), which are located in the centre of two meshes. In this project, we have simplified all concrete walls into two types, facade, 24 cm (10 cm + 4 cm insulation + 10 cm), and all other types, dividing walls, partition walls, and cabinets, 10 cm. All are load-bearing.

Once the mesh and insulation are mounted, all installations are placed in the thickness of the 10 cm walls, except heating, which is distributed on the perimeters of the slab.

The next step is the placement of the aluminium formwork which comes piece by piece from the adjoining house and its concrete works.

At the end come the windows, painting and laying floating wood floors on a self-levelling slab, and tiling bathroom and kitchen.

The rhythm of completion is daily, as stripping, forming and pouring can be done on the same day, as can the rest of the work on the assembly line. In this way one housing unit can be done per day.

The advantage of this industrialised system is the quickness of on-site installation, which speeds up execution time and eliminates debris in the construction process. However, one must bear in mind the increase in material cost as the concrete used is of a larger quantity than usual.

The system has another disadvantage for the user. Future renovation in the housing units will be difficult, since it is all structure. However, this possibility was not considered in this project for two reasons. Firstly, since the housing units are quite small (between 42 and 66 m^2), spatial possibilities are limited to the proposed layout. Secondly, the main reason is that these are rental flats, which would not allow for renovation anyway.

The final exterior finish depends on the direction the facade faces to offer an appropriate climatic response and promote a more sustainable energetic behaviour.

The main rooms, living room and bed room, of each housing unit face southeast and southwest. Kitchens, bathrooms and secondary bedrooms face northeast and northwest.

Insulation takes up most of the inside mass, to increase thermal inertia of the permanent-use houses and keep in heat accumulated in winter. It also serves to keep heat from unnecessarily accumulating in the summer.

Besides the integral insulation, there is a facade of stretched galvanised sheet metal, lacquered in white (the most reflective colour, thus the least absorbent of solar radiation) on south facades. This sheet makes up a double ventilated skin which is placed horizontally on the southwest facade and vertically on the southeast facade. In this way, winter horizontal radiation is allowed to pass through and the building is protected from summer vertical radiation. On the southwest facade it is vertical to protect from strong rays at sunset during the Madrid summer, which are less exposed when the sunset moves northeast (21 June).

On north facades, concrete is only regulated with white paint and overhanging bedrooms are covered by white galvanised sheet metal, in this case simply perforated, as it is a ventilated facade which also protects the sprayed insulation.

Installations are centralised and distributed to each housing unit through access platforms without interfering with the main concrete section. There is energy support on the roof, also centralised, and a preinstalled air conditioning which is planned for the terrace/utility area, hidden from exterior view.

The centralisation of the heating and water system is organised on basement level, which will open up to the exterior by means of large patios where trees will be planted and cars will be able to park.

For the most part, the direction of the sun was a main factor in organising the housing units and distributing spaces. This was conditioned by the layout of land available for the construction of the building. An exterior cladding by the system name ETICS was chosen to work with the whole of the window structure to cover the entire perimeter of the building.

Cleaning the facade every five or ten years, depending on pollution, will be enough. Window frames will also require no special maintenance.

Energy production of the building is centralised, takes advantage of the energy supplied by solar panels on the roof. These solar panels and their use will be managed by the owning company itself, billing users directly for calories consumed.

The inclination on the central entrance patio, though they have steps at certain points, also have long ramps for people with reduced mobility to be able to independently access the entrance and gardens.

From the very beginning, this project followed the criteria of economy, viability and sustainability that the property owners requested. Spans of around 5.5 m have been used, the facade was done in modules of different coloured, single-layer mortar which not only reduces production costs, but also prevents having to repaint after time.

A large number of sustainability measures have been taken, which led to a high level of sustainability: Groninger Housing Quality II (highest category)
Key factors are:
· Adaptability of the groundplan of the apartments (besides the 3 standard options) (to the changing needs of inhabitants as they grow older and or become disabled)

· Ventilation: natural supply, mechanical ventilation (although the building is 63 metres high, we could do without balanced ventilation (due to the groundplan of 4 apartments per layer, in a cross-shape)
· Heating: central low temperature floor heating, adjustable per room, per apartment.
· Relative small building footprint on the site; hardly any trees needed to be cut. Closed loop system for soil during the construction.
· Vertical sunscreens keep out the summersun
· With the above ground parking making use of daylight and natural ventilation, the need for artificial lighting is reduced to just the nightly situation and costly energy-inefficient mechanical ventilation can be done without.
· Prefabricated elements were used where possible, (balconies, circular windows, steel reinforcement) reducing cutting-waste of material.

The most important obligatory requirement for social housing in Catalonia is an hour of sunlight between 10 and 12 o'clock during the winter solstice in the living rooms of at least 80% of the housing units. This block has 91% and the other 9% has at least 45 minutes.

In addition, construction solutions must demonstrably fulfil certain parameters of eco-efficiency which must reach 10 points. This project obtained 30 points.

1. Ventilated, +/- 90 degree southwest-facing facade (5 points)
2. One hour of sunlight on the winter solstice (5 points)
3. Natural cross ventilation (6 points)
4. Pre-industrialised systems in 80% of the structure (alveolar panels) (6 points)
5. Reduction of the average coefficient of thermal transmittance Km of vertical cladding by 30% of 0.70 w/m^{2}K, Km 0.49 w/m^{2}K (8 points)

LÓPEZ-RIVERA ARQUITECTOS BARCELONA.ES 2007 118-127

Both natural ventilation and abundant natural light are guaranteed in each space by the interior layout and by each unit having two opposite open facades. Taking advantage of the Mediterranean climate, the entrance to the apartments will be by means of a partly elevated street at the back of the building which looks toward an interior patio like those typical of Barcelona.

Natural light and ventilation
The kitchen and bathroom are placed adjoining to this facade, while the main living area is

on the opposing southwest facade, to comply with the local eco-efficiency ordinance. This ordinance requires 80% of housing units to have at least one hour of direct sunlight between 10 o'clock a.m. and two o'clock p.m. on the winter solstice.

South and west windows have adjustable exterior solar protection. The kitchen window and the summer terrace space face northwest, always in the shade.

Gallery as a passive solar energy collector
We placed a small gallery on the south side of the living room, to serve as a cushion between the outsider and the living room and to bring back a Barcelona tradition. This gallery is generated between two glass surfaces and works as a passive solar collector in winter. In summer, due to the verticality of the sun, if exterior glass slats are opened and interior folding door is closed, the gallery becomes a balcony.

Solar panels for hot water production
Ventilated facade facing North-west.

ROLDÁN + BERENGUÉ BARCELONA.ES 2009 170-183

Housing units face East and West. The facade has thermal inertia which provides protection and makes energy savings possible. The apartments all have exterior-facing rooms and cross ventilation.

Roof: solar energy collectors (solar thermal energy) to preheat water used for bath and heating. The other part of the roof is an ecological solarium.
Treatment of water flow at all supply points. Low consuming sanitary devices. Low consuming lifts.
Use of ecological paint on interior and exterior and wood of controlled origin.

POOLEN ARCHITEKTEN CULEMBORG.NL 2008 184-197

Sustainable architecture is an essential part in our design process. This isn't just about the technique and materialisation of the building, where special attention is paid to the environment and energy consumption.

Sustainability is also about the durability and flexibility of the design during time. The building should be easy-manageable, low in maintenance and energy use. For as far as possible the rainwater should be kept and collected or infiltrated into a nearby water stream.

BonVie is a low-energy building with a high insulation class and constructed of environmental friendly materials. In addition the plan is very flexible, the very diverse programme is translated into a flexible modular construction system

MVRDV, BLANCA LLEÓ MADRID.ES 2009 198-217

The complete mould system allows the prefabricated construction of this singular structure to be solved in the right amount of time and price. The 146 housing units are settled into a base unit and two variations. This allows one, two and three-bedroom units with versatile rooms and especially generous spaces for bath, leisure and storage.

Some of the benefits of the mould system include industrialisation, agility and simplicity. It is sustainable and does not produce on-site damage or debris. It is versatile, practical and revolutionary. It allows a house to be built in a day. It facilitates flexible organisation and the simultaneous execution of structure, cladding and installations. The assembly of the aluminium formwork is light and manageable for workers. It produces quality construction in little time and at a low cost.

The high-rise patios guarantee cross ventilation by means of two or three opposite facades for all of the units. A system of power efficient boilers is used for the entire building, reducing energy use. These systems are combined with solar panels to heat water.

The balcony layer runs all around the block.
The wooden ornamental construction elements in front of the balconies and loggias

are designed in the same sense as traditional hayracks; wooden objects in function of storing and drying the grass. They provide first entry temperature zone to the main living and sleeping areas and also creates shading to the balconies.
Additional aluminum shading panels are placed on the outer sides of the winter loggias and balconies.
The service and communication spaces are reduced to minimum thus the daylight is provided on the shafts. The monthly basic energetic and service costs are very low; so also economic for the users since the apartments are social type.

· Small axe measure and reduced elevation surface (effective ratio surface/elevation surface)

· Low energy standard with 'whole-house balanced ventilation system' (mechanical ventilation)

· Photovoltaic panels are disposed on the roofs of the building units R+9 and R+11 to reduce electricity costs for the inhabitants.
· Type of panels = monocristallin.

· Panels dimensions = 1.00 x 1.30 m
· Number of panels = 63.
· Total = around 82 m².
· Capacity of production = 11,6 Kw.
· There is a water retention tank placed in the basement, used for the terrace plants and the cleaning of the building.
· Placed in the centre of the building, the hanging gardens reduce thermal shocks.
· Use of self-compacting bulk-dyed, cast-in-place and untreated concrete. This material has dealt with the noise pollution efficiently during the construction phase.

Sustainable felling
The wooden deck of the courtyard of the Het Kasteel is made of FSC certified wood.
We have chosen to make the deck from six different types of wood. This way they could use the sustainable way of felling. Together with the wood supplier we searched for the most environmentally friendly combination.

In addition to using a mix of wood, the use of different sizes of timber benefits the felling.

Natural engineering
Het Kasteel is equipped with a soundproof wall. This facade was one of the conditions that this project had to comply to and is also used in the plan as a thermal buffer space.
The facade, which is specially developed for this project, provides natural ventilation and air refreshment. By using the natural force of the heated air, the houses are also very good to keep cool in the summer.

Water retention
The roofs of the building are equipped with moss-sedum vegetation, which contains the rainwater for a longer time. Moss-sedum is not only more durable than bitumen roofs it also looks much better.

Base rule : SIA 112/1 2004

Social environment

Life in common:

· Integration, mixing: creation of optimal conditions for social, cultural and intergenerational integration and mingling (city centre, keeping families in the city)

· Social relationships: creation of meeting points that encourage exchange and communication (semi-public spaces, patios and play areas)

Planning:

· Identity of the location, sense of belonging: promotion of the orientation and identity of the location (feeling of security and belonging, environmental responsibility)

Operating, viability:

· Near provisions, mixed effect: reduction of distances, creation of an attractive mixed effect inside the neighbourhood (promoting neighbourhood life, urban density)

· Smooth mobility: guaranteed access to a satisfactory transport network (safe, well-lit pedestrian walkways, bicycle parking, good public transport connection)

· Accessibility and use for all: building design and adaptation for the disabled.

Comfort, health:

· Safety: increase in sense of safety, reduction of potential dangers.

· Light: optimise use of daylight, guarantee adequate lighting.

· Protection from the summer sun: high comfort due to effective solar protection in summer.

· Noise, vibrations: reduction of noise and vibration problems.

Economy

Regarding the building:

· Location: guaranteed long-term economic operation adapted to the location (accessibility and high density).

· Constructed object: obtaining a lasting, high quality value in terms of usable life (construction conforming to technique)

Investment cost:

· Costs and usable life: investment according to cost of the whole of usable life (reduction of operation costs)

· Financing: choice of a financing system that, over time, would guarantee investment, renovation and demolition costs (redemption of investments according to duration of use)

· External costs: maximum reduction and internalisation of external costs (external effects of pollution from air, noise and debris resulting from construction, operation, maintenance and demolition)

Operation and maintenance expenses:

· Operation and maintenance: reduction of maintenance costs through preliminary planning and taking continuous measures (decrease in operation costs by means of initial itemised investments)

· Renovation: Reduction of renovation expenses by paying attention to accessibility and optimum quality.

Environment

Construction materials:

· Pollutants: reduction of pollutants in construction elements.

Energy in operation:

· Needs for heating and cooling: reduction of necessary energy consumption for heating by taking technical measures and measures in construction. (high quality cladding and heat production)

· Energy needs for hot water: decrease in energy consumption by taking technical measures and measures in construction.

· Electricity: reduction of consumption of electricity by taking technical measures and measures in construction.

Sun, landscape:

· Land surface: reduction of land consumption (rezoning industrial land, promotion of the creation of new zones in the city)

Infrastructure:

· Mobility: implementation of mobility compatible with the environment (lot well connected to transport and located near businesses, schools, work and recreational sites)

Sustainability

In the Lootsbuurt project we dealt with the theme of sustainability in three ways. The Dutch building laws dictate various measurements in order to obtain a high level of sustainability in each project build in the Netherlands. Off course the Lootsbuurt Project is built completely according to the building rules. The Lootsbuurt project moreover has some features concerning sustainability that are not written down in any law or rule. Yet, these features enhance the sustainable qualities of the project.

Lifespan

We are very much concerned by the question how buildings can adept to future demands for dwelling-types. We think that there are two principle answers to this question: Flexibility vs. specificity. Flexibility offers the possibility to change a floorplan in the future according to future demands. Specificity is about creating unique floorplans with extraordinary qualities as a result of which this floorplan will be appealing at any time. As a comparison, check out our project 'Multifunk' that is about a building that is totally flexible and multi-functional during time. The facade is made of recycled plastic
In this project, the answer is specificity.
The project aims for a natural 'shortage' of dwelling types by offering only three dwellings of the same kind as a maximum. At the same time, each dwelling has specific special and/or programmatical qualities (e.g. a giant outdoor space, a veranda, a roofgarden, a void, a working space etc.) By doing so, the unicity of each dwelling is guaranteed, which makes the dwelling and therefore the building as a whole appealing also in the future.
Besides this, special care has been taken in order to give the casco of the building a sustainable quality. The concrete casco is over dimensioned. Floors and walls are in fact thicker as legally requires, which enhances the constructional qualities as well as the sound reduction between dwellings. This benefits the quality of living in the building and therefore the sustainability.

Environmental friendly

In the building, as much as possible durable materials are used. The casco is made of concrete. The outer walls along the street are made of brick. Brick is a very durable material, that becomes more beautiful during time. The south facade is made of FSC-wood (Forest Stewardship Council). This organisation is submitted in order to enhance the use of durable forest, specifically the tropic rainforests. The aims of the organisation are to exploit the forests in a social, environmental and economically responsible way. The infill is made entirely out of glass (even the closed panels are glass) and stucco.

Saving energy

The building has a very low Rc-value, because of various energy-saving measurements. Most helpful (and least 'catchy') is the south orientation of the dwellings. All the living-rooms are oriented to the sun, whilst the bedrooms are oriented to the North-West. The glass is with the highest quality energy-saving characteristics.

The plot chosen to construct this building was occupied by a three-bedroom house inhabited by a family made up of an elderly woman and her daughter. Once the plot was acquired, the demolition of the old house went underway, exponentially multiplying the density of inhabitants per square metre. We trust that the increase in density makes our cities more sustainable.

EcoHomes rating Excellent; use of certified and low-embodied energy materials; excellent sound insulation; good daylight; communal outdoor spaces; comprehensive recycling facilities; mixture of tenures to facilitate social integration; naturally cross-ventilated flats; water collection for plant irrigation in communal garden; car-free development with off-street bike storage.

Adelaide Wharf is currently with BREEAM for validation, targeting an Excellent rating (subject to the outcomes of acoustic and daylighting reports)

The key drivers have been affordability and efficiency, with a pre packaged central plant on the roof providing heat to all flats, which may be easily replaced should the energy source need changing.

Domestic hot water is also generated by the central plant from localised heat exchangers avoiding the energy losses of central hot water

storage. Lighting throughout the building has been designed to be low energy use. All flat types have 50 - 60% low energy fittings and occupancy sensors control landlord areas. Water saving devices such as aerated taps, dual flush cisterns and low-flow showers are specified to reduce consumption.

Situated next to the Wildlife corridor of the Regent's Canal, the north block has a brown roof which over time will be colonised by local flora, and 40 bird boxes designed for various different species.

Rainwater from the roof is harvested and stored for landscape irrigation, and a strip of land between the building and the canal is planted and left to grow into wildflower grassland.

All the timber used in the construction of Adelaide Wharf was FSC certified, including the untreated Larch cladding, internal floors, doors, joinery and timber used for temporary works. The development has 183 secure bike spaces and a children's play area.

HPE 2000 Cref -8% Label: Thermal insulation, external sunshading (by shutters, louvres or blinds) for all windows on the new building, green planted roofs, central gas powered heating, double glazed windows with high level (42 db) accoustique ventillation vents.

The Brunnenhof development is ideal in terms of health and ecology and is the first in Zurich with the Minergie-Eco certificate (one grade higher than the *Minergie-Standard*). The health and ecological criteria of the Standard make reference to use of natural light, noise protection, exposure to radiation and pollution, use of high quality raw materials, expenses in the building process and a debris removal process that respects the environment.

In terms of energy, Brunnenhof also passes the test. The two sections hardly lose heat thanks to their compact form and the 20 cm of rock wool which insulates facades. Residues are treated and recycled at the Hagenholz incineration plant. Both hot water and heating use a long distance heating system.

There is one other relevant factor of the energy quality of the whole: ventilation, typical of buildings with the Minergie certificate. The ventilation not only guarantees air quality inside the building, but also has advantages in terms of energy. The heat given off in the ventilation process goes back to the housing units on its own (heat recovery ventilator)

Costs

Family friendly also includes reasonable prices. In the Brunnenhof development even houses that are not subsidised are economical. A 5.5 bedroom, 140 m^2 flat costs around 2000 FCH (net), plus maintenance costs. This low rent is only possible because of the owner's budget limit, set from the very beginning: 37 million FCH, or 3600 FCH per usable square metre.
The council of housing for large families also set the acquisition of the *Minergie-Standard* certificate as an initial requirement in the conditions of the project.
For the project leader, Markus Seiller, from the Gigon-Guyer architectural firm, the strict budget did not create limitations, but additional motivation. 'We wanted to show that, with the money available, it was absolutely possible to make something special: for example a glass facade'.

Surface for energy data: 13904 m^2.
Building cladding: 0.96.
Heat needs:
Required by Minergie (until 2007): 36 kwh/m^2.
Building: 31.4 Kwh/m^2.
Adjusted energy indicator:
Required by Minergie (until 2007): 42 Kwh/m^2.
Building: 32.8 Kwh/m^2.

Thin Flats is an 8-unit Sustainable Urban Community. Located in the heart of Northern Liberties, Philadelphia, Thin Flats will be the nation's first LEED-Homes Platinum Certified residential duplex project.

Eco features:

· Solar Thermal panels provide in-floor radiant heat and domestic hot water.
· Green roof on building decreases thermal heat gain, prolongs roof life, assists with storm water management.
· Rainwater harvesting cisterns for irrigation of yards/gardens.
· FSC certified White Tiger hardwood flooring
· Low flow faucets and fixtures reduce water consumption.
· Concrete containing a minimum of 25% recycled fly ash content.
· Double pane, low E, argon insulated, thermally broken, aluminum clad wood windows/doors.
· Home automation technology by Colorado vNet: centralized and programmable lighting, heating, cooling, security, and audio/video entertainment system maximizes convenience and minimizes energy use.
· Grade 1 insulation package including foam sealing of all joints to minimize air infiltration and closed cell spray-in foam insulation in exterior walls.

· Maximum use of sustainable framing materials.
· Maximum use of locally sourced/manufactured materials.
· Hydronic radiant in-floor heating system
· HVAC system designed to ACCA Manual recommendations.
· HRV (Heat Recovery Ventilation) system.
Indoor air quality system.
· Insulated hot water supply pipes.
· Low or No VOC (Volatile Organic Compounds) emitting paints, adhesives, and sealants.
· Located within one block of public transportation
· Private car park with electric car charging port (electric car optional)
· Detailed Homeowner's Manual included for maximum usage and enjoyment of home's features.

Appliances/fixtures/finishes:

· Italian designed kitchen.
· Air Dual Fuel oven and cooktop.
· Refrigerator (Energy Star Rated)
· Dishwasher (Energy Star Rated)
· Washer/dryer (Energy Star Rated)
· Windows & doors (Energy Star Rated)
· Glass/Ceramic tile bathrooms.
· Low flow faucets.
· Dual flush toilets.
· Bain Ultra/Kohler tub.
· Custom vanities.
· Custom vessel sinks.
· Custom steel/glass stair & bridge.

Garden/outdoor space:

· Private yard/garden.
· Private outdoor decks.
· Permeable hardscaping.
· Drought tolerant landscaping.

Sustainable Design Elements/LEED Credits
Sustainable Site
· Reduce heat island effect with garden roofs.
· Light pollution reduction.
· Storm-water management (reduce run-off to municipal system with garden roofs)
· Covered parking spaces provided and integrated into building (reduces heat island effect)
Alternate Transportation
· Site is near public transportation –close proximity to subway & buses.
· Zip car located in the garage for resident use
· Providing 4 electrical car chargers in the garage & storage space for bikes.

Water Efficiency
· Capture/store run-off and cooling tower water for irrigation.
· Low water use fixtures: dual flush toilets.

Materials/Resources
· On-site recycling management for residents.
· Construction waste recycled.
· Materials with recycled content:
  Concrete (piles and structural)
  Structural steel/re-bars.
  Steel deck.
  Exterior sheathing board/interior GWB.
  Aluminum siding panels.
  Rigid insulation.
  Cotton insulation.
  Interior steel studs.
  Carpet.
  Floor underlayment.
  Bicycle racks.

· Rapidly renewable materials:
  Bamboo.
  Cork wallpaper.
  Grasscloth wallpaper.
  Tectum ceiling tile.
  Linoleum flooring.
  Wheatboard core used for all millwork.
  Cotton insulation.
· Use local/regional materials obtained within 500 miles.
· Certified wood sustainably grown and harvested.
Rough and finish wood.
Veneers.
Decking and landscape furniture.

Energy/Atmosphere
· Optimize energy performance 15% target (building envelope engineering, lighting control, etc.)
· All HVAC equipment uses zero HCFC and Halon.
· Using an independent commissioning agent to verify proper equipment operation/green power.
· All Energy Star water/energy efficient appliances (including condenser dryers)

Indoor air quality
· Management of construction air quality.
· Control of tobacco smoke and indoor chemicals/pollution.
· Monitoring of CO_2 levels.
· Effective fresh air ventilation system with energy recover units to capture energy form exhaust sources.
· Low emitting (VOC) paints.
· Low emitting (VOC) adhesives & sealants.
· Low emitting (VOC) carpet.
· Low emitting (VOC) composite wood.
· Increase daylight and views to the outdoors.
· Individual units control thermal, ventilation & lighting (including operable windows)

Innovation credits
· Dolphin treatment system: treat & process water without chemicals.
· Acoustic Mitigation at South Facade.
· Sovent plumbing.
· Educational program with local design schools.

ADAMO-FAIDEN ARQUITECTOS
....75 330-339
Architects: Adamo-Faiden Arquitectos
Collaborators: Luciano Intile, Aldana Rizza.
Structures: AHF, Alberto Fainstein.
Installations: Julio Blanco.
Window frames: Alumplast
Client: Fideicomiso Conesa 4560
Contractor: Adamo-Faiden
Photos: Sergio Pirrone, Adamo-Faiden

AGUINAGA Y ASOCIADOS ARQUITECTOS
....05 88-95
Architects: Eugenio Aguinaga Churruca, José
María Jiménez Urrutia, Ignacio López Fernández
Collaborators: Belen Benavides, Javier Barrero,
Laura Trejos, Juan Pablo Bajuk, Román Martínez
del Cerro, Blanca López de Armentia
Client: Empresa Municipal de la Vivienda de
Madrid (EMV)
Contractor: IMASATEC, S.A.
Quantity Surveyor: Manuel López Lara
Structural Engineer: Otep
Installations: Dicyp, S.A.
Photos: Jose Latova

ALLFORD HALL MONAGHAN MORRIS
....27 348-357
Architects: Allford Hall Monaghan Morris
Client: First Base Ltd & English Partnerships
RSL Landlord: Family Mosaic with Housing
Corporation funding
Main Contractor: Bovis Lend Lease
Structural Engineers: Adams Kara Taylor
Services Engineers: Waterman Building Services
Quantity Surveyors: Faithful and Gould
Building Manager: Tower Homes
Landscape Architect: Charles Funke Associates
Artist: Richard Woods
Fire Consultant: Warrington Fire
Acoustic Consultant: Sandy Brown Associates
Access Consultant: David Bonnett Associates
Approved Inspector: Butler & Young
Planning Supervisor: Bovis Lend Lease

Planning Consultant: DP9 Planning Consultant
Transport Consultant: ARUP, Transport
Ecological Consultant: Ecology Solutions
Party Wall & Rights of Light: Goodman Mann
Associates
Real Estate Consultant Savills
Trade Contractors: Sipral (cladding), AJ
Morrisroe & Sons Ltd (concrete frame),
PAD Contracts Ltd (balconies), Swift Brickwork
Contractors
Ltd, Cubitt Building & Interiors Ltd (landscape
& lobbies),
Prater Ltd (roof), Southdown Construction Ltd
(metalwork),
OTIS Ltd (lifts), Axiom Contract Flooring
(flooring), M&S
Contractors Ltd (joinery), Handrail Design Ltd
(internal)
balustrades), OCP-Ratgrad Ltd (bathroom pods),
A&H
Contractors Ltd (kitchens)
Photos: Tim Soar

ANA ARCHITECTEN......................22 2998-307
Architects: ANA architecten
Authors: Marcel van der Lubbe and Jannie
Vinkecollaborators: Gert Anninga, Simea Knip
and Sander Monteiro
Client: De Alliantie
Art (fences): Andy Scott
Contractor: Vink Bouw Nieuwkoop BV
Structural engineer: Adams Bouwtechniek
Installation engineer: RTA, 's Hertogenbosch
Building costs adviser: Theo Laan
Bouwkostenadvies
Photos: Rolf Bastiaans

ARONS EN GELAUFF ARCHITECTEN
Architects: Floor Arons, Arnoud Gelauff, arons en gelauff architecten
Architectural team: Jan Bart Bouwhuis, Rianne Kreijne, Adrie Laan, Florian Schrage, Joost van Bergen, Aldrik Stegenga, Mahir Dündar, Claudia Temperilli, Mariska Koster-Berbé
Client: Housing association De Huismeesters
Contractor: Schutte Bouw
Architectural engineer: Ingenieursbureau Wassenaar
Advisor building physics and installations: Adviesburo Nieman
Photos: Allard van der Hoek

ATELIER KEMPE THILL
Architects:
Atelier Kempe Thill architects and planners
André Kempe, Oliver Thill, Teun van der Meulen with Takashi Nakamura
Urban planner: De Nijl architecten, partner-in-charge Endry van Velzen
Supervisor: Endry van Velsen and Michael van Gessel
Building Physics: DGMR Bouw
Structural Engineer: ABT
Quantity Surveyor: BBN
Building contractors: Smit's Bouwbedrijf SBB
Client: DeltaForte
Photos: Ulrich Schwarz, Kempe Thill

AVA ARCHITECTS
Architects: Carlos Jorge Coelho Veloso, Gil Miguel Monte Gonçalves, Hélder Manuel Reis Coelho
Client: GOP – Câmara Municipal do Porto, E.M.
Photos: Joao Ferrand

BECKMANN-N'THÉPÉ ARCHITECTES
Architects: Architects: Beckmann-N'Thépé
Project manager: Nicolas Gaudard
Architects: Stéphane Maîtrejean, Mathilde Malher
Assistant architects: Amélie Authier, Maïté Dupont, Caroline Huybrechts, Tiphaine Leclère, Aimé-Issa N'Thépé
Client: SEMIDEP
ZAC (mixed development zone) planner: SEMAPA
ZAC architect coordinator: Atelier Christian de Portzamparc
BET TCE (all building trades technical design office): COTEC
Fire protection: BTP Consultants
Landscaping consultant: Ecovégétal
Control bureau: VERITAS
Health and safety coordinator: ANM Consultants
General contractor: HERVE SA
Concrete provider: Holcim
Photos: Stephan Lucas, Laurent Julliand

BEVK PEROVIC ARHITEKTI
Architects: Matija Bevk, Vasa J. Perovic, Jernej Bevk, Spela Jerin, Andrej Mercina, Mitja Zorc, Sanja Škrinjar
Client: Housing Fund Maribor and Housing Fund of Slovenia
Photos: Miran Kambic, Petr Smidek

Architects: Matija Bevk,Vasa J. Perovic, Ana Celigoj, Ursula Oitz (project team)
Client: Ministry of Education and Sport
Photos: Miran Kambic

BIG+JDS
Architects: Partner-in-Charge: Bjarke Ingels
Project Architect: Jakob Lange
Project Leader: Finn Nørkjær
Project Manager: Jan Borgstrøm
Construction Manager: Henrick Poulsen
Contributers: Annette Jensen, Dariusz Bojarski, Dennis Rasmussen, Eva Hviid-Nielsen, Joao Vieira Costa, Jørn Jensen, Karsten V. Vestergaard, Karsten Hammer Hansen, Leon Rost, Louise Steffensen, Malte Rosenquist, Mia Frederiksen, Ole Elkjær-Larsen, Ole Nannberg, Roberto Rosales Salazar, Rong Bin, Sophus Søbye, Søren Lambertsen, Wataru Tanaka
Collaborator: JDS, Moe & Brødsgaard, Freddy Madsen Rådgivende Ingeniører ApS
Photos: Jakob Boserup, Jens Lindhe, Ulrik Jantzen, a+t

COLL-LECLERC ARQUITECTOS
Architects: Jaime Coll, Judith Leclerc
Collaborators: Narcis Font, Cristian Vivas
Consultants: Guillen Gonzalez (Structure), RC-Gustavo Crespo (Installations), Jordi Carbonell (Budget),
Angela Vidal (NAXAL, Technical Supervisor)
Client: Instituto Catalán del Suelo
Photos: José Hevia

DOSMASUNO ARQUITECTOS
Architects: Ignacio Borrego, Néstor Montenegro, Lina Toro
Quantity Surveyors: Javier González, Javier Mach
Structural Engineer: José Luis de Miguel
Installations: Grupo JG
Client: EMVS. Empresa Municipal de la Vivienda y el Suelo de Madrid
Contractor: Begar
Photos: Miguel de Guzmán

dRMM
Architects: Philip Marsh, Jonas Lencer, Michael Spooner, Myrtille Ferte Fogel
Client: Southern Housing Group; Elephant and Castle Regeneration
Main contractor: Wates Construction
Project manager: Southern Housing Group
Structural engineer: Bradbrook Consulting
Services engineer: Scott Wilson incorporating Cameron Taylor
Acoustics consultant: RBA Acoustics
Sustainability consultant: XCO2
Cost consultant: Martin Associates
Photos: Alex de Rijke, Jonas Lencer

EDOUARD FRANÇOIS
Architects: Edouard François
Collaborators: Marika Lemper, Randa Kamel, Julien Odile
Project manager (design and construction): Julien Odile architect
Landscape: Sophie BarbauxC
Contractor: SICRA
Client : Paris Habitat
Photos: David Boureau, Javier Arpa

EMMANUEL COMBAREL DOMINIQUE MARREC ARCHITECTES
Architects: Emmanuel Combarel & Dominique Marrec (ECDM)
Client: RIVP (Régie Immobilière de la Ville de Paris)
Engineering: BETIBA
Project manager: Dario Oeschli
Contractor: LES MAÇONS PARISIENS (general contractor)
Photos: Benoît Fougeirol

FOREIGN OFFICE ARCHITECS

Architects: Farshid Moussavi, Alejandro Zaera Polo with:
David Casino, Leo Gallegos, Joaquim Rigau, Caroline Markus, Nerea Calvillo
On-site team: David Casino
Detail Project: David Casino, Leo Gallegos, Joaquim Rigau, Caroline Markus
Basic project: Nerea Calvillo
Client: EMVS
Contractor: ACCIONA
Structural Engineer: Jesús Hierro
Quantity Surveyor: Alfonso Cuenca Sánchez
Electrical Engineer: FASEVEN
Mechanical Engineers: ASETECNIC
Telecomunication Engineer: Raúl Heranz , S.D.C
Photos: Francisco Andeyro García, Alejandro García González, Sérgio Padura, Javier Arpa

FREI ARCHITEKTEN

Architects: Frei Architekten
Civil engineer : Rothpletz, Lienhard & Cie.
Electricity engineer: Herzog Kull Group
Structure engineer: Hans Abicht
Client: Immobilien Anlagestiftung Turidomus
Photos: Roger Frei

GIGON / GUYER

Architects: Annette Gigon / Mike Guyer,
Collaborators: Markus Seiler (Project Architect), Rolf-Werner Wirtz, Lorenzo Igual, Ulrike Horn, Thomann Mireille, Anja Widmer
Project Manager/Costing:
B+P Baurealisations AG
Colour Concept: Adrian Schiess
Landscape Architect: Hager Landschaftsarchitektur
Civil Engineer: Dr. Lüchinger & Meyer
Mechanical Engineer: 3-Plan Haustechnik, Winterthur
Electrical Engineer: Elkom Partner AG
Structural Physiks Engineer: Lemon Consult
Client: Stiftung Wohnungen für kinderreiche Familien
Photos: Georg Aern, Gigon/Guyer

HAMONIC + MASSON

Architects: Hamonic + Masson (Gaëlle Hamonic, Jean-Christophe Masson, Julien Gouiric, Cédric Bregeot)
Engineering and quantity surveyors: SIBAT
Construction company/Contractor: Capaldi
Client: Paris Habitat
Photos: Hervé Abbadie, Javier Arpa

HVDN ARCHITECTEN

Architects: design team: Arie van der Neut, Albert Herder, Vincent van der Klei
Project team: Arie van der Neut, Albert Herder, Vincent van der Klei, Monika Pieroth, Pascal Bemelmans
Structural Engineering: Jean-Marc Saurer, Vincent van der Klei
Photos: Luuk Kramer, John Lewis Marshall

KASPER DANIELSEN ARCHITECTS FUTURE SYSTEMS

Architects: Design architect: Kasper Danielsen Architects, in collaboration with Future Systems
Architect of Record: Kasper Danielsen Architects
Engineer: Moe & Brødsgaard, Consultant Aarsleff
Main Contractor: KPC- byg, Consultant Aarsleff
Developer: Nordkranen with Co-investor: Cargill (now Carval) and Real Estate company Metropolis
Photos: Kontraframe, Jesper Ray Manley, Soeren Aagard

KOKO ARCHITEKTID

Architects: Raivo Kotov, Andrus Kõresaar / KOKO architects
Interior designers: Liis Lindvere, Raili Paling; Lembit Tork etc.
Construction Engineer: Ago-Allan Kuddu
Client: Koger Kinnisvara
Photos: Andrus Kõresaar, Fred Lau, Arne Maasik, Kaido Haagen

LEHMANN FIDANZA & ASSOCIÉS

Architects: Philipp Lehmann and Alain Fidanza
Collaborators: Karin Schultze, Andres Goetz, Simon Monnier, David Wyss, Stefan Frei, Christian Waldvogel
Landscape Architecutre: Robin Winogrond
General Contractor: Losinger Construction with Thomas Schaller, Benoit Demierre, Jean-Christophe Gauthier
Client/Investor: Schweizerische Mobiliar Insurance (project manager: Donald Vogt)
Photos: Corinne Aeberhard, Thomas Jantscher

LÓPEZ-RIVERA ARQUITECTOS

Architects: Emiliano López & Mónica Rivera Arquitectos
Office Collaborators: Florencia Grieco, Sandra Hernandez , Álvaro Solís
Structures Consultant: BIS Arquitectes
Engineering Consultant: PGI Grup
Quantity Surveyor: Rafael Huertes
Contractor: Constructora D'Aro
Client: Institut Català del Sòl
Photos: José Hevia, Javier Arpa

MVRDV, BLANCA LLEÓ

Architects: MVRDV y Blanca Lleó asociados S.L.
Team: Camilo García, Maria Espinosa, Miguel Tejada, Constanza Temboury, Néstor Montenegro, Belén Butragueño, Sandor Naus, Patricia Mata, Ignacio Borrego, Raquel Martinez, Florián Jenewein, Marjolijn Gudemond, Fabien Mazenc, Alfredo Cadenas
Quantity Surveyors: Enrique Gil, Apartec
Structural Engineer: Estudio de José Luis de Miguel
Installations: Emilio González, JG Asociados.
Contractor: BEGAR Construcciones y Contratas
Client: EMV del Ayuntamiento de Madrid.
Photos: Ricardo Espinosa

OFFICE dA, BURT HILL

Architects: Design Architect Firm Staff:
Design Architect: Office dA
Architect of Record: Burt Hill
Principals in Charge (Office dA): Monica Ponce de Leon, Nader Tehrani
Project Architect (Office dA): Dan Gallagher
Project Manager (Office dA): Lisa Huang
Project Team (Office dA): Ghazal Abassy, Remon Alberts, Hansy Luz Better, Scott Ewart, Katja Gischas, Anna Goodman, David Jeffries, Krists Karklins, Ethan Kushner, Christine Mueller, Julian Palacio, Penn Ruderman, Ahmad Reza Schricker, Harry Lowd
Architect of Record Firm Staff:

Principals in Charge (Burt Hill): Steven Brittan, Harry Gordon
Project Manager (Burt Hill): Ed Bourget, AIA
Project Team (Burt Hill): Thomas Urtz, Millescent Lizares, Zander Shaw, Ginelle Lang, AIA, Robert Graf, PE, Edward Wunderley, PE, Bruce Kvarta, PE, Douglas Ellsworth, Gerry Lebrato, Greg Torchia,
General Contractor: Bovis Lend Lease,
Project Manager: Jason Burrell, LEED AP Engineers
Structural Engineer: Simpson Gumpertz & Heger (James Parker, Senior Principal; Michael Louis, Principal; Matthew H. Johnson, P.E., Senior Project Manager; Stan Zagajeski, Staff Consultant; Peter Babaian, Staff Engineer; Michael Peddie, Senior Engineer; Paul Schuman, Senior Engineer)
MEP Engineer of Record: Burt Hill
Design MEP Engineer: C3 (Commercial Construction Consulting)
Civil Engineer: BSC Group Consultants
Acoustical: Acentech
Landscape Architect: Landworks Studio
Exterior Envelope Consultant: Simpson Gumpertz & Heger
Specification Consultant: Falk Associates
Hardware Consultant: William Elliot
Code Consultant: Schirmer Engineering Corporation
Parking Consultant: Walker Parking Consultants
Elevator Consultant: Lerch Bates Associates
Pool Consultant: North East Aquatic Design
Audio/Visual Consultant: Audio Visual Designs
Cost Estimating Consultant: Rider Hunt Levett & Bailey
Geotechnical Engineer: GEI Consultants
Illustrator: bhch, LLC
Client: Timothy Pappas, Pappas Enterprises, Inc.
Photos: John Horner

OFIS ARHITEKTI 218-229
Architects:
Project leaders: Rok Oman, Spela Videcnik
Design team: Nejc Batistic, Martina Lipicer, Andrej Gregoric
Client: Gradis G group,
Photos: Tomaz Gregoric

ONION FLATS 0392-401
Architects: Tim McDonald, Howard Steinberg, AIA, James Sanderson, Ted Singer, Linda Montanile, MaGrann, AEC, Roofscapes Inc.
Photos: Onion Flats

POOLEN ARCHITEKTEN 184-197
Architects: Jan Poolen
Collaborators: Severine Kas, Gert van Eijden, Sander Kok, Sander Vredeveld
Contractor: Slokker Bouwgroep
Structural Engineer: Ingenieursbureau Smit Westerman
Installations Engineer:
Technisch Adviesbureau Crone
Client: Betuws wonen / W6
Photos: Paul Smulders, Robert Oerlemans, Your Captain

ROLDÁN + BERENGUÉ 170-183
Architects: José Miguel Roldán y Mercè Berengué (Roldán + Berengué, arqts.)
Collaborators: Vincenç Sanz, Annick Branders
Structural Engineer: Javier Monte
Installatione: Manel Comas y Javier Mateos
Quantity Surveyor: Encarna García Ramiro
Contractor: Corsan-Corviam
Client: Patronat Municipal de l'Habitatge de Barcelona.
Photos: Jordi Puig, Pedro Pegenaute, Jordi Darder, Javier Arpa

URBANUS ARCHITECTURE & DESIGN
.... 128-143
Architects: Urbanus Architecture & Design inc.
Chief Architect: Liu Xiaodu, Meng Yan
Project Team: Li Da, Yin Yijun, Huang Zhiyi, Li Hui, Chen Yun, Huang Xu, Zuo Lei
Landscape Architect: Li Jing, Wei Zhijiao
General Contractor: Shenzhen Jiasheng construction Co.,Ltd
Structural Engineer: Wu Zhou engineering and research institute
M/E/P Engineer: Ni Guoming, Zhou Lijuan,
Civil Engineer: Tian Wenfeng,
Lighting Consultant: Urbanus Architecture and Design
Curtain Wall Design Consultant: Architecture precast grc(HK) LTD
Client: Vanke Real Estate Co., Ltd
Photos: Chaoyin Yang, Yan Meng, Iwan Baan